T0329524

IN THE
SHADOW
OF **POLICY**

IN THE
SHADOW
OF **POLICY**

EVERYDAY PRACTICES IN SOUTH AFRICAN
LAND AND AGRARIAN REFORM

EDITED BY

Paul Hebinck & Ben Cousins

WITS UNIVERSITY PRESS

Wits University Press
1 Jan Smuts Avenue
Johannesburg
South Africa
www.witspress.co.za

Published edition copyright © Wits University Press 2013
Compilation copyright © Edition editors 2013
Chapter copyright © Individual contributors 2013

First published 2013

ISBN   978-1-86814-745-8 (print)
ISBN   978-1-86814-746-5 (digital)

Project managed by Inga Norenius
Edited by Inga Norenius
Proofread by Lisa Compton
Index by Tina Mössmer
Cover design by Peter Bosman
Layout and DTP artwork by Robin Yule
Printed and bound by Creda Communications

Contents

Part 1   Setting the scene: land and agrarian reform in post-apartheid South Africa

Part 2   'Mind the gap': discrepancies between policies and practices in South African land reform

Part 3 Competing knowledge regimes in communal area agriculture

Tables and figures

Acknowledgements

In the Shadow of Policy is the outcome of a collaborative project called CAPRI (Cape Rural Innovation Project) that was implemented between 2008 and 2012. The project brought together different institutions to discuss and study rural development and to reflect on the role of rural extension in social and economic transformation in post-apartheid South Africa. The focus of the project was on the Cape provinces, Northern, Eastern and Western, and on initiating collaboration between the provincial departments of agriculture and Wageningen University in the Netherlands. The project was initiated by the three departments of agriculture (DOAs). Over time, the project expanded to include collaborators from the University of the Western Cape and Rhodes University. The project was funded by a grant from NUFFIC (Netherlands University Foundation for International Cooperation) which operates under the mandate of the Ministry of Foreign Aid. NUFFIC administers a capacity-building programme (NICHE) from which the CAPRI project received funding.

CAPRI funded the Master's studies at Wageningen University of nine members of staff of the collaborating DOAs. Two PhD students are currently finishing their theses. Another part of the CAPRI project was to engage with rural extension and its frontline workers. Together with the collaborating DOAs, a rural extension training programme was designed and implemented ('The Big Five'), training over 1 000 extension officers at diploma level, updating their skills and exploring new forms of rural innovation in South Africa. The core of this book consists of the Master's and PhD theses of the CAPRI-funded graduates. Additional authors have contributed chapters on topics not covered.

The book could not have been written without the financial support CAPRI received from NUFFIC. Many others need to be mentioned for their valuable role in CAPRI: Marius Paulse, Ruud Ludeman, Nomakhaya Stemele, Joyene Isaacs, Patience Tamba, Gertrude Gayiya and Waldo Weimers. Carin Vijhuizen at NUFFIC needs specific mentioning, as she championed the compilation of this book.

It is equally important to acknowledge Michael Wessels for his enduring support and patience in assisting most of the authors to write their chapters, commenting on style and argumentation, and correcting spelling.

The book was reviewed by two anonymous reviewers whose reflections on the book as a whole and critical comments on individual chapters were most helpful. In addition, Marc Wegerif, Alberto Arce and Jan Douwe van der Ploeg commented on earlier draft versions of various key chapters of the book. Their comments and suggestions have improved the book considerably.

The support and advice rendered by Roshan Cader, commissioning editor for the Wits University Press, has been extremely important. She successfully guided the book through its process from manuscript submission and reviewing, rewriting and final production of the published product.

Acronyms and abbreviations

ABET	Adult Basic Education and Training
Agri-BEE	agricultural sector code for black economic empowerment
ANC	African National Congress
ARC	Agricultural Research Council
BEE	Black Economic Empowerment
CASP	Comprehensive Agricultural Support Programme
CLRA	Communal Land Rights Act
CPA	Communal Property Association
CRDP	Comprehensive Rural Development Programme
CSG	Child Support Grant
DBSA	Development Bank of Southern Africa
DLA	Department of Land Affairs
DOA	Department of Agriculture
DRDLR	Department of Rural Development and Land Reform
ECRLCC	Eastern Cape Regional Land Claims Commission
EDD	Economic Development Department
EO	extension officer
FWES	Farmer Worker Equity Share
GEAR	Growth, Employment and Redistribution programme
GM	genetically modified
HFPP	Homestead Food Production Programme
LRAD	Land Redistribution for Agricultural Development programme
LRC	Legal Resources Centre
MAFISA	Micro-agricultural Financial Institutional Scheme of South Africa
MFPP	Massive Food Production Programme
MLAR	market-led agrarian reform model
MST	*Movimento dos Trabalhadores Rurais Sem Terra*
NAFU	National African Farmers Union
NCP	Northern Cape province
NDA	National Department of Agriculture
NGO	non-governmental organisation
NPC	National Planning Commission
PDA	Provincial Department of Agriculture
PGDP	Provincial Growth and Development Plan
PLAS	proactive land acquisition strategy
PTO	Permission to Occupy
RDP	Reconstruction and Development Programme
SLAG	Settlement/Land Acquisition Grant
SSDP	Settlement Support and Development Planning
TRANCRAA	Transformation of Certain Rural Areas Act

VIS	Vaalharts Irrigation Scheme
VOC	Dutch East India Company
WCDOA	Western Cape Department of Agriculture
ZRA	Zweledinga Residents' Association

Map of the Cape provinces, showing the location of the case studies

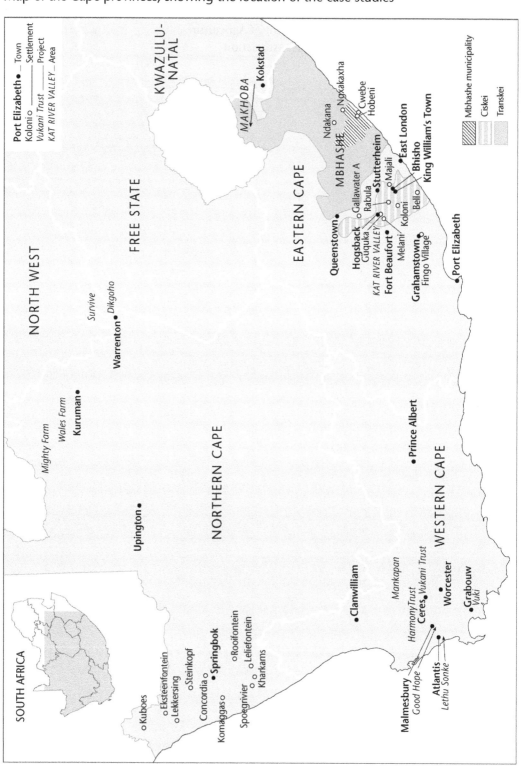

Part 1

Setting the scene: land and agrarian reform
in post-apartheid South Africa

1   Post-apartheid land and agrarian reform policy and practices in South Africa: themes, processes and issues

Paul Hebinck

This book critically examines land and agrarian reform policies in post-apartheid South Africa. Notions of land and agrarian reform are well entrenched in the everyday life of a significant number of people in post-apartheid South Africa, as is evident when one visits government departments and meets policymakers and practitioners, attends academic and policy-oriented seminars, reads newspapers and media reports, or interacts directly with land reform beneficiaries and people in villages. What reform actually means for everyday life, however, varies considerably, as do the ways in which we study and understand land and agrarian reform processes. There are contrasting theoretical frameworks; the field of study is inherently multidisciplinary and complex, and varying experiences of historical events and situations colour our interpretations. Moreover, it is often forgotten that agrarian development policies have been designed and implemented in South Africa since the nineteenth century and that the current crop of policymakers had little or no experience in dealing with land and agrarian reform when the reform process started.

The purpose of the book is neither to provide an extensive review of academic debates, nor to argue that land reform has failed outright to achieve its objectives. Rather, the book aims to set out a number of themes that are drawn from the broader literature on land and agrarian reform as well as from empirical case studies that reconstruct everyday experiences of land and agrarian reform, and how both may inform policy and research agendas. The debates revolve around a number of pertinent issues, informing and shaping the collection of papers brought together in this book. The title of the book – *In the Shadow of Policy: Everyday Practices in South African Land and Agrarian Reform* – is suggestive of its methodology: by elucidating how a range of social actors (such as policymakers, state officials, beneficiaries, extension workers and so on) involved in the land and agrarian reform process engage with the ideas and actions of policy institutions, we will be able to document, as Long (2004a: 26 ff.) phrases it, 'how these ideas are transmitted, contested, reassembled, and negotiated at the points where policy decisions and implementations impinge upon the life circumstances and everyday life-worlds of so-called "lay" or "non-expert" actors'. The title also suggests that policies may hide informal and unofficial objectives that, as Ferguson (1990), De Sardan (2006) and many others suggest, intrude on the formally stated objectives. There is always, as much of the book will indicate, a fair degree of rhetoric at play. What drives the momentum of this book, then, is a commitment to making visible what is happening in the fields and homesteads on the land reform projects and what this potentially means for different actors in different places in South Africa. This is intimately linked to the debate on the land question (Bernstein 2004, 2007; Ntsebeza and Hall 2007; O'Laughlin et al. 2013). With Hammar (2007), I argue that there is a plurality of co-existing land and agrarian questions articulating with one another within specific sites, and across space and time. This in turn urges us to rethink the land question; the book sets out to provide empirical data for that.

The title specifically reflects the three major aims of the book:
- to illuminate the interactions between the role and position of the state and its assumed capacity to design and implement policies;
- to elucidate whether and how the actions derived from these interactions resonate meaningfully with everyday realities. As the book documents, there is a lot more going on at grass-roots level and in the villages than is often assumed by state officials, policymakers and experts;
- to contribute to the debate on land and agrarian reform beyond the South African experiences by unpacking and analysing how policies and everyday practices get intertwined and mutually shape each other.

This analysis identifies a number of important analytical issues for the debate on how to study land and agrarian reform processes and practices.

This chapter briefly reviews some of the major emerging themes within land and agrarian reform processes. It explains the structure of the book and provides an overview of the themes addressed in each chapter. Drawing on these provides substantial scope for both a synthesis of arguments and the formulation of a number of methodological points of departure for further analysis and debate in the study of land reform and agrarian change.

Land and agrarian reform: themes and topics

How to understand and design land reform has generated heated debates between scholars and practitioners. The nub of this book is that land and agrarian reform are both needed in view of the high degree of rural and urban poverty, and the socio-economic and political inequalities that largely, but not exclusively, revolve around ownership of land and access to productive assets and income. It is a matter of undoing past injustices, given the long history of racialised land dispossession and forced removals, as well as the continuing inability of the industrial and service sectors to absorb the abundant rural and urban labour force. These two agendas have increasingly become connected in the policy discourse and everyday practices of land and agrarian reform in South Africa. This is expressed – in varying ways and tones – in government documents (DLA 1996, 1997; DRDLR 2009, 2011), in public statements by African National Congress (ANC) dignitaries and politicians and in publications by South African scholars (for instance, Ntsebeza and Hall 2007; Van Zyl et al. 1996; Walker 2008; Walker et al. 2010); it also finds recognition in the international literature (Bernstein 2002, 2003, 2007; Borras 2008; Lipton 2009; O'Laughlin et al. 2013; Rosset 2006; Thiesenhusen 1989a). What is questioned by this book is what *kind* of land reform, *how* implemented and by *whom*.

Any attempt to lay out some of the major themes and controversies and formulate a methodological framework for the critical analysis of land reform in South Africa must take into account that experiences of land reform are contextual and historically specific. Clearly, these experiences are many and cannot be accounted for fully in this introductory chapter. Nevertheless, I argue that some general lessons can be drawn, which can be broadly summarised as pertaining to the interconnected role of the state and market(s) and the rhythms of agrarian change, as well as the tensions and contradictions that are generated as a result of this. These are as yet unresolved, as we will see, in both theory and everyday practice. Lipton (2009: 8) considers land reform 'unfinished business' which should remain a feature of the political agenda. The motivations, however, for addressing land issues have shifted considerably over time.

Thiesenhusen (1989b: 488) succinctly summarises over 50 years of land reform in Latin America: '… reform programmes have been too small, too late, too underfunded, too dictated from above, too hierarchically organized, and too infrequently responsive to pressure from the grassroots'. In addition, Thiesenhusen points to a number of processes and key issues that are also relevant for the South African case: (i) 'if land reform is to be a substitute for rural welfare programmes and affirmative action … it fell short of the mark' (1989b: 483). (ii) '… the technological imperative came partially to replace the social rationale as the predominant force shaping and moulding the defining features of Latin American agrarian structure' (1989b: 484). He specifically points to labour tenants becoming smallholders and landless labourers: (iii) 'a group of large- to middle-sized, entrepreneurial, capitalised farms resulted' (1989b: 484); (iv) a range of reform bottlenecks emerged: inputs supply was constrained; political interest in reforms waned as new economic growth points emerged; bureaucratic procedures, negative and critical public opinion, inadequate post-settlement support and a top-heavy bureaucracy smothered the process and progress; and (v) reform is 'betting on the strong': the 'overall number of peasants accommodated in land reform was relatively small …' (1989b: 486, 487).

Despite such critical evaluation of land and agrarian reform, it still is a relatively legitimate item on the agenda in many countries and for many donor agencies, and relevant for social movements to engage with. Land reform has been designed, planned and implemented in many different ways and for many different reasons. Two of these modes stand out clearly in the literature and both emerge from relatively contrasting ontologies: the 'land to the tiller' perspective, which gradually became incorporated in neo-liberal discourses of development, and those that flow from the 'agrarian question' debate.

'Land to the tiller' has long been a guiding and popular slogan to legitimise and carry out land reform in Latin America. Redistributing land more equally was to reduce poverty by providing the poor with access to their main productive asset, thereby increasing rural employment and incomes. 'Land to the tiller' has also been favoured as a vehicle to increase and render production more efficient as productivity on smallholdings is seen by some as much higher than that on large farms (Lipton 1993, 2009; Mafeje 2003; Wiggins et al. 2010). Securing their land rights would sustain expanded production and increased welfare (Smith 2003) as well as a democratisation of land–society relations (Wittman 2009). Recently, De Janvry and Sadoulet (2010) provided substantial evidence that rural poverty reduction has been associated with growth in agricultural yields and labour productivity; they warn, however, that this relation varies sharply across regional contexts. Land reform, then, should set out simultaneously to provide access to land and to increase production through the increased use of new technologies and integration into commodity markets. This discourse of modernisation, in which market institutions and relations play a key role, is preferred by most land reform protagonists (Deininger and Binswanger 1999; Ellis 1993; Lipton 2009; Lipton and Lipton 1993; Van Zyl et al. 1996). One must hasten to add that a pro-market stance does not automatically mean an uncritical embracing of neo-classical economic growth models. Smith (2003) thoroughly critiques the neo-classical economic assumptions about land markets and people–land relations, which according to many (Ferguson 2013; Hebinck and Van Averbeke 2007; Shackleton et al. 2001) do not revolve only around the production of agricultural goods.

The argument for land reform also has its roots in the classic 'agrarian question' debate. Does land reform help to solve the major agrarian questions? What is or will be the direction of agrarian transformation? Smallholders, small- and large-scale farmers, subsistence and market-oriented farmers, peasants and entrepreneurs, capitalist and petty commodity production are some of the social categories and concepts that are used to debate the direction and trajectories of agrarian change. Chayanov (1966) and Kautsky (1988) represent opposing theoretical and ideological positions in the debate about the role of smallholders in the context of capitalist encroachments in agriculture. A Chayanovian tradition has emerged which views smallholders, or rather peasants, as a central factor in rural economic development (Van der Ploeg 2008, 2010, 2013). Kautsky's entry point is that smallholders are transitionary in the process of capitalist development in the rural agrarian economy; peasants inevitably disappear as a result of ongoing processes of class differentiation, a view which has been adopted by Leninist schools of thought (Bernstein 2009). Bernstein (2007) and also Sender and Johnston (2004) link this with the land reform debate by questioning, for instance, whether land reform alone is able to absorb the unemployed which, in essence, are an outcome of capitalism and industrialisation processes.

Chayanovian views are classified by political economists as a populist tradition that ignores the class character of development (Bernstein 2010a, 2010b), but they continue to play an important role in the land reform debate and future visions of the countryside. This is echoed in the 'land to the tiller' slogan. Contemporary social movements, in particular peasant organisations such as *Via Campesina* and the Brazilian *Movimento dos Trabalhadores Rurais Sem Terra* (MST), echo in their struggles that family farms and peasant cooperatives are viable options to fight for (Borras 2008; Rosset 2006). However, as Rosset et al. (2006) and Wolford (2010) point out, the smallholder option for land reform has been assimilated by global considerations of equity and production efficiencies and as such incorporated into World Bank neo-liberal land and agricultural discourses. Much of the original land reform discourse has been incorporated into the neo-liberalisation of agrarian policy, which has also gradually encroached on the land reform programme in, for instance, South Africa and Brazil. State-driven development has been replaced by neo-liberalism, which is considered by many as the predominant, global discourse of development (Kydd and Dorward 2001; Gore 2000). For Gore (2000), neo-liberalism involves not only a shift from state-led to market-oriented policies, but also a discursive shift in the ways in which development problems become framed (for example, more market-oriented) and in the types of explanation through which policies are justified. A major consequence of neo-liberalism is that development policy analysis and evaluations by the state and its monitoring institutions revolve around applying a standardised set of methodologies, which tends to disconnect dynamics from context and history, as well as from power relationships. In that sense neo-liberalism emerges as the logical follower of the modernisation discourse of the post–World War II era, with a strong belief in planned development.

Both state and market are subject to critical analysis in the land reform litera-ture and both are also debated in the villages and on land reform farms. Since they often work against development, markets and their role occupy a central place in critical analyses, not least of all in South Africa. Marsden (1998) and Van der Ploeg et al. (2002), for instance, point to the 'squeeze on agriculture' that stands for the increased pressure on farm income which is an outcome of unequal terms of trade and power relations between the agricultural sector on the one hand and the indus-trial and financial sectors on the other. Lipton (2009), who is not against market options per se, is, however, critical of neo-liberalism and the uncritical embracing of the market that follows. Based on a comparative worldwide study, he argues that under certain conditions a degree of market regulation is required to counteract the impact of market and market relations on land reform practices (see also Lipton and Lipton 1993). Land and agrarian reform should address existing unequal power relations between agriculture and industry – a position, given the extent of deregu-lation, that is not shared by the current South African government, which is wary of any form of state subsidy for the agricultural sector (Hall 2009b).

Binswanger and Deininger (1996), Deininger and Binswanger (1999) and Deininger (1999) are critical of state-led market reform because of political and financial problems with enforcing a ceiling on land ownership. Experiences else-where, they argue, show that state-led reforms generate 'corruption, tenure insecu-rity, and red tape' (Deininger and Binswanger1999: 263). They plead instead for a market-led agrarian reform model (MLAR) which has become the much-favoured approach of the World Bank. MLAR involves a negotiated land reform that relies on voluntary land transfers based on negotiations between buyers and sellers ('willing buyer, willing seller'), where the government's role is restricted to establishing the necessary framework and making available a land-purchase grant to eligible beneficiaries. MLAR is defined as a land reform strategy fostering a productive and market-oriented agricultural sector. Deininger (1999) argues that becoming a bene-ficiary of land reform should be self-selective. The role of the state, then, should be limited to providing land-purchase grants and settlement support services, which demands both budget and human resource capacity, both of which appear to be critically lacking in the course of the land reform programme in South Africa.

Borras (2003: 390) in turn questions MLAR and maintains that the MLAR approach to land reform disconnects 'the technical/administrative issues in project/policy implementation (like post-settlement support, PH) from the political contexts (such as those in South(ern) Africa, PH) within which MLAR operators and clients are embedded'. Neither history and everyday social realties nor technological choices present themselves as neutral. This book documents in detail that neither market nor self-selection of beneficiaries is a neutral process.

To escape neo-liberal tendencies, Huizer (1999), Rosset (2006) and Borras (2008) call for an agrarian reform 'from below'. Their plea is for a land reform under the leadership of the state but controlled by social movements that have led the social struggle for land and are experienced in devising ways to improve liveli-hoods. Not the market but people's livelihoods and their well-being should inform the state's reform agenda. It is often argued that a precondition for 'development from below' is an active social movement capable of mobilising and driving the process and acting as a creative broker. Brazil, where the MST has pushed land reform, is a good example; experiences show, however, that such involvement can also turn out to be ambiguous, where, for example, the leadership of social move-ments push their own agendas (Caldeira 2008; Wittman 2009).

Cousins (2007, 2011, 2013) argues in the same vein that 'accumulation from below' is a more relevant trajectory to pursue in land reform. Applied to the South African context, 'accumulation from below' should help to create situations whereby elites cannot run away with the benefits of the reforms. Thiesenhusen (1989b) points at a similar dynamic in Latin America. Moreover Cousins (2007: 240, 241) maintains that 'what is required is a radical restructuring of agrarian economic space, prop-erty regimes and socio-economic relations, premised on the potential for accumula-tion from below in both agricultural and non-agricultural forms of petty commodity production, and expanded opportunities for "multiple livelihoods strategies"'. Phrasing it differently, in Chayanovian terminology (Van der Ploeg 2013), land and agrarian reform in south(ern) Africa should facilitate the construction of self-owned and self-controlled resource bases which fit in with multiple livelihood strategies.

Overview of *In the Shadow of Policy*

The book is divided into three parts. The first, comprising three chapters, provides an analysis of context. The second part consists of ten chapters that examine the gaps between policy and practice, and the final part, with seven chapters, draws on empirical research to critically assess policy-led initiatives in the Eastern Cape. What follows is a brief overview of the chapters in each section.

Part 1 Setting the scene: land and agrarian reform in post-apartheid South Africa

This part provides an analytical context as well as a policy one. Whereas chapter 1 (this chapter) debates land reform and identifies key issues, chapters 2 and 3 specifically address the policy dimensions of land and agrarian reform in South Africa. Key among the arguments in this part is that next to discontinuities in the policy domain, important and strategic continuities in official thinking remain a predominant feature of institutional repertoires and intervention practices.

This chapter reviews the land reform debate in South Africa and elsewhere, and works towards a synthesis of the book. The themes that emerge from the international debate, and analytical lessons learned from agrarian studies more broadly, appear meaningful for understanding the complexities of South Africa's land reform practices.

In chapter 2, Paul Hebinck reviews agrarian and rural development policies in South Africa and charts the changes and shifts that have taken place over the years. He summarises over 100 years of rural and agricultural development policy and analyses the ideas and ideologies that shaped these policies. They appear to have many common characteristics even though they have emerged from contrasting political ideologies and governance regimes. These continuities often constrain the dramatic structural changes and transformations that post-apartheid policy-makers would like to achieve.

Ben Cousins's chapter 3 discusses why and how post-apartheid land and agricultural policies have been uncoupled, partly as a result of the unwillingness of policy-makers to tamper with the perceived strengths of large-scale commercial farming, as well as unexamined assumptions about the nature of 'modern agriculture'. The chapter assesses the consequences of these policy choices, including, most damagingly, the lack of a coherent strategy to reform the inherited agrarian structure.

Part 2 'Mind the gap': discrepancies between policies and practices in South African land reform

The second part explores how agrarian reform policies are transmitted, implemented and experienced at the grass-roots level of projects and villages. Chapters 4–13 draw heavily on empirical investigations of land and agrarian reform practices after land has been redistributed and/or returned to the original owners and new institutional and property relations come into play. The land tenure reform dimension is addressed specifically, to show how history complicates current reform initiatives. The chapters stress that social inequality embedded in relations of class, gender and generation are important ingredients of land reform practices. In addition, there is ample evidence of new forms of inequality that derive from the social categories the reform discourse has introduced. At the same time, beneficiaries make their own selections from among the opportunities and resources land reform policy has to offer, thus unpacking policy components and repackaging them, as it were, to suit the needs of their everyday practices. All of this happens against a background of multiple livelihood strategies.

Francois Marais explores, in chapter 4, the degree to which land reform beneficiaries rework the expert advice provided by land reform consultants. The case material of two farms in the Western Cape shows that beneficiaries are not passive recipients of expert knowledge. They actively redesign knowledge to accommodate their own ideas and experiences. The expert belief that farming should consist solely of cultivation and livestock production is deeply flawed.

In chapter 5, Yves van Leynseele examines the dynamics of project planning in land restitution and explores how land reform beneficiaries contest project viability. An ethnographic study of the different stages of the Makhoba land restitution case provides evidence that land restitution bureaucrats often wish to protect 'their claimants' from an unforgiving market. The chapter calls for a critical analysis of the ways in which restitution officials play a brokerage role in the land restitution process, operating as mediators in a field of power in which they occupy an ambivalent position as both local translators of dominant farming models and as engaged bureaucrats. Van Leynseele maintains that state-induced intervention is not implemented by a coherent bureaucracy, nor does it follow a straight road from design through to implementation.

Modise Moseki provides, in chapter 6, an account of everyday life at a land reform farm near Queenstown. Making use of previous studies, his account contrasts starkly with the abstract and quantitative ways in which policymakers and land reform analysts generally evaluate land reform projects. Moseki argues that sweeping policy statements and evaluations based on prescribed outcomes fail to register a lot of what is actually happening on the ground, which hinges on multiple livelihoods. He also points out what the basis is for the new inequalities that have emerged in the South African countryside in the wake of land reform.

Chapter 7, by Harriët Tienstra and Dik Roth, examines cases of market-led land reform in the Western Cape. The cases represent the two dominant forms of land reform in the province: 100 per cent ownership projects and Farmer Worker Equity Share projects. They explore the ongoing dynamics on both kinds of land reform farms from a property rights and relations perspective, and show that when these are transformed on the farms, beneficiaries' 'bundles' of rights and obligations change simultaneously.

Limpho Taoana scrutinises land reform cases in chapter 8 to provide proof that land reform has led to the formation of new social categories in the urban and rural landscapes of South Africa: land reform beneficiaries and non-land reform beneficiaries. These categories are policy-induced categories that only become real in land reform situations. Non-active land reform beneficiaries form a third category, comprised of the disenchanted people that have left a project due to the low performance of the newly acquired farm, or conflict with fellow beneficiaries, or the hard work and exposure to risks involved in participating in a land reform project. Most of them have returned to their previous places of residence.

Malebogo Phetlhu addresses two general but fundamental questions in chapter 9: what is happening on land reform farms, and how do different actors develop strategies to make sense of land reform policies? The chapter provides an everyday life account of the experiences and ideas of those actors who are directly involved with land reform. There is no single answer to the question about how land reform has reshaped people's lives. Phetlhu builds on the idea that land reform is often a conflictual and ambiguous process, and that it is important to understand that beneficiaries are not a homogeneous group. Indeed, one of the tasks of land and agrarian reform is to deconstruct social categories such as 'beneficiary' or 'extension worker'.

Petunia Khutswane's chapter 10 concerns the role of youth in land reform. By exploring land reform from a generational point of view, combined with a view of land as a resource, she shows the processes that constrain or inhibit the participation of youth in the South African land reform programme. Little is known about why very few young people engage in land reform projects. The youth dimension of land reform has mainly been associated with mobilisation. The majority of land reform beneficiaries in South Africa are older people whose livelihoods combine land ownership and old age pensions. This raises questions about the future of land reform.

Robert Ross argues in chapter 11 that land restitution is, by definition, about history. Claims to land, and thus to compensation, have to be made on the basis of historical events and not those of a court of law. History, however, has sometimes developed in too complicated a way for the simple assumptions of the Land Claims Commission to be fulfilled. Ross explores the history of land ownership and allocation in the upper Kat River valley in particular, to show the extraordinarily complex nature of land relationships which inform the settlement of restitution claims.

Rosalie Kingwill focuses in chapter 12 on the problems of conjugating customary and common-law notions of ownership. The argument hinges on the complex way in which customary approaches to land ownership articulate with the legal prescripts of ownership in South Africa, the latter derived mainly from common law. Drawing on case material from two Eastern Cape sites, one urban and one rural, she argues that customary practices cannot be reduced to 'official' customary law. The chapter charts the lived interpretations of land ownership and identifies how normative practices engage a hybrid of custom and state law, which, for strategic reasons, many scholars, officials and legal practitioners ignore.

In chapter 13, Karin Kleinbooi delivers an account of women's experiences with exercising their land rights in Namaqualand. She explores the gendered customs and practices surrounding land rights and how women demand, assert or realise their land rights. The chapter shows that women are farming on land allocated for their own use and on land controlled by male relatives, while a few better-off women engage in independent livestock farming. Women gain access to land mainly through relationships of dependency on husbands, fathers and sons. Unmarried and divorced women are extremely vulnerable to loss of land rights and other resources.

Part 3 Competing knowledge regimes in communal area agriculture

Chapters 14–20 in this part draw on empirical research and critically examine the attempts of the state to rejuvenate agriculture and to address food security and well-being in the former homelands of Ciskei and Transkei, now part of the Eastern Cape. The chapters focus on recent policy initiatives such as Siyazondla, the Massive Food Production Programme (MFPP) and Siyakhula, as well as the revitalisation of irrigation and the reintroduction of Nguni cattle. These are taken as examples to address the tensions generated by the policy reforms, which attempt to redesign and modernise communal areas and communal farming, and to assess whether and how this resonates with local conditions. Together these chapters show that land reform occurs in contexts where livelihoods are multiple and practices are embedded in complex and dynamic cultural repertoires.

Chapter 14, by Paul Hebinck and Wim van Averbeke, problematises the notion of 'agrarian' in the Eastern Cape. Land and agrarian reform and rural development presupposes an agrarian identity from which to tap. This chapter examines the practical and discursive content and meaning of the terms 'farming' and 'agrarian' in two settlements in the former Ciskei homeland region of the central Eastern Cape. The analysis draws on ongoing research that started in 1995 in two villages in the central Eastern Cape, and more specifically on data collected in 1996/1997 and 2010/2011.

Klara Jacobson and Zamile Madyibi deal in their respective chapters with the intentions and dynamics of the MFPP, designed to revive agriculture in the former Transkei. Jacobson, in chapter 15, identifies that the programme aims to reduce rural poverty through increasing agricultural output and the environmental sustainability of farming. The MFPP aims to transform subsistence-oriented farming into commercially oriented mechanised agriculture using agrochemical inputs, and hybrid and genetically modified maize seeds Conditional grants are provided to financially assist smallholders. The MFPP's record, Klara Jacobson argues, is meagre and she offers an explanation based on an analysis of how policymakers perceive and understand smallholder or communal agriculture. She unpacks the MFPP discourse by making use of MFPP documents and interviews with policymakers. Case material from three villages provides background data on smallholder agriculture and how the MFPP plan works in practice.

Chapter 16, by Zamile Madyibi, elaborates the MFPP as a planned development intervention which strongly reminds one of the homeland policies. He considers the theoretical assumptions that underpin the MFPP. The chapter explores the multiple realities of the rural Eastern Cape province to show the different ways in which beneficiaries have accommodated the MFPP in their agricultural activities. Three selected cases reflect the different labour patterns and land tenure systems that prevail in the province. The analysis shows the MFPP as rigidly adhering to ideas connected with economies of scale and the pursuit of state-driven green-revolution-style strategies. The MFPP has largely strengthened the trend set in motion in the 1930s, whereby a few elites manage to combine wage income with cultivating more land and obtaining high(er) yields.

Henning de Klerk describes, in chapter 17, the implementation of the Siyazondla Homestead Food Production Programme in Mbhashe. He takes the experiences of women's groups, who see themselves as prospective participants and beneficiaries, as a starting point to analyse Siyazondla. De Klerk convincingly argues that unfulfilled expectations and experiences of exclusion have a major impact on social relationships among homestead food producers at village level and on the relationships between homestead food producers and local Department of Agriculture (DOA) officials. This needs to be taken into account in debates about governance and development interventions at local municipal level, particularly when these aim at outcomes that are sustainable in the long run.

Derick Fay's chapter 18 offers another perspective on the dynamics of Siyazondla, by including the Child Support Grant (CSG). Since 1998, CSG has expanded to reach nearly two-thirds of the households in Hobeni, while Siyazondla began to assist households in southern Hobeni in 2007, with production inputs and training. Fay engages in this way with two debates: the potential of direct cash transfers and the potential of subsidised inputs for smallholders to serve as strategies for rural development and poverty alleviation. Fay's analysis draws on ethnographic fieldwork and points at both recent change – a sharp decline in the cultivation of remote fields since 1998 – and long-term continuities – the expansion and intensification of cultivation in homestead gardens. Concurrently, the contribution of formal employment to livelihoods has declined considerably, while the contribution of welfare has expanded.

Chapter 19, by Wim van Averbeke and Jonathan Denison, provides an insightful overview of smallholder irrigation in South Africa, with a particular focus on the Cape provinces, and shows clearly that irrigation cannot be disconnected from years of racial segregation policies. They explore the factors that play a role in the success of smallholder irrigation. These include a range of interventions driven by conflicting objectives, the limited role of agriculture in rural people's livelihoods, and the legacy of apartheid that continues to cause exclusion from input and output markets. These factors are critical but often ignored.

The last chapter, by Ntombekhaya Faku and Paul Hebinck, explores the tensions and dynamics generated by the reintroduction of Nguni cattle in the Eastern Cape. Nguni projects are meant to address some of the colonial and apartheid legacies and to transform communal area livestock farming. Laudable as this goal might be, a critical examination of the Nguni project reveals that planners fail to take into account the fact that communal farmers' view of cattle stems from experience and knowledge that has been accumulated over long periods of time. These include the experience of past state efforts to 'upgrade' their herds. In contrast to rural realities, projects like the Nguni projects work within a fixed time frame of about eight years and draw their knowledge from a mixture of scientific and idealistic, even romantic, views.

Themes, points of departure and synthesis

The themes and pertinent issues that emerge from the chapters together present a vivid picture of contemporary land reform dynamics experienced in South Africa. These themes can be recapped and synthesised as follows:

- there is a considerable discrepancy between policy discourse and practices;
- next to discontinuities, continuities in official thinking remain a predominant feature of institutional repertoires and intervention practices;
- processes of social differentiation and unequal power relations include relations of class, gender and competing intergenerational interests;
- beneficiaries contest, reassemble and negotiate land and agrarian reform policies;
- multiple and diverse livelihood strategies continue to be important.

These processes and practices are hardly recognised in contemporary land and agrarian reform models. I would argue that what emerges from the experiences documented and analysed in this book is that the state and its support network of experts is unable to engage meaningfully, through its land and agrarian reform policies and programme design, with the action space of people at the local level (for example, in villages and land reform projects) and is equally unable to tackle the inherited structural inequalities in the agricultural sector. In constructing such an argument I will elucidate some key analytical and methodological points of departure for the analysis of land and agrarian reform and agrarian change at the same time as I synthesise the findings of the book at a more abstract, theoretical level. These are multidimensional, overlapping points which I number below in order to facilitate cross-referencing.

1 Policy, processes and practices

Studying the discrepancy between policy and practice requires making a distinction between (land and agrarian) development as a *field of policy* and development as a *practice* and a *set of processes* (Keeley and Scoones 2003; McGee 2004; Van der Ploeg et al. 2012). Land and agrarian development as a *practice* refers to the many grass-roots level activities, that is, what happens in communal area farming and on land reform farms and projects. *Processes* refers to the aggregate flows that are constituted by the many development practices; *policies* denotes the coordinated efforts of the state and its bureaucracy to stimulate, direct, attempt to control, regulate and govern development practices (Ferguson 1990; Li 2007; Scott 1998).

State policies are rooted in discourses of development that believe that economic growth, social change and the reduction of poverty can be achieved through the design and implementation of a series of concrete, time-bound development policies and intervention programmes; this is debated in the literature as 'planned development' (De Sardan 2006; Long 2001; Long and Van der Ploeg 1989). The leading role of the state in development assumes a coherent bureaucracy; the analyses of the empirical material brought together in this book clearly challenge such Weberian assumptions about state bureaucracies (see also point 3 below).

2 Policy as narrative and the centrality of resources

Policies usually come into being as broadly stated narratives which have the capacity to mobilise the state to act and allocate public resources (Grindle and Thomas 1991; Keeley and Scoones 2003). These narratives are formulated not exclusively by policymakers, bureaucrats and politicians but also by well-situated beneficiaries, corporate interests, organised labour, practitioners, consultants, non-governmental organisations (NGOs), churches, and so on. The outcome and nature of political processes shape which of the narratives make it to an accepted and shared discourse of development that forms the core of state policies.

Policy essentially is about tangible and non-tangible resources (such as land, markets, capital, knowledge, agricultural inputs, sociocultural repertoires, memories, and so on). Policies entail (re)distribution, preventing or smoothing, and privileging access to resources (for example, legal restrictions to ownership and rights, and land redistribution). Policy is also about the power and knowledge to (re)define what constitutes resources: where they originate from (for example, the market), as well as how to deploy and how to redistribute the wealth emanating from their use (Peach and Constatin 1972; Ribot and Peluso 2003). State policies manifest and are transmitted as programmes (such as the social grants and welfare schemes, the Land Redistribution for Agricultural Development programme and the Massive Food Production Programme in the Eastern Cape) that define the key resources for development, often in the form of packages and services (Ferguson 1990; Mango and Hebinck 2004), and to make them available to beneficiaries and safeguard their (re)production. Policies are also supported and legitimised by a range of laws which become real as rules and regulations, acts and decrees.

3 Neo-liberalism and the role of the state

Neo-liberalism has thus become an important dimension that shapes the current debate, in South and southern Africa as well as in Brazil. The importance is, as Cousins argues in chapter 3, that neo-liberalism has provided the organising framework for the transition from apartheid to post-apartheid and the reforms ensuing from that process. Embracing neo-liberalism is a matter of political choice and orientation – the ANC has embraced neo-liberalism (Habib and Padayachee 2000) – as well as a matter of economic strategy – the deregulation of the agricultural sector which is embedded in the historical position the South African economy occupies in the global economy. But is the impact of neo-liberalism pervasive and determining, or is it only shaping land reform practices, and what ambiguities have transpired? Wolford (2010) examined the outcomes of neo-liberalism for land reform in Brazil: the marriage between the state and MST turned out to be not an easy one, not necessarily pro-poor, and often ended up as privileging the most powerful, thereby reinforcing prior inequalities, a phenomenon also pointed out by Thiesenhusen (1989b). South Africa is a good example of what the obscurities are when development policies are situated in a neo-liberal economic policy context. There is, on the one hand, a considerable reliance on (and belief in) the market and on development ideas, models and technologies that are often, but not exclusively, externally sourced and that do not resonate well with local conditions and experiences. On the other hand, there remains a considerable degree of state influence on reforming the conditions for agricultural production in communal agriculture. The role of the state in beneficiary selection is not left to the market but is also embedded in paternalistic practices. Land reform has certainly retained populist tendencies and low-ranking officials (extension workers and bureaucrats) often try to find options outside the market by bringing beneficiaries under the ambit of the state, or find ways to use land reform brokerage space for themselves (James 2007, 2011; and chapters 6, 8 and 9, this volume).

Whereas the practice in Brazil is that social movements mediate in the selection of beneficiaries (Wolford 2010), South African experiences are rather different. This book provides ample evidence of the dynamics involved in the self-selection approach adopted and implemented by the South African Department of Agriculture (DOA 2001) from the start, and continued by the current Department of Rural Development and Land Reform (DRDLR). Beneficiaries apply for land reform grants, and since 2001, in the context of policy changes envisaged in the Land Redistribution for Agricultural Development (LRAD) programme, beneficiaries themselves have to contribute, either in kind or in cash. The experiences can be summed up as a combination of beneficiaries pooling their cash and/or in-kind resources ('renting a crowd'), financial viability criteria to engage with commercial agriculture (Cousins and Scoones 2010), and a continuation of a system of patronage steered by state officials (Wegerif 2004). Chapter 3 reflects critically on the process; chapters 8 and 9 show how self-selection works out at the grass roots. Moreover, the practices of planning and beneficiary selection of the Department of Land Affairs (DLA), the provincial departments of agriculture and the current DRDLR, with regard to reviving and transforming communal agriculture, reveal continuities with their apartheid-era predecessors, the Department of Native Affairs and the Native Agricultural and Lands Branch. The book is ample evidence of continuities as embedded in state institutions' approaches to planning (see point 7), personnel, relationships and policy languages (see points 4, 5 and 6). This has remained despite the movement of many former NGO staff into the state's institutions.

4 Gap between discourse and practice

There is a considerable gap between discourse and practice. This can be explained with reference to the nature of the state, or rather governance practices, but it also has much to do with the strong belief that development can be planned through the implementation of policies. The governance dimension is elaborated in the next section. Here we consider planned development policies from the central argument that policies are seldom translated as designed. Policies are not blue-prints (Roe 1991) nor do they follow a coherent, linearly implementable script which is laid out by the state and its experts (Hebinck and Shackleton 2011; Long 2004b; Scott 1998). Two processes are important to consider in this respect.

First, projects on paper 'have little in common with the project itself as it exists in practice, once into the hands of the people to whom it is destined' (De Sardan 2006: 4). Development interventions inevitably encounter and simultaneously give rise to emerging and robust practices that attempt to redesign or oppose and sometimes blatantly resist them. We observe in South Africa, for instance, that land reform beneficiaries become disenchanted with the land reform process and/ or that resource use does not follow the expert-designed business models, often leading to a particular entanglement of practices and new resource use patterns. Chapters 4–10 in the second part of this book show that land reform beneficiaries do not simply sit back and wait for 'development' to be delivered to them in the form of post-settlement support; instead they actively redesign post-settlement support by contesting expert-designed business plans. Beneficiaries try to make things work for themselves even though their efforts might be contested by the state and their fellow beneficiaries, often for different reasons. Similar processes are documented in the third part of the book, in chapters 15–20.

Second, policies are frequently (re)negotiated and rewritten by policymakers and are redesigned in the context of consultations and negotiations between the various representatives of state institutions, farmers' organisations, politicians, political parties, NGOs, bilateral foreign aid donors, World Bank experts, private consultants and agribusiness companies. Nor is there always consensus within and among state institutions and the policy community itself about the future and direction of land and agrarian reform (Cousins 2007; Hall 2004; Lahiff 2007; Van den Brink 2003). Land and agrarian reform are uncoupled, as Cousins argues in chapter 3. The market-led land reform model (MLAR) appears not to be the vehicle to address the fundamental restructuring of the agrarian economy (Lahiff 2007). The decision of the state, for instance, to deregulate and open up agriculture to global markets had a stabilising effect on the agricultural sector, putting pressure on the profitability of farming (the 'squeeze on agriculture' alluded to earlier in this chapter) and in turn negatively impacting on the economic success rates of land reform projects and influencing the extent to which farmers comply with new labour legislation and minimum wage rates. We see large landowners paying wages that are set at a low level, and subsequent increases in the rates have not kept up with increases in the prices of food and fuel. 'The lack of full enforce-ment,' as Naidoo (2011: 206) argues, 'of the minimum wage leads to … little or no gains for low-paid workers that will alleviate poverty ... Moreover, full compliance with minimum wages and increases in the rate of pay may well result in dis-employment.' The strikes for higher wages by farm workers in the De Doorns region in the Wine District Municipality in the Cape is the most recent manifestation of that process, which was predicted by Ewert and Hamman (1999). In addition, the analyses of Van Leynseele and De Klerk in chapters 5 and 17 in particular critique the notion of a development bureaucracy as a coherent institution; state officials in fact act as brokers navigating between various interests and positions (see also James 2011). Taoana, in chapter 8, and Phetlhu, in chapter 9, problematise the brokerage role of extension officers. The implication of these processes is that the state does not act as a monolithic, Weberian institution. Rather, it has multiple layers which act according to their own interpretations of the state's reform discourse, which often turn out to be contrasting interpretations of state policies, directives and objectives. Next to the state there are many other coordinating mechanisms and practices that shape the dynamics and outcomes of land and agrarian reforms. This helps to explain why policies generate unexpected and perhaps unwanted outcomes in practice.

5 Governance practices

'The will to' initiate, to partially quote Li (2007), new forms of governance and citizenship that might be expected to come about in periods of change such as the post-apartheid era in South Africa has not (yet) really come to fruition. Innovative policy processes, as explored by McGee (2004), that would be capable of replacing and transforming colonial and apartheid-era policy-planning mechanisms have not emerged since 1994. Several observers and commentators have criticised (agrarian) policy and its implementation in, for instance, the Eastern Cape. Hadju (2006) points to the still existing unequal power relations between policymakers and local actors, leaving the latter with the feeling that they have limited control over their own fate. The homeland style of governance is reproduced rather than discontinued. Monde (2003) notes that the record of the post-1994 interventions to promote agriculture in the former homelands is long on new initiatives but short on measurable success stories. Both Ainslie (2005) and Kepe (2002) argue that the Eastern Cape Department of Agriculture has failed to table a comprehensive and consistent livestock development plan.

It is not just the state and its prostrate institutions, as Scott (1998) labels and understands them, that require critical analysis. Civil society organisations, social movements (such as the Landless People's Movement; see James 2007 for a critical view on LPM and Greenberg 2004 for a glorifying assessment) and NGOs also appear to be ineffective and incapable of leading the reform 'from below' that Rosset (2006) and Borras (2008) call for. The few experiences with mobilisation, such as the land occupations in Mahlahluvani, are not organised into any movement that even NGOs engage with, let alone the state (Wegerif 2010). In addition, as some of the chapters (notably chapters 6, 9 and 16) elucidate, processes through which elites capture development potentials at village or project level colour the outcomes of the reforms.

6 The knowledge base of policy

All actors construct knowledge and they do so in different and contrasting ways. Not all knowledge, but particular bodies of knowledge, however, feed and shape the policy process. Policies are generally informed by knowledge generated by experts and scientists that derive from ill-conceived assumptions about empirical (rural) realities and development that have not been tested in the conditions in which the policies will be applied. Such knowledge results in received wisdoms, which, as Leach and Fairhead (2000) argue, lead to erroneous interpretations of urban and rural change in Africa and also to 'bad' or ill-informed policy choices. This helps to explain why most development policies fail to bridge the gap between the perceptions of the experts and the day-to-day experiences of people at grass roots (Keeley and Scoones 2003; McGee 2004; Scoones 1992). Moreover, the national statistics that inform policies are not always reliable, available and up to date (Jerven 2010), and frequently fail to adequately reflect developmental trends at grass-roots level. One of the most influential pieces of 'received wisdom' that today shapes land and agrarian reform practices is that agricultural development in communal areas can be realised only by following the 'commercial' farming model (Cousins and Scoones 2010; Scoones 1992), which adopts strict notions of what constitutes the agrarian. The latter is brought to the fore in chapters 14, 17, 19 and 20. Scott (1998) describes this phenomenon as 'seeing like a state', which reinforces the critical conclusion various chapters draw that the land and agrarian reform policies have not taken into account how land reform beneficiaries – 'communal farmers', women, youth and pensioners, understand and enact development. In their response to past and present state interventions, their ability to redesign programme components and their autonomous practices, local actors expose the limitations of policymakers' assumptions about contemporary rural realities, questioning in turn the capacity of the state to design and deliver services and intervene.

7 Post-settlement support dynamics

What this book substantiates is that post-settlement support has often failed to deliver relevant knowledge and information to the 'new' landowners. Post-settlement support advice and project and business plans are often irrelevant to the needs of the beneficiaries (Cousins and Scoones 2010; Hall 2009a; Hebinck et al. 2011). The dissonance between the type of support that is required – assuming that this is voiced in some way – and what is offered can largely be explained by the predominance of a particular paradigm as to what constitutes 'viable' farming. This paradigm, as chapter 3 details, is based on the planning models that are associated with large-scale, capital-intensive farming. It also defines agriculture rigidly and narrowly. It assumes, too, that agriculture is rural people's only livelihood source. Chapters 14, 17 and 18, among others, have shown that this assumption does not reflect rural realities. It is also important to take into account that agriculture in the real world includes more than simply cultivation and livestock. More and more scholars maintain that 'doing' agriculture includes harvesting from the natural environment (Hebinck and Lent 2007; Shackleton et al. 2001). Agriculture, they argue, supplements a range of livelihood sources, including wages and, increasingly, state grants. Chapters 4–10 provide accounts of what happens when post-settlement advice does not resonate with local conditions: outsiders blame beneficiaries for the failure of projects. Their style of 'doing agriculture' is not recognised or seen by the state as productive. State actors often oppose and misunderstand local development trajectories and 'accumulation from below'. The prevailing view is that rural people should walk the path of modernisation as defined by Siyakhula and Siyanzondla. The authors of chapters 15, 16, 17 and 18 make this clear in their account of the disenchantment and disappointment that follow when modernisation is forced on people, leading them to withdraw from land-reform-related developments. In addition, some of the chapters also document the way in which bureaucratic procedures hamper the inclusion of a range of potential participants in the reform programmes. De Klerk and Van Leynseele, in particular, draw attention to rigid bureaucratic procedures that exclude people from benefits and meaningful participation. The red tape that attends DOA interventions makes it difficult to execute plans for farm operations in the allocated time frames. These are only two examples of the sort of top-down planning that allows little room for participation and flexibility.

8 The importance of historical continuities

Policies not only 'have left their historical traces', as James (2010: 222) argues, which are visible and still felt to this day; they also have many common characteristics even though they have emerged from contrasting political ideologies and governance regimes. This book demonstrates that the overriding reality is that old ideas and institutional repertoires continue to prevail. These often constrain reform programmes from achieving the stated objectives. Both past and present development policies limit local people's capacity to use the resources made available to them in the ways that they see fit, but as argued earlier, these do not completely prevent local people from manipulating and redesigning land reform interventions. An important continuity that hinders reform from coming to fruition is that, as in the past, policymakers, experts, extension workers and many – but not all – students and scholars of agricultural and rural development link local practices with 'underdevelopment'.

While there are significant continuities with the past (chapters 2 and 3), post-apartheid policies have also contributed a new set of ideas and institutional practices, as parts 2 and 3 of this book show. For a start, these policies have produced new social categories and terms for them: 'emergent farmers'; 'land reform beneficiaries', which requires a further distinction between those that contribute their own capital, those that contribute in kind to acquire a farm, and 'collective property associations'. Experience also informs us about non-land reform beneficiaries looking for opportunities, which were previously almost non-existent, to somehow access land. These terms are used alongside the terms for existing social categories, such as 'commercial' and 'subsistence' farming and 'small-' and 'large-scale' farmers. It cannot be denied that the state has deployed key resources in its efforts to generate rural transformation. It should be noted, however, that budgets have been very small relative to the scale and complexity of the problem (Aliber and Hall 2012). The state has made new policies and passed land laws and acts. Because of land reform and land restitution people can now acquire land. The controls on the movement of labour have been removed. Post-settlement support is organised and, notwithstanding the critique (Aliber and Hall 2012), it has created opportunities – perhaps only for some well-situated beneficiaries – to engage with markets and access loans, inputs and technology.

9 History and processes of transformation

History as a complicating factor and context runs throughout the book. As Ross argues in chapter 11, land reform in certain areas in the Cape has not resulted in the deracialisation of land ownership because of intricate historical factors. Lahiff (2011) presents a similar argument. Rights to land continue to be vested in the hands of men while their spouses work the land in their absence. This leads Kleinbooi to assert in chapter 13 that women's rights to land are not being addressed in an appropriate manner. Moreover, as Kingwill shows in chapter 12, when land laws conjugate customary and common-law notions of ownership, the historical complexities of customary claims become even greater. Historical processes of transformation, such as the de-agrarianisation processes referred to by Hebinck and Van Averbeke (chapter 14) and Fay (chapter 18), complicate the current attempts of the state to resuscitate agriculture. Although there are considerable local differences, it is appropriate to refer to the majority of rural African people as rural dwellers or villagers, and not as peasants, smallholders, communal farmers or farmers *sensu strictu*. We are often dealing with what F. Wilson (1975) characterises as an 'industrial proletariat domiciled in the country', and what Beinart (2001) refers to as a 'pensionariat'. Along with retrenched workers and urban drifters, pensioners make up the largest proportion of people in many villages; this varies sharply, however, across regional contexts.

10 Social heterogeneities

It would be a mistake to treat land reform and rural development processes homogeneously and the beneficiaries as an undifferentiated group of social actors. Several chapters, notably those by Marais, Moseki, Taoana, Phetlhu and Khutswane, provide detailed accounts of how existing social inequalities (based, for example, on the ownership of resources such as livestock, capital and contacts, but also on gender and age) among groups of beneficiaries shape land reform dynamics and outcomes. Post-apartheid forms of inequality are strengthened by the politics of land reform, especially since the state distinguishes between beneficiaries and/or non-beneficiaries. The much alluded-to intrinsic problems of the collective property associations (James 2007) and the 'rent-a-crowd strategies' (Lahiff 2007) of some of the beneficiaries, aimed at expanding and strengthening their control over assets, undermine the ability of people to devise commonly shared strategies and result in struggles and disenchantment, and winners and losers. Existing inequalities, based on assets and skills, are strengthened. At the same time collective property organisations and the rent-a-crowd strategies that have given shape to land and agrarian reform in South Africa were imposed by the state and state officials to achieve results and to show the public that land reform proceeds as planned. The social forms and strategies also emerged to achieve, with the limited state grants that have become available, scales of operation that would fit with their idea of commercial agriculture.

Conclusion

This chapter has provided a summary as well as a synthesis of the book against the background of some of the major theoretical and empirical lessons land and agrarian reform processes have generated in South Africa as well as elsewhere in the world. Land and agrarian reform does not unfold as a neat and straightforward process; societies in which reform is launched and bureaucracies and states that give hands and feet to these processes appear far more complex than is often assumed or dreamed of. The lessons learned from land reform are synthesised in a series of conceptual starting points; these help us to disentangle the complexities, ambiguities and contradictory realities and experiences that land and agrarian reform has generated and will continue to generate.

In the Shadow of Policy conveys many ideas and suggestions. By making a distinction between policies and (everyday) practices, it offers scope to study the discrepancy between theory and policy (that is, design and implementation, including budgeting) and practice (what is implemented, how and by whom, and how reworked by beneficiaries). It reflects on the politics of land and agrarian reform and challenges those involved to ensure a genuine role for reforms on the political agendas of governments and international development agencies. What is questioned is whether these agendas take note of the realities at grassroots level and whether an organised social movement is there to channel land reform processes. *In the Shadow of Policy* simultaneously critically engages with the assumptions that the South African state has the capacity to provide budgets, to design meaningful programmes and to deliver services to beneficiaries. The experiences of reform that are elucidated in this book severely critique that capacity. Yet the idea that beneficiaries sit back and wait for government to deliver, and do not enact development, is not in line with the findings from empirical research in South Africa's rural areas. At the same time, land reform experiences are varied and heterogeneous, from both a social and a livelihood point of view. But beneficiaries do not become disenchanted only with the process; elites 'capturing' benefits for themselves, internal fights, abuse and new forms of social inequalities signify that beneficiaries contest the socio-political spaces of land reform.

This chapter has provided food for thought about land reform policy and practices and has captured land and agrarian reform policies, practices and processes as messy and often as unordered. When we begin to view land reform as messy and structurally unordered, new modes of thinking, new designs and social action are required. *In the Shadow of Policy* provides some ideas to facilitate progress beyond rhetoric.

References

Ainslie, A. 2005. 'Keeping cattle? The politics of value in the communal areas of the Eastern Cape province, South Africa', unpublished PhD thesis, University of London.

Aliber, M. and R. Hall. 2012. 'Support for smallholder farmers in South Africa: challenges of scale and strategy', *Development Southern Africa*, 29(4): 548–562.

Beinart, W. 2001. *Twentieth-century South Africa. New edition*, Oxford: Oxford University Press.

Bernstein, H. 2002. 'Land reform: taking a long(er) view', *Journal of Agrarian Change*, 2(4): 433–463.

Bernstein, H. 2003. 'Land reform in southern Africa in world-historical perspective', *Review of African Political Economy*, 30(96): 203–226.

Bernstein, H. 2004. '"Changing before our very eyes": agrarian questions and the politics of land in capitalism today', *Journal of Agrarian Change*, 4(1–2): 190–225.

Bernstein, H. 2007. 'Agrarian questions of capital and labour: some theory about land reform (and a periodisation)', in L. Ntsebeza and R. Hall (eds) *The land question in South Africa: the challenge of transformation and redistribution*, Cape Town: HSRC Press.

Bernstein, H. 2009. 'V.I. Lenin and A.V. Chayanov: looking back, looking forward', *Journal of Peasant Studies*, 36(1): 55–81.

Bernstein, H. 2010a. 'Rural livelihoods and agrarian change: bringing class back in', in N. Long, Y. Jingzhong and W. Yihuan (eds) *Rural transformations and development – China in context: the everyday lives of policies and people*, Cheltenham: Edward Elgar.

Bernstein, H. 2010b. *Class dynamics of agrarian change*, Nova Scotia: Fernwood Publishing Company.

Binswanger, H. and K. Deininger. 1996. 'South African land policy: the legacy of history and current options', in V. J. Zyl, J. Kirsten and H. Binswanger (eds) *Agricultural land reform in South Africa: policies, markets and mechanisms*, Oxford: Oxford University Press.

Borras, S. 2003. 'Questioning market-led agrarian reform: experiences from Brazil, Colombia and South Africa', *Journal of Agrarian Change*, 3(3): 367–394.

Borras, S. 2008. 'La Vía Campesina and its global campaign for agrarian reform', *Journal of Agrarian Change*, 8(2–3): 258–289.

Caldeira, R. 2008. '"My land, your social transformation": conflicts within the landless people movement (MST), Rio de Janeiro, Brazil', *Journal of Rural Studies*, 24(2): 150–160.

Chayanov, A. 1966. *The theory of peasant economy*, Homewood: American Economic Association.

Cousins, B. 2007. 'Agrarian reform and the "two economies": transforming South Africa's countryside', in L. Ntsebeza and R. Hall (eds) *The land question in South Africa: the challenge of transformation and redistribution*, Cape Town: HSRC Press.

Cousins, B. 2011. 'What is a "smallholder"? Class-analytic perspectives on small-scale farming and agrarian reform in South Africa', in P. Hebinck and C. Shackleton (eds) *Reforming land and resource use in South Africa: impact on livelihoods*, London: Routledge.

Cousins, B. 2013. 'Smallholder irrigation schemes, agrarian reform and "accumulation from above and from below" in South Africa', *Journal of Agrarian Change*, 13(1): 116–139.

Cousins, B. and I. Scoones. 2010. 'Contested paradigms of "viability" in redistributive land reform: perspectives from southern Africa', *Journal of Peasant Studies*, 37(1): 31–66.

Deininger, K. 1999. 'Making negotiated land reform work: initial experience from Colombia, Brazil and South Africa', *World Development*, 27: 651–672.

Deininger, K. and H. Binswanger. 1999. 'The evolution of the World Bank's land policy: principles, experience and future challenges', *The World Bank Research Observer*, 14(2): 247–276.

De Janvry, A. and E. Sadoulet. 2010. 'Agricultural growth and poverty reduction: additional evidence', *The World Bank Research Observer*, 25(1): 1–20.

De Sardan, O. 2006. *Anthropology and development: understanding contemporary social change*, London: Zed Press.

DLA (Department of Land Affairs). 1996. *Land Affairs Green Paper*, Pretoria: Department of Land Affairs.

DLA. 1997. *White Paper on South African land policy*, Pretoria: Department of Land Affairs.

DOA (Department of Agriculture). 2001. *Land redistribution for agricultural development*, Pretoria: Department of Agriculture.

DRDLR (Department of Rural Development and Land Reform). 2009. 'Comprehensive rural development programme: the concept', Pretoria: Department of Rural Development and Land Reform.

DRDLR. 2011. *Green Paper on land reform 2011*, Pretoria: Department of Rural Development and Land Reform.

Ellis, F. 1993. *Peasant economics: farm households and agrarian development*, Cambridge: Cambridge University Press.

Ewert, J. and J. Hamman. 1999. Why paternalism survives: globalization, democratization and labour on South African wine farms, *Sociologia Ruralis*, 39(2): 202–221.

Ferguson, J. 1990. *The anti-politics machine: 'development', depoliticization, and bureaucratic power in Lesotho*, Cambridge: Cambridge University Press.

Ferguson, J. 2013. 'How to do things with land: a distributive perspective on rural livelihoods in southern Africa', *Journal of Agrarian Change*, 13(1): 166–174.

Gore, C. 2000. 'The rise and fall of the Washington Consensus as a paradigm for developing countries', *World Development*, 28(5): 789–804.

Greenberg, S. 2004. *The Landless People's Movement and the failure of post-apartheid land reform*, Centre for Civil Society and the School of Development Studies, University of KwaZulu-Natal, Durban.

Grindle, M. and J. Thomas. 1991. *Public choices and policy change: the political economy of reform in developing countries*, Baltimore: Johns Hopkins University Press.

Habib, A. and V. Padayachee. 2000. 'Economic policy and power relations in South Africa's transition to democracy', *World Development*, 28(2): 245–263.

Hadju, F. 2006. 'Local worlds: rural livelihood strategies in Eastern Cape, South Africa', unpublished PhD thesis, Linköping University.

Hall, R. 2004. 'A political economy of land reform in South Africa', *Review of African Political Economy*, 31(100): 213–27.

Hall, R. (ed.) 2009a. *Another countryside? Policy options for land and agrarian reform in South Africa*, Cape Town: Institute for Poverty, Land and Agrarian Studies, University of the Western Cape.

Hall, R. 2009b. 'Dynamics in the commercial farming sector', in R. Hall (ed.) *Another countryside? Policy options for land and agrarian reform in South Africa*, Cape Town: Institute for Poverty, Land and Agrarian Studies, University of the Western Cape.

Hammar, A. 2007. '"The Day of Burning": land, authority and belonging in Zimbabwe's agrarian margins in the 1990s', unpublished PhD thesis, Roskilde University, Copenhagen.

Hebinck, P., D. Fay and K. Kondlo. 2011. 'Land and agrarian reform in South Africa's Eastern Cape province: caught by continuities', *Journal of Agrarian Change*, 11(2): 220–240.

Hebinck, P. and P. Lent (eds). 2007. *Livelihoods and landscape: the people of Guquka and Koloni and their resources*, Leiden/Boston: Brill Academic Publishers.

Hebinck, P. and C. Shackleton. 2011. 'Livelihoods, resources and land reform', in P. Hebinck and C. Shackleton (eds) *Reforming land and resource use in South Africa: impact on livelihoods*, London: Routledge.

Hebinck, P. and W. van Averbeke. 2007. 'Livelihoods and landscape: people, resources and land use', in P. Hebinck and P. Lent (eds) *Livelihoods and landscape: the people of Guquka and Koloni and their resources*, Leiden/Boston: Brill Academic Publishers.

Huizer, G. 1999. *Peasant mobilization for land reform: historical case studies and theoretical considerations*, Discussion Paper No. 103, Geneva: UNRISD.

James, D. 2007. *Gaining ground? Rights and poverty in South African land reform*, Johannesburg: Wits University Press.

James, D. 2010. 'Doing business with a development ethic: "new look" land redistribution in South Africa', in B. Freund and H. Witt (eds) *Development dilemmas in post-apartheid South Africa*, Pietermaritzburg: University of KwaZulu-Natal Press.

James, D. 2011. 'The return of the broker: consensus, hierarchy, and choice in South African land reform', *Journal of the Royal Anthropological Institute*, 17(2): 318–338.

Jerven, M. 2010. 'The relativity of poverty and income: how reliable are African economic statistics?', *African Affairs*, 109(434): 77–96.

Kautsky, K. 1988. *The agrarian question*, London: Zwan.

Keeley, J. and I. Scoones. 2003. *Understanding environmental policy processes: cases from Africa*, London: Earthscan.

Kepe, T. 2002. 'The dynamics of cattle production and government intervention in communal areas of the Lusikisiki District', in A. Ainslie *Cattle ownership and production in the communal areas of the Eastern Cape, South Africa*, PLAAS Research Report No.10, Cape Town: Programme for Land and Agrarian Studies, University of the Western Cape.

Kydd, J. and A. Dorward. 2001. 'The Washington Consensus on poor country agriculture: analysis, prescription and institutional gaps', *Development Policy Review*, 19(4): 467–478.

Lahiff, E. 2007. '"Willing buyer, willing seller": South Africa's failed experiment in market-led agrarian reform', *Third World Quarterly*, 28(8): 1577–1597.

Lahiff, E. 2011. 'Land reform and poverty reduction in South Africa', in P. Hebinck and C. Shackleton (eds) *Reforming land and resource use in South Africa: impact on livelihoods*, London: Routledge.

Leach, M. and J. Fairhead. 2000. 'Fashioned forest pasts, occluded histories? International environmental analysis in West African locales', *Development and Change*, 31(1): 35–59.

Li, T. 2007. *The will to improve: governmentality, development, and the practice of politics*, Durham, NC: Duke University Press.

Lipton, M. 1993. 'Land reform as unfinished business: the case for not stopping', *World Development*, 21(1): 1–58.

Lipton, M. 2009. *Land reform in developing countries: property rights and property wrongs*, London: Routledge.

Lipton, M. and M. Lipton. 1993. 'Creating rural livelihoods: some lessons for South Africa from experience elsewhere', *World Development*, 21(9): 1515–1548.

Long, N. 2001. *Development sociology: actor perspectives*, London: Routledge.

Long, N. 2004a. 'Contesting policy ideas from below', in M. Bøås and D. McNeill (eds), *Global institutions and development: framing the world?* London: Routledge.

Long, N. 2004b. 'Actors, interfaces and development intervention: meanings, purposes and powers', in T. Kontinen (ed.) *Development intervention: actor and activity perspectives*, Helsinki: Helsingfors.

Long, N. and J.D. van der Ploeg. 1989. 'Demythologizing planned intervention: an actor perspective', *Sociologia Ruralis*, 29(3–4): 226–249.

Mafeje, A. 2003. *The agrarian question, access to land, and peasant responses in sub-Saharan Africa*, Civil Society and Social Movements Programme Paper No. 6, Geneva: UNRISD.

Mango, N. and P. Hebinck. 2004. 'Cultural repertoires and socio-technological regimes: a case study of local and modern varieties of maize in Luoland, West Kenya', in H. Wiskerke and J.D. van der Ploeg (eds) *Seeds of transition: essays on novelty production, niches and regimes in agriculture*, Assen: Royal Van Gorcum.

Marsden, T. 1998. 'Agriculture beyond the treadmill? Issues for policy, theory and research practice', *Progress in Human Geography*, 22(2): 265–275.

McGee, R. 2004. 'Unpacking policy: actors, knowledge and spaces', in B. Brock, R. McGee and J. Gaventa (eds) *Knowledge, actors and spaces in poverty reduction in Uganda and Nigeria*, Kampala: Fountain Publishers.

Monde, N. 2003. 'Household food security in rural areas of central Eastern Cape', unpublished PhD thesis, University of Fort Hare.

Naidoo, L. 2011. 'Poverty and insecurity of farm workers and dwellers in post-apartheid South Africa', in P. Hebinck and C. Shackleton (eds) *Reforming land and resource use in South Africa: impact on livelihoods*, London: Routledge.

Ntsebeza L. and R. Hall (eds). 2007. *The land question in South Africa: the challenge of transformation and redistribution*, Cape Town: HSRC Press.

O'Laughlin, B., H. Bernstein, B. Cousins and P. Peters. 2013. 'Introduction: agrarian change, rural poverty and land reform in South Africa since 1994', *Journal of Agrarian Change*, 13(1): 1–15.

Peach, W. and J. Constatin. 1972. 'Meaning and nature of resources', in W. Peach and J. Constatin (eds) *Zimmerman's world resources and industries*, New York: Harper and Row.

Ribot, J. and N. Peluso. 2003. 'A theory of access', *Rural Sociology*, 68(2): 153–181.

Roe, E. 1991. 'Development narratives, or making the best of blueprint development', *World Development*, 19(4): 287–300.

Rosset, P. 2006. 'Conclusion: moving forward: agrarian reform as a part of food sovereignty', in P. Rosset, R. Patel and M. Courville (eds) *Promised land: competing visions of agrarian reform*, Oakland, CA: Food First Books.

Rosset, P., R. Patel. and M. Courville (eds). 2006. *Promised land: competing visions of agrarian reform*, Oakland, CA: Food First Books.

Scoones, I. 1992. 'The economic value of livestock in the communal areas of southern Zimbabwe', *Agricultural Systems*, 39(4): 339–59.

Scott, J.C. 1998. *Seeing like a state: how certain schemes to improve the human condition have failed*, New Haven, CT: Yale University Press.

Sender, J. and D. Johnston. 2004. 'Searching for a weapon of mass production in rural Africa: unconvincing arguments for land reform', *Journal of Agrarian Change*, 4(1–2): 142–164.

Shackleton, C., S. Shackleton and B. Cousins. 2001. 'The role of land-based strategies in rural livelihoods: the contribution of arable production, animal husbandry and natural resource harvesting in communal areas of South Africa', *Development Southern Africa*, 18(5): 583–604.

Smith, R. 2003. 'Land tenure reform in Africa: a shift to the defensive', *Progress in Development Studies*, 3(3): 210–222.

Thiesenhusen, W. (ed.) 1989a. *Searching for agrarian reform in Latin America*, Boston: Unwin Hyman.

Thiesenhusen, W. 1989b. 'Conclusions: searching for agrarian reform in Latin America', in W. Thiesenhusen (ed.) *Searching for agrarian reform in Latin America*, Boston: Unwin Hyman.

Van den Brink, R. 2003. *Land policy and land reform in sub-Saharan Africa: consensus, confusion and controversy*, Pretoria: World Bank South Africa.

Van der Ploeg, J.D. 2008. *The new peasantries: struggles for autonomy and sustainability in an era of empire and globalization*, London: Earthscan.

Van der Ploeg, J.D. 2010. The peasantries of the twenty-first century: the commoditisation debate revisited, *Journal of Peasant Studies*, 37(1): 1–30.

Van der Ploeg, J.D. 2013. *Peasants and the art of farming: a Chayanovian manifesto*, Nova Scotia: Fernwood Publishers.

Van der Ploeg, J. D., A. Long and J. Banks. 2002. *Living countrysides: rural development processes in Europe: the state of the art*, Doetinchem: Elsevier.

Van der Ploeg, J.D., J. Ye and S. Schneider. 2012. 'Rural development through the construction of new, nested, markets: comparative perspectives from China, Brazil and the European Union', *Journal of Peasant Studies*, 39(1): 133–173.

Van Zyl, J., J. Kirsten, J. and H. Binswanger (eds). 1996. *Agricultural land reform in South Africa: policies, markets and mechanisms*, Oxford: Oxford University Press.

Walker, C. 2008. *Landmarked: land claims and land restitution in South Africa*, Johannesburg and Athens: Jacana and Ohio University Press.

Walker, C., A. Bohlin, R. Hall and T. Kepe (eds). 2010. *Land, memory, reconstruction and justice: perspectives on land claims in South Africa*, Pietermaritzburg and Athens: University of KwaZulu-Natal Press and Ohio University Press.

Wegerif, M. 2004. *A critical appraisal of South Africa's market-based land reform policy: the case of the Land Redistribution for Agricultural Development (LRAD) programme in Limpopo*, Cape Town: Programme for Land and Agrarian Studies, University of the Western Cape.

Wegerif, M. 2010. 'The right to land restitution as inspiration for mobilization', in C. Walker, A. Bohlin, R. Hall and T. Kepe. (eds) *Land, memory, reconstruction and justice: perspectives on land claims in South Africa*, Pietermaritzburg and Athens: University of KwaZulu-Natal Press and Ohio University Press.

Wiggins, S., J. Kirsten and L. Llambí. 2010. 'The future of small farms', *World Development*, 38(10): 1341–1348.

Wilson, F. 1975. 'Farming, 1866–1966', in M. Wilson and L. Thompson (eds) *The Oxford history of South Africa. Vol. II. South Africa 1870–1966*, Oxford: Clarendon Press.

Wittman, H. 2009. Reframing agrarian citizenship: land, life and power in Brazil, *Journal of Rural Studies*, 25(1): 120–130.

Wolford, W. 2010. 'Participatory democracy by default: land reform, social movements and the state in Brazil', *Journal of Peasant Studies*, 37(1): 91–109.

2 Land and agrarian reform policies from a historical perspective

Paul Hebinck

The purpose of this chapter is to review land and agrarian development policies in South Africa and to chart the changes that have taken place over the years. This overview spans the period before the native reserves came into being as result of the infamous 1913 Land Act, to the recent post-apartheid land and agrarian reform policies.

A historical analysis of policy structures the chapter. Land and agrarian reform policies are not designed and implemented in a socio-political and historical vacuum. Policies 'have left their historical traces' as James (2010: 222) points out and these are still visible and felt to this day. Notably, the residual effects of colonial and apartheid policies constrain the social transformations that post-apartheid policymakers would like to facilitate. An account of policies and their formulation requires a chronology, preferably one which intertwines the nature of state power with advancements in the sciences.

The history of South Africa clearly did not begin in 1652 with the colonisation of a small piece of land near present-day Cape Town by Dutch settlers instigated by the Dutch East India Company (VOC). Our concern is with the role the colonial state and state policies have played since 1654 in the reordering of what is currently South Africa and how this concurred with the interests of the state, white settlers and later those of the mining sector. A common periodisation is one that distinguishes the colonial from the Union era and apartheid from post-apartheid. State policies, acts and degrees do not neatly fit these four periods, but they nevertheless have some degree of distinctiveness. During the colonial period policies were implemented to expand and control the frontier and that laid the foundation for racial segregation. The second period roughly covers the Union years (1910–1948) during which key land, labour and land-use legislation was passed that exclusively favoured white land ownership and large-scale farming. The apartheid period (1948–1994) hinged on a continuation of betterment and the implementation of homeland policies and a fine-tuning of discriminatory laws. In the post-apartheid era, all discriminatory laws, acts and decrees previously passed to limit the mobility of black people and their access to land have been repealed, and reform policies have been initiated.

The increasing ability of the state to master the social and natural environment, however, is not only attributable to its political and military power to extend its frontiers and enforce rules and regulations. It is also shaped by the advancement in (notably agrarian) sciences and technology and the gradual formation and expansion of an associated expert system (Beinart 2003; Scott 1998). The technological advances progressing over time that assisted the state in its attempts to reorder (rural) society, with a view to intensifying agricultural and rural production, are significant. Laws that regulated use of and access to land came into being after a series of state-appointed special commissions, consisting of known experts (notably reputable scientists) in their field, had advised the state on why and how to deal with matters that reduced environmental risks (erosion, insects and pests) and enhanced productivity of land, cattle and crops. The commissions were always known by the names of their chairmen (see Cross 1988 for more details). The Beaumont Commission, for example, delivered its report about the actual delimitation of land for black people in 1916, while the Tomlinson Commission of 1955 rejected the one-man-one-plot principle and argued instead for a move towards large(r)-scale farming. The Swart Report of 1983 advocated moving all the black people in the Ciskei to urban areas, arguing that the rural areas were unable to sustain their present populations. This would also have opened the way for large-scale farming. The knowledge and institutional culture of each generation of experts has laid the foundations for the next. In this way, expert practice and knowledge has been reproduced in its own image (Hebinck et al. 2011). Some of these experts are non–South Africans by birth and training (see chapter 3, this volume).

Tracing the policy histories serves to show that over the years, apart from changes and shifts (that is, discontinuities), the policies retained many common characteristics (that is, continuities in design and the knowledge repertoires that underlie them) even though they emerged from contrasting political ideologies and governance regimes. This chapter argues that the degree of continuity between past and present policy is surprisingly large, and significant to an understanding of current land and agrarian reform dynamics. The chapter draws attention to three important continuities: (i) The state, whether colonial, apartheid or post-apartheid, has taken the lead in agrarian development and coordinating agrarian transformation; (ii) In doing so, the state always relied heavily on expert discourses for the design of its planned interventions; (iii) State-led and expert-designed agrarian development discourses uncritically embraced linear, neo-liberal views of development, consistently relying on a paradigm of modernisation to define what constitutes resources, even though lip service has been paid to the value of indigenous knowledge systems.

The colonial and Union eras

During the early years of the colony, the state alienated the original inhabitants from their land. Its geographical reach was rather limited then. The early Dutch colonial state was preoccupied with extending its control over the immediate social and physical environment so that it could procure meat. Penn (2005: 30 ff) uses the term 'policy' to describe the creation and expansion of the frontier into the Cape interior. The search for meat for the VOC was supported by commando raids that 'encouraged' the Khoi and San to barter for meat. The granting of farms and issuing of grazing licences (in the form of loan farms) to Dutch settlers had a tremendous effect on pastoral production in the region but guaranteed the supply of meat to the Cape Town market. The advent of the loan farm system institutionalised a form of land tenure which provided cheap and easy access to vast tracts of precious grasslands for the semi-nomadic, cattle-keeping *trekboers* in the early eighteenth century. *Trekboers* lived, like the Khoi and the San, by harvesting wild resources. The intensification of land use that gradually emerged facilitated the cultivation of crops, sedentary cattle farming and capitalist accumulation. This was accompanied by the establishment of a vivid rural Afrikaner culture and the dispossession of the land of the Khoi, the San and, much later, also African peoples. Sending missionaries into the Cape hinterland was part of a deliberate policy to pacify the region and achieve political closure (Penn 1986: 67). The Khoi and the San were left with little choice but to hunt illegally for cattle and game on the land that had once been theirs.

The reach of the colonial state also expanded dramatically towards the east. Around 1770 the *trekboers* encountered the Xhosa, who had crossed the Kei River and were moving south. The Xhosa and the *trekboers* soon competed for the same resources (pasture, labour and cattle); both relied heavily on pastoral cattle farming (Mostert 1992; Penn 2005). Although their co-existence was relatively peaceful initially, it was always inherently unstable. In contrast to the northern frontier during the early eighteenth century (Penn 2005), where the Khoi and the San were brutally subjugated and absorbed as labourers, the Xhosa were, after an initial period of resistance during the 1820–1889 border wars, defeated, settled and incorporated as migrant labourers into the colonial economy.

The mindful and coordinated efforts of the state during the colonial period clearly aimed not just to establish control over land and labour but also to facilitate early forms of agricultural commodity production. Legislation, such as the Fencing Acts of 1883 and 1910, enabled measures to be taken to increase the productivity of pasture and livestock and in turn laid the ideological foundations for private property and commoditisation in the countryside (Van Sittert 2002). The state's mindset in favour of agriculture is a response to its being the backbone of wealth production in the country, which has expanded to become the chief source of commodities for national and global markets. Even when diamonds and gold became the key sectors of the colonial economy, agriculture remained the major source of accumulation, albeit in different ways, for both African people and white farmers, most of whom were Afrikaners of Dutch descent.

Towards the end of the nineteenth century, a range of measures were taken that especially affected African agriculture, fundamentally reshaping the rural livelihoods of African people (Bundy 1988, Mayer 1980). In addition, the discovery of diamonds (1867) and gold (1880) marked the emergence of the mining sector in the country, which had a profound impact on the agricultural sector, both white and African (F. Wilson 1975). The mining and white agricultural sectors held considerable political power at the time (Legassick 1977). Together they pushed for the promulgation of legislation that would give them control over African labour (Seekings and Nattrass 2006; F. Wilson 1975). State revenue from the mines was spent on developing the commercial capacity of white capitalist farming, which had moved beyond nomadic livestock to become sedentary. The economic conditions encouraged white farmers to abandon the practice of keeping peasant squatters on their farms in favour of the development of their farms for large-scale production of crops and livestock. To facilitate further expansion of commodity, white farmers required access to and control over a permanent workforce. Legislation was enacted that denied Africans access to white-owned land by prohibiting different forms of tenancy. Various anti-squatting laws culminated in the Natives Land Act No. 27 of 1913. The 1913 act, which was followed by the Native Trust and Land Act No. 18 of 1936, identified the areas that should be set aside for black people. This was the first legislation to apply the principle of territorial segregation and separate land rights for 'natives' and 'non-natives', preventing Africans from purchasing land outside the 'reserves' and restricting accumulation within them. The 'native' areas were gradually reshaped so as to serve as labour reserves, which in turn had devastating consequences for black farming. By the late 1950s, African farming had declined substantially. A vicious cycle of overpopulation, deterioration of natural resources, migration and impoverishment increasingly manifested itself. Despite these segregation policies, some black people managed to purchase land (referred to as 'black spots'), but they were often forced to allow others – officials, the church, missionaries – to hold the land in trust for them. These groups became subject to forced removals during the apartheid era (see Claassens and Cousins 2008; Van Leynseele forthcoming; Walker 2008).

A second set of legislation, including the Glen Grey Act (Cape Act No. 25 of 1894), was aimed at limiting the amount of land Africans could hold. The 'one-man-one-plot' principle and the intention to extend private tenure was of central importance and served the purpose of securing notions of individually owned property and drawing people into the monetary economy. Limiting the size of plots compelled landholders to seek additional income off-farm elsewhere so that '... during the coming generation a limited number will be agriculturalists, i.e., native farmers – and ... the rest will have to go out and work' (M. Wilson 1975: 65). Making the plots indivisible meant that all but the landowner's eldest son had to find off-farm livelihoods, which they found *en masse* in the mines, factories, large farms and in the transport sector. Women were predominantly drawn into the commodity economy as domestic labourers. Raising taxes also served to increase the need for cash among rural Africans (Bundy 1988; Lewis 1984). A strict land-use model was implemented, hinging on land use in distinct categories of land, combined with tenure arrangements such as freehold, quitrent and communal (see chapter 14, this volume). However, the tenacity of local practices, rural opposition to tax increases and the limits of state capacity meant that tenure reform 'fell away as a central administrative objective ...', (Beinart and Bundy 1987: 141).

Before the early twentieth century, the state had actively intervened only to address land and labour questions and issues. At the turn of the nineteenth century and during the early years of the Union, Afrikaner nationalism drove land policy and was instrumental in the formation of specific agrarian institutions whose mandate and orientation were largely shaped by the political and economic needs of the then ruling elite and the state. The state was often resented by white farmers because of the interference of state officials who arrived at their farms to implement 'corrective' measures (such as preventing soil erosion, or stock control to prevent diseases from spreading). Nonetheless, the state implemented a series of interventions that gradually led to the situation where white farmers increasingly looked to the state to solve their problems. After the establishment of the Union of South Africa in 1910, the state started to support white-dominated, large-scale capitalist agriculture more aggressively. Mbongwa et al. (1996) point out that between 1910 and 1935, 87 acts were passed to legitimise the provision of state support to white farmers. The policies raised the price of agricultural commodities to well above market levels. The formation of the Land Bank in 1912, providing credit to capitalise white agriculture, was soon followed by a range of initiatives effectively subsidising white farming (see F. Wilson 1975: 136–153). Poor white farmers received state support to rationalise their enterprises and were provided with cheap credit. Cooperatives were formed and railway extensions, which largely bypassed black farming areas, were constructed. The state assisted the institutionalisation of an agricultural expert system by establishing a national Department of Agriculture (DOA) in 1924 and agricultural training colleges and research stations (F. Wilson 1975; Beinart 2003). This is also the period when numerous 'white' and 'black' universities (notably faculties of agriculture) and other agricultural institutions of higher learning were created, with the support of the state and corporate lobby groups.

Beinart (2003: 336) argues that the agricultural expert system became associated in rhetoric and policy with attempts to forge a unified and modern white nation from the early years of the twentieth century onwards (see also Anker 2001). Heinrich Sebastian Du Toit, a highly committed senior official in the DOA, played a key role in the construction of an agricultural (expert) discourse and practice. Du Toit travelled worldwide, and his experiences convinced him that the advances of science should be incorporated into farming. This would stimulate production and secure conditions for the proper tilling of the land in difficult and marginal environments. These advances were intended to benefit the mass of white Afrikaner landowners, rather than white farmers in general. Du Toit felt that many rural Afrikaners had been bypassed by the department's research and publicity initiatives (Beinart 2003: 237). State support in irrigation cannot be disconnected from the poor white question. Brown (2001) situates the formation of the veterinary department, which dealt with animal diseases and breeding, and an entomology department at the turn of the twentieth century in a similar perspective.

As in Europe and the United States, expert knowledge was brought together in these institutions in order to facilitate agricultural and rural development (Brown 2001). Agricultural development, the leading role of the state, experts and expertise, Afrikaner nationalism and modernisation became intertwined. The frame of reference for most agricultural experts became the white settler farm. Black or African farming was either virtually absent from or on the margins of agricultural expert knowledge, even though some experts drew on African farming techniques (see Bundy 1988).

Land degradation in the 'native reserves' (for example, soil erosion, land denudation and the drying-up of springs) attracted the attention of the South African government. The 1932 Native Economic Commission called for a development programme to teach Africans how to use their land more economically and to halt resource degradation (M. Wilson 1975; Yawitch 1981). The Native Trust and Land Act No. 18 of 1936 provided the legal framework for government services to begin the reclamation and rehabilitation of the so-called native areas. The Act had two important objectives: to address the problem of overcrowding in the native areas by allocating additional land and to halt or prevent degradation on both old and new land allocations by means of land-use (betterment) planning. The South African Native Trust handled the allocation of additional land which became known as 'trust land'. The Act 'prevented the emergence of a stratum of rich or small capitalist farmers by rigidly insisting on a combination of communal grazing and one-man-one-plot agriculture' (Cross and Haines 1988: 83).

The chief concern of betterment planning between 1936 and 1950 was the protection and rehabilitation of natural resources. The government introduced policies that were aimed at limiting livestock in order to arrest the perceived denudation of the rangeland. It also engaged in the construction of contour banks in an attempt to prevent soil erosion. The planning for these measures started in the late 1930s. Things proceeded slowly because there was much resistance to the plans. Substantial opposition to betterment became widespread in the mid-1950s, partly because betterment was implemented by the hated new system of Bantu Authorities (Cross and Haines 1988; De Wet 1987, 1989; Mager 1999; McAllister 1988, 1989; Yawitch 1981). Betterment angered people not only because it was externally imposed but 'because it undermined the sense of security for old age which was one of the prerequisites of traditional tenure' (Cross and Haines 1988: 83, citing Davenport 1956). Betterment elicited mixed reactions in the Ciskei. Reallocations and culling, for example, were disliked but education was welcomed (Hebinck and Smith 2007).

The African population especially resisted the restrictions on livestock numbers. Their opposition to limiting livestock numbers was shaped by their views about carrying capacity and the significance of cattle, views which contrasted markedly with those of the experts. The limiting of stock numbers and subsequent measures to cull were instigated by scientists and agricultural experts arguing that overstocking

ruined the land and weakened cattle. The interplay of inadequate tenure, population pressure, lack of education and skills, and little scientific grounding of farming
practices was held responsible for erosion (Laker 1975; Trollope 1985). The widespread system of *kraaling*, used by both white and black farmers, was seen as a prime
example of ignorant farming that led to both overgrazing and selective grazing.
These views emerged during the great drought at the beginning of the twentieth
century, which brought environmental concerns to the fore in state circles and
among the general public (Beinart 2003; F. Wilson 1975). Such views, held by many
government officials and experts, were also sustained by the idea that communal
farming was an inefficient means of raising cattle and crops as an economic resource
and was destined to trigger ecological collapse. These views persisted for a long
time. They still drove betterment planning 30 years later. This is not to say, though,
that degradation and overgrazing never presented a problem. Gullies have resulted
from overgrazing and ploughing in the Eastern Cape and in the rest of the country
(Beinart 2003; Bundy 1988; Hoffman and Todd 2000; Lent and Mupakati 2007).

Apartheid, betterment planning and homelands

The apartheid era saw a consolidation and fine-tuning of the laws, acts and
degrees issued before. The advent of the National Party government in 1948,
however, changed the nature of state intervention dramatically. The Group
Areas Act No. 41 of 1950 signalled the beginning of complete segregation. Native
reserves were gradually transformed into independent 'homelands' with which
white South Africa could maintain economic and political relationships. In 1955,
the Commission for the Socio-Economic Development of the Bantu Areas within
the Union of South Africa, headed by Tomlinson, released its report based on
the most comprehensive investigation of socio-economic conditions in the native
reserves ever undertaken (Tomlinson Commission 1955). The Commission's brief
had been to develop a rural policy of separate development. One of its key recommendations was that the rural population needed to be divided into a landless
group and a group of progressive farmers. The Tomlinson Commission rejected
the 'one-man-one-plot' principle of land allocation. Instead, it called for the allocation of landholdings that were large enough to form economic farming units.
It also recommended the abolition of communal tenure and its replacement by a
system of private tenure. This would be subject to restrictions, however, in order
to avoid the accumulation of land. The commission recommended the development of urban centres and industries in the 'native areas' in order to accommodate people that were already landless as well as those who would become landless because of the plans. The commission's plans would entail a fundamental
restructuring of society in the 'native' areas, and called for a massive investment
by the state to make this possible. The South African government rejected two of
the commission's key recommendations: the abolition of communal tenure and
the establishment of white-owned industries. The financial implementation of

the original plan was considered far too costly. Politically, too, the recommendations were unacceptable. The removal of 50 per cent of the population would lead to massive resistance. However, the Verwoerd government realised that it would have to make provision for the influx of vast numbers of people into the homelands, in any event. After all, its own grand apartheid plan envisaged that all non-white South Africans would become citizens of an ethnic homeland. Betterment planning after 1955 became part of a complex set of policies that were developed in response to the government's desire to maintain control over the population in the 'native areas'. Two key elements of betterment planning after 1950 contributed to improving control over the 'surplus people' residing in the homelands. Firstly, people were moved from dispersed homestead clusters to villages. Secondly, the government interfered with traditional leadership. Chiefs and headmen became government employees. They were expected to support government policy in order to maintain their status and benefits. Those who opposed the government were replaced (Westaway 1997). Together with the removals, this created a general atmosphere of distrust and protest.

In accordance with the objectives of apartheid, native areas or homelands were encouraged to adopt self-governance and become independent states. The general policy goal of controlling the African population in these areas was maintained by the governments of these new states, but there was also an effort to provide local livelihood opportunities for the resident people. African farming was supported by the state in the form of subsidised tractor services (called 'Trust tractors'), an increase in public extension services and services supporting production, marketing and providing access to finance – services which would be supplied by parastatals. Several studies, however, have demonstrated that the implementation of betterment planning had an adverse effect on agricultural production largely because it separated homesteads from natural resources and disrupted the cooperative work arrangements that had been based on kinship relations (De Wet 1989; McAllister 1988). Large capital investments in agriculture, most notably the irrigation schemes in the valleys of major rivers, aimed to increase agricultural production. Many of these investments had limited success or were financially unsustainable. Agricultural banks were restructured to reduce their reliance on state subsidies, making access to finance by small-scale farmers more difficult than before. The public agricultural extension service was criticised for its lack of impact (Bembridge 1985; Steyn 1988), and its budget was reduced progressively.

Land and rural development policies under apartheid were ambiguous, to say the least. Cross and Haines (1988: 88–90) argue that state-designed and -funded programmes had little impact on poverty and land use. Programmes were designed in a 'top-down, top-heavy management' manner, and their benefits tended to accrue to elites. Instead of seeking inputs from the grass roots, a style of imposing reforms from above became the norm. Interventions were entangled with patron–client relationships. The approach to land questions was frequently overly technical and misdirected, because it tended to ignore actual constraints (see also McAllister 1988).

Post 1994: land and agrarian reforms and social policies

Land and agrarian reform has been one of the main areas in which the post-apartheid state has asserted itself since 1994. Land and agrarian reform were initiated alongside expanding the social security network. The scale and reach of social grants has expanded considerably since 1994 and has become a more significant factor in rural development (Devereux 2007; Francis 2002), in budget and in magnitude, surpassing the role of land and agrarian reforms.

Land reform and agrarian reform

Land reform in South Africa began even before the new government led by the African National Congress (ANC) took control of the country in 1994, albeit with more limited objectives. In March 1991, De Klerk's government passed the Abolition of Racially Based Land Measures Act (No. 108), which repealed the 1913 and 1936 Land Acts and all the other provisions that regulated ownership of land according to race. The differences between pre-1994 and post-1994 land reforms were both strategic and substantive. The post-1994 land and agrarian reform objectives were more comprehensive and overarching, encompassing restitution, redistribution and security of tenure.

Land and agrarian reforms entrenched, for the first time in history, equal rights to land, documented in the Constitution of the Republic of South Africa 1996 (Act 108). An early initiative of the Mandela administration after the first democratic elections in 1994 was the articulation of the Reconstruction and Development Programme (RDP) 1994–1996 that set out to undo the legacy of apartheid, including the skewed distribution of land and income, racially discriminatory laws and regulations, and immense poverty. Land and agrarian reforms were initiated in order to correct and transform the agrarian structure (DLA 1996, 1997; DOA 2001). Government budgets for its land and agrarian reform programmes have grown since the mid-1990s, and some budgets have even tripled in size, but critique of the quantity and quality of service delivery soon surfaced (Aliber and Hall 2012; see chapter 3 in this volume for more details).

The state has shifted its policies and the allocation of its budgets over time from a more populist approach, which emphasised human and citizenship rights and gender and racial equity principles (during the period in which Derek Hanekom was minister of Agriculture and Land Affairs), to a more neo-liberal and paternalistic one (under ministers Thoko Didiza, Lulu Xingwana and Gugile Nkwinti). During the first years of the Mbeki administration the RDP was succeeded by the Growth, Employment and Redistribution (GEAR) programme reiterating the importance of employment, with redistribution to be achieved through a neo-liberal economic framework of state intervention (Habib and Padayachee 2000; see also chapter 3 in this volume). The change in focus is also apparent in the move away from the Settlement/Land Acquisition Grant (SLAG), which provided grants of R16 000 to people to access land if their monthly income was below R1 500 (Lahiff 2007: 1580; Williams 1996; see also chapter 3, this volume), and the introduction of the Land

Redistribution for Agricultural Development (LRAD) programme, which demands contributions from potential land reform beneficiaries themselves (DOA 2001; see chapter 3, this volume). LRAD has initiated *ex post* audits (replacing lengthy *ex ante* audits) and monitoring to make sure that its objectives are met (DLA 2008: 2). Land reform shifted from simple redistribution to market-led and assisted land reform, hinging on a policy of 'willing buyer, willing seller'. The market-led reform is, according to many commentators (Hall 2004; Lahiff 2007; Naidoo 2011), little more than a programme of assisted purchase under which the main beneficiaries are likely to be white landowners and a small minority of better-off black entrepreneurs. GEAR in particular emphasised the productive use of redistributed land and public–private partnerships (Derman et al. 2010) to secure the continuation of a highly capitalised, globally well-connected, commercial agricultural sector in South Africa. However, in contrast to what was expected from GEAR in terms of efforts to increase employment and to restructure the commercial agrarian economy, the post-apartheid state also took steps to deregulate the economy and liberalise trade, generating opposite outcomes. The reforms led to a withdrawal of the subsidies white farmers had enjoyed for years but also instigated changes that were not foreseen: landholdings remained consolidated as large; farming became more capital-intensive; and agricultural employment decreased substantially (Hall 2009). These tendencies clearly shape the success of the objective of land reform to propel 'emergent' farmers beyond subsistence and encourage them to access markets, technology and capital. They reinforce, on the one hand, the views that small-scale ('communal') farming is incapable of supporting anything more than a life of poverty. On the other hand, particular, normative notions of viability emerged, denoting that good farming is embodied in technical recommendations around 'minimum farm sizes', 'economic units' and 'carrying capacities' (Cousins and Scoones 2010; see chapter 3, this volume).

The Zuma administration reaffirmed the commitment to land and agrarian reform objectives (redistributing 30 per cent of the land by 2013) but with a much stronger emphasis on rural development and simultaneously confirming the prominence of a productivist land reform discourse. The transformation of the old Department of Agriculture and Land Affairs into the new Department of Rural Development and Land Reform (DRDLR) was emblematic of this change of emphasis. DRLDR formulated a Comprehensive Rural Development Programme (CRDP) 'to create vibrant, equitable and sustainable rural communities. [This] will be achieved through a three-pronged strategy based on a coordinated and integrated broad-based agrarian transformation, rural development infrastructure, and an improved land reform programme' (DRDLR 2009; Gwanya 2010: 11). The National Planning Commission (NPC) is responsible for developing a long-term vision for South Africa. It recently published its 'Vision 2030', which, together with *The New Growth Path* compiled by the Economic Development Department (EDD) in 2010, provides insight into how land and agrarian reform should proceed. Like the aborted *Green Paper on Land Reform* (DRDLR 2011), both documents target a transformation in the social relations of production to achieve social cohesion and development with a focus on supporting and expanding the smallholder sector – including communal farming – to 500 000 producers by 2020. The transfer of new technology to fuel productivity increases, tenure security and above all the creation of links into markets constitutes the rural insfrastructure to enable this transformation (NPC 2011: 145). These plans build on the expert discourse that poor farming practices, lack of markets and inefficient land tenure are the root of the problem. The NPC envisages vertical integration into existing markets but argues that preferential procurement strategies such as school feeding programmes and other institutional catering (food services to hospitals, correctional services and emergency food packages), in which the state is the main purchaser, should be put in place to serve as a market for small-scale producers. Such markets, however, are often situated in small- and medium-sized towns, away from where potential producers live. Such integration inevitably leads, as Li (2009) and Amanor (2009) argue, to the exclusion of the very people who are targeted by such development policies – smallholders and the poor – thus enforcing unequal development. A good example is the Agri-Park of the University of Fort Hare in Alice which facilitates the process whereby the added value of producing crops in the villages is realised elsewhere, in the towns. Farmer access to such markets is constrained by transport costs, quality standards, and lack of proper post-settlement support and adequate service delivery for smallholders (Aliber and Hall 2012). The NPC/EDD development discourse typically ignores that the markets that are formed, for instance, in the framework of the Massive Food Production Programme are beyond the control of small producers. Moreover, although supermarkets have become big players in rural food markets, they hardly procure from local small-scale producers. They prefer to buy from a limited number of producers, almost always large-scale farmers (D'Haese and Van Huylenbroeck 2005; Louw et al. 2007). Local, small-scale producers instead tend to 'supply' local, village-based 'informal' or nested (Van der Ploeg et al. 2012) markets which are largely absent from policy models.

State social policies: old age pensions and social grants

Old age pensions and a range of social grants constitute the core of the South African post-apartheid state's social policy, which can be conceptualised as state transfers to rural people and regions. The central argument here is that these state transfers in combination with rural production, which includes both crops and livestock production as well as natural resource harvesting, form the backbone of the current rural and urban economy (see chapters 14, 17 and 18, this volume; Devereux 2007; Hebinck and Lent 2007; Neves and Du Toit 2013).

The establishment and institutionalisation of the old age pension goes back to white miners' struggle for security in 1911 (Bhorat 1995). The grant scheme that was negotiated slowly evolved and was later broadened by the Verwoerd government to include Africans. From the mid-1940s onwards, various grants for blindness and invalidism were introduced. Child support and grants for HIV/AIDS affected people are a recent, but significant, addition to the social-grants system. Until 1993, however, the monetary value of old age pensions was determined by race. Black people received about half the amount that whites did. This was implemented by paying black people their pensions every second month. In 1993, the then government increased the value of welfare grants paid to African people by removing racial disparities. To qualify for an old age pension, South African males had to be 65 and females 60. This changed only in 2010, when the age of eligibility for males was lowered to 63.

The cash transfers have significant redistributive and welfare effects. They allow people to purchase food, clothes and other essentials of life but are also socially and symbolically significant. State transfers became even more significant during the 1990s, when the South African economy was restructured and deregulated. Unemployment rates increased because the economy failed to absorb new entrants into the formal labour market, and existing jobs were lost due to retrenchments in the private and public sector. As a result, social grants and old age pensions became a major source of income. As the size of the grant has increased over the years, these recipients have gradually achieved the status of 'earners'. In some areas, widows account for 80 per cent or more of the beneficiaries. Consequently, old age pensions are often referred to as widows' pensions (Sagner 2000: 547). The predominance of pensioners in the rural areas prompted Beinart (2001) to coin the term 'pensionariat'. Pensions and grants support three generations in many homesteads (Lund 2009; Van Averbeke and Hebinck 2007). Over time, grants have become a major component of the monetary economy in many rural villages, varying in degree of importance amongst homesteads. This does not mean that land and/or food production is unimportant. In many homesteads food is grown to supplement wages and grants, and for petty cash (chapters 14–18, this volume; Aliber and Hart 2009; De Wet 2011; Hart 2007).

Conclusion

This chapter has drawn attention to the birth of a range of policy measures that, taken together, have shaped (but not determined) past and present agrarian development processes. A common thread has been the continuous reliance of the state on expert discourses of development. Expert consultants and scientists have come to play a significant role in the identification of key resources and how to deploy them in development models with broader application. This has allowed experts to give direction to pre-apartheid, apartheid and post-apartheid agrarian policy and to shape the domain of the applied agrarian sciences.

Another common element in agrarian and rural development policies is the consistently held premise that modern technologies, markets and related institutions represent the only relevant and productive path for development. This is manifested in the noted ideological shift from a human rights perspective to productionism and rationalism. This, in turn, can be explained by the influence on key policymakers of the commercial farming lobby and economists advocating a conventional linear model of agricultural development uplifting the emergent farmers from subsistence to commercial producers. Most policies are derived from what might be called 'received wisdoms' (Leach and Fairhead 2000) commonly based on untested assumptions about empirical reality. It is important, therefore, to question the nature of the knowledge that informs current agrarian reform and rural development policies, as well as the quality and quantity of service delivery and the slow pace of land restitution and redistribution.

A significant issue is that the productivist discourse that underlies these does not take sufficiently into account that the state's social policies have been by far the most significant factor in (rural) development and that the role of agriculture, as narrowly defined by experts, has diminished dramatically. What this means for revitalising agriculture under the banner of the current CRDP is a critical question.

The trend that has emerged over the years is that more than ever, state and expert notions sanction projects or elements of projects both before and after a project has been established or a programme has been launched. Land reform increasingly is couched in terms of the conventional transfer of knowledge, manifested in the advice from expert-consultants, mentorship programmes and transformed institutional arrangements, as providing access to markets. Land reform, as Ben Cousins argues in chapter 3, is not meaningfully engaging with agrarian reform. After all these years, land and agrarian reforms are still at the crossroads.

References

Aliber, M. and R. Hall. 2012. 'Support for smallholder farmers in South Africa: challenges of scale and strategy', *Development Southern Africa*, 29: 548–562.

Aliber, M. and T. Hart. 2009. 'Should subsistence agriculture be supported as a strategy to address rural food insecurity?' *Agrekon*, 48(4): 434–458.

Amanor, K. 2009. 'Global food chains, African smallholders and World Bank governance', *Journal of Agrarian Change*, 9(2): 247–262.

Anker, P. 2001. *Imperial ecology: environmental order in the British Empire, 1895–1945*, Cambridge, MA: Harvard University Press.

Beinart, W. 2001. *Twentieth-century South Africa. New edition*, Oxford: Oxford University Press.

Beinart, W. 2003. *The rise of conservation in South Africa: settlers, livestock, and the environment 1770–1950*, New York: Oxford University Press.

Beinart, W. and C. Bundy. 1987. *Hidden struggles in rural South Africa: politics and popular movements in the Transkei and Eastern Cape, 1890–1930*, London: James Currey.

Bembridge, T. 1985. 'Agricultural and rural development in LDCs with special reference to South Africa', *Development Southern Africa*, 2: 287–296.

Bhorat, H. 1995. 'The South African safety net: past, present and future', *Development Southern Africa*, 12(4): 595–604.

Brown, K. 2001. 'Political entomology: the insectile challenge to agricultural development in the Cape Colony, 1895–1910', *Journal of Southern African Studies*, 29(2): 529–549.

Bundy, C. 1988. *The rise and fall of the South African peasantry*, London: James Currey.

Claassens, A. and B. Cousins (eds). 2008. *Land, power and custom: controversies generated by South Africa's Communal Land Rights Act*, Cape Town and Athens: UCT Press and Ohio University Press.

Cousins, B. and I. Scoones. 2010. 'Contested paradigms of "viability" in redistributive land reform: perspectives from southern Africa', *Journal of Peasant Studies*, 37(1): 31–66.

Cross, C. 1988. 'Introduction: land reform and the rural black economy in South Africa', in C. Cross and R. Haines (eds) *Towards freehold? Options for land and development in South Africa's black rural areas*, Kenwyn: Juta.

Cross, C. and R. Haines. 1988. 'An historical overview of land policy and tenure in South Africa's black areas', in C. Cross and R. Haines (eds) *Towards freehold? Options for land and development in South Africa's black rural areas*, Kenwyn: Juta.

Derman, B., E. Lahiff and E Sjastaad. 2010. 'Strategic questions about strategic partners: challenges and pitfalls in South Africa's new model of land restitution', in C. Walker, A. Bohlin, R. Hall and T. Kepe (eds) *Land, memory, reconstruction and justice: perspectives on land claims in South Africa*, Pietermaritzburg and Athens: University of KwaZulu-Natal Press and Ohio University Press.

Devereux, S. 2007. 'Social pensions in southern Africa in the twentieth century', *Journal of Southern African Studies*, 33(3): 539–560.

De Wet, C. 1987. 'Betterment planning in South Africa: some thoughts on its history, feasibility and wider policy implications', *Journal of Contemporary African Studies*, 6(1/2): 85–122.

De Wet, C. 1989. 'Betterment planning in a rural village in Keiskammmahoek District, Ciskei', *Journal of Southern African Studies*, 15(2): 326–345.

De Wet, C. 2011. 'Where are they now? Welfare, development and marginalization in a former bantustan settlement in the Eastern Cape, post 1994', in P. Hebinck and C. Shackleton (eds) *Reforming land and resource use in South Africa: impact on livelihoods*, London: Routledge.

D'Haese, M. and G. van Huylenbroeck. 2005. 'The rise of supermarkets and changing expenditure patterns of poor rural households: case study in the Transkei area, South Africa', *Food Policy*, 30: 97–113.

DLA (Department of Land Affairs). 1996. *Land Affairs Green Paper*, Pretoria: Department of Land Affairs.

DLA. 1997. *White Paper on South African land policy*, Pretoria: Department of Land Affairs.

DLA. 2008. *Land redistribution for agricultural development: sub-programme of the land redistribution programme*, Pretoria: Department of Land Affairs.

DOA (Department of Agriculture). 2001. *Land redistribution for agricultural development*, Pretoria: Department of Agriculture.

DRDLR (Department of Rural Development and Land Reform). 2009. 'Comprehensive rural development programme: the concept', Pretoria: Department of Rural Development and Land Reform.

DRDLR. 2011. *Green Paper on land reform 2011*, Pretoria: Department of Rural Development and Land Reform.

EDD (Economic Development Department). 2010. *The new growth path: framework*. Pretoria: Economic Development Department.

Francis, E. 2002. 'Rural livelihoods, institutions and vulnerability in North West province, South Africa', *Journal of Southern African Studies*, 28: 531–550.

Gwanya, T.T. 2010. *South Africa position paper on rural development: a model for the Comprehensive Rural Development Programme*, Pretoria: Department of Rural Development and Land Reform.

Habib, A. and V. Padayachee. 2000. 'Economic policy and power relations in South Africa's transition to democracy', *World Development*, 28(2): 245–263.

Hall, R. 2004. 'A political economy of land reform in South Africa', *Review of African Political Economy*, 31(100): 213–227.

Hall, R. 2009. 'Dynamics in the commercial farming sector', in R. Hall (ed.) *Another countryside? Policy options for land and agrarian reform in South Africa*, Cape Town: Institute for Poverty, Land and Agrarian Studies, University of the Western Cape.

Hart, T. 2007. 'The socioeconomics of subsistence farmers and the contribution of the social sciences to agricultural development', in S. Ntutela and W. Gevers (eds) *Science-based improvements of rural/subsistence agriculture*, Pretoria: Academy of Science of South Africa.

Hebinck, P., D. Fay, and K. Kondlo. 2011. 'Land and agrarian reform in South Africa's Eastern Cape province: caught by continuities', *Journal of Agrarian Change*, 11(2): 220–240.

Hebinck, P. and P. Lent (eds). *Livelihoods and landscape: the people of Guquka and Koloni and their resources*, Leiden/Boston: Brill Academic Publishers.

Hebinck, P. and L. Smith. 2007. 'History of settlement: processes and patterns', in P. Hebinck and P. C. Lent (eds) *Livelihoods and landscape: the people of Guquka and Koloni and their resources*, Leiden/Boston: Brill Academic Publishers.

Hoffman, T. M. and S. Todd. 2000. 'A national review of land degradation in South Africa: the influence of biophysical and socio-economic factors', *Journal of Southern African Studies*, 26(4): 743–758.

James, D. 2010. 'Doing business with a development ethic: "new look" land redistribution in South Africa', in B. Freund and H. Witt (eds) *Development dilemmas in post-apartheid South Africa*, Pietermaritzburg: University of KwaZulu-Natal Press.

Lahiff, E. 2007. '"Willing buyer, willing seller": South Africa's failed experiment in market-led agrarian reform', *Third World Quarterly*, 28(8): 1577–1597.

Laker, M. (ed.) 1975. *The agricultural potential of the Ciskei: a preliminary report*, Alice: University of Fort Hare.

Leach, M. and J. Fairhead. 2000. 'Fashioned forest pasts, occluded histories? International environmental analysis in West African locales', *Development and Change*, 31(1): 35–59.

Legassick, M. 1977. 'Gold, agriculture, and secondary industry in South Africa, 1885–1970: from periphery to sub-metropole as a forced labour system', in R. Palmer and N. Parsons (eds) *The roots of rural poverty in central and southern Africa*, Berkeley and Los Angeles: University of California Press.

Lent, P. and G. Mupakati. 2007. 'The view from above: a history of land use in Guquka and Koloni, 1938–1996', in P. Hebinck and P. Lent (eds) *Livelihoods and landscapes: the people of Guquka and Koloni and their resources*, Leiden/Boston: Brill Academic Publishers.

Lewis, J. 1984. 'The rise and fall of the South African peasantry: a critique and reassessment', *Journal of Southern African Studies*, 11(1): 1–24.

Li, T. 2009. 'Exit from agriculture: a step forward or a step backward for the rural poor?' *Journal of Peasant Studies*, 36: 629–636.

Louw, A., H. Vermeulen, J. Kirsten and H. Madevu. 2007. 'Securing small farmer participation in supermarket supply chains in South Africa', *Development Southern Africa*, 24(4): 539–551.

Lund, F. 2009. *The provision of care by non-household institutions, South Africa*, Research Report 3, Geneva: UNRISD.

Mager, A. 1999. *Gender and the making of a South African bantustan: a social history of the Ciskei, 1945–1959*, Portsmouth/Oxford/Cape Town: Heinemann/James Currey/David Philip.

Mayer, P. 1980. 'The origin and decline of two rural resistance ideologies', in P. Mayer (ed.) *Black villagers in an industrial society*, Cape Town: Oxford University Press.

Mbongwa, M., R. van den Brink and J. van Zyl. 1996. 'Evolution of the agrarian structure in South Africa', in J. van Zyl, J. Kirsten and H. Binswanger (eds) *Agricultural land reform in South Africa: policies, markets and mechanisms*, Oxford: Oxford University Press.

McAllister, P. 1988. 'The impact of relocation in a Transkei betterment area', in C. Cross and R. Haines (eds) *Towards freehold? Options for land and development in South Africa's black rural areas*, Kenwyn: Juta.

McAllister, P. 1989. 'Resistance to "betterment" in the Transkei: a case study from Willowvale District', *Journal of Southern African Studies*, 15(2): 346–368.

Mostert, N. 1992. *Frontiers: the epic of South Africa's creation and the tragedy of the Xhosa people*. London: Pimlico.

Naidoo, L. 2011. 'Poverty and insecurity of farm workers and dwellers in post-apartheid South Africa', in P. Hebinck and C. Shackleton (eds) *Reforming land and resource use in South Africa: impact on livelihoods*, London: Routledge.

Neves, D. and A. Du Toit. 2013. 'Rural livelihoods in South Africa: complexity, vulnerability and differentiation', *Journal of Agrarian Change*, 13(1): 93–115.

NPC (National Planning Commission). 2011. *National development plan 2030: our future – make it work*, Pretoria: National Planning Commission.

Penn, N. 1986. 'Pastoralist and pastoralism in the Northern Cape frontiers during the eighteenth century', *South African Archeological Society Goodwin Series: Prehistoric Pastoralism in Southern Africa*, 5(1): 62–68.

Penn, N. 2005. *The forgotten frontier: colonist and Khoisan on the Cape's northern frontier in the 18th century*, Athens/Cape Town: Ohio University Press/Double Storey Books.

Sagner, A. 2000. 'Ageing and social policy in South Africa: historical perspectives with particular reference to the Eastern Cape', *Journal of Southern African Studies*, 26(3): 523–553.

Scott, J.C. 1998. *Seeing like a state: how certain schemes to improve the human condition have failed*. New Haven, CT: Yale University Press.

Seekings, J. and N. Nattrass. 2006. *Class, race and inequality in South Africa*, Pietermaritzburg: University of KwaZulu-Natal Press.

Steyn, G. 1988. A farming systems study of two rural areas in the Peddie District of Ciskei, unpublished PhD thesis, University of Fort Hare.

Tomlinson Commission. 1955. *Summary of the report of the Commission for the Socio-Economic Development of the Bantu Areas within the Union of South Africa*, Pretoria: Government Printer.

Trollope, W.S.W. 1985. 'Third world challenges for pasture scientists in southern Africa', *Journal Grassland Society of Southern Africa*, 2(1): 14–17.

Van Averbeke, W. and P. Hebinck. 2007. 'Contemporary livelihoods', in P. Hebinck and P. Lent (eds) *Livelihoods and landscapes: the people of Guquka and Koloni and their resources*, Leiden/Boston: Brill Academic Publishers.

Van der Ploeg, J.D, J. Ye and S. Schneider. 2012. 'Rural development through the construction of new, nested, markets: comparative perspectives from China, Brazil and the European Union', *Journal of Peasant Studies*, 39(1): 133–173.

Van Leynseele, Y. forthcoming. 'Landscaping people: spatial politics and territorialisation in South Africa', Wageningen: Wageningen University.

Van Sittert, L. 2002. 'Holding the line: the rural enclosure movement in the Cape Colony, c. 1865–1910', *Journal of African History*, 43(1): 95–118.

Walker, C. 2008. *Landmarked: land claims and land restitution in South Africa*, Johannesburg/Athens: Jacana/Ohio University Press.

Westaway, A. 1997. 'Headmanship, land tenure and betterment in Keiskammahoek, c. 1920–1980', in C.J. de Wet and M. Whisson (eds) *From reserve to region: apartheid and social change in the Keiskammahoek District of (former) Ciskei: 1950–1990*, Occasional Paper no. 35, Grahamstown: Institute of Social and Economic Research, Rhodes University.

Williams, G. 1996. 'Setting the agenda: a critique of the World Bank's rural restructuring programme for South Africa', *Journal of Southern African Studies*, 22(1): 139–166.

Wilson, F. 1975. 'Farming, 1866–1966', in M. Wilson and L. Thompson (eds) *The Oxford history of South Africa. Vol. II. South Africa 1870–1966*, Oxford: Clarendon Press.

Wilson, M. 1975. 'The growth of peasant communities', in M. Wilson and L. Thompson (eds) *The Oxford history of South Africa. Vol. II. South Africa 1870–1966*, Oxford: Clarendon Press.

Yawitch, J. 1981. *Betterment – the myth of homeland agriculture*, Johannesburg: South African Institute of Race Relations.

3 Land reform and agriculture uncoupled: the political economy of rural reform in post-apartheid South Africa

Ben Cousins

Restructuring of the rural economy has been somewhat on the margins of political and policy debate in post-apartheid South Africa, but recently this has begun to change. A wide-ranging resolution adopted by the ruling African National Congress (ANC) at its watershed Polokwane conference in 2007 asserted the vital importance of land and agrarian reform for the reduction of rural poverty. Land reform and rural development were identified as priorities by the Zuma government after the 2009 election.

This chapter traces the evolution of post-apartheid policies on land and agrarian reform in South Africa, with a particular focus on land redistribution and agricultural production. It examines the influence of different interest groups on emerging policies, and assesses the impact of these policies to date. The chapter argues that the fundamental flaw in post-apartheid rural reform policies has been the failure to couple land and agricultural reform in a coherent and effective manner, with the latter hamstrung by policymakers' uncritical acceptance of the superiority of large-scale commercial farming and scepticism about the 'commercial viability' of small-scale systems of production. The state has thus attempted to implement *land reform* without engaging in meaningful *agrarian reform*, thus severely constraining its impact on rural poverty and inequality.

Policy processes in the transition to democracy

The period of multiparty negotiations between 1990 and 1994 saw a number of shifts taking place in the South African political landscape which influenced the stances of different political groupings in relation to land and agriculture. The ANC had not seen rural areas as a priority for many years (Dolny 2001: 33; Levin and Weiner 1996: 97–98, 107), and in 1990 the party brought few concrete proposals for rural reform to the negotiating table. The Freedom Charter of 1955 had stated that 'the land shall be shared by those who work it. Restrictions of land ownership on a racial basis shall be ended, and all the land re-divided among those who work it, to banish famine and land hunger. The state shall help the peasants with implements, seeds, tractors and dams' (ANC 1955). Although imprecise, the Charter clearly envisioned radical transformations in both the nature of property land rights and their distribution, perhaps even implying nationalisation of land. In the early 1990s, as multiparty negotiations began, nationalisation was still seen as a possibility by some activists (Dolny 2001: 50), but by 1993 it was clearly off the agenda of the ANC. Under discussion, rather, was the wording of a property clause that would protect existing property rights, but at the same time allow for land reform (Levin and Weiner 1996: 108).

Hall (2011) describes the convoluted and contested process of formulating policy stances on land and agriculture in the early 1990s. Agricultural policy and economic rationales for land reform were domains captured by the World Bank, other foreign advisors, and a grouping of South African agricultural economists based largely at the Development Bank of Southern Africa and at the University of Pretoria, who positioned themselves as politically neutral experts with local knowledge. The World Bank and other foreign agricultural economists favoured redistribution to small-scale farmers, citing the inverse relationship (IR) between farm size and productivity, but their arguments were met with scepticism by many of the South African economists (Hall 2011: 172). According to Hall, a middle ground emerged, a vision of a 'mix of farm sizes, which could offer opportunities for entry by the poor while taking advantage of the economies of scale where they did exist, and making possible mutual support and equipment sharing between white and black, large and small farmers' (Hall 2011: 172–173). There was also agreement amongst the economists on the need for further deregulation and liberalisation of the agricultural sector.

The World Bank also strongly promoted its favoured model of 'market-assisted' land reform, in which grants would be provided by the state for applicants to purchase land on the open market, with 'willing buyers' negotiating prices with 'willing sellers'. At a Land Policy Options conference in 1993, convened jointly by the ANC-aligned Land and Agriculture Policy Centre (LAPC) and the World Bank, this was effectively the only model on the table. A target of transferring 30 per cent of commercial farmland from whites to blacks in five years was proposed, and later accepted as policy. Hall (2011: 186) argues that by 1994

> … the policy discourse was internally contradictory, an amalgam of competing visions. It embraced efficiency and equity, the state and market, 'the poor' and 'emerging farmers', women and men, agricultural and non-agricultural land uses, commercial and non-commercial production, allowing the remaining fundamental differences to be elided.

The negotiated settlement decisively altered the framework of debate on land reform. In particular, it saw an accommodation of the interests of large-scale commercial farming interests, through acceptance of a 'willing seller, willing buyer', 'market-assisted' approach to land acquisition and redistribution. The dominant discourse of the time was 'feasibility', referring not only to how coherent, practical and affordable policy proposals were, but also how realistic in political terms, given the negotiated (and compromised) character of the political transition (Cousins 2004). Tellingly, an anodyne notion of 'rural development' was what land reform would contribute to, rather than a thorough going *agrarian* reform aimed at addressing structural inequality (Wildschut and Hulbert 1998).

Land redistribution and agricultural policies and their implementation, 1994–1999

The 1997 *White Paper on South African Land Policy* set out the rationale for land reform, and outlined how it would seek to achieve its ambitious goals: addressing the injustices of dispossession in the past; creating a more equitable distribution of land ownership; reducing poverty and contributing to economic growth; providing security of tenure for all; and establishing a sound system of land management. Its vision was of 'a land reform which results in a rural landscape consisting of small, medium and large farms; one which promotes both equity and efficiency through a combined agrarian and industrial strategy in which land reform is a spark to the engine of growth' (DLA 1997: 7).

Land reform would have three sub-programmes: restitution, tenure reform and redistribution, the latter aiming to address the highly skewed ownership of land along racial lines. The purpose of the redistribution programme was defined as 'the redistribution of land to the landless poor, labour tenants, farm workers and emerging farmers for residential and productive uses, to improve their livelihoods and quality of life. Special attention would be given to the needs of women' (DLA 1997: 36). Land redistribution would not be rights-based, and people wanting land would have to apply for land acquisition grants, which 'willing buyers' would use to purchase farms from 'willing sellers'.

A Settlement/Land Acquisition Grant (SLAG) was set at R15 000 per household, in line with the state housing grant, and could also be used to invest in farm infrastructure and equipment (DLA 1997: 41). Qualification for the grant included a maximum household income of R1 500. It was expected that many land purchases would be undertaken by groups, whose members would 'pool their resources to negotiate, buy and jointly hold land under a formal title deed' (DLA 1997: 36).

Various types of small-scale farming that the SLAG grant might help establish were listed in the White Paper, including irrigated cropping, small stock and feedlot enterprises, timber and fruit production, rain-fed cropping, extensive grazing, and contract farming (DLA 1997: 42). Opportunities for beneficiaries to engage in small-scale agricultural production, characterised as land-and-labour intensive, was one of six 'economic arguments for land reform', along with reducing unemployment (DLA 1997: 13). A section of the White Paper discussed financial services for land reform beneficiaries, for establishing small-scale agricultural production or related rural enterprises. The recommendations of the Presidential Commission of Inquiry into Rural Financial Services (the Strauss Commission) were accepted and summarised, including the rejection of subsidised interest rates, the provision of 'sunrise' subsidies such as graded and flexible repayments of loans and discounted subsidies, state-supported financial packages for land reform beneficiaries, and the use of parastatals such as the Land Bank and the Post Office as rural financial service providers.

The White Paper referred to investigation of 'measures to expedite subdivision of land to encourage individual or smallholder ownership' (DLA 1997: 42), and stated that 'there is general agreement that the Subdivision of Agricultural Land Act be phased out to free up the land market', accompanied by regulations to protect high-potential agricultural or environmentally sensitive land (DLA 1997: 25). The Act would 'not be allowed to frustrate land reform', with draft regulations allowing for exemptions. The Provision of Certain Land for Settlement Act No. 126 of 1993 would be used as the legal framework for land transfers, and this exempted such transfers from the requirement of ministerial permission for subdivision. The Subdivision Act was meant to be repealed in 1998, but despite its approval by parliament it has never been signed into law, and in practice very little subdivision of farms for land reform purposes has taken place, for financial, institutional and ideological reasons; see Lahiff (2007: 1589) and Hall (2009: 39) for analyses of these.

The White Paper made little mention of how land reform objectives would be supported by agricultural policies, and the issue of agrarian structure and its reform was addressed in only one sentence. This disconnect was mirrored in a corresponding failure to integrate land reform into agricultural policy. The Department of Agriculture prioritised policies of deregulation and liberalisation, focused on the abolition of subsidies on credit, inputs and exports, and the dismantling of the system of marketing through single-channel schemes and fixed prices. A new Marketing of Agricultural Products Act (No. 47) of 1996 aimed to increase market access for all 'market participants' (a euphemism for new black commercial farmers), promote efficiency, optimise export earnings and enhance the viability of agriculture (Van Schalkwyk et al. 2003: 128). The *White Paper on Agriculture* of 1995 (RSA 1995: 12) declared that state interventions in marketing should be 'limited to the correction of market imperfections and socially unacceptable effects'.

These policy frameworks enabled the continued consolidation of agrarian capital, in both farm production and agribusiness. Farmer-owned cooperatives, many centred in the grain industry, were privatised and became major companies supplying goods and services along agro-produced value chains (Amin and Bernstein 1996). There were already high levels of concentration in seeds, fertilisers, agrochemicals, machinery, farm finance, milling, food processing and food retailing, and these saw further processes of vertical integration and the extension of 'private regulation' in parallel to the reduction of public regulation (Bernstein 1996).

The land redistribution programme began slowly and gradually accelerated: by 1999, it had yielded 472 projects, 48 176 households and 635 599 hectares (Turner 2002: 12) – but involved the transfer of only 0.73 per cent of commercial farmland. More than half of the land transferred was arid or semi-arid rangeland in the Northern Cape province (Hall 2011: 237). Groups acquiring land had to develop business plans before transfers were approved; these were generally undertaken by government-appointed consultants, and few provided for subdivision. Typically, the plans provided 'ultra-optimistic projections for production and profit, based on textbook models drawn from the large-scale commercial farming sector and further influenced by the past use of the land in question' (Lahiff 2007: 1588). This approach meant that group-based or collective ownership and production projects dominated, although this was not at all the intended outcome (Hall 2011: 221). Projects did not receive post-transfer support in the form of training, infrastructure, credit, extension or market access, with the Department of Land Affairs assuming, incorrectly, that these would be provided by provincial departments of agriculture (Jacobs 2003: 5). Similar problems beset land restitution projects where land was restored to claimants (Turner 2002: 9).

Reviewing and remaking policy, 1999–2009

In response to both the slow pace of land reform and the mounting evidence that it was yielding few positive impacts on rural livelihoods, government reviewed its policies and programmes in 1998 and 1999 (Hall 2011: 241). The use of the SLAG grant for production purposes was permitted, a land reform credit facility was established, new grants to support production and multiple livelihoods were proposed, and a move away from group projects and towards individual farmers was considered. Before these new ideas could be implemented, however, a national election took place and the incoming president, Thabo Mbeki, appointed a new minister of agriculture and land affairs, Thoko Didiza, who imposed a moratorium on new SLAG projects and initiated a review of land reform policies. Redistribution policies were heavily criticised for creating large and unwieldy groups of beneficiaries (the so-called rent-a-crowd syndrome) and for not supporting emerging black commercial farmers, who now became a key target group for land redistribution.

In 2001 a new policy framework for redistribution was announced: the Land Redistribution for Agricultural Development (LRAD) programme. Its stated intention was to integrate land reform and agriculture, which had previously been poorly linked. The new LRAD grants would range from a minimum of R20 000 to a maximum of R100 000 per beneficiary, with own contributions ranging from R5 000 at the lower end (which could be paid in kind, including 'sweat equity' labour) to R400 000 at the upper end of the scale. One of the stated aims of the new policy was to create a significant class of black commercial farmers – but without abandoning the rural poor, for whom a food security net programme would cater; support for farming in communal areas would also be provided

(Jacobs et al. 2003: 4). The intention was that individuals rather than groups would be the main beneficiaries.

In relation to agricultural policy, a market-friendly orientation and a strong focus on 'efficiency' was retained, with a new emphasis on 'partnerships' between established and 'emerging' farmers. A *Strategic Plan for South African Agriculture* was published in 2001 (DOA 2001), with the goal of promoting 'equitable access and participation in a globally competitive, profitable and sustainable agricultural sector' (DOA 2001: viii). There was a strong emphasis in the document on deracialising the commercial farming sector – but mainly through 'partnerships' rather than extensive land redistribution. A process of developing a black economic empowerment (Agri-BEE) code for the sector was also set in motion.

The LRAD programme saw a rise in the number of redistribution projects, beneficiaries and hectares transferred, but the latter never amounted to more than around 250 000 hectares a year, or 10 per cent of that required to achieve the overall target of 30 per cent of farmland by 2014 (Lahiff 2008: 23). The focus on nurturing black commercial farmers failed to bear fruit, with relatively few grants provided to individual applicants, and very few at the upper end of the sliding scale. In its first two years, the programme provided 41 per cent of its grants at the lowest end (R20 000), and 40 per cent at the R30 000 level (Lahiff 2008: 3).[1] Most applicants continued to pool their grants, unsurprisingly, given the small size of the grant relative to the cost of large farms and the absence of any thrust to subdivide. Group size declined in some provinces, but remained large in others. Grant size was not adjusted for inflation, yet land prices across the country increased in the early 2000s, and grants decreased in value in real terms as a result (Hall 2010: 181). Available evidence suggested the persistence of 'the dichotomy of large group projects for the poor and small (household or individual) projects, albeit with relatively large per capita land areas, for the better-off' (Lahiff 2008: 26).

Inadequate post-settlement support continued to be a problem, in part because investment in farm infrastructure through the Comprehensive Agricultural Support Programme (CASP) was not 'synchronised' with LRAD (Lahiff 2008: 37), suggesting that poor coordination between different government departments and different levels of government had not yet been addressed. Within the programme, bureaucratic and time-consuming processes for lodging and approving applications, establishing legal entities, identifying farms for sale, writing business plans, negotiating prices, reaching sale agreements and paying for land meant that the process of acquiring land was daunting for beneficiaries, the so-called willing buyers, and unattractive to landowners, the 'willing sellers' (Lahiff 2007: 1585–1589). It was also challenging for officials, who were expected to meet numerical targets for land transfer rather than for well-planned projects likely to be sustained over time (Walker 2008: 144).

Dissatisfaction with land redistribution continued to be expressed by beneficiaries, the NGO sector, commercial farmers, analysts and commentators, and this led to the organisation of a National Land Summit in 2005. The summit agreed on a review of the 'willing seller, willing buyer' approach, the expanded use of expropriation, and a more prominent and proactive role for the state in land redistribution. The following year saw several new policy thrusts: area-based planning, a proactive land acquisition strategy, a review of 'willing seller, willing buyer', a draft Expropriation Bill designed to help speed up restitution, and reports being commissioned on foreign land ownership, land ceilings and land taxes (Lahiff 2008: 7–9). The radical tone was maintained in a resolution adopted at the ANC's National Conference in Polokwane in December 2007, which emphasised the need for an 'integrated programme of rural development, land reform and agrarian change'; support for smallholder farmers, farm dwellers and women and a review of market-based land redistribution.[2]

Nothing came of the review of 'willing seller, willing buyer', or of proposals for land ceilings and land taxes, and the draft Expropriation Bill was withdrawn after receiving a hostile reception from landowners, farmers and opposition parties. Area-based planning, which was intended to integrate land reform into local development plans drawn up by municipalities, was implemented from 2007, and the proactive land acquisition strategy (PLAS) was adopted as policy in 2006. In the latter, the state purchases farms directly from landowners rather than providing grants to beneficiaries, and these are then allocated to redistribution applicants on the basis of three- to five-year leasehold agreements, after which the lessee may be offered an option to purchase outright (Lahiff 2008: 8). The LRAD grant range was increased to a maximum of R431 000 in 2007 (Aliber and Hall 2010: 20), indicating renewed attention to the needs of emerging farmers.

These new programmes fared little better than their predecessors. The impact of large increases in the land reform budget from 2003/04, perhaps due to political pressure arising from numerous reports of failure, was eroded by rising land prices (see figures 3 and 4 in Greenberg 2010: 5–6), and underspending on redistribution continued to be a problem.[3] Area-based planning was outsourced to consultants, a common response to capacity weaknesses in government, and there was little indication that land reform had been integrated into the development plans of local government bodies, which are also often undertaken by consultants, reflecting the continuing crisis of capacity within rural local government. By late 2009 the area-based process was still in the planning stage, with no plans having been implemented as yet (Umhlaba Rural Services 2009: 111).

Funding for agricultural development by provincial departments increased considerably after 2005 while remaining a very small proportion (less than 3 per cent) of the national budget (Aliber and Hall 2010: 5). Spending took various forms, including spending on extension services, infrastructure development via CASP, loans through the Micro-agricultural Financial Institutional Scheme of South Africa (MAFISA), and research. In relation to the first three of these, around 13 per cent derived benefits from 58 per cent of provincial spending. Aliber and Hall (2010: 8) estimate that between 2005 and 2008 there was an annual average of 61 000 CASP beneficiaries and about 2 500 farmers per annum received loans from MAFISA. These figures mask a highly skewed distribution:

in 2009, for 322 national CASP projects, 50.7 per cent of funds went to 2.6 per cent of beneficiaries; taking all small-scale farmers into account, 'the lion's share of state funding ... goes to less than 0.02 per cent of them' (Aliber and Hall 2010: 12). The bulk of funds went to land reform projects, and communal areas were largely excluded. The implicit criterion for CASP funding was 'commercial viability', and the imperative to spend large budgets resulted in officials scaling down the number of projects and scaling up the size of each project (Aliber and Hall 2010:16).

Redistributive land reform and rural development under the Zuma government, 2009–2012

After the elections of 2009 the Zuma government identified rural development, food security and land reform as priorities, and a Comprehensive Rural Development Programme (CRDP) was launched (DRDLR 2009). At its core was a job creation model through which para-development specialists would train community members to be gainfully employed in rural development projects. The overall goal is to create 'vibrant and sustainable rural communities'. The new Department of Rural Development and Land Reform (DRDLR) was to have a key coordinating role in partnerships with other government departments and local government bodies. A series of CRDP pilots was launched in selected sites, one in every province. New land reform policies had not been announced by the end of 2012, but a moratorium on LRAD projects was imposed in 2010 and only the PLAS programme appears to be operational at present. Restitution claims continued to be approved, but in 2011 spending on new projects was suspended due to the mounting backlog of unpaid claim settlements (Kleinbooi 2011: 7).

The long-promised *Green Paper on Land Reform* was finally published for comment in August 2011, but was only eleven pages long and contained only general statements of principle. Its main focus was on a possible alternative, 'four-tier' tenure system, comprising leasehold on state land; freehold 'with limited extent', possibly implying restrictions on land size; 'precarious' freehold (that is, with obligations and restrictions) for foreign owners; and communal tenure. It also contained proposals for several new institutions such as a Land Management Commission, a Land Rights Management Board, and a Valuer-General. Two of the measures proposed – a recapitalisation programme aimed at investing in failing land reform projects, and partnerships with commercial farmers – do not resolve the systemic failure to provide effective support to smallholder farmers. Only a few sentences in the 2011 Green Paper address the connections between land reform and agriculture, and these are extremely vague.

Land redistribution continued to falter. Aliber and Hall (2010: 10) show that in 2007/8 the PLAS programme contributed the largest share of land acquired for redistribution, but it benefited 'larger-scale beneficiary farmers'. A midterm review report released in May 2012 reports that a total of 882 238 hectares was redistributed to 10 447 beneficiaries between 2009 and 2012, but does not disaggregate these by type of programme (DRDLR 2012: 20). Case studies suggest that many PLAS beneficiaries are relatively well off and have other business interests, but nevertheless often fail to pay rent, without this proving to be a barrier to renewal of their leases (Ranwedzi 2011). The midterm review reports that a number of established (white) commercial farmers are acting as either 'strategic partners' or 'mentors' (264 and 117 respectively) to land reform beneficiaries, and that some have been appointed in order to 'graduate smallholder farmers into commercial farmers' (DRDLR 2012: xx). The underlying presumption that large-scale, capitalist agriculture is the desirable norm is clear.

An early assessment of the CRDP pilots (Umhlaba Rural Services 2009: 7–8) found the following weaknesses: lack of an agreed overall vision and strategic plan; insufficient conceptual understanding of the CRDP; lack of clarity on the constitutional mandate and legislative framework; lack of alignment and integration of budgets; failure to integrate relevant government policies and programmes; lack of clarity on authority and accountability; uncertainty and confusion as to who is leading the pilots; insufficient community participation; and lack of clear time frames or a functioning system of monitoring and evaluation. The conception of rural development embodied in the CRDP is highly problematic. The programme involves funding of a plethora of micro-projects within selected districts within the former 'homelands', and it is not clear how multiplying such projects is envisaged to lead to 'the emergence of rural industrial and financial sectors marked by small, micro and medium enterprises and village markets' (DRDLR 2009: 18).

It is unclear how these projects link up with or contribute to the 'agrarian transformation' component of the CRDP, which focuses on improved levels of agricultural production in communal areas, or to the land reform component – which appears to be prioritising 'emerging commercial farmers' on medium- to large-scale farm units (in practice, if not in theory). A coherent overall strategy to reconfigure the inherited (and largely intact) unequal agrarian structure, and the associated spatial divide between sparsely settled commercial farming areas and very densely settled 'communal areas', is conspicuous by its absence.

Recent agricultural sector reform initiatives

Within the agricultural sector, 'reform' has been taken to mean the opening up of opportunities for black business interests and emerging farmers. A policy framework for black economic empowerment was published in 2004, followed by an Agri-BEE Charter in 2008, the key objectives being to encourage black ownership and control of agribusinesses. A scorecard establishes targets for variables such as equity ownership, employment of senior managers and employment equity, the main incentive for companies being to secure procurement contracts from government. A survey of 30 large companies by the Agricultural Business Chamber in 2010 revealed that 30 per cent had completed a scorecard with a further 50 per cent 'in progress'. Half of the businesses had black owner-ship of between 14 and 35 per cent, and there were high scores for enterprise development, average scores for preferential procurement and low scores for management control, employment equity, and skills development (Van Rooyen et al. 2010: 4). Some companies were attempting to support emerging farmers, but in most cases this was limited to a few individuals and small groups in the former 'homelands' and it appeared that many of these initiatives would not be sustained (Van Rooyen et al. 2010: 5).

A range of private sector actors within the agro-produce sector, from large sugar and forestry companies to individual commercial farmers, have embarked on farmer support programmes, some involving land reform beneficiaries (Kleinbooi 2009; Mayson 2003). It is unclear just how many farmers or land reform beneficiaries are benefiting from these private sector projects, but indi-cations are that only limited numbers are involved. There appear to be few examples of successful contract farming schemes, with the much-vaunted sugar industry subject to precipitous declines in smallholder cane production in recent years (Dubb 2012), and negative experiences abound in Limpopo province irriga-tion schemes (Tapela 2005). This seems to be the case for fresh produce contracts with supermarkets too: apart from a few localised examples (Louw et al. 2007; Vermeulen et al. 2008), the character of these value chains means that 'in the absence of a wider set of procurement regulations and incentives, the practices and requirements of dominant market actors exclude small-scale farmers' (Aliber and Hall 2010: 35).

In summary, attempts to 'transform' agriculture by supporting the entry of significant numbers of emerging black commercial farmers appear to have met with limited success to date. This outcome probably has much to do with the highly competitive nature of the sector, as well as sector-wide policies, such as deregulation, which have been distributionally regressive. The sector has become increasingly integrated into global markets for both inputs and outputs, and profits are strongly influenced by global conditions and exchange rates. Trends such as the growing concentration of farm ownership and declining levels of employment have been noted above.

Some government policy documents stress the potential for agriculture to create new jobs and help reduce unemployment. The New Growth Path docu-ment published by the Economic Development Department, for example, suggests that opportunities for 300 000 households in 'agricultural smallholder schemes' can be generated by 2020 (EDD 2010: 18), and the National Development Plan (NPC 2011: xx) asserts that one million new jobs can be created in agriculture and related industries over the next two decades. Many will come from labour-inten-sive forms of small-scale farming in communal areas and on redistributed land. The National Planning Commission suggests that there is potential to expand the area under irrigation from 1.5 million hectares to 2 million hectares (NPC 2011: 197), and asserts that market opportunities exist for increased production of fruit for export and vegetables for the domestic market, as well as niche crops such as nuts, olives and berries which are small-scale and labour-intensive in character (NPC 2011: 201–204). Both documents assert that more effective land reform policies will also be required, but there is little that connects their proposals to those set out in the 2011 Green Paper. The lack of overall coherence in government policy, and the absence of any attempt to identify the reform of agrarian structure as a central challenge, persists.

The incoherence of post-apartheid policymaking on land and agriculture

How have the key challenges of rural reform been responded to by post-apartheid policies on land redistribution and agriculture? Firstly, in relation to *an unequal and spatially divided agrarian structure*, land and agricultural policies have not been conjoined within a coherent, overall strategy aimed at reconfiguring both the distribution of land and current systems of production and marketing; if anything, these policies have pulled in opposite directions. The key thrust in agricultural policies has been liberalisation and deregulation – that is, on state withdrawal and the promotion of 'market efficiency' (which, its advocates in the early 1990s argued, would create opportunities for efficient small farmers). Land reform, in contrast, was premised on state intervention in land markets, in order to acquire land for black South Africans unable to afford to do so themselves. Despite rhetoric to the contrary, land reform policies have not actively promoted small-scale farming. The withdrawal of state subsidies to commercial farmers has boosted increasing concentration within the sector, and if anything, has raised, rather than reduced, barriers to entry by small-scale farmers.

Secondly, in relation to the challenge of *defining the beneficiaries of land redistribution*, the early emphasis in policy was on a broad and ill-defined category, 'the rural poor', but also included were women, farm workers, labour tenants and 'aspirant farmers'. Emerging black commercial farmers were identified as an additional key target group after 1999. Given the hegemony of the large farm model, the latter have been the main focus of the limited 'transformation' initiatives undertaken in the agricultural sector to date. In recent years a rhetoric of supporting 'smallholders' through land reform and agricultural development in communal areas has emerged, but the term is poorly defined, and the means whereby they will be enabled to overcome barriers to entry, and compete with large-scale capitalist enterprises in an increasingly competitive and concentrated sector, remain unclear. In practice, the recent evolution of the PLAS programme suggests that land redistribution may be subject to elite capture by black business people.

Thirdly, in relation to the *mechanisms for land redistribution*, a combination of political, ideological and pragmatic considerations was probably responsible for the ANC's acceptance of the protection of property rights in a new constitution, and also for the adoption of a 'willing seller, willing buyer' (market-friendly) approach to the acquisition of land. The primary mechanisms until 2006/07 were grants to land reform beneficiaries for land purchase and land development, the establishment of legal entities to hold land for groups, and business planning to ensure 'viable' farm plans for large farm units (in other words, without subdivision). The state played the central role in negotiating prices with landowners and approving grants and plans, through long-winded bureaucratic procedures; consultants played key roles in writing constitutions for legal entities and producing business plans, which were often poorly aligned with the needs or desires of beneficiaries; landowners who were unwilling to sell were able to veto land transfers in specific locations; the lack of capital and ineffective post-settlement support measures have hamstrung the ability of beneficiaries to engage in commercial farming; and the absence of area-based planning meant that land acquisition lacked any kind of spatial logic. In effect, the least effective aspects of both state and market-driven approaches to land redistribution were combined in a programme that worked within, rather than confronted, the overarching context of an agrarian structure dominated by large-scale agrarian capital.

Figure 3.1 depicts the key land reform policy choices made by the South African government since 1994 in relation to two policy 'axes' – state versus market mechanisms, and large farms versus small farms. Also shown are the policy stances advocated by a range of interest groups outside of the state. Farmer unions such as Agri-SA and the Transvaal Agricultural Union (TAU), and private sector think tanks such as the Centre for Development and Enterprise (CDE 2005, 2008), continue to argue for a market-driven, large-farm orientation within land reform, and the National African Farmers Union (NAFU) and similar formations urge high levels of state support for commercial black farmers on large farms. Land-sector NGOs such as the National Land Committee in the 1990s, or the Trust for Community Outreach and Education over the past decade, have consistently advocated state-driven approaches aimed at redistributing land to smallholder and subsistence farmers (Andrews 2009). The World Bank's policy stance has been closer to that of government, but has consistently identified smallholder farmers as the key beneficiaries (while continuing to argue that liberalisation of agriculture is necessary for efficiency).

In contrast, on the 'state versus market' axis, government policy since 1994 has retained its position at the midpoint, or crossroads: the 'willing seller, willing buyer' mechanism is still in place; land reform is still state-funded, market-friendly and lacking any effective instruments for a wide-ranging agrarian reform; and it continues to combine bureaucratic ineptitude with market processes that undermine strategic planning. On the large farms versus small farms axis, government policy (at least rhetorically) favoured small-scale farming in the 1990s, shifted emphasis to 'emerging' large-scale commercial farming in the early 2000s, and then shifted back to 'smallholders' after the 2009 national elections.

Figure 3.1 Land reform policy stances in South Africa

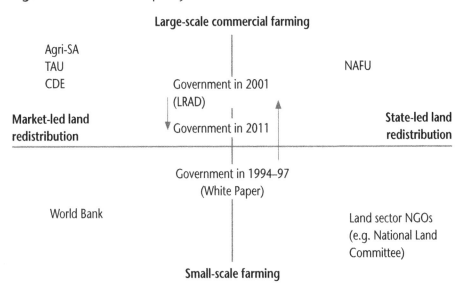

In the absence of agrarian reform, the impact of government policies is that (i) some poorer beneficiaries of land reform and rural development are able to enhance their (marginalised) livelihoods to some degree; and (ii) a small minority of better-off beneficiaries, often those with access to income from non-agricultural businesses, is being provided with significant funding and support by the state and elements of agrarian capital.

Conclusion: the political economy of policymaking on land and agriculture

According to Lahiff (2007: 1583–1584), South Africa's reform programme should be seen as 'the outcome of competing imperatives and contending political forces', but with low levels of mobilisation amongst the rural poor, resulting in 'a messy compromise'. Hall (2010: 189) emphasises 'uneasy truces between competing interests', resulting in 'internal ambiguity, tension and even contradiction within policy'. The incoherence of land reform policy thus originates within the contested politics of policy processes, a key outcome being the effective decoupling of land reform and agricultural policy and consequent failure to advance a coherent strategy of agrarian reform.

Understanding the underlying logic of this choice and assessing possibilities for alternative choices means looking beyond the land and agricultural sectors and locating it within the political economy of South Africa's transition to majority rule. Marais (2011: 139) argues that neo-liberalism has provided the 'organising framework' for the transition. Following Harvey (2005), I understand neo-liberalism as 'the contemporary form of global capitalist accumulation' (2005: 134) characterised by the 'expansion of opportunities and options for private capital accumulation' (2005: 136). On coming to power the ANC adopted a neo-liberal path, restructuring the economy on the terms of conglomerate capital, hoping for a trade-off of corporate support for programmes of socio-economic redress, the compatibility of corporate ambitions and the creation of a black bourgeoisie (Marais 2011: 389).

However, given that poverty and inequality continue to be reproduced and the economy is 'structurally incapable of providing jobs on remotely the scale and quality required' (Marais 2011: 427), the dilemma for the ANC, the state and capital 'is how to reproduce and maintain power and achieve social and political stability' (Marais 2011: 388). This is the context for ongoing contests for hegemony, and for the tendency for the as yet unresolved land question to periodically resurface as a symbol of dispossession and deprivation more generally.

Notes

1   Departmental reports from 2003 onwards do not contain a disaggregated analysis of LRAD grants (Lahiff 2008: 3).

2   'ANC 52nd National Conference 2007 – resolutions: rural development, land reform and agrarian change', available at http://www.anc.org.za/ancdocs/history-conf/ conference52/resolutions-f.html.

3   This is in contrast to restitution, where budget constraints began to impact negatively on the resolution of large and costly rural restitution claims from 2009 (Greenberg 2010: 5).

References

Aliber, M. and R. Hall. 2010. 'Development of evidence-based policy around small-scale farming', paper commissioned by the Programme to Support Pro-poor Policy Development, Pretoria: The Presidency, Republic of South Africa.

Amin, N. and H. Bernstein. 1996. *The role of agricultural co-operatives in agricultural and rural development*, Johannesburg: Land and Agriculture Policy Centre.

ANC (African National Congress). 1955. *The Freedom Charter*. Adopted by the Congress of the People, Kliptown, Johannesburg, 26 June 1955.

Andrews, M. 2009. 'Piloting participatory needs-based land reform in the Breede River/ Winelands Municipality', in R. Hall (ed.) *Another countryside? Policy options for land and agrarian reform in South Africa*, Cape Town: Institute for Poverty, Land and Agrarian Studies, University of the Western Cape.

Bernstein, H. 1996. 'The agrarian question in South Africa: extreme and exceptional?' *Journal of Peasant Studies*, 23(2–3): 1–52.

CDE (Centre for Development and Enterprise). 2005. *Land reform in South Africa: a 21st century perspective*. Research Report No. 14, Johannesburg: Centre for Development and Enterprise.

CDE. 2008. *Land reform in South Africa: getting back on track*. Research Report No. 16, Johannesburg: Centre for Development and Enterprise.

Cousins, B. 2004. 'Grounding democracy: the politics of land in post-apartheid South Africa', paper presented to an IDASA roundtable on 'Lessons from the field: a decade of democracy', Pretoria, August 2004.

DLA (Department of Land Affairs). 1997. *White Paper on South African land policy*, Pretoria: Department of Land Affairs.

DOA (Department of Agriculture). 2001. *The strategic plan for South African agriculture*, Pretoria: Department of Agriculture.

Dolny, H. 2001. *Banking on change*, Johannesburg: Viking.

DRDLR (Department of Rural Development and Land Reform). 2009. 'Comprehensive rural development programme: the concept', Pretoria: Department of Rural Development and Land Reform.

DRDLR. 2012. *Midterm review of the Department of Rural Development and Land Reform*, Pretoria: Ministry of Rural Development and Land Reform.

Dubb, A. 2012. *Social reproduction, accumulation and class differentiation: small-scale sugar growers in Mtubatuba, KwaZulu-Natal*, Working Paper No. 25, Cape Town: Institute for Poverty, Land and Agrarian Studies, University of the Western Cape.

EDD (Economic Development Department). 2010. *The new growth path: framework*, Pretoria: Economic Development Department.

Greenberg, S. 2010. *Status report on land and agricultural policy in South Africa, 2010*, Research Report No. 40, Cape Town: Institute for Poverty, Land and Agrarian Studies, University of the Western Cape.

Hall, R. (ed.) 2009. *Another countryside? Policy options for land and agrarian reform in South Africa*, Cape Town: Institute for Poverty, Land and Agrarian Studies, University of the Western Cape.

Hall, R. 2010. 'Two cycles of land policy in South Africa: tracing the contours', in W. Anseeuw and C. Alden (eds) *The struggle over land in Africa: conflicts, politics and change*, Cape Town: HSRC Press.

Hall, R. 2011. 'The politics of land reform in post-apartheid South Africa, 1990 to 2004: a shifting terrain of power, actors and discourses', unpublished PhD thesis, Oxford: St Antony's College, University of Oxford.

Harvey, D. 2005. *A brief history of neoliberalism*, Oxford: Oxford University Press.

Jacobs, P. 2003. *Support for agricultural development*. Occasional Paper No. 4, Evaluating land and agrarian reform in South Africa series, Cape Town: Institute for Poverty, Land and Agrarian Studies, University of the Western Cape.

Jacobs, P., E. Lahiff and R. Hall. 2003. *Land redistribution*. Occasional Paper No. 1, Evaluating land and agrarian reform in South Africa series, Cape Town: Institute for Poverty, Land and Agrarian Studies, University of the Western Cape.

Kleinbooi, K. 2009. 'The private sector and land reform', in R. Hall (ed.) *Another countryside? Policy options for land and agrarian reform in South Africa*, Cape Town: Institute for Poverty, Land and Agrarian Studies, University of the Western Cape.

Kleinbooi, K. 2011. 'Reopening restitution', *Umhlaba Wethu*, 12: 7, Institute for Poverty, Land and Agrarian Studies, University of the Western Cape.

Lahiff, E. 2007. '"Willing buyer, willing seller": South Africa's failed experiment in market-led agrarian reform', *Third World Quarterly*, 28(8): 1577–1598.

Lahiff, E. 2008. 'Land reform in South Africa: a status report 2008', Cape Town: Institute for Poverty, Land and Agrarian Studies, University of the Western Cape.

Levin R. and D. Weiner. 1996. 'The politics of land reform in South Africa after apartheid: perspectives, problems, prospects', in H. Bernstein (ed.) *The agrarian question in South Africa*, London: Frank Cass.

Louw, A., H. Vermeulen, J. Kirsten and H. Madevu. 2007. 'Securing small farmer participation in supermarket supply chains in South Africa', *Development Southern Africa*, 24: 539–551.

Marais, H. 2011. *South Africa pushed to the limit: the political economy of change*, Cape Town: University of Cape Town Press.

Mayson, D. 2003. *Joint ventures*. Occasional Paper No. 7, Evaluating land and agrarian reform in South Africa series, Cape Town: Institute for Poverty, Land and Agrarian Studies, University of the Western Cape.

NPC (National Planning Commission). 2011. *National development plan 2030: our future – make it work*, Pretoria: National Planning Commission.

Ranwedzi, E. 2011. 'The potential and limits of the Proactive Land Acquisition Strategy (PLAS): land reform implementation in Gauteng province of South Africa', presentation to the New Researchers' Workshop on Land and Agrarian Studies, University of the Western Cape, 27–28 October.

RSA (Republic of South Africa). 1995. *White Paper on agriculture*, Pretoria: Ministry of Agriculture.

Tapela, B. 2005. *Joint ventures and livelihoods in emerging small-scale irrigation schemes in greater Sekhukhune District: perspectives from Hereford*, Research Report No. 21, Cape Town: Institute for Poverty, Land and Agrarian Studies, University of the Western Cape.

Turner, S. 2002. *Land and agrarian reform in South Africa: a status report*, Research Report No. 12, Cape Town: Institute for Poverty, Land and Agrarian Studies, University of the Western Cape.

Umhlaba Rural Services. 2009. 'National assessment of the comprehensive rural development pilots', report submitted to the Department of Rural Development and Land Reform, Umhlaba Rural Services.

Van Rooyen, J., S. Hobson and J. Kirsten. 2010. 'The contribution of agribusinesses to broad-based black empowerment in South African agriculture', Pretoria: Agricultural Business Chamber.

Van Schalkwyk H., J.A. Groenewald and A. Jooste. 2003. 'Agricultural marketing in South Africa', in L. Nieuwoudt and J.A. Groenewald (eds) *The challenge of change: agriculture, land and the South African economy*, Pietermaritzburg: University of KwaZulu-Natal Press.

Vermeulen, S., J. Woodhill, F. Proctor and R. Delnoye. 2008. *Chain-wide learning for inclusive agrifood market development: a guide to multi-stakeholder processes for linking small-scale producers to modern markets*, London: International Institute for Environment and Development (IIED) and Wageningen: Wageningen University, the Netherlands.

Walker, C. 2008. *Landmarked: land claims and land restitution in South Africa*, Johannesburg and Athens, Jacana and Ohio University Press.

Wildschut, A. and S. Hulbert. 1998. *A seed not sown: prospects of agrarian reform in South Africa*, Johannesburg: Deutsche Welthungerhilfe/Interfund.

Part 2

'Mind the gap': discrepancies between policies
and practices in South African land reform

4 Consultants, business plans and land reform practices

Francois Marais

I visited the Lethu-Sonke farmers in September 2007, accompanied by Willem, the agricultural specialist employed by the provincial agricultural ministry. He had been involved with the Lethu-Sonke beneficiaries since the inception of the project. 'These beneficiaries do just what they want ... and normally they plainly just do nothing,' sighed Willem. 'The conditions are right for planting, but you will not find anybody working the fields now ... Just look at this place ... they do not use that broiler house you see there ... it was recommended by the consultant and constructed brand new for them ... government spent a lot of money on it.' Certain that the beneficiaries would not be busy elsewhere on the farm, he led me straight to the house. He was right. We found Mama Zukisa[1] and several other people there, not all of them land reform beneficiaries. I later found out that these 'other' individuals were tenants living and working on the farm. No one was planting crops or tending cattle. This pattern was repeated on subsequent visits to Lethu-Sonke, and was also regularly observed on the Good Hope farm. Beneficiaries were often to be found relaxing next to the fireplace, on the *stoep* or under a tree. They were clearly not following the experts' recommendations as detailed in their respective business plans.

Beneficiaries are advised by experts who compile a detailed business plan for each project. Much of the advice contained in the business plans concerns agricultural production and the management of the farm as an (agri)business. The plans detail what should be produced and how an optimum return on investments can be made. These plans are compulsory and used to judge the viability of a project before it begins. They are typically compiled by consultants, who believe that projects will be viable, efficient and productive if their plans are followed. The business plans are scrutinised by agricultural officials and expert committees before they are approved. The Western Cape provincial government uses the economic viability of projects to measure the success of agricultural support programmes in land reform: recipients of land are expected to make productive use of their land or lose it (Ministerial Media Release 2009: 3).

Business plans play a key role in fostering efficient production (N. Vink, personal communication, November 2010). They have to meet minimum requirements and, along with the extensive application procedure, necessitate the use of consultants. These consultants typically receive the most substantial component of their remuneration when the business plans they have devised are approved by the officials. This encourages them to design project plans that will satisfy the wishes of those officials.

Business plans and their role in both shaping land reform projects and disciplining beneficiaries have been critiqued severely as being imposed without much consultation (Hall 2004; Lahiff 2007: 15). The main concern is that a plan should guarantee returns on (public) financial investments. The 'commercial' logic applies also to loans. If beneficiaries are unable to repay loans and other debts, they can lose their newly acquired land. This happens quite frequently (Hall 2004: 58).

The 'land lost' phenomenon has drawn attention to the question of whether beneficiary needs are accommodated in the business plans. Do beneficiaries agree with the expert recommendations and prescriptions? Is it not likely that the lack of beneficiary involvement in the construction of business plans contributes to their failure to follow the plans and, ultimately, to the land reform process itself being seen as a failure (Agri SA Media Release 2009; Lahiff 2008: 32)? Research confirms that land reform projects rarely succeed in developing an economic performance that matches expectations (Agri-Africa Consultants 2005: iv). Beneficiary interpretations of expert prescriptions could help to indicate what beneficiaries can realistically be expected to accomplish with their available resources, networks, experience and competencies.

Theoretical points of departure

I have employed an ethnographic study of the Lethu-Sonke and Good Hope projects in order to explore what land reform pratices are emerging, as well as how and whether beneficiaries of land reform relate to one another, to consultants and to government officials. This actor-oriented and constructivist approach has led me to see development-cum-land-reform as many-sided, complex and often contradictory in nature, encompassing multiple realities. The key is attributing agency – 'the capacity to make a difference' (Long 2001: 3) – to all those who are involved in land reform, including beneficiaries, experts, consultants, policymakers and extension agents. The idea of agency also expresses the capacity of social actors to change and adapt their situations and to create something new and unexpected from existing conditions (Long 2001: 15). Experts tend to ignore or dismiss people's agency and their ability to shape social life (Arce and Long 2000: xv).

The experts who are involved in the land redistribution process are frequently referred to in policy documents as 'key stakeholders' with 'key responsibilities' (DLA 2008: 3, 11, 13). Together they constitute a system 'of technical accomplishment or professional expertise that organises large areas of the material and social environments in which we live today' (Giddens 1990: 27). Expert systems possess typical characteristics. They value those actions that contribute towards the goals they have set (Giddens 1990: 10). They create the rules by means of which participants in a project are selected, and authorise the continued involvement of these participants in a project's activities. They allocate resources such as grants and possess the authority to sanction or prescribe different forms of activity and conduct. They have 'the power to define behaviour as rational, and therefore as desirable, whereas alternatives will appear as less rational, if not irrational' (Giddens 1990: 230). An expert system develops a clear picture of the solution to problems, as well as what the future looks like (Van der Ploeg 2003: 229).

The 'key stakeholders', 'developers' and 'those that comment and elaborate on draft versions' of land reform policy and working documents form the core element of this expert system. The main actors are officials of the Department of Land Affairs (DLA – renamed the Department of Rural Development and Land Reform in 2009), the National Department of Agriculture (NDA) and the Western Cape Department of Agriculture (WCDOA), as well as private consultants and academics contracted by these departments, some of whom had worked at WCDOA before they became private consultants. Consultants are inclined to design project plans to satisfy the wishes of the officials who engage their services and can, therefore, be regarded as an integral part of the expert system (Hebinck et al. 2011). Other key actors include the 'assessment committees' of the WCDOA, representatives of the departments of environmental affairs, nature conservation, water affairs and forestry, minerals and energy, public works, housing and social services, non-governmental organisations, farmers' unions and financial institutions (such as the Land Bank).

Experts, as I argue in this chapter, operate within a given mindset. Their ideas have been shaped in a context in which modernisation constitutes the chief discourse of development. This discourse is articulated at the level of the state and specialised agricultural research institutions. The Land Redistribution for Agricultural Development (LRAD) programme and the Comprehensive Agricultural Support Programme (CASP) both promote specialised, commodity-oriented production that can achieve high yields and high levels of sustained productivity. Production of this kind typically requires high levels of input and skill and the use of modern, mechanised techniques. In addition, LRAD encourages beneficiaries to increase their own contribution to a project by taking out a loan. The only way to service the loan is for beneficiaries to increase production and to focus on trading agricultural commodities in commercial markets. The expert has become established as part of a network aiming to prevent the modification of what are considered viable projects. The structures that judge these plans are firmly established and make use of an extraordinary degree of planning. In order to attain predetermined outcomes, the experts endorse mentors, management standards, proven production records, expected annual returns and other factors that promote 'proper commercial production'. They reinforce dominant discourses and build networks that aim to prevent the 'unpacking' of the encrypted project plans and support the sanctioning of beneficiaries who do not apply the innovations as proposed. The vision of the future that is 'inscribed' is thus protected.

The kind of advice given by experts is, however, only partly guided by land and agrarian policies. Experts' views are also shaped by their own experiences and by what they define as problems. They assess who is capable of achieving the goals they have established for land reform and define people as 'winners' or 'losers' on the basis of their ability or inability to attain these goals. By rating beneficiaries according to their capacity to produce for the market, experts effectively ignore forms of agriculture and land use which, in their view, are unsustainable because they do not lead to optimum commercial production.

The cases I present show land reform beneficiaries engaged in practices that do not necessarily follow experts' advice or the scenarios set out in the different projects' feasibility reports. Experts, beneficiaries argue, are unlikely to find solutions to the problems identified by the beneficiaries themselves as long as they consider alternative practices to be unacceptable deviations from the dominant agrarian regime.

Two case studies

The two projects that I discuss in this chapter intersect the borders between the City of Cape Town and the West Coast District Municipalities in the Western Cape province. I collected data during two periods of field research (August to October 2007 and January 2008) on two land redistribution farms, the Good Hope Farming Trust and the Lethu-Sonke Farmers' Association. The Good Hope Farming Trust occupies 31 hectares of land. Good Hope is seen as a model farm for 'small farmers' in the Western Cape and has attracted many visitors, including politicians, government officials and academics.

The conveners of the Good Hope Farming Trust group started planning to access land through the land reform programme in 1994. They were not interested in taking out a loan from a financial institution to top up their own contribution and access a bigger grant. The participants were adamant that they should avoid debt. It was decided to limit membership of the group to people who knew one another and/or to people with farming experience. The logic of this decision was based on the idea that limiting membership in this way would reduce the likelihood of tension and conflict within the group. The beneficiaries identified conflict as one of the main reasons for the failure of other land reform projects. The group was limited to 32 members, divided into eight 'family' groups. The Good Hope farm was acquired for R410 000 and each of the 32 beneficiaries received a grant of R20 000. The land was officially subdivided into eight equal-sized areas. Apart from a borehole and fencing, the land did not have any infrastructure. There were no structures or occupants on it and it had no electricity supply. The land was a subdivision of a larger farm. The previous landowner had used it mainly as a source of gravel and sand. He continued farming on the neighbouring farm after the beneficiaries had taken over Good Hope.

The Lethu-Sonke Farmers' Association was formed in 1992 with the aim of acquiring agricultural land of its own. About 50 people joined the association.

The members of this group were initially part of a larger association called the Western Cape Disadvantaged Farmers, which was established by a businessman and entrepreneur from Cape Town. He had no objection to a large group of people acquiring a farm together:

> One commercial farmer may have a large number of farm workers, but the Lethu-Sonke Farmers are many owners who would be performing their own labour requirements … it is thus to their advantage. While the farm belongs to everybody, the labour is divided. They can then even sell together which will be to their advantage.

The Lethu-Sonke Farmers' Association asked a woman working as a private consultant in the field of enterprise development to compile their business plan. She recommended that the number of members should be halved. In her opinion, there was 'a need to be realistic when approaching issues of managing group dynamics and a group of 50 people [would] create a management crisis for the group'. Membership was accordingly reduced to 26 people. Only those who had attended the short courses organised for the group were selected. Some of the initial 50 members had lost interest by this time, because it had taken approximately ten years to acquire land.

Expert prescriptions

Although the LRAD policy declares that '*ex post* audits and monitoring will substitute a lengthy *ex ante* approval process' (DLA 2008: 2), both methods are regularly employed. They are used in order to secure better control of the process of sanctioning a project, or elements of it, both before and after it is established. The *ex post* audits (devised by the experts as an 'evaluation of the desirability of the project when operational') are used in combination with careful scrutiny of the business plan before a project is approved. A project's financial state, the training attended and farming activities undertaken are also instruments of *ex post* control. These are compared to the business plan to see if the project is still on the 'right track'. The experts use various means to control and sanction projects (or elements thereof) and to promote the broader macro-project that underlies land reform in its present form.

The changes requested by the expert system to the initial business plans of both the Good Hope and Lethu-Sonke projects are revealing. They suggest that the needs and wishes of beneficiaries are seldom accepted as part of an approved business plan without significant modification. The initial Good Hope business plan, compiled by the beneficiaries, declared that production would be geared towards growing crops familiar to the project members. Home gardens would be the major focus initially. Production on a bigger scale would start only when the necessary infrastructure was in place. In contrast, the plan that was approved by the experts stipulated that two hectares would be cultivated in the first year, followed by four in the second year. The approved income and expenditure analysis was based on a planting programme that was scheduled to start only two months after the infrastructure had been put in place. The formal subdivision of the farm into eight units was ruled out, a mentor had to be incorporated and production had to start as soon as possible after the establishment of the project. The intention behind the final plan is clearly the transformation of the beneficiaries into 'real' agriculturalists as quickly as possible. While projects might begin as small-scale farming operations, they are expected to expand rapidly and become commercially viable. The focus is on training the farmers so that they get to 'the right level'. Anything which is too alternative or which might jeopardise the envisioned outcome of a project is unacceptable.

The beneficiaries' desire to formally subdivide the land into eight equal-sized areas was not allowed because the experts maintained that the cost of subdividing the land would be too high and the subdivided areas would be too small to be sustainable. According to the 'Concept policy for subdivision and changed use of agricultural land' of the provincial agricultural ministry (WCDOA 2002), the sustainability of a unit of land is determined by the input costs and the long-term prices received for its products. A sustainable unit of land for irrigated vegetable production should not be less than 15 hectares. These calculations are based on a model of farming that depends on high-cost inputs. The cost and benefit of vegetable production is measured solely in financial terms. Its advantageous social and environmental benefits, or its unique contribution to the livelihoods of beneficiaries, is not taken into consideration.

The initial Lethu-Sonke business plan was approved by the experts. The proposed 8 000-layer hen unit and the application for a Land Bank loan were in line with commercial standards. A consultancy drew up a new business plan for the Lethu-Sonke farmers free of charge when their project was threatened with closure due to insufficient progress and conflict. This plan depended on the use of modernised and mechanised techniques. The consultants knew that this would be the only way to secure the support of the experts for the plan. They encouraged a style of farming that would produce high volumes of produce for the markets since the beneficiaries had to pay off crippling debts.

How and why the beneficiaries changed the experts' plans

On the Good Hope farm, Mr Seppie October is regarded as one of the most successful of the new farmers. He and his family cultivate a relatively large area with good-quality vegetables. Close investigation reveals that the way in which the family practises agriculture does not follow the recommendations of the experts in many ways. Seppie is the only one in the family who actually works on the farm. His wife prefers to stay in Atlantis. His two daughters follow their own careers: one is an engineer and the other is a municipal administrator. Apart from acting as scribe during beneficiary meetings, Seppie's wife is not directly involved with the farm. It is clear that many individuals become beneficiaries for the sole purpose of accessing a grant from government so that enough funds can be accumulated to buy the land. The Good Hope farmers subscribed more beneficiaries than they needed to buy the land and used the excess funds to cover their operational costs.

When he was a teenager, Seppie's family made a living from a small piece of land, known as Richmond, approximately 20 kilometres to the south of Good Hope Farm. They were evicted from the land in 1978 in terms of the Group Areas Act. Seppie describes his love of farming and the desire he had to access land through the land reform programme. He participated in an organised protest in Cape Town carrying a banner with the slogan 'No Land, No Vote'. His efforts to access land were rewarded. Not long after the protest march the applicants were informed by the Department of Land Affairs that money from the unspent budget of another province had become available to buy Good Hope farm.

Policymakers envisioned that all the beneficiaries who were provided with land in terms of the land redistribution programme would be involved on a regular basis with agricultural production. In reality, only a small percentage of the beneficiaries are actively involved in farming the land. Of the 32 members of the Good Hope Farming Trust, only 13 are directly involved in production on the farm, while another two indirectly provide support. Beneficiary involvement on the Lethu-Sonke farm is even lower: only four beneficiaries are directly involved in production on the farm, while six others are kept informed about strategic decisions.

The approved business plan of the Good Hope project was very ambitious and required the beneficiaries to cultivate 1.7 hectares of vegetables in the first year and 3.4 hectares in the following few years. Financial projections were based on these quantities. As it turned out, the planting of the first crop was delayed by more than a year due to a combination of government red tape, budget allocation problems and a lack of adequate infrastructure. A comparison of the area that the experts expected to be cultivated with the area that was actually cultivated is revealing. The beneficiaries cultivated 0 per cent of the prescribed area in the first year, 2.65 per cent in the second year, 6.15 per cent in the third year and only 12.63 per cent in the fourth year. While the quantities produced per hectare and the quality of the produce were of acceptable standard, the overall production levels were much lower than expected.

The time devoted to agricultural activities differs tremendously from beneficiary to beneficiary. Only a handful spend a typical working day on the farm. Many are only involved part-time. Some never visit the farm and some do not even know where it is. Sometimes a previously uninvolved beneficiary might unexpectedly become active on a farm, or a non-active beneficiary might claim some of the assets that have been produced. This can disrupt the social dynamics on the farm and have a detrimental effect on production. Different beneficiaries might also have very different ideas about how to make a living from the land.

The experts were reluctant to allow the Good Hope beneficiaries to live on the land. They argued that it would be problematic to provide services such as refuse removal and sewerage. After the beneficiaries had acquired the land, however, they moved into the wooden sheds that had been provided for the storage of their equipment. They rejected the suggestion that they should travel from Malmesbury or Atlantis to the farm. It was too expensive to travel the 40 kilometres every day. Over time, more and more wooden and corrugated iron houses were erected on the land, and the number of structures that served as houses almost doubled.

Similarities exist between the ways in which the Lethu-Sonke and Good Hope farmers interpreted and adopted the plans that the experts had devised for them. The beneficiaries of both the projects rejected enterprises (or components thereof) that required technology and expensive, specialised techniques. The Lethu-Sonke beneficiaries declined the fish farming operation and the roll-on lawn enterprise suggested by the business plan. The new broiler house that was built for them is still not in use. The chickens that were provided through government funds were sold. They rejected the organic production of vegetables and pigs. They also ignored other suggestions in the plan such as the expansion of the pig herd, the establishment of a 'nursery stock production base', the establishment of farm tourism and the production of value-added products. Even the experts' suggestion that the beneficiaries elect one person as farm manager 'to manage water use, feeding and negotiating with buyers' was not followed. They accepted the idea of vegetable production, but only on a much smaller scale than proposed. The pig-production unit was accepted, but not on the large, technologically advanced scale that was proposed. The idea of harvesting wood from the Port Jackson forest on the property was also accepted. The experts recommended that a mentor should be appointed for both projects. The Good Hope project was welcomed by the managers of the neighbouring vegetable-production unit, who were earmarked to act as its mentors, stating that they had 'no objection against them as new farmers as long as they use[d] good production techniques'. Most of the beneficiaries indicated that they would like to work on their own and that they did not 'have the desire to work under a mentor and be taught how to farm'.

None of the individuals involved with production on the two projects relies solely on the land to provide for their daily livelihood needs. They all augment their livelihoods by other means. Four of the Good Hope members and one from Lethu-Sonke receive a social welfare grant. Most of the beneficiaries are involved in entrepreneurial activities that are not related to agriculture at all.

Each beneficiary possesses unique skills and experience. Seppie's neighbour, Mr Johnson, uses his technical and mechanical skills to maintain the Good Hope farmers' tractor. He does not charge the other beneficiaries for his labour but admits that he does expect to gain favour with the group, as well as some sort of reciprocation. Seppie continues to repair refrigerators and cooling units at the same time as he produces crops that meet the standards set by the experts. He uses networks linked to his refrigeration repair business to market his and other beneficiaries' vegetables. He stores old refrigerators and air conditioners, which he uses as spare parts, on part of his land. It is not unusual to find land being used for purposes other than agriculture.

Beneficiaries use second-hand production inputs or make their own production inputs in innovative ways. They might save money, for example, by recycling old building materials. In one case, precast slabs were provided for building pigsties. Some of the beneficiaries chose not to build the structures using this long-lasting, quality material because it required the hiring of labour. Instead they built the sties themselves, using old wooden beams and rusted corrugated roofing sheets that they acquired cheaply, and sold the precast slabs for cash to buy animal feed and other necessities. The beneficiaries also tend to use cow and pig manure to fertilise their gardens, or greens from their gardens as feed for pigs, instead of buying modern, sophisticated and costly production inputs.

The participants in land reform projects pursue a great variety of 'mini-projects'. The Lethu-Sonke beneficiary Xolile rented out the pigsties on the farm to a local entrepreneur in order to earn money to pay the farm's electricity account. Some of the Lethu-Sonke beneficiaries also sell the leftover vegetables collected on a neighbouring farm to motorists travelling on the N7 road. Beneficiaries often find ways of accessing cheap labour and/or rental income. Tenants might be invited to live on the land in exchange for labour, a situation that was not anticipated by the politicians and experts. Although new types of exploitation may result from such arrangements, all the tenants interviewed said that they preferred their lifestyle on the farm to living in a township.

Participants sometimes coordinate their projects. The Lethu-Sonke farmers commonly negotiate cooperative work arrangements among themselves, known as *ilima*. These work parties are arranged when there is too much work for an individual to do alone. An example might be weeding. Food is usually provided after the work party has finished weeding a garden. The party will then move on to the garden of the next participant. As mentioned earlier, Seppie helps to market the other Good Hope beneficiaries' vegetables. They return the favour by helping him with mundane tasks on his vegetable plot.

Conclusions

Although the activities on the projects were planned in extensive detail, many obstacles to attaining efficient and sustainable production appeared in practice. Limited access to finance, a lack of technical knowledge, unexpected costs and the complexities of communal decision-making and farming all caused problems. Limited access to approachable support networks and the apprehension with which established farmers viewed the land reform beneficiaries were also a factor.

The beneficiaries clearly interpreted the experts' prescriptions in their own way and in accordance with their knowledge, skills and capabilities. They possessed unique aspirations, informed by different life experiences and visions for the future. The experts anticipated that the beneficiaries would engage full-time in agricultural production. This did not occur as the beneficiaries did not discard their existing ways of creating livelihoods.

The expert belief that farming should consist solely of agricultural production, exemplified by calculations of financial viability, is deeply flawed. It is time that expert planners realised that the establishment of an agricultural production unit is extremely complicated, especially when prospective producers have limited access to capital and are poorly connected to established commodity networks. Land beneficiaries should not be expected or encouraged to disengage from their existing livelihood strategies. It should be accepted that the typical beneficiary will engage in various livelihood activities, many of which will be unrelated to agriculture. Cross-subsidisation will take place, not all of which is measurable in monetary terms. The value of social networks, including friends not involved in agriculture, and of unconventional marketing opportunities and unexpected windfalls should not be underestimated.

Financial criteria alone should not be the measure of the success of a project. The achievement of greater social equality, for example, is vitally important. Niches like informal marketing opportunities, the use of unique labour arrangements as well as the use of alternative or unconventional technologies escape conventional financial accounting. These have a value, however, since they save on high input costs. Experts need to start using alternative methods to determine the viability and sustainability of specific projects and of the broader land reform initiative. Amartya Sen's 'Capability Approach', which measures overall well-being rather than simple profit, is one such method (Sen 1993).

Actors in land and agrarian reform, be they experts, beneficiaries or policy-makers, attach multiple meanings to land and land reform. They engage in multiple social relationships and follow various livelihood strategies. None of this is considered when judging the success or failure of a project at present. Instead, projects are judged according to strict financial criteria and, inevitably, are found to be 'unsustainable' and 'failing'. While the beneficiaries on the two projects that I have discussed in this chapter have not performed as expected, it would be inaccurate, in my opinion, to describe the projects as downright failures. Many of the beneficiaries report that their lives have improved as a result of the projects and their access to land.

It is time for the experts to reconsider their stance towards the kind of development that beneficiaries desire and the way beneficiaries engage with the land in order to create livelihoods. The desires of land reform beneficiaries need to be taken into consideration when articulating the goals and future of land reform in South Africa. Possible innovative solutions are ignored when land is seen solely as an agricultural production factor. The experts should begin to embrace the idea of an 'innovation system', which involves processes that go beyond the sort of linear thinking that is centred on research systems and predetermined outcomes. The focus should be on the successful introduction of new products and processes that are socially and economically relevant (Davis et al. 2008: 35, 37).

The innovation system concept requires a paradigm shift in how the experts conceive of land and agrarian reform. It acknowledges that agents have the ability to learn, to gather information and to be creative. It recognises that successful innovation depends on the capacity of individuals and organisations to learn and innovate (Davis et al. 2008: 37, 38). The different roles that farmers play, as well as their micro-projects and the resulting niches, are an indispensable part of an innovation system. The expert system, however, often rejects beneficiary niches because they do not fit the conventional paradigm, which advocates a specialised, commodity-oriented and rapidly expanding form of production that relies on high levels of input and skill and the use of modernised and mechanised techniques. In its present form, the expert system is in fact almost the antithesis of everything that makes an innovation system successful.

The empirical evidence described in this chapter strongly suggests that extension delivery to land reform beneficiaries should also focus on the human component of land reform projects. It should support the innovations of the new farmers and the niches they create, rather than blindly following the 'expert' paradigm. The long-term stability and sustainability of the land redistribution programme as a whole will be jeopardised if the desires, resources and skills of the beneficiaries continue to be ignored.

Note

1   Names have been changed to protect the identity of the interviewees.

References

Agri-Africa Consultants. 2005. 'Assessment of agricultural land reform projects in the Western Cape', Final report, Western Cape Department of Agriculture Tender No. 493-2004/2005.

Agri SA Media Release. 2009. 'Land claims pose headache for agriculture', 5 February. Accessed 7 March 2009, http://www.agrisa.co.za/Verklarings/V2009-02-05.pdf.

Arce, A. and N. Long. 2000. *Anthropology, development and modernities: exploring discourses, counter-tendencies and violence.* London: Routledge.

Davis, K.E., J. Ekbboir, and D.J. Spielman. 2008. 'Strengthening agricultural education and training in sub-Saharan Africa from an innovation systems perspective: a case study of Mozambique', *Journal of Agricultural Education and Extension*, 14(1): 21–34.

DLA (Department of Land Affairs). 2008. *Land redistribution for agricultural development: a sub-programme of the land redistribution programme*, Pretoria: Department of Land Affairs.

Giddens, A. 1990. *The consequences of modernity*, Oxford: Polity Press.

Hall, R. 2004. *Land and agrarian reform in South Africa: a status report 2004*, Cape Town: Programme for Land and Agrarian Studies, University of the Western Cape.

Hebinck, P., D. Fay and K. Kondlo. 2011. 'Land and agrarian reform in South Africa's Eastern Cape province: caught by continuities', *Journal of Agrarian Change*, 11(2): 220–240.

Lahiff, E. 2007. *State, market or the worst of both? Experimenting with market-based land reform in South Africa*, Cape Town: Programme for Land and Agrarian Studies, University of the Western Cape.

Lahiff, E. 2008. 'Land reform in South Africa: a status report 2008', Cape Town: Institute for Poverty, Land and Agrarian Studies, University of the Western Cape.

Long, N. 2001. *Development sociology: actor perspectives*, London: Routledge.

Ministerial Media Release. 2009. Minister of Agriculture and Land Affairs, South African Government. Accessed 22 April 2009, http://www.dla.gov.za/Documents&Publications/Publications/2009/Ministers%20Statement%20on%20Land%20Reform.pdf.

Sen, A. 1993. 'Capability and well-being', in M. Nussbaum and A. Sen (eds) *The quality of life*, Oxford: Claredon Press.

Van der Ploeg, J.D. 2003. *The virtual farmer: past, present, and future of the Dutch peasantry*, Assen: Royal van Gorcum.

WCDOA (Western Cape Department of Agriculture). 2002. *Konsepbeleid vir die onderverdeling en veranderde gebruik van landbougrond in die Wes-Kaap*, Cape Town: Western Cape Department of Agriculture.

5 'Seeing like a land reform agency': cultural politics and the contestation of community farming at Makhoba

Yves van Leynseele

Land reform policy has been increasingly criticised for its narrow concern with economic growth at the expense of more equitable, pro-poor development strategies (James 2010). Observers of the programme highlight the significant shift after 1997, when the ANC adopted 'the extremely conservative set of macro-economic policies under the misleading acronym of GEAR (growth, employment and redistribution), and the entrenchment of the market-based "willing buyer, willing seller" principle as the basis for land reform' (Ntsebeza and Hall 2007: 13). The state, in this view, was primarily concerned with creating the conditions for market-led development and the formation of a new class of African farmer-entrepreneurs (Lahiff 2007).

The principle of 'letting the market do its work' has certainly taken hold in the land redistribution programme (Naidoo 2011; chapters 2 and 3, this volume). Land restitution, however, implies a more proactive state intervention in terms of land acquisition and the selection of beneficiaries on the basis of their having a rightful claim to land as opposed to their having the 'right attributes' (such as skills and access to capital) to replace exiting white commercial farmers. This is not to say that restitution policies are inherently better-suited to servicing the rural poor than land redistribution policies. Even when market conditions and state commitments coincide, and land is restored to claimants – when 'willing sellers' are forthcoming and government funds are released for land purchase – state demands frequently lead to inequitable outcomes.

In cases where the reclaimed land is considered to be highly productive farmland which it is in the national interest to preserve, state functionaries may set conditions on land use and business options. An extreme manifestation of this occurs when the state insists that claimant groups enter into joint ventures with agribusiness partners (Fraser 2007). In such instances, project planning focuses on the maintenance of the status quo on the farms at the expense of the diverse needs of the beneficiaries. As Lahiff (2011: 69) comments, 'Great attention is paid to the physical features of the land, its recent history and its agricultural potential, as seen through the eyes of the commercially oriented planners who have been appointed by the state. Little or no attention is paid to the resources, skills and even the expressed wishes of the intended beneficiaries.'

Planning and evaluation tools are then used to replicate the dominant view of viability, which 'is embodied in technical recommendations around "minimum farm sizes", "economic units" and "carrying capacities"' (Cousins and Scoones 2010: 32). The latest business models in land restitution measure 'success' on the basis of farm profitability and how many farm workers can be retained on redistributed farms. The cult of large-scale commodity farming and its underlying neo-liberal logic has apparently colonised the state bureaucracy and is replicated through normative and technocratic planning. This trend obscures alternative, smallholder solutions, which are relegated to history's graveyard as 'backward', subsistence-oriented farming methods.

The notion of state expansion by means of refined yet exclusivist planning practices is explored in James Scott's seminal work, *Seeing like a State* (1998). The state's tendency to simplify and regiment social relationships in order to reach a measure of bureaucratic legibility is apparent in the South African state's approach to land restitution. Scott argues that modern statecraft works through a politics of 'othering'; it constructs groups such as peasants as high modernity's 'other' and denounces their demands as unrealistic at best, or destructive at worst. States need this 'other' to justify their versions of high modernity; they even sometimes create sanitised spaces where 'backwardness' or 'tradition' can be enjoyed by citizens. In my view, Scott's position, notwithstanding its subtlety, is subject to some of the same shortcomings that characterises much of the literature on neo-liberal trends in South African land reform. Problematically, the state is conceived of as an abstract yet discrete entity whose underlying logic can be identified by examining its macro-political orientations and policy statements.

This chapter examines the contours of project planning in land restitution and explores the contestation of project viability as a decentred process that undergoes various stages of articulation. This is done through a study of the different stages of the Makhoba land restitution case and the policy environment from which it emerged as the 'flagship project' of the Eastern Cape Regional Land Claims Commission (ECRLCC) in 2002 and 2003. I argue that planning orientations are central to post-apartheid land reform. There is undoubtedly a continuity with the pre-democratic past in the state's reliance on technical solutions for resolving agrarian questions (Hebinck et al; 2011, chapter 3, this volume). At the same time, though, land restitution bureaucrats often wish to protect 'their claimants' from an unforgiving market and initiate an 'ethics of implementation' that retains elements of redistributive justice (Attfield et al. 2004). Without glamorising these efforts as radically pro-poor, the ways in which restitution officials rescale state-induced interventions in order to adapt them to local contexts and extra-programmatic settings (outside of land restitution) need to be understood. At Makhoba, as we shall see, lower-ranking and senior restitution officials turned to public programmes such as housing and education to provide services to their beneficiaries. They used planning in an effort to construct a more 'community-friendly' business model, which at once exhibited their social agency in steering outcomes but also the problematic assumptions that accompany much rural development thinking when solutions projects are designed outside of the market and within the ambit of the state.

The brokerage role of officials in land restitution implies a less confident and mono-lithic description of the state and a coherent bureaucratic 'legibility'. In land restitu-tion, bureaucrats muddle through a labyrinthine policy environment that offers no coherent vocabulary of project viability or redistributive justice. They also do not act alone in shaping policy outcomes as hired consultants; other state departments and community leaders (temporarily) engage with planning processes and strive to control the interpretation of concepts such as the 'right to land', 'beneficiary community' and 'project viability'. As Li (2005: 386) puts it: 'Rather than emerging fully formed from a single source, many improvement schemes are formed through an assemblage of objectives, knowledges, techniques, and practices of diverse provenance.'

I argue for conceptualising land restitution as an arena of contested, cultural politics. Restitution is not implemented by a coherent bureaucracy nor does it follow a straight road from design through to implementation. Although a particular interpretation might seem to be 'winning the day', consecutive plan-ning stages around the construction of a beneficiary group and land-use planning mean that alternative readings may (re)surface and continue to exist as possible resources for well-positioned actors. The remainder of this chapter explains how the ECRLCC's 'developmental approach' was applied in the Makhoba case and how this project never quite integrated competing demands and categories in the way that was indicated in its original planned objectives.

The 'developmental approach' to land restitution in the Eastern Cape province[1]

The post-development focus in land restitution emerged around 1999 against the backdrop of wide-scale criticism of the state's lack of commitment to its promise of land restoration and the slow pace of delivery (Du Toit 2000). One major draw-back was the lack of government vision about how to promote rural development during and after settling land claims. The reason for this lay in the programme's narrow focus on land rights: 'it has been designed as a stand-alone, legally driven programme without linkages to other planning or development processes' (Turner and Ibsen 2000: 12). A significant shift in orientation came with the arrival of Thoko Didiza as minister of the Department of Land Affairs (DLA) in 1999. She initiated an administrative reform that gave more authority to regional land claims commissions in settling land claims and mapped out a development strategy that aimed at maintaining a strong commercial farming sector.

The new direction drew on a policy discourse of 'failure' and 'success'. Chief Land Claims Commissioner Wallace Mgoqi invoked the bitter lessons learnt from 'failures' such as the Riemvasmaak case, 'where little regard was given to what happens after people, coming from different and divergent life experiences, are restored to land' (CRLR 2000: 4). This reorientation went hand in hand with a focus on planning: 'Both the Minister and the Land Claims Court now insist on development and settlement plans as a prerequisite for finalising a land restitution claim where people are restored to previously dispossessed land. This approach will ensure that the mistakes of the past are not repeated' (CRLR 2000: 4). The Settlement and Planning Grants that are part of the restitution awards (R1 440 per beneficiary household) could be used to hire business consultants and land-use planners.

It was against this backdrop of devolved powers and a focus on planning that the ECRLCC received an open letter from the new minister, in which it was invited to take a more proactive stance towards securing sustainable land deals. Commissioner Gwanya of the ECRLCC grasped the opportunity to expand his mandate to include post-settlement support and identified a brokerage role for his officials in order to link their 'clients' to latent state funding. He pioneered the 'integrated development approach' in 2001 by creating a new division that was responsible for post-settlement support: the Settlement Support and Development Planning (SSDP) unit. A new, final stage in land restitution duly appeared in policy documents, defined as 'settlement implementation facilitation' (ECRLCC 2002). By using the planning grants, the new unit could supervise the outsourcing of feasibility studies and business plans to third parties. It was envisioned that this improved planning would commit parastatals such as the Land Bank and the Agricultural Research Council (ARC), as well as provincial and local government departments, to restitution projects. As a senior commission official explained in 2002, the new approach is 'the key' to 'unlock the money the [provincial] DLA, Department of Housing and the Department of Agriculture are sitting on'. In short, land restitution would screen and link up groups of rural and urban poor (the rightful claimants) who had previously remained invisible to other public authorities.

Commission officials went about shaping their developmental approach without clear guidelines. The ECRLCC therefore required demonstration projects that could illustrate the new approach in practice. In this endeavour, the Makhoba restitution project held great promise. There was ample archival evidence of a forced removal and land for redistribution also became readily available. Officials were able to purchase an unprecedented 11 000 hectares of 'high-potential' agricultural land for restoration to the Makhoba community of 1 400 households. The final ingredient was the willingness of the neighbouring white farmers to assist with the 'transformation' of the Makhoba beneficiaries into commercial farmers and the community leadership's assurance that it would maintain the farm's productivity.

Old and New Makhoba:
competing landscapes of meaning

While the forced removal of the Makhoba group in 1946 could be reconstructed straightforwardly by ECRLCC investigators, reading into the present situation proved more problematic. In the 63 years between displacement and land reclamation in 1999, the ancestral land of 'Old Makhoba', as the claimants affectionately call it, was integrated into a political economy of white-owned family farms oriented towards commercial livestock rearing. The 'New Makhoba' location, to which the community was forcibly resettled, lies in the north-western corner of the former Transkei homeland, an area in which land is held communally and traditional leaders still control key administrative functions. New Makhoba is the picture of a rural area that is overcrowded and overgrazed, where the population relies heavily on pensions and other social grants for income. In bureaucratic-speak it is one of South Africa's 'deep rural areas', interstitial spaces between the legacy of former 'homeland' consolidation and a yet-to-be-realised inclusive citizenship.

While the white landowners whose land was under the claim tried to avert the claim by echoing Zimbabwe-like doom scenarios and fears about squatters in complaint letters to the ECRLCC, the Makhoba claimants demanded the full restoration of land ownership. The land claim form the community submitted to the ECRLCC in 1995 emphasised the problem of land shortage for residential and agricultural uses at their current location. Interestingly, it also provided a counterclaim to the white landowners' concerns about efficiency, stating that 'the land we are claiming has enough space for what we need and the farmers that are owning it are doing nothing to the land at the moment'.[2] It also reinforced the tribal status of the claim by nominating Chief Ambrose Makhoba as the applicant on behalf of the community.

The ECRLCC investigative report summarised the community's resettlement desires strategically, by noting the claim as 'tribal' and showing a preparedness to maintain the farm's productivity:

> The claimants would like to start their lives where their forefathers are resting. There is a feeling that as the area is used for farming most graves have been desecrated and for the Africans their lives cannot be stable. They would like to continue with farming operations as they used to do in the past. The Makhoba Community would like to get their respect back and resume the life of enjoying culture under their leader. If they can get financial support in order to conduct their farms as commercialised farms they will be able to compete on the open market. (ECRLCC 1999)

Translating this repatriation narrative into reality presented problems for the bureaucracy. Two main questions arose. How could community representation and membership be organised, and how would resettlement impact on the reclaimed commercial farms? Addressing the former question meant recognition of the traditional leadership and deciding whether or not to take a proactive role in democratising community decision-making. Following the principle that communities themselves should bring forward their leaders, the commissioners accepted the place of Chief Makhoba as head of the newly formed Makhoba Trust (the legal entity to which the land is restored). The so-called settlement agreement of 2002,[3] entered into between the trustees and the DLA, summarises the ECRLCC position: 'the claimant[s] warrant that the trust shall make provision for all persons who are members of the community to benefit from the restitution award in accordance with traditional custom and in accordance with the constitution of the Republic of South Africa'.

The second question involved viable livelihood options and what it meant to 'continue with farming operations as they used to do in the past'. Should the commercial farms be converted to other 'traditional' land uses or should the current status quo be maintained?

Planning for the future: merging community needs and commercial farming

Following the validation of the claim based on the evidence, intense negotiations ensued between the community leadership and the ECRLCC. The empowered chief emphasised the right of all claimants to resettlement on the ancestral land but also argued a willingness to maintain the farm's productivity. From a planning perspective, however, these divergent demands seemed irreconcilable. ECRLCC officials tried to dissuade the community from its resettlement plans, and suggested that monetary compensation be given in order to develop 'community projects' at the current residence. This option met with fierce resistance from the group of claimants. Popular support for the claim relied on accessing land for residential purposes and off-farm jobs in a more affluent region.

A twist in the negotiations with the white landowners made land restoration possible. Since the listing of the private properties under the restitution claim in the Government Gazette in 1998, the ECRLCC had been silent with regard to the farmers whose land was 'gazetted'. It acknowledged the white farmers' letters of protest and diverted its attention from the claim investigation for three years. This lull in communication divided the white farming community. Whereas some landowners tried to formulate a concerted response through the KwaZulu-Natal Agricultural Union, others offered their land for sale to the ECRLCC. Suspicion grew amongst the white farmers, and even those who had initially resisted the claim offered their properties for sale.

With this unexpected surge in 'willing sellers', the ECRLCC agreed to the purchase of 10 986 hectares. Approximately one-fifth of this was bought as additional land – land that was not part of the original claim – 'in order for the farms to remain a viable farming unit and to continue the present status quo on the farms'.[4] In the run-up to the formal handover of land in December 2002, the fledgling SSDP unit assembled a project steering committee consisting of community trustees, members of a local white farming union and various state departments involved in service provision and the training of beneficiaries. The services of the ARC were enlisted to draw up the development plans.

ARC planners visited the New Makhoba location in mid-2002 for a socio-economic analysis of local conditions and farming skills. The report noted the demise of peasant farming and the predominance of poor management practices that had resulted in periodic veld fires and overgrazing. It stated that 'traditional farming systems are followed, with livestock and subsistence maize, sorghum and beans, as well as vegetables in home gardens as the main enterprises' (ARC 2002a: 6). A follow-up report outlined the required transformation: 'the [community] trust could, with the available financial support, mentoring and training, very soon move from the negative trends and implications of subsistence and small-scale farming into the benefits of effective and rewarding commercial farming' (ARC 2002b: 2).

ARC's development plan duly laid out a 'phased approach' to farm development. It held that an interim period of mentorship by an external farm manager – preferably a commercial farmer from the area – was necessary in order to transfer commercial farming skills to restitution beneficiaries. Central to the plan was the consolidation of the farm, meaning that the 20 reclaimed family farms would be managed as one farm economic unit of 11 000 hectares. Financial projections for the mega-farm noted its strong position as collateral for taking out loans. If managed expertly, it could be debt-free, fully stocked with livestock and equipped with farm implements within three years. Upon reaching this future 'viability threshold', benefits in the form of farm profits could be distributed to the wider beneficiary group in the form of community projects.

Although the plan stated that housing development should not compromise the 'farm's net income', it also developed resettlement plans for 1 400 households. Planners recommended that an agri-village settlement could reduce the costs of service provision and limit impact on farm productivity by concentrating resettlement around two existing farmhouses. The Kokstad municipal housing department, having recently joined the steering committee, would be responsible for administering the housing according to its Reconstruction and Development Programme (RDP). However, a complication arose, in that the SSDP had come to a compromise with the claimants: relatively large 50 by 50 metre residential plots had been planned for, which diverted from the RDP standard of 35 by 35 metre plots in rural areas.

In awaiting approval by the municipality, interim plans were developed with an eye to consolidating the status quo. Planners insisted that the grazing land be leased to local white farmers for a period of two years, although some grazing land was reserved for the introduction of 200 'community cattle' from New Makhoba (goats were not welcome). It was foreseen that the community stock – owned by individual members – would be gradually upgraded by inter-breeding with a commercial stock, which would be purchased once the farm was profitable. For now, the thinking went, the interests of the community would be best served if only 23 permanent workers from the community, the number necessary for running the farm, occupied the existent farmhouses to protect them from vandalism and illegal squatting.

The explanation of the interim plans to the Makhoba leadership fell to SSDP officials. They occupied ambivalent roles as the custodians of beneficiary interests on the one hand, and the disciplining body ensuring that community demands did not compromise development objectives on the other. Although officials convinced the claimant leadership to accept the temporary leases, they also took it upon themselves to make the ARC business model more 'community-friendly' through a number of adjustments to the development plan that aimed to decrease dependency on private sector partners and broaden the scope of livelihood activities.

In responding to the initial planning, the SSDP project coordinator argued against the plan to capitalise the farm with loans, have it fully stocked with cattle and ready for commercial operations within two years. Her input to the final document noted that 'a debt position [for the Makhoba Trust] is morally unacceptable, taking cognisance of the skills and experience levels of the trustees and beneficiaries' (ARC 2002c: 28). A more gradual transition was called for, where the community's assets would be protected by separating the business end of the farm from the land title. At a 2002 workshop with the trustees, the SSDP project coordinator stressed the necessity of creating a separate operating company besides the community trust to act as 'a buffer to expropriation: if the business fails, the operating company alone will fall' (ARC 2002c: 28). The operating company could be used to attract business partners who would have a minority stake in it, but the redistributed land would not be part of the company's asset base and would remain vested in the community trust. A further protective measure that implied yet more state involvement was her insistence that the substantial restitution award (R6.2 million) would not be deposited into the trust's or the operating company's account but be managed by Kokstad Municipality as an 'independent party'.

In her reassessment of the revised plans, the SSDP coordinator further expressed concerns about the overemphasis on commercial livestock farming. In the final 'Strategic Plan' a wider set of 'additional' income-generating activities outside of commercial farming were included so as to 'reduce the initial financial and business risks contained in the said plan' and 'assist them [the beneficiary community] to supplement their anticipated commercial agricultural income streams' (ARC 2002c: 1). The ensuing list of 27 additional activities will be familiar to anyone with any experience of rural, community-oriented planning in South Africa. It includes sewing, knitting, baking, beekeeping, carpentry, broilers for chickens and traditional medicine. Only a few of these activities had actually been defined as community preferences during the preceding socio-economic analysis. Most of them reflected the assumptions of the responsible officials, who saw these activities as representing low entry costs in terms of skills and the types of project that could be managed by community members themselves. An example of the officials' discretionary definition of community interests and orientation to gender equity relates to how each activity was allocated to a gender (male, female or M/F), with the two highest projected earners – the vegetable production tunnels and the production of essential oils – reserved for women.

The provision of ample (albeit low-paying) jobs was the main objective of the community-based projects, with the additional projects employing an esti-mated 230 people. Highlighting the problematic planning orientation prevalent amongst the restitution officials, however, we found that these projects were rele-gated to the future with the notification that each activity required a 'detailed market evaluation' in order to ensure its viability. The well-intentioned projects were thus effectively placed outside the scope of the farming operation and made the responsibility of state-led poverty relief programmes, access to whose funding was contingent on the claimants' capacity to form collectives and submit business plans for each project.

The housing scheme witnessed a similar mix of good intentions and poor linkage to state programmes. On the surface the trajectory seemed clear enough. The Makhoba Strategic Plan confidently proclaimed that the 'Greater Kokstad Municipality is already tasked to execute the above studies [the Environmental Impact Assessment] to enable finality regarding the allocation of stands to the beneficiaries' (ARC 2002c: 5). SSDP officials were, however, acutely aware of the institutional constraints and additional costs involved in linking up the restitu-tion beneficiaries to the housing programme. In a steering committee meeting in 2002, the SSDP coordinator recognised that the restitution procedures for regis-tering the beneficiaries had been inadequate, which meant that the Makhoba Trust could not act as a legal entity in dealings with the municipal service providers. In addition, the informal way in which the 1 400 beneficiary house-holds had been arrived at meant that a second verification process would have to be conducted, which entailed checking each claimant's ID document. There was also the question of the compulsory Environmental Impact Assessment called for when 'appropriate planning' procedures are followed. This planning exercise is costly in monetary terms and implies risky renegotiations due to the fact that it gives neighbouring landowners an opportunity to contest the designation of 'prime' agricultural land for residential purposes. These obstacles could be over-come only with firm political commitment from the Kokstad Municipality and the prioritisation of Makhoba claimants over its established constituency, in its Integrated Development Plans.

With the handover of the farms to the trust approaching in December 2002, rumours started circulating that the new chief and trustees had sold the land back to the white farmers. ECRLCC officials feared that popular discontent with the 'phased approach' that the trustees had grudgingly accepted could entice radical elements amongst the claimant group to embark on spontaneous settlement of what they regarded as their land. In the weeks preceding the handover, two workshops were held at the buildings of the Cedarberg Farmers' Association (Old Makhoba) in order to help prepare the community leadership for assuming management tasks and to get a firm commitment to the handover process from involved stakeholders.

In order to enhance community ownership of the process and their capacity to monitor farm operations in the new operating company, 12 trust members took a training course in financial record-keeping for rural groups: 'Basic Financial Management for Community-based Organisations'. Discussions were held about the immediate tasks that the trustees would have to perform in the transitional stage. The trustees were asked to find suitable people for the 23 budgeted jobs – 3 operational managers and 20 farm workers. They were also tasked with selecting youngsters from Makhoba to enrol in job training programmes, run by the provincial Department of Agriculture, which the SSDP still had to identify. Selected trustees, now equipped with basic accounting skills, would be asked to check the financial reports coming from their Kokstad Municipality account manager and run a shadow administration for an undisclosed period until they had proven their competency. A concession was also made to the chief. He would be guaranteed a seat on the board of directors in the new operating company.

The December 2002 handover passed calmly. Some trustees and the chief moved into the 11 farmhouses at Old Makhoba and brought with them the required number of workers to mind the cattle. The main element of the plan that gave the community some ownership of the project was the agreement that some 200 'community cattle' would be brought over from New Makhoba. Unfortunately, this early form of beneficiation exposed the costs that would be involved in the new landowners' making the transition to commercial farming. The cattle owners had to pay for vaccinations and dips so as not to infect the commercial herds of their neighbours. They were also informed that in terms of the new livestock policy on the farm they would have to contribute 20 per cent of the income that was earned from newborns to the community trust.

A visit to the Old Makhoba farm in 2006 confirmed that the features of the transitional stage had become entrenched. Whilst the resettlement plans and the additional projects remained on hold, the management had entered into five-year lease agreements with neighbouring farmers. Chief Makhoba had survived several challenges to his leadership and emerged as the managing director of Ntlangwini Makhoba Farming. Two other trustees occupied paid management positions and a third worked as full-time operational manager for livestock. Day-to-day management fell to a local white farm manager who was paid by the KwaZulu-Natal Department of Agriculture. Business planning remained open-ended and speculative; the managing director's report of July 2006 described how he had been approached by two agribusiness companies that specialised in maize production and dairy, and that wanted to become involved in the farm. The farm was also waiting for a large grant from the provincial Department of Agriculture for purchasing the high-quality livestock called for in the original planning.

Conclusion

The Makhoba case represents an early experiment in applying development planning to complex land restitution deals involving the transfer of commercial farmland to large beneficiary groups. It was embraced in 2001 by the ECRLCC as a flagship project that aimed to stifle mounting criticism of land restitution as a stand-alone, legalist programme that offered little post-settlement support to its beneficiaries. The project exemplifies a recent trend in land reform, which seeks to replicate the large-scale commercial farming model on land claim farms. Commission officials – in conjunction with invited stakeholders – opted for consolidating what were 20 private properties into a single economic unit comprising 11 000 hectares.

Consultants from the ARC argued for following this route chiefly on the grounds of the lack of management skills among the Makhoba beneficiaries. They suggested a 'phased approach' in terms of which the community leadership would be mentored by white commercial farmers until they were able to manage the farms themselves. From 2002 to 2006, the temporary phase of mentorship, however, became solidified. Community leaders settled into management positions, accepted medium-term leases with neighbouring private landowners for the community's grazing land, and successfully curtailed community demands for houses and arable plots, postponing these to a distant point in the future when the consolidated farm had become 'viable'.

On first inspection, restitution authorities have helped promote forms of paternalism by endorsing the tribal leadership and attributing key roles in skills transfer and farm management to white mentors. Closer analysis of the ways in which the lower-ranking functionaries set about planning the project reveals that the logic of commercial farming did not go unchallenged. As self-styled custodians of beneficiary interests, restitution officials assumed ambivalent and reflexive positions. They often adopted an ethical stance towards redistributive justice, which entailed trying to guide project planning towards more equitable outcomes. Officials tried to protect the claimants from some of the entrepreneurial risks involved in the project and transferred these to future investors by ensuring that the community land was not put down as collateral. They insisted that the housing option and a more diverse range of income-generating activities besides commercial farming be incorporated in the development plans.

These attempts at making plans more 'community-friendly' exposed the problem of attaining bureaucratic legibility across government programmes. ECRLCC planners believed that the state could provide the beneficiaries with certain key requirements that the commercial farm could not deliver itself. The adjusted plans also betrayed the officials' subjective notions of community skills and needs; the alternative projects would have to be low-risk and low-entry but at the same time promote gender equity. The historical demands of the wider group of beneficiaries were thus reconceptualised so that they could be made the responsibility of governmental poverty relief programmes that promised jobs, land and houses. The contentious and speculative nature of this strategy is illustrated by the planners' unrealistic expectation that the resettled Makhoba community, newcomers in the area, would be given priority access to the RDP housing programme of the Kokstad Municipality.

The way planning married competing demands of resettlement and 'community-friendly projects' with a commercial farming orientation also highlights the manner in which planners construed restitution beneficiaries according to technocratic, hierarchical and ahistorical preconceptions. On the one hand, they regarded them as a 'blank slate upon which increasingly sophisticated entrepreneurial modernity and private ownership could be drawn' (James 2007: 171). On the other hand, beneficiaries were reconstituted as tribal subjects whose constraining rural backgrounds and experiences necessitated the creation of a separate space of rural development – outside of the commercial farming project – where income is derived from projects such as beekeeping and vegetable farming.

Against this backdrop of good intentions, ambitious planning and the difficulties of linking restitution communities, we can rethink the role of the state in land reform. In their planning efforts, officials muddle through a labyrinthine policy landscape. They struggle with and help constitute what Nuijten (2003: 16) describes in her study of Mexican land reform as the 'hope generating machine', which is 'based on the fact that the bureaucracy offers endless openings and that officials are always willing to initiate procedures'. Officials from the Department of Housing and Agriculture were glad to be listed as key stakeholders in the Makhoba project and dutifully attended workshops in which time frames were formulated. Community representatives went along with these speculative plans. In appeasing the rank-and-file community members, they too – by sheer political necessity – became enrolled as 'hope-generators' and extensions of the (not-yet) developmental state. A picture emerges of land restitution as a decentred, open-ended process that offers plural pathways and in which the thesis of the dominant presence of a commercial farming orientation in the state bureaucracy can be nuanced.

Notes

1   The primary data collection for this section was conducted as part of the author's internship at the Eastern Cape Regional Land Claims Commission in September and October 2002. It was completed during a stay with the Transkei Land Service Organisation (TRALSO) in Umtata from October to December 2002.

2   Commission on Restitution of Land Rights, 'Makhoba Land Claim Form', received 24 November 1995. Material in private possession.

3   Settlement Agreement in Terms of Section 42D of the Restitution of Land Rights Act No. 22 of 1994 as amended, made and entered into between the DLA, the Commission on Restitution of Land Rights and the Makhoba Community, dated 2002. Material in private possession.

4   Settlement Agreement in Terms of Section 42D of the Restitution of Land Rights Act No. 22 of 1994 as amended, made and entered into between the DLA, the Commission on Restitution of Land Rights and the Makhoba Community, dated 2002. Material in private possession.

References

ARC (Agricultural Research Council). 2002a. 'Makhoba Land Restitution Project: situation analysis report, September 2002', consultancy report for the Eastern Cape Regional Land Claims Commission, Pretoria: Agricultural Research Council.

ARC. 2002b. 'Makhoba Land Restitution Project: development plan', consultancy report for the Eastern Cape Regional Land Claims Commission, Pretoria: Agricultural Research Council.

ARC. 2002c. 'Makhoba Trust: strategic business plan', consultancy report for the Eastern Cape Regional Land Claims Commission, Pretoria: Agricultural Research Council.

Attfield, R., J. Hattingh and M. Matshabaphala. 2004. 'Sustainable development, sustainable livelihoods and land reform in South Africa: a conceptual and ethical inquiry', *Third World Quarterly*, 25(2): 405–421.

Cousins, B. and I. Scoones. 2010. 'Contested paradigms of "viability" in redistributive land reform: perspectives from southern Africa', *Journal of Peasant Studies*, 37(1): 31–66.

CRLR (Commission on Restitution of Land Rights). 2000. *Annual report*, Commission on Restitution of Land Rights, Pretoria: Government Press.

Du Toit, A. 2000. 'The end of restitution: getting real about land claims', in B. Cousins (ed.) *At the crossroads: land and agrarian reform in South Africa into the 21st century*, Cape Town and Johannesburg: University of the Western Cape and National Land Committee.

ECRLCC (Eastern Cape Regional Land Claims Commission). 1999. 'Makhoba Land Claim report', unpublished report, Eastern Cape Regional Land Claims Commission.

ECRLCC. 2002. *Umhlaba Wethu Eastern Cape*, Newsletter 1, Eastern Cape Regional Land Claims Commission.

Fraser, A. 2007. 'Hybridity emergent: geo-history, learning, and land restitution in South Africa', *Geoforum,* 38(2): 299–311.

Hebinck, P., D. Fay and K. Kondlo. 2011. 'Land and agrarian reform in South Africa's Eastern Cape province: caught by continuities', *Journal of Agrarian Change*, 11(2): 220–240.

James, D. 2007. *Gaining ground? 'Rights' and 'property' in South African land reform*, Johannesburg: Wits University Press.

James, D. 2010. 'Doing business with a development ethic: "new look" land redistribution in South Africa', in B. Freund, and H. Witt (eds) *Development dilemmas in post-apartheid South Africa*, Pietermaritzburg: University of KwaZulu-Natal Press.

Lahiff, E. 2007. '"Willing buyer, willing seller": South Africa's failed experiment in market-led agrarian reform', *Third World Quarterly,* 28(8): 1577–1597.

Lahiff, E. 2011. 'Land reform and poverty reduction in South Africa', in P. Hebinck and C. Shackleton (eds) *Reforming land and resource use in South Africa: impact on livelihoods*, London: Routledge.

Li, T.M. 2005. 'Beyond "the state" and failed schemes', *American Anthropologist*, 107(3): 383–394.

Naidoo, L. 2011. 'Poverty and insecurity of farm workers and dwellers in post-apartheid South Africa', in P. Hebinck and C. Shackleton (eds) *Reforming land and resource use in South Africa: impact on livelihoods*, London: Routledge.

Ntsebeza L. and R. Hall (eds). 2007. *The land question in South Africa: the challenge of transformation and redistribution*, Cape Town: HSRC Press.

Nuijten, M. 2003. *Power, community and the state: the political anthropology of organisation in Mexico*, Sterling, VA: Pluto Press.

Scott, J.C. 1998. *Seeing like a state: how certain schemes to improve the human condition have failed*, New Haven, CT: Yale University Press.

Turner, S. and H. Ibsen. 2000. *Land and agrarian reform in South Africa: a status report*, Research Report No. 6, Cape Town: Institute for Poverty, Land and Agrarian Studies, University of the Western Cape.

6 Land reform and newly emerging social relations on Gallawater A farm

Modise Moseki

This chapter provides an account of everyday life on a land reform farm and paints a vivid picture of the multiple realities that emerge during the process of land restitution, and after beneficiaries have acquired their land. If the day-to-day dynamics of land reform are to be adequately understood, one needs to engage with beneficiaries frequently by means of a situational analysis, participatory observation, and formal and informal interviews. This provides a contrast with the abstract and quantitative ways in which policymakers and land reform analysts generally evaluate land reform projects. The chapter argues that sweeping policy statements and evaluations that are based on prescribed outcomes fail to register much of what is actually happening on the ground. It is essential that the voices and opinions of the social actors directly and indirectly involved in land reform – beneficiaries, frontline extension workers, consultants, commercial farmers – are heard and respected.

Newly settled land reform beneficiaries tend to ignore approved business plans or find them too difficult to implement. Many of the beneficiaries explore alternative ways of improving their lives and combine new livelihood activities with the ones that they pursued before they became farmers. Land reform produces many kinds of beneficiaries and multiple livelihood scenarios. It is too simplistic to claim that it merely produces a new class structure among the rural poor (Davis et al. 2004; Driver 2007; Greenberg 2003; Hall 2007; Kariuki and Van der Walt 2000; Wegerif 2004: 43).

Conceptualising the land reform programme

The South African land reform programme brings together a range of social actors and produces a kaleidoscope of experiences. Different actors encounter one another in a context that is new to most of them. The multiple encounters between different social actors together constitute the land reform arena, in which fierce struggles over the future and nature of the land reform project occur.

Land reform does not represent a single, linear set of experiences. In fact, only a small percentage of the experiences that it does produce are consistent with policy expectations. This chapter seeks to capture and present some of these multiple experiences in the form of life-history accounts which are offered as vignettes of the social realities that are emerging on land reform farms in South Africa.

James (2007: 255) points out that 'it is important to recognise that policy initiatives and planned social change are often productive of new social, cultural and political identities rather than simply acting upon pre-existing ones'. Social interactions in new environments produce multiple meanings and interpretations of activities and situations (Long 2001, 2004). Social actors create room to manoeuvre and ultimately create new projects in such contexts. There is thus a need to develop a form of analysis that centres on understanding actors' everyday life struggles, the semi-autonomous fields of action in which they operate and the creativity they display in resolving the problems they face. Encounters and social interactions between various actors occur on both the narrow (the immediate day-to-day struggle for a decent livelihood) and broader (the market and the state) levels of land reform, resulting in the coalescence of interests and practices that constitute new, interlocking projects. These projects in turn create new sets of relationships. New social spaces provide the medium in which individuals (re)create new social relationships and/or transform existing ones (McGee 2004; Vivian and Sudweeks 2003).

I will show, in the next section of this chapter, how social relationships are constructed and contribute towards meeting the needs of the different actors in relation to the Gallawater A land reform project. This will contribute to the emergence of a clearer picture of the multiple realities taking place on land reform farms more generally.

Gallawater A farm

Gallawater A farm is situated 31 kilometres north of Queenstown and 15 kilometres south of the small town of Whittlesea. It covers 900 hectares and is one of the oldest land reform projects in the Eastern Cape province. It was purchased for R285 000 in 1995. The government paid 85 per cent of the price, and the beneficiaries had to pay a 5 per cent deposit before officially moving onto the farm, with the agreement that the remaining 10 per cent loan would be repaid over a period of five years.

A study conducted by Vetter and Goqwana (2000) shortly after the farm was purchased revealed that it was not completely clear from the beginning whether the land was going to be used primarily for farming and related activities or for residential purposes, with some access to surrounding communal rangelands. Vetter and Goqwana found that few of the beneficiaries had the means or motivation to invest their money and/or labour in farming. The area's natural resources were also badly depleted.

The Gallawater A farm beneficiaries have a common history (Wells 1995). They are a group of people who left the Glen Grey area in 1975 after they had learnt that it was to be incorporated into the former Transkei homeland under President Mathanzima. They feared that they would be victimised and become even poorer than they were already. The group were relocated to the village of Zweledinga (which means 'promised land' in isiXhosa), near Queenstown. They were promised their own land at a later stage. Zweledinga village was incorporated into Lennox Sebe's Ciskei homeland in 1981. The Zweledinga Residents' Association (ZRA) always resisted the leadership of the Ciskei government. They repeatedly asked the government to give them the land that they had been promised. When Zweledinga became overcrowded, the ZRA decided to invade white-owned farms. Gallawater A farm was invaded in 1993. Mr King, the owner, opened negotiations with the state, proposing that it buy his farm for the group that had occupied it. A local non-governmental organisation (NGO), the Border Rural Committee (BRC), negotiated on behalf of the occupants and provided them with administrative services and legal advice.

Although 102 households contributed financially to the purchase of Gallawater A farm, only 26 have moved onto the farm. Members of four other households remain in Zweledinga but farm on Gallawater. Six households moved to Gallawater but later returned to Zweledinga. Sixty-four households have never moved to Gallawater. An unknown number of people who are not beneficiaries have also moved onto the farm. They are given land on which to settle in exchange for providing cheap labour to some of the beneficiaries on the farm. They also contribute to increasing the number of residents; this is an advantage when it comes to claiming services and sustaining the school farm.

Gallawater actor projects: multiple realities

The case studies presented in this chapter are all drawn from Gallawater A farm. They illustrate the fact that a land reform project such as Gallawater represents multiple realities and consists of diverse sets of interlocking projects. The cases are representative of the different social categories to which the Gallawater beneficiaries belong. Each case tells a unique story of the complex manner in which actors engage with each other in the course of their daily activities, both on and off the farm. The cases reflect the ways in which the different social actors make a living and influence one another's lives while exploring new livelihood avenues. Taken together, the cases show Gallawater A farm as a social space that is constituted by the interlocking of various actor projects. Beneficiaries, government officials, neighbouring farmers, people from the surrounding areas and informal settlers engage with each other in new ways. They search for common values and ideas and find ways of working together.

Case 1: the Bokwe family

This family is actively involved in the general operation of the farm. Mrs Bokwe is a 64-year-old pensioner. Her husband, Mr Bokwe, passed away in 2006. His name was frequently mentioned in interviews with beneficiaries and other actors connected to the project. Most of them maintained that things on the farm would be better if he were still alive. 'He was a man of initiative; he would go to any government office and present the needs of the community, and things happened when he took action,' said the school principal. The late Mr Bokwe was at the forefront of all the activities on the farm from the period of the farm invasions until the time that the farm was transferred. Although he was the deputy chairperson of the ZRA, he took on the role of chairperson as well because the elected chairperson was largely inactive.

Mr Bokwe was the only person who knew everything about the farm. Unfortunately not all of his knowledge has been passed on. His family has inherited his status, however. They form something of an elite on the farm. Their house is the only electrified building on the property. Mrs Bokwe is the main link between outside institutions, especially government departments, and the community. Since she has access to electricity, she can keep her cellphone charged at all times. Many of the beneficiaries see Mrs Bokwe as their leader. The interviewees frequently referred me to her for answers to my questions.

Mrs Bokwe's family owns about 200 sheep. Sandile, her youngest son, heads the family's sheep business. He is assisted by Vusi, who is employed to take care of the animals. The sheep are kept mainly for their wool but are also sometimes sold for slaughtering. Even though only four beneficiaries engage in wool production on Gallawater farm, Sandile indicated that it is a good business. The Department of Agriculture is actively involved in the wool enterprise, having undertaken to equip the farm with the necessary infrastructure such as a shearing shed, a generator to pump drinking water for the livestock, dams, and fencing for the camps. The beneficiaries had been waiting for 12 months for the promised infrastructure, however, when I last interviewed them. Both Mrs Bokwe and Sandile complained that the government seldom fulfilled its promises.

The government did carry out its promise to repair the bridge on the farm. But this occurred only after the intervention of a neighbouring farmer. He had provided access to Gallawater farm through his farm after the bridge had collapsed and devised a strategy to galvanise the government into action when it failed to repair the bridge. He locked his gates. The strategy worked. Within a week a municipal delegate had visited the farm and employed the residents of Gallawater A to assist a contracted engineer to rebuild the bridge. The residents decided that at least one member from each household should get a chance to work on the bridge rebuilding project, for two weeks a month for each of the three months of the project's duration. Mrs Bokwe was the only person who was employed full-time. Since Sandile also worked on the project, the family received a double income from it.

After matriculating in 1994, Sandile moved to Cape Town in the hope of finding a job. He worked as a petrol attendant in Khayelitsha township before returning home when his father's health deteriorated. He has lived with his mother on Gallawater farm since his father's death. All his siblings live elsewhere. Sandile earns a living from a range of activities besides sheep farming. He makes R300 a month from operating the generator that pumps clean water from the farm's borehole to the rest of the property. The fuel for the generator is supplied by the local municipality. He also generates income by recharging other people's cellphones. He charges R5 a time for this service. He cuts down trees and sells the wood to people in the neighbouring townships of Shilo and Sada. Encouraged by a season of good rainfall, Sandile planted one and a half hectares of potatoes. Even though he has to hire a tractor from Zweledinga at a rate of R500 a hectare, he intends to plant potatoes when the rainy season arrives.

Case 2: Mr Njabulo

Mr Njabulo's father was one of the initial beneficiaries of Gallawater A farm. Mr Njabulo was 41 when his father died and left him 100 sheep. He moved from Lady Frere, where he had been working as an electrician, and settled on the farm. He has since increased the stock of sheep to 400. He still works as an electrician and also owns two taxis. Mr Njabulo's wife is one of three teachers who work in the community's farm school.

The residents of Gallawater depend on Mr Njabulo's taxis for transport. He is contracted by the Department of Education to transport schoolchildren from the farm to schools in the neighbouring townships of Sada and Shiloh. He also transports children from the townships to the school on Gallawater farm. During the day, when the learners are at school, Mr Njabulo's taxis run between Gallawater, Whittlesea and Queenstown. He checks whether the sheep are in the kraal when he returns to the farm at the end of the day. If necessary, he will then go out to the veld to look for missing sheep.

Mr Njabulo employs two young men and an old man who is one of the registered beneficiaries. Like the other wool producers on Gallawater A, Mr Njabulo is assisted by almost all the residents during the peak season when people come together to shear, sort, grade and pack the wool before it is collected for the markets. He complains that the government has not fulfilled its commitment to provide water, fences and dipping tanks. 'For us to receive government services, we have to struggle by going to the offices and it takes a very long time before anything can be done,' he says.

Case 3: Mrs Qongo

I interviewed 91-year-old Mrs Qongo while she was deboning the meat of a cow. She described her experiences of life in Glen Grey, which she had left in 1975, with obvious enjoyment. Her three teenage grandchildren sat behind her as she spoke. They were all off school with flu. Mrs Qongo blamed this on the fact that the children had got wet from crossing the river on their way to school. Mrs Qongo was satisfied with the work of the agricultural extension officer but complained that other departments were inactive. She saw the repair of the bridge and the installation of electricity as priorities. She also wanted more people to live on the farm: 'But things will only be better if those people [beneficiaries not living in Gallawater] will come and stay on the farm; we need them to get more services here,' she said.

Mrs Qongo owns about 20 cattle and a few goats, which she sells at an auction when the need arises. Her son manages the livestock. She claims that the amount that she receives when selling her livestock at the auctions does not equal the value of her animals, leaving her feeling cheated. She also receives a government old age grant. Her daughter, who is a primary school teacher in Tambo village and comes home only at weekends, also gives her some money. Overall, Mrs Qongo is happy to be part of Gallawater A farm: 'I have a farm which belongs to me, my livestock is safe and increasing in number each year'. She feels safe living on the farm. She likes to participate in all the community's activities and contributes to decision-making. She feels as though the Gallawater community is one big family.

Case 4: Mrs Mqo

I interviewed 55-year-old Mrs Mqo in front of the two-roomed brown mud house that she shares with two teenage daughters, a son and four grandchildren. She was clearly well informed about things on the farm even though she had only moved there in 2006. Although she had not been part of the initial group that contributed to buying the farm, she had always had good connections with the Gallawater A beneficiaries. She explained, 'I only remained in Zweledinga when the ZRA took a decision to invade white farms; my children were in school and I did not want them to lose out by taking them out of school, but later I negotiated my way into Gallawater and the community here was very happy to welcome me.'

Mrs Mqo owns a few goats and cattle. Her teenage son helps her look after them. They form an important part of her livelihood: 'Being part of Gallawater farm is a great opportunity for me because my livestock are increasing and I can sell whenever the need arises. This livestock becomes very helpful since I am unemployed. My three children go to school in Shiloh; at least their transport to school is taken care of by the government. I care for four grandchildren. I get a social grant of R160 a month for two of them'. The other two grandchildren are her eldest son's children. He lives in Cape Town. Mrs Mqo doesn't know where the children's mother is, 'but wherever she is, she is the one receiving the grants for the other two children'. Her husband works in Cape Town. He depends on casual jobs there and only comes home in December.

Although she thinks that 'the government just drops land reform beneficiaries on farms and leaves them there', Mrs Mqo indicated that the government had good programmes in place and was confident that things would improve. The state would eventually provide farm machinery, clean water, a new bridge, electricity, and Reconstruction and Development Programme (RDP) houses, as they had done elsewhere in the area.

Mrs Mqo's connections with the 'legal farm owners' led to her settling on the land. The Gallaway A beneficiaries do not attach much importance to whether a person contributed to the purchase of the farm or not. They are more concerned with their relationship with the person. Another factor that motivates them to accept people moving onto the land is the fact that the larger the population on the farm, the more eligible the community becomes for better service delivery. Mrs Mqo is a resident of Gallawater and receives the same recognition, benefits, support and right to participate in the farm activities as everyone else. Her grand-children attend the farm school. Her household was included in the bridge recon-struction project. Her livestock is safe and has grazing on the farm. She feels that she is more a part of the farm than the absentee beneficiaries. In her opinion, they should not be included in decision-making processes because they have no involvement in the farm.

Case 5: Mr Saku

Mr Saku, who is 49 years old, was born in the Glen Grey District, but like many other Gallawater residents, he left the area in 1975 when it was incorporated into the Transkei homeland. He is an epileptic. He received a disability grant but it has been stopped. He is not sure why. His wife is a volunteer at the preschool on the farm. She cooks for the children and runs the school when the government-paid teacher is away.

I found Mr Saku fixing an empty kraal when I went to interview him. He owned four cows when he moved to Gallawater, but they had all died in 2003 from red heart disease. He hopes that one day his kraal will be in good shape and have some cattle in it. He is not optimistic about the future, though. 'Currently nothing is promising,' he says. Mr Saku derives some income from helping people who move onto the farm build houses and from assisting with sheep-shearing during the season. Otherwise his family depends solely on the R160-a-month government child support grant that they receive for their nine-year-old son, who is in grade three in the farm school.

Mr Saku says life on Gallawater is better than it was in the other areas in which he has lived. There is no crime and there are many opportunities for making a living: 'For people interested in farming there is plenty of land to do that on. But there can only be developments in Gallawater if the government buys us farm implements, builds RDP houses and provides electricity'. He sees sustainable agri-culture as the way forward on the farm. But for this to happen, in his opinion, the government needs to supply the beneficiaries with equipment or someone needs to rent the farm and employ the residents as workers.

Case 6: Mr Boy

Mr Boy is a 63-year-old retired school principal who lives in Embokweni, one of the villages that comprise Zweledinga. He has a home garden and also keeps some sheep. Although he has some livestock at Gallawater, he is opposed to keeping livestock on the farm: 'Gallawater A farm was intended for agricultural practices but now people are turning it into a residential area'. The farm, in his view, was in perfect condition when Mr King moved out. It has been vandalised by its new owners, who want to turn the farm into a village. He sees the farm school as proof of this. Mr Boy has no intention of moving to Gallawater. Nor does he think that implementing a Comprehensive Agricultural Support Programme (CASP) on Gallawater would solve the farm's problems: 'For as long as the government is making promises it does not implement and people are unemployed, then there is no solution to the problems experienced on that farm and everywhere else'.

The man hired to tend Mr Boy's cattle and goats on Gallawater lives on the property with his wife and two children in a two-bedroomed house that he built himself. His eldest child attends the farm school. He was employed by the bridge construction project since he is considered a resident of Gallawater.

Case 7: Mr Neli

Mr Neli, a 65-year-old pensioner, expressed strong views about the farm when I interviewed him in his house in Zweledinga: 'The failures of Gallawater were obvious from the beginning when the government decided to settle 102 house-holds on a farm previously owned by one household. The only reason for so many people to buy the farm together was to raise enough own contribution in order to qualify for this programme. There are no implements on the farm; an agricul-tural farm is now being turned into a village'. Mr Neli keeps some of his livestock on the farm, though, employing a man named Melusi to look after them. Melusi lives in a small mud house on the farm. Mr Neli considers himself part of the farm even though he visits only to check on his animals. He also obtains firewood from Gallawater. He hopes that one of his children will farm on Gallawater on a full-time basis one day. He is in regular contact with people on the farm and appreci-ates being kept in touch with developments. Despite his concerns about whether Gallawater A is a farm or a residential area, Mr Neli is happy to know that he owns a piece of land somewhere.

Case 8: Mrs Nomsa

Fifty-three-year-old Mrs Nomsa grew up in Lady Frere but moved to Zweledinga with her parents, who were part of the group that resisted being incorporated into the Transkei. She grew up in a rural area where everyone kept livestock and culti-vated some fields. Her family derived enough of an income from their agricultural activities to be able to send her to a teacher training college.

Mrs Nomsa does not live on Gallawater A farm. She has entered into a verbal agreement with a family on the farm in terms of which they occupy her portion of land. She is a primary school teacher in the neighbouring village of Tambo. She told me that the land had been in good condition when it was transferred. Unfortunately, though, it was never made clear whether the farm would be used for agricultural or residential purposes, or a combination of the two. She had been keen to farm at first but complained that the government had not supplied Gallawater with the necessary implements. She had clearly lost interest in the farm: 'What will I benefit from leaving a place where I have transport, live comfortably and have all the basic services, to go and suffer on that farm? No normal person can do that'.

The fact that she had contributed to buying the farm entitled her to some rights in the farm, though: 'If I need firewood, I will come and get it from the farm'.

Case 9: Mr Nza

Mr Nza began the interview by telling me that the reason for acquiring Gallawater A farm was that Zweledinga had become overcrowded. The people from Glen Grey had only settled there temporarily in any case. They needed their own place for their children and livestock. Mr Nza had been elected the chairperson of Gallawater A farm at the time of the transfer. According to several residents, he had never carried out his responsibilities. His late deputy, Mr Bokwe, had taken on the duties of chairperson.

Mr Nza lived on the farm with his livestock until 2006. He then decided to go back to Zweledinga. His small house on the farm remains unoccupied. He intends going back to Gallawater A farm only when it is safe for his livestock and the infrastructure has been improved. He claims that he lost three cows in one year due to the big, loose rocks on the farm. He complained: 'The government just dumped us on Gallawater; there is no farm infrastructure. For me to even dip my animals, I had to move to another place. Services, such as electricity, are available in Zweledinga. The government should have not given us the farm without the proper infrastructure and other basic services that are needed on a farm, like an irrigation system and tractors.'

He told me that he intended to call a meeting to discuss issues on the farm and choose a new committee. He accused the people living on Gallawater of doing as they pleased and ignoring the owners of the farm who lived elsewhere. He was against people who had not contributed to purchasing the land settling on it.

Case 10: Mr Zondi

Mr Zondi also lives in Zweledinga. It is better than Gallawater, he maintains, because it has electricity and dipping tanks. He would farm on Gallawater if the necessary infrastructure and services were in place, but he wouldn't live on the farm. He wants the Department of Agriculture to install the CASP infrastructure it promised the beneficiaries. Mr Zondi is in regular contact with the residents on the farm. He is kept informed of developments by relatives and friends who live on the land.

Making sense of Gallawater A farm

The cases show that the beneficiary networks that exist on the farm are under-pinned by a common historical background. The beneficiaries fall into different social categories, the result of intricate sets of relationships and histories. Certain key members wield unequal power and influence. The way in which the different categories of beneficiary, including those who live on or off the farm, interact produces a particular kind of social space characterised by diverse sets of interlocking projects. These projects are influenced by their participants' various interests, social relations and choices. They exemplify the multiple realities produced by land reform in South Africa.

The Gallawater A project illustrates how land reform beneficiaries shape projects organically. They do not conform to the intentions of policymakers or the parameters of programme designs. Different expectations, views and interests among the stakeholders, especially the beneficiaries, give rise to new and unexpected forms of activity and a variety of small projects. As the cases illustrate, a great variety of livelihood strategies are pursued by different actors in order to meet both their own needs and the needs of others.

Mrs Bokwe and Mr Njabulo are typical of a rural elite 'who are better off since they have good access to markets, education facilities and all sorts of information, and their ability to speak foreign languages presents them [elites] with opportunities to be recognised or tasked with some responsibilities within their communities' (Platteau and Gaspart 2003: 1690). These beneficiaries might be privileged, but they also mobilise opportunities that help other community members. The transport that they provide and the jobs they create help everyone. They also strengthen the social ties on the farm through their activities. The shearing and grading of wool, for example, when the elite employs the other beneficiaries as labour, constitutes a social event in which the residents work, talk and eat together. Political economists emphasise that land reform creates inequalities and new elites. In the case of Gallawater A farm this is not a bad thing. It has produced a win–win situation for all the beneficiaries.

The case of Mrs Qongo exemplifies the way in which many beneficiaries pursue multiple sources of livelihood. She is a proud landowner. The connection with the land provides her with psychological security and a strong sense of identity (see also James 2007). Her testimony points to the importance of land reform projects as social spaces.

Access to land and security of tenure are major land reform objectives. Tenants and labourers also live on Gallawater, however. They provide cheap labour. While this constitutes an exploitative relationship and is not consistent with the policies that underpin land reform,[1] many of these people manage to access free land on which to settle as part of the transaction. Mrs Mqo's and Mr Boy's employees are a case in point.

In practice, land reform projects such as Gallawater work in ways that might be very different from the intentions of policymakers. Newcomers are welcomed as an asset. They contribute to the sustainability of the school and the growth of the area, making the farm more eligible for the provision of services. Even though most of the beneficiaries do not live on Gallawater A farm, they retain close ties with the farm. Non-resident owners like Mr Nza influence how the farm is run. Many of these beneficiaries use resources from the farm and have been instrumental in the movement of people onto the land.

Conclusions

Various actors and different voices come together on Gallawater A farm. This produces a complex social space in which diverse forms of agency can be exercised. Life on Gallawater A displays features of social embeddedness, a self-organising process that is characterised by the interpersonal networks and informal normative commitments that are necessary for accessing resources, developing livelihood strategies and managing enterprises or projects (Long 2001).

The newly created social spaces constituted by land reform projects are differentially occupied. This is evident from the nature and dynamics of the interlocking projects. New meanings and identities are continually produced by land reform projects. Judgements about land reform projects therefore need to be based on empirical evidence. Policy statements and ideologies do not mean much in such a fluid social context.

It is evident from the case of Gallawater that a much more flexible policy design and implementation process needs to be followed by the South African land reform programme if it is to cater for the diverse (and sometimes contradictory) needs of different categories of beneficiary.

Note

1   The Land Reform (Labour Tenants) Act (Act No. 3 of 1996) was passed by parliament to protect the rights of labour tenants and to make a land acquisition grant available for this purpose. According to this act, a 'labour tenant' is defined as a person who resides or has the right to reside on a farm that is owned by someone else as a result of his/her parents or grandparents' having resided on the farm. They receive grazing and cropping rights in exchange for provision of labour to the farm owner. The Act defines a farm worker as 'a person who is employed on a farm in terms of a contract of employment. In return for the labour which he or she provides to the owner or lessee of the farm, he or she shall be paid predominantly in cash or in some other form of remuneration, and not predominantly in the right to occupy and use land; and he or she is obliged to perform his or her services personally' (DLA 1997).

References

Davis, N.C., A.C. Horn, and S. Govender-Van Wyk. 2004. '"Invisible women": making the case for supply-led, class-based, gender-targeted land redistribution in South Africa', *GeoJournal*, 61(3): 273–279.

DLA (Department of Land Affairs). 1997. *White Paper on South African land policy*, Pretoria: Department of Land Affairs.

Driver, T. 2007. 'South African land reform and the global development industry', *African Studies Quarterly*, 9(4): 59–72.

Greenberg, S. 2003.'Land reform and transition in South Africa', *Transformation*, 52: 42–67.

Hall, R. 2007. 'Transforming rural South Africa? Taking stock of land reform', in L. Ntsebeza and R. Hall (eds) *The land question in South Africa: the challenge of transformation and redistribution*, Cape Town: HSRC Press.

James, D. 2007. *Gaining ground? 'Rights' and 'property' in South African land reform*, Johannesburg: Wits University Press.

Kariuki, S. and L. van der Walt. 2000. 'Land reform in South Africa: still waiting', *Southern Africa Report*, 15(3): 19–20.

Long, N. 2001. *Development sociology: actor perspectives*, London: Routledge.

Long, N. 2004. 'Actors, interfaces and development intervention: meanings, purposes and powers', in T. Kontinen (ed.) *Development intervention: actors and activity perspectives*, Helsinki: Helsingfors.

McGee, R. 2004. 'Unpacking policy: actors, knowledge and spaces', in B. Brock, R. McGee and J. Gaventa (eds) *Knowledge, actors and spaces in poverty reduction in Uganda and Nigeria*, Kampala: Fountain Publishers.

Platteau, J.P. and F. Gaspart. 2003. 'The risk of resource misappropriation in community-driven development', *World Development*, 31(10): 1687–1703.

Vetter, S. and W. Goqwana. 2000. 'Grazing management and sustainability in a land reform pilot project: a case study of Gallawater A farm, Eastern Cape province', in S. Vetter, W. Goqwana, J. Bobo and A. Marsh, *Land reform, sustainable rural livellhoods and gender relations: a case study of Gallawater A farm Vol. 2*, Research Report No. 5, Cape Town: Programme for Land and Agrarian Studies, University of the Western Cape.

Vivian, N. and F. Sudweeks. 2003. 'Social networks in transnational and virtual communities', paper presented at the Informing Science and Information Technology Education Joint Conference, 24–27 June, Pori, Finland.

Wegerif, M. 2004. *A critical appraisal of South Africa's market-based land reform policy: the case of the Land Redistribution for Agricultural Development (LRAD) programme in Limpopo*, Research Report No. 19, Cape Town: Programme for Land and Agrarian Studies.

Wells, T. 1995. 'The people, the ideas, the action in the fight for global justice: promised land', *New Internationalist*. Accessed February 2008, http://www.newint.org/issues265/Promised.htm.

7 Property rights and land reform in the Western Cape

Harriët Tienstra and Dik Roth

In this chapter we examine cases of market-led land reform in the Western Cape. The case material is derived from a study conducted during the period January to April 2010 (Tienstra 2010). The Western Cape has a long history of exporting fruit and wine produced on large farms and estates. Most land is owned by white farmers and estate companies. This may explain why land reform in the area mainly takes the form of land reform beneficiaries purchasing agricultural land (100 per cent ownership projects) or acquiring equity shares in an existing farming enterprise (Farmer Worker Equity Share projects, or FWES). This chapter explores the ongoing dynamics on both forms of farms, from a property perspective. We examine how the changing 'bundles' of rights and obligations experienced by the actors involved are transforming property rights and property relations on the farms.

Property relations and ordering modes of property

Land reform involves the transfer of property. In the legal anthropological approaches that are critical of mainstream economic approaches to natural resource management, property refers to the many ways in which people attribute value and meaning to goods or elements of their environment, and how they define rights and obligations, organise their social relationships, legitimise claims, and deal with conflicts pertaining to such valuables (Benda-Beckmann et al. 2006; Hann 1998, 2007). Property is regarded as a broad set of arrangements, not just a specific type of right or relationship such as 'ownership' (Benda-Beckmann et al. 2006). Property rights are in fact 'bundles' of rights and obligations, benefits and burdens, duties, freedoms and restrictions. Recent work on property has paid specific attention to the transformation of property. Changes of property regimes may generate a variety of new property relations. While attention is usually focused on the benefits of the resources that are transferred, risks, responsibilities, obligations and restrictions can also be transferred (Verdery 2004). Verdery

(2004) and Hann (2007) associate this with the 'bads' of property. To understand the property dimensions of the socio-political and economic changes initiated by land reform in South Africa, it is necessary to give greater attention to the complexities that attend the transformation of property rights and the relationships that accompany them.

We argue that how people experience new property rights varies significantly and that these variations can be understood as different modes of ordering property. We borrow the notion of modes of ordering from Law (1994), coined to characterise the nature of networks. Networks, in his view, are materially heterogeneous: they consist of a mix of social, economic, material, human, 'natural' and technical elements. The specific ordering of a network creates particular opportunities, as well as problems, for those who are involved in it. The logic of network ordering, Law (1994) argues, is not determined by single actors; the network itself establishes this ordering. Van der Ploeg (2003) describes how the projects of different actors interlock in the organisation of a network. The concrete nature and practice of the interlocking of these projects shape the opportunities that are generated by what Reich (1964) has referred to as 'new property'.

The networks in the context of land reform involve complex sets of social relationships that have emerged between the state, experts, markets, land and estate owners, and land reform beneficiaries. These are the post-settlement government support programmes, Land Redistribution for Agricultural Development (LRAD) programme subsidies and other payments to which land reform beneficiaries are entitled. The new property relations on the farms provide the focal point of our analysis. We divide the farms that we have studied into two categories: the 100 per cent ownership or smallholding projects and farms, and the FWES or shareholding farms and projects. In our view, these reflect two distinct modes of ordering property.

Land redistribution in the Western Cape

We begin this section by discussing the context of land reform in the Western Cape and explaining why land reform policy has assumed a specific character here. We argue that land tenure histories are key to understanding recent transformations and current conditions. This is followed by a discussion of the two modes of ordering property that have been employed in land reform projects in the Western Cape.

Land tenure histories in the Western Cape

The Western Cape was the first region where Dutch colonists settled. They gradually moved inland and began using the indigenous Khoisan inhabitants as labourers to work their land. The Khoisan lost their land and became completely dependent on the white farmers (Penn 2009). Most farms in the Western Cape are owned and managed by a mixture of estates, companies and families, many of which originated in settler times. The land was alienated long before the infamous Land Act of 1913, by which time it was already concentrated in the hands of the few. The farms and estates in the Western Cape are renowned for their fruit and wine, produced chiefly by a large workforce of permanent but predominantly seasonal farm workers. Production is largely geared towards the global market. The UK has been an especially important export market since the early eighteenth century (Barrientos et al. 2000).

The predominant ownership and management structure means that land reform primarily takes the form of land redistribution. Black people can buy land on the land markets created according to the 'willing buyer, willing seller' principle. They can ask for an LRAD grant from the Department of Rural Development and Land Reform to purchase land in order to start a farm or acquire shares in an existing agricultural enterprise, as long as security of tenure is ensured (DRDLR 2009). This means that beneficiaries can either become full owners of land (the 100 per cent ownership projects, referred to from now on as *smallholdings*), or become shareholders and form a joint venture with other shareholders (the FWES projects, referred to as *shareholdings* from now on). The rationale behind the FWES projects is that they will benefit both farm owners and farm workers. FWES projects offer farm owners an opportunity to invest new capital in their businesses, to expand and to score Black Economic Empowerment (BEE) points, while farm workers can expect to receive additional income, gain experience and expertise from the farm owner, and develop a better sense of self-esteem and belonging (MCA Urban and Environmental Planners 2008). Black farmers who want to become 100 per cent owners should be full-time farmers with an interest in commercial farming. This was confirmed by interviews we held with government officials, who stated clearly that they 'do not believe in farming as a side business'.

The two new modes of ordering property that have emerged in the Western Cape are distinguishable not only by their specific 'bundles' of rights and obligations and the transfer of certain risks, but also by the nature of the networks in which the two kinds of farm become embedded. The smallholdings are transferred *in toto* to new black farmers. They are expected to become commercial farmers and 'black entrepreneurs'. The government provides them with some support, mostly financial. Their farms, however, are not always on the most desirable pieces of land. This is a direct consequence of the 'willing seller, willing buyer' principle. The risks transferred to the new farmers create serious difficulties in the start-up phase. They are responsible for the development of their farms. Most of them prefer to operate independently and do not like too much government interference. They tend to search for additional support elsewhere. Other income-generating activities remain important to them as a source of capital and livelihood. The smallholding entrepreneurs tend, therefore, to be part-time farmers, despite the intentions of the government.

Shares in a farm are transferred to farm workers in terms of the shareholding model. This turns them into co-owners and the former farm owners into their commercial partners. Officially this means that farm workers have the right to a share of the profits and can influence long-term decision-making through their representation on the board of directors. Our case material shows, though, that in practice only a few shareholders gain direct control of a property. Only this select group of shareholders attend the meetings of the board of directors, are mentored by their new partners and receive relatively better-paid positions in the shareholding. Nevertheless, most farm workers do benefit financially and materially from their shares. The previous owners, now holders of the majority of the shares, generally accept the implications of the change in the way that the property is owned. They usually embark on this route in a positive spirit and accept the changing social and political climate in South Africa. They are susceptible to government pressure to implement a BEE strategy. This is partly because it has become increasingly difficult to find enough casual farm workers to supplement the permanent workforce. The new shareholding property arrangement makes this easier. It also gives the farmers access to new sources of funding and offers new business opportunities. The government does not interfere directly in the running of this kind of farm. The shareholding property arrangement implies that there is a mentoring relationship in place that facilitates the transfer of the knowledge, skills and experience of commercial farmers to a new generation of owners. The government, as a result, considers its role as chiefly providing financial support.

Smallholdings

We discuss two smallholdings in this section.[1] Each case illustrates the challenges that arise when starting a new farm, especially during the years immediately after the transfer of land. The two farmers have different backgrounds and different access to resources and networks, and choose their own ways to farm and make their enterprises sustainable.

The first case is Salmon Mankapan, a 'coloured' farmer in an area dominated by white farmers. Mankapan exemplifies the struggle of new farmers in finding the right institutions to support them. Mankapan has lived in the area all his life. He worked as a shepherd before he started a borehole service for farmers, fixing pumps and irrigation systems. With the help of government subsidies, he has acquired 1.652 hectares of land in the central Karoo (WCDOA 2006). It is rocky land and lacks water. He planned to keep sheep and plant crops such as vegetables and lucerne but the land has proved unsuitable. He continues running his borehole service.

Vukani Trust is quite distinct from the other case, in terms of its ownership structure. It clearly demonstrates how risks can be transferred along with property rights. The Vukani Trust consists of a group of 20 people from N'Duli, the township next to Ceres. Most members were employed to do piecework on surrounding farms. The trust was able to buy 6.5 hectares as part of a water reform project and receives support from a mentor. The mentor and trust members decided to plant vegetables. Even though the business plan predicted enough income for all, most members regard the farm only as a source of additional income and still rely on off-farm work and social grants.

Mankapan acquired many hectares of land, situated in an isolated and rocky place, with limited water availability. Having lived and worked in this area all his life, he knew that the soil in the area was dry and required a specific type of farming. Yet he did not predict the difficulties that his lack of access to water was to give him. Soon after he had realised the scale of the problem, he started looking for better land in the same area. He also requested assistance from the Department of Water Affairs to construct a dam on his land. He then ran into an institutional problem: Mankapan's farm is situated in an area that falls between the areas of responsibility of two offices of the department, one in Worcester and the other in Clanwilliam. The officials in Worcester informed him that there was money for a dam and boreholes but that he would need the approval of the Department of Water Affairs in Clanwilliam. The office in Clanwilliam found him ineligible for funding as only groups, not individuals, are allowed to apply. He sums up the situation: 'I feel I am constantly knocking on the wrong door. I'm talking to the wrong people.' Until his water scarcity problems are resolved, Mankapan can only keep sheep. His plans for planting pomegranate trees and vegetables are now on hold.

Mankapan's problems with water scarcity not only show the inherent risks of transferred property but also illustrate the difficult relationships that a farmer like Mankapan has to negotiate with various stakeholders. According to an official from the provincial Department of Agriculture, the Cape Winelands' farmer support and development programme has given Mankapan some basic support in the form of funding from the Comprehensive Agricultural Support Programme (CASP). His farm has also been visited and he has been offered some general advice. The official explained:

> We have made a business plan for him and provided him with a shed. The department has, however, not gone through his farming operation. Also he seemed relatively satisfied with how things were going and believed he knew better himself. Mankapan is now growing a little bit of lucerne on rocky soil, even though we advised him not to plant it there. He thinks it will grow there.

He added that the department could not provide Mankapan with additional support because of a lack of capacity – a staff member of the Ceres office had recently left and had not yet been replaced. Mankapan, however, is not very pleased with the support he has received from the government:

> Those people do not understand the Karoo. The soil is dry here. It requires a different type of farming. The people of the Department of Agriculture don't know anything about farming in such an area. When they come to this farm

> they ask me questions about why I am doing certain things. I have years of knowledge by just doing it, by farming in the area for so many years.

Mankapan might not receive much support from the government, but he makes sure that he finds support elsewhere. He has good connections with his white neighbours and, as a borehole expert with his own company, he can fix the irrigation pumps of the other farmers. They are more than willing to help him if he needs a worker, an extra tractor or certain implements. This means that he has access to implements when he needs them. He recognises the importance of his borehole service company: 'My work as a bore man is actually paying for my work on the farm.' Without his borehole service business he would not be able to continue farming. It allowed him to purchase his farm and it continues to provide food and cash for his family and capital to invest in his farm. Mankapan works on the farm only on weekends. Two people work on the farm in his absence. He aspires to become a full-time farmer one day, however.

Before the Vukani Trust could receive subsidies for the purchase of land, a business plan had to be set up. A consultancy company was hired by the government to draw up business plans for the land reform projects of the Koekedouw small farmers' project, including Vukani. Nevel Grobbelaar, who got involved as a mentor, believed from the start that the business plan was unrealistic:

> When I read the business plan I knew it was a lot of rubbish. It is white people who make the plan for money. Therefore they write a plan that looks like a successful venture. This project would only have been possible for a commercial farmer who already owns implements.

Grobbelaar did not believe that 6.5 hectares of land could support 20 people. Yet the business plan predicted that enough vegetables could be produced for both the farmers' own consumption and to sell locally (Ceres Development Consultants 2002). The mentor proved to be right about the unsustainability of the project. The members of the Vukani Trust work on the farm themselves. However, most of them also continue to do piecework on neighbouring farms because, as Grobbelaar puts it, 'They prefer to work for a salary'. Only five people are actually engaged in the day-to-day management of the farm. 'Fourteen trust members did not participate from the start,' according to Mkile, the chair of the trust. Grobbelaar himself provides not only financial and planning advice but also contributes physical labour to the project.

There have been problems with vandalism and stealing. This is part of the risk that was transferred along with the property. The land of the Vukani Trust is near the township of the trust members. It belonged to a neighbouring white farmer who wanted to create a buffer between his farm and the residents of N'Duli by selling the land solely for agricultural purposes. According to Grobbelaar, 'This was put in the contract since the previous owner wanted to sell the plot to create a buffer between his farm and the township. If they would start building houses on the plot the township would only move closer to the border of his land.' The risk of vandalism and theft has, in effect, been transferred to the new owners. The members were aware of the risks and hired a watchman. The watchman, though, became increasingly scared and finally quit his job. Things were stolen even when the guard was there. Even the roof and doors of the storeroom were taken. This was one among the many reasons why the members of the Vukani Trust eventually decided to sell the project.

Smallholdings as a new mode of ordering

The smallholding cases illustrate the varying dynamics of smallholding as a mode of ordering property. The new owners are the sole decision-makers and have to bear the consequences of their choices. While the individual actors who own the smallholdings make their own decisions, they are also subject to networks that order and structure the outcome of their endeavours to a significant degree. Mankapan continues to run a business that helps sustain his farming, and is able to tap into networks that are not state-sponsored. This helps him deal with the risks that attend his new activities. The government provides him with only some financial support and general advice. The members of the Vukani Trust have to face the consequences of a bad business plan, as well as the transfer of risk attached to their property.

Shareholdings

Shareholding is the second mode of ordering property that has emerged. The shareholding case we discuss here – the Harmony land reform project on the Môrester Estate – illustrates how land reform alters decision-making power and the division of profits, but does not really transform labour patterns on the farms.

The Harmony land reform project on the Môrester Estate is considered a success story by both the estate management and most beneficiaries themselves. The beneficiaries receive their dividends and some of them have become managers. Nevertheless, for most beneficiaries, daily life has not changed markedly. It is clear that many of them do not understand what being a shareholder means.

The Harmony project is situated on one of the farms that make up the Môrester Estate in the Koue Bokkeveld, a fruit-producing area. The farm started at the beginning of the twentieth century and has grown into a large company, consisting of several farms and employing hundreds of permanent and casual workers. The owners initiated talks to start a joint venture with some of the permanent farm workers in 2002. The workers were organised into a trust, which was represented by a number of trustees. Later, with the help of LRAD subsidies, the trust purchased land from the Môrester Estate and shares in one of company's farms. This land is now under production and the profits are shared.

According to Hein Jurries, the production manager at Harmony and chair of the Harmony Trust, a joint venture is the way to successful farm ownership, since it facilitates the transfer of skills and knowledge acquired over more than 100 years of experience in farming Môrester. When management, workers and others describe the Harmony project at Môrester Estate, they refer to it as their BEE project. Land reform on this farm is closely linked to the goals of BEE policies. Môrester Estate follows a 'SEB Ondernemings Ontwikkeling' strategy, a BEE enterprise development initiative. This is important for a farm like Môrester, which exports its fruit to supermarkets in the UK and the US via retail companies such as Colors and Capespan (Van der Merwe 2007). Supermarkets in the UK are under pressure to pay more attention to environmental and labour standards. Their suppliers, the fruit farms in the Cape, are pushed, in turn, to adhere to particular codes of conduct (Barrientos et al. 2000).

The property change at Môrester has provided the company with new sources of funding. The Harmony Trust has received CASP funds from the Department of Agriculture for irrigation and the purchase of other assets. An extension officer visited the farm to offer advice about soil erosion. The Department of Water Affairs has also visited the project a few times to work on the dam. The project's management, however, has not been very impressed with the government's contribution. According to Hein Jurries, government officials make promises that they don't fulfil. But the fact is that the government does not see a big role for itself in the project. Jurries puts it this way:

> There has been very little involvement in this project. There is already much service delivery from the fruit industry, and the department cannot assist much. The only thing we have done for this project is to facilitate getting Water Affairs to the table. The project wants to start doing some fruit farming and therefore water is needed.

The officials of the Western Cape Department of Agriculture are of the opinion that there is little they need to contribute because all the necessary knowledge and capital are already available on the farm. Their role is primarily to provide financial support.

Land reform has initiated a shift in the property relations between the different stakeholders at Harmony. The Harmony Trust is represented by two trustees, Hein Jurries and Griffith Sowa, who have the right to attend the meetings of the board of directors of the Môrester Estate. In theory, this should give them the opportunity to participate in decisions about what happens on the farm and offer them opportunities for personal development. The two men have very different backgrounds and also hold very different views about the opportunities and difficulties their new role involves.

Hein Jurries studied agricultural education at Elsenburg Agricultural Training Institute. He has managed different parts of the farm at Môrester and other farms as well. Jurries is very enthusiastic about the project. He would like to manage his own farm one day and considers this project as an opportunity to develop his managerial skills:

I believe we are a healthy project because we are a joint venture with Môrester. You cannot make up for their 100 years of experience and knowledge. I would like to be independent one day, but I cannot afford it. Taking decisions for the long term is quite hard.

Griffith Sowa does not have the same level of education as Jurries. He has always worked on one of the Môrester farms. He finds his new role as a trustee challenging. The board meetings present special difficulties: 'The level of communication is very high. They use all kinds of terms and figures that don't mean anything to me. I need to start understanding them'.

Both men hold management positions in the daily operation of the farm and are mentored by other production managers. They also receive special training at a training centre. A government official wondered, though, about the level that Jurries would be able to reach as a manager. He thought that there could be vested interests involved:

The question is if he will have the chance to develop into an MBA-level manager. That would also mean that his market value would rise and he could easily get a job at another place. In five years his market value has risen enormously. That is also the reason why the management may be reluctant to give too much training. They might lose their investment then.

Despite the opportunities that the role of trustee offers, not many trust members want to be a trustee. Trustees are chosen every two years but most people are reluctant to stand. Recently someone stepped down as trustee because he considered the work pressure too high. He needed to do his work as a trustee on top of his regular work. At present, the wives of both the vice chair and the chair of the Harmony Trust serve as trustees. This is not considered ideal.

Generally, the farm workers are most concerned about the dividends from their shares. They have received these four or five times already. I asked the trust members of Môrester what owning shares meant to them. One member replied, 'Now I am doing something not just for the money anymore.' Another said, 'We are working on something together. It is not only about wages anymore. I am happy that the project is now also growing.' Some trustees said that they had felt more motivated since becoming shareholders. Despite the positive attitudes of these trust members, some people have already left the project. About 12 people from Middeltuin farm have left the trust. Hein Jurries explains: 'A problem with the Farm Worker Equity Share project is that they think they can make money fast. However, when people leave they need to be bought out. This takes years. The trust deed states that trust leavers will also lose their equity share.'

It is not clear whether the FWES project on this farm enterprise has actually changed most people's daily lives for the better. The reactions of trust members who were asked whether the FWES arrangements had altered relations between management and farm workers were mixed. 'Nothing has changed in the attitude of the management towards the workers,' said one trustee. Hein Jurries disagreed: 'Some of the people in the top management were not so nice, but this has changed now. This is because the trust now judges them on their behaviour towards the shareholders. This judgement influences their bonus from the profits of Harmony.' Another trust member from Middeltuin farm agreed with Jurries: 'The project has changed many things. Firstly, the relation between the board and the workers changed. There is much more communication now.' He explains this is because he now gets all the information directly from the highest level: 'Every three months a report is made on what is happening on the work floor. That wasn't the case in the past'.

The living conditions on the farms have undoubtedly changed for the better during the last few years. The workers at Môrester all stay on the farm now. Their houses have recently been upgraded. Hein Jurries argues that this is because of regulations such as Eurepgap and the new labour laws. Eurepgap standards demand a higher standard of living for farm workers. These changes have also benefited the seasonal and permanent workers who are not part of the trust.

Shareholdings as a new mode of ordering property

The case material presented in this section illustrates how global discourses and national policies interact and shape one another. Land reform has initiated a new mode of ordering property, referred to as shareholding. This property change on the farms has resulted in new opportunities for several stakeholders. Global labour standards and demands from buyers have also played a part. Môrester has adapted so as to meet labour standards nationally and internationally. Financial support from the government has been made available for the trust to invest in its business. The government has not needed to give support in other ways, as much knowledge and experience is already available on the farm. Despite the changes, though, farm operations have continued much as before. Some workers have moved into management positions and attend meetings of the board of directors, but most continue to work as before. The majority of workers are more interested in the financial benefits of their shares than in changing their status on the farms. In addition, farm workers have not simply received new rights, but also have new responsibilities and risks to contend with.

Conclusion

The Western Cape, with its export-oriented, large-scale fruit and wine farms, is an important and dynamic economic region. The government wants the local black population to profit from the region's economic opportunities. It also seeks to promote black ownership. Land redistribution is the vehicle for obtaining these policy objectives. The government expects the agricultural industry to play a major role in land reform. It wants to confine its own role to the provision of financial support and basic advice. It remains a moot point as to whose interests have been best served by the type of land reform that has been implemented in the Western Cape.

We examined two smallholdings and one shareholding as new forms of property that generate different dynamics. The new smallholders have control over their properties but find it hard to reap the benefits. The situation might change in future but for now the smallholders depend on additional sources of income. They have also inherited risks along with their new property rights. While the new shareholders have obtained partial ownership of the farms on which they work, this does not translate into direct control of the farms or even into a desire for more control. The management of the farms now includes some of the new shareholders, but most of them seem to be more interested in the financial benefits they stand to get than in the managerial opportunities that their new position affords them. The new shareholders, too, have acquired new risks along with their new opportunities.

Both the smallholding and shareholding models illustrate the discrepancy between policy and practice in South African land and agrarian reform. These new modes of ordering property have not dramatically transformed the nature of farming in the country. The success of smallholdings largely hinges on pluriactivity, the combination of agricultural and non-agricultural activities, contrary to government and expert ideas and expectations, while labour relations remain largely unchanged on the shareholdings.

As this chapter has shown, the state has played a major role in the design of the current ordering of property rights on the farms. However, smallholders prefer to stay away from government expertise, interacting instead with other farmers and networks in order to obtain advice and support. The government does not want to be closely involved on the farms, apart from providing funding. It encourages the transfer of knowledge from white to black farmers and entrepreneurs. Finally, the case studies reveal that the new modes of ordering property generate opportunities and hopes. However, the (re)construction of new networks of property relations have not only transformed ownership but have also created new risks and responsibilities.

Note
1   For both the section on smallholdings and that on shareholdings, more cases have been researched, but cannot be discussed here for lack of space.

References

Barrientos, S., S. McClenaghan and L. Orton. 2000. 'Ethical trade and South African deciduous fruit exports, addressing gender sensitivity', *The European Journal of Development Research,* 12(1): 140–158.

Benda-Beckmann, F. von, K. von Benda-Beckmann and M. Wiber. 2006. 'The properties of property', in F. von Benda-Beckmann, K. von Benda-Beckmann and M. Wiber *Changing properties of property,* New York/Oxford: Berghahn Books.

Ceres Development Consultants. 2002. 'Besigheidsplan vir die onderneming N'Duli Vukani small farmers deelnemerstrust, als deel van die Koekedouw beginnersboer projek fase 2: N'Duli & Bella Vista, Ceres, een component van die Koekedouw besproeingskema vanuit die groter Ceresdam'.

DRDLR (Department of Rural Development and Land Reform). 2009. *Comprehensive rural development programme: the concept*, Pretoria: Department of Rural Development and Land Reform.

Hann, C.M. (ed.) 1998. *Property relations: renewing the anthropological tradition*, Cambridge: Cambridge University Press.

Hann, C. 2007. 'A new double movement? Anthropological perspectives on property in the age of neoliberalism', *Socio-Economic Review*, 5(2): 287–318.

Law, J. 1994. *Organizing modernity*, Oxford: Blackwell.

MCA Urban and Environmental Planners. 2008. 'Final report, area-based land sector plan', Cape Winelands District, Stellenbosch Municipality.

Penn, N. 2009. 'Labour, land and livestock in the Western Cape during the eighteenth century: the Khoisan and the colonists', in W.G. James and M. Simons (eds) *Class, caste and color: a social and economic history of the South African Western Cape*, New Brunswick, NJ: Transaction Publishers.

Reich, C. 1964. 'The new property', *Yale Law Journal*, 73(5): 733–787.

Tienstra, H. 2010. '"Ons kan in besit wees van eie grond": analysing property change and the role of post-settlement support on six farms in the Cape Winelands', unpublished MSc thesis, Wageningen University, the Netherlands.

Van der Merwe, D., in cooperation with the Harmony Trust. 2007. 'Besigheidsplan Harmony Trust en Middeltuin boerdery, aansoek by Department Grondsake'.

Van der Ploeg, J.D. 2003. *The virtual farmer: past, present and future of the Dutch peasantry*, Assen: Royal van Gorcum.

Verdery, K. 2004. 'The obligations of ownership: restoring rights to land in postsocialist Transylvania', in K. Verdery and C. Humphrey *Property in question: value transformation in the global economy*, Oxford: Berg.

WCDOA (Western Cape Department of Agriculture). 2006. 'Farming business plan: Mankapan boerdery projek', Western Cape Department of Agriculture.

8 'Rent a crowd' land reform at Survive and Dikgoho land reform projects

Limpho Taoana

This chapter focuses on the redistributive dimension of land reform in the Northern Cape province (NCP), which is both South Africa's largest province and its least populous (approximately 840 000 people). About 80 per cent of the NCP is classified as farmland. Crop production requires irrigation and water is taken from the Vaalharts Irrigation Scheme (VIS). Most of the available farmland is suitable only for extensive farming (Low and Rebelo 1998). Large, white-owned farms have been the norm since commercial farming began in the area in the 1930s.

The farms I studied are situated in Frances Baard, which is one of the five districts that make up the NCP. The market-assisted land reform, or 'willing buyer, willing seller' model, has been employed in the province's land distribution programme. The aim is to buy land for redistribution and to support beneficiaries to become independent commercial farmers. More than 700 000 hectares of agricultural land have been redistributed in the province since 1994, including 78 500 hectares that have been redistributed to 505 beneficiaries on 29 land reform projects (NCPG 2007). At this rate, the province will meet the government's target of redistributing 30 per cent of white commercial agricultural land by 2014. Despite these impressive figures, however, research suggests that only a handful of the implemented land reform projects have achieved their goals (Bradstock 2005 a, b, c; 2011; Khwene et al. 2004).

Khwene et al. (2004) observe that the majority of the land reform projects in the area have been characterised by low agricultural production, poor infrastructure, a lack of farming implements and machinery in good working order, and too many beneficiaries. Bradstock (2011) concludes that the land reform programme in the Northern Cape is producing a number of dysfunctional groups who are not 'fit for purpose'. It is evident that the land reform programme in its current form is unlikely to have a significant effect on poverty reduction in the province, nor will it lead to the creation of a black commercial farming class. Even if the government did manage to create such a class, agriculture would remain a risky livelihood activity for the great majority of people in the province. These conclusions are consistent with those reached in this chapter, which will also offer an explanation as to why land reform has failed to achieve its goals. The study on which this chapter is based has relied more heavily on the collection and interpretation of actor narratives than those of Khwene et al. and Bradstock, cited above. This qualitative study has enabled me to examine the actual practices of the beneficiaries in more detail. It has also provided me with first-hand information about whether or not the land reform programme has adequately provided the beneficiaries with the means to purchase the land and to work it productively.

The Northern Cape is a typical example of a region that has been caught between a rock and a hard place. Its structural and physical features – the great distances between places, insufficient infrastructure, market imperfections, a semi-arid environment – make agriculture a risky undertaking. Although people manoeuvre strategically to reduce or soften the impact of these conditions, I argue in this chapter that their manoeuvring can result in the emergence of new structures and sets of social relationships and social categories that limit the individual's freedom to act.

This dynamic makes land reform a complex, multifaceted project that does not evolve in a linear way. The outcomes of land reform cannot be predetermined and should not be studied as though they can. The consequences of land reform emerge in a context of negotiations that take place between a range of actors. This chapter documents this process by exploring the dynamics and opportunities that land reform presents to beneficiaries. It is based on case studies that were conducted in the Frances Baard District to examine the actual practices of people and their interpretations of land reform. It shows how land reform beneficiaries redesign elements of state policy so that it fits their own lives and experiences. In particular, the chapter explores the history and everyday workings of the Survive and Dikgoho projects as an aggregation of the individual stories of the social actors who are involved in them and whose strategies may or may not complement each other as they collectively try to manage their respective land reform projects.

Survive and Dikgoho have been selected as representative of two types of Land Redistribution for Agricultural Development (LRAD) project that have been implemented in the Frances Baard District. Looking at the two projects in depth provides a way of understanding the position of the LRAD projects and their beneficiaries in the area more generally. The Survive and the Dikgoho projects differ in a number of ways. The beneficiaries of the Survive project started farming in 2006. None of them had worked on a farm before. The Dikgoho beneficiaries started farming on their own in 2002. They were all familiar with poultry farming since they had worked on the farm for its previous owner. The two projects also display certain similarities. In both cases, many of the original beneficiaries left the project because it did not generate sufficient income, or because of conflict and a lack of trust.

The data that forms the basis for the analysis that is conducted in this chapter is derived from both participant observation and semi-structured interviews with the land reform beneficiaries, extension staff and the previous owners of the land. Documents, minutes of meetings, annual reports, strategic plans and business plans were also consulted. The data suggests that the 'rent-a-crowd' phenomenon, as described by James (2007), is a useful notion with which to explore the dynamics of many of the land reform projects in the area. Typical of rent-a-crowd projects, the beneficiaries generally do not have much in common. Many of them did not even know one another when the idea for a land reform project was born. The Survive project fits the rent-a-crowd profile very well; Dikgoho conforms to this profile to a lesser degree. Two important themes that emerge from the rent-a-crowd perspective are addressed in this chapter: leadership and the nature of the social relationships between the beneficiaries.

The chapter begins with a short description of how the two projects originated. The crucial role of chairpersons or leaders is examined. They act as 'big men' (see Platteau 2004) whose role in land reform projects cannot be ignored. The implementation of the Comprehensive Agricultural Support Programme (CASP), a core part of post-settlement support, is also discussed. It has created tension among land reform beneficiaries because there is no consistency when it comes to the distribution of resources such as farm implements. In the words of one of the beneficiaries: 'We received the land before the other project and now the government assists them before us and we have been waiting for a tractor for almost two years.'

Both the Survive and Dikgoho cases provide proof of the fact that land reform has led to the formation of new social categories in the urban and rural landscapes of South Africa: land reform beneficiaries and non-land reform beneficiaries. These categories are policy-induced categories that become real only in land reform situations. Non-active land reform beneficiaries form a third category, comprised of the disenchanted people that have left a project due to the low performance of the newly acquired farm, conflict with fellow beneficiaries, or the hard work and exposure to risks involved in participating in a land reform project. Most non-active land reform beneficiaries return to their previous places of residence.

Multiple realities in the Survive and the Dikgoho projects

The Survive project

Survive is one of the LRAD projects that falls within the area of the Vaalharts Irrigation Scheme (VIS). It is situated close to Hartswater, a town in the municipality of Phokwane. There are many black- and a few white-owned farms in the VIS area. Survive was handed over to 36 beneficiaries in 2006. When I started to collect data at the end of 2007, there were only six people who were still actively engaged on the project. I interviewed five of them. Three of the original beneficiaries had passed away since 2006, while 27 had left. The non-active beneficiaries all lived in Taung township. I interviewed 18 of them. Table 8.1 lists the beneficiaries and makes a distinction between active and non-active beneficiaries.

Table 8.1 Survive land reform beneficiaries

Active	Not active
Lindi, Shield, Freddy, Palesa, Clifford	Jerry, Patisiwe, Morwa, Matshediso, Modise, Montsheng, Sebini, Josina, Mantenya, Tafita, Joan, Uphill, Mary, Mathabo, Zama, Bohentse, Madipudi, Jakobo

I arranged the visit to the Survive land reform beneficiaries by telephone. At first they were reluctant to meet me because they thought I was a government official. They said that they were sick and tired of government employees who always failed to fulfil their promises. I informed them that I was a foreign student pursuing research. This convinced them, and they were ready to host me. I visited Survive for the first time on 23 November 2007. The beneficiaries were eager to share their challenges with someone and to exchange views about best practices. The meeting was cheerful and quite traditional in that the two women who were present sat apart from the two men and Mr Shield, the chairperson, did most of the talking. I had to encourage the other beneficiaries to participate in the discussion. I gained the impression that the four men cultivated and irrigated the land, while the two women performed the household chores – cooking and cleaning the house. Mr Shield did not work on the land himself, but supervised the work. He acted as if he were the owner of the project.

Survive covers 20.95 hectares of land. Five hectares were being used for lucerne and ten hectares were planted with wheat at the time of my study. The remaining five hectares were not under cultivation. Most of the produce of the Survive project achieved only first- or fourth-grade quality. The first wheat harvest was third grade and generated very little income as a result.

Survive was previously owned by a Mr Johnson, who had bought the farm in 1981. He sold the farm to the Department of Land Affairs (DLA) in 2004 because he 'was having financial problems'. These were partly attributable to drainage difficulties that had occurred on parts of his farm following heavy rainfall. The willing buyer, willing seller policy offered him the chance to get reasonable financial compensation. Like the current owners, Mr Johnson had planted lucerne, cotton, maize and wheat. He had always managed to produce first-grade crops, however, and obtained much higher yields than the land reform beneficiaries managed to realise. When I compared his yield data with those of the land reform beneficiaries, Mr Johnson was not surprised:

> The new owners don't plough in the proper way. If the field is not levelled, there will be no good production, as the water will be concentrated in one area. There are many bosses and they can't manage properly. I once advised them about planting, but Mr Shield doesn't listen as he thinks he knows it all. I sometimes offer to help them but they decline my offer, and they told me that they want to farm their way and they also know everything about farming.

After the group members settled on Survive, they formed themselves into three groups of 12. The plan was to rotate the cultivation of the land between the groups on a six-monthly basis. The proceeds from each harvest would be shared equally among all the members of the project. The first group, under the chairmanship of Mr Shield, managed to produce a harvest of lucerne. This was rated as third grade and did not generate a satisfactory income. The proceeds from the harvest were used to pay the electricity bill and the contractors who were hired for ploughing and harvesting. The balance was shared out among the members of the group. Each received a sum of R500. The members of the other groups did not receive any money. The second group failed to take their turn at cultivating the land because distrust and a lack of communication created a rift between the three groups of the Communal Property Association (CPA) and generated a series of disputes between them. Planned meetings failed to materialise. The other two groups complained that they did not have a sense of ownership of the land. Survive belonged only to the first group. A combination of lack of communication, mismanagement and conflict resulted in 27 beneficiaries leaving the project.

The story of the Survive project started in 2005, when Mr Tafita heard about the sale of the farm Plot 2G5 in Hartswater: 'I started to inform other people at Taung township. Quite a number showed an interest and we formed a group'. Tafita (34 years old at the time of the first interview in Taung) had been retrenched from the mines in 2004 and had received a lump-sum payout. He saw the acquisition of the land as an opportunity when he first heard about the sale. He was at the forefront of the project for a while but then lost interest. A group of 36 potential beneficiaries, 16 men and 20 women, was eventually formed. The members were not related to each other. The group approached the DLA in Kimberley to apply for the land in 2005. The DLA decided that the group met the requirements for an LRAD grant as stipulated in the White Paper: they were historically disadvantaged people, and they were also landless (DLA 1997: 38). It approved their application in 2006. The project was handed over to the group after a CPA statute had been written up and agreed to. The contribution of the beneficiaries to the project would take the form of labour. This was given a monetary value of R720 000. The land was purchased for R520 000, excluding farming implements. The remaining R200 000 was used to obtain an electricity connection and to purchase a weedkiller, a small tractor, a tiller, a plough and row planter, a wagon, a baler and disc, diesel, pesticides, seed and fertiliser.

Although the beneficiaries all hailed from Taung township, they came from a variety of backgrounds and had different reasons for joining the land reform project. None of them had prior knowledge of commercial farming. However, as Palesa, Matshediso and Sebini informed me, they all had a love for agriculture. Palesa said that she had aspired to study agriculture at tertiary level but her mother could not afford the fees. A major reason for joining the group was unemployment. Many of the beneficiaries had been recently retrenched. Mr Shield told me that he had become interested in the project because he had wanted to earn an income and not depend on his wife. Freddy developed an interest because he had lost his job and was looking for opportunities. Other unemployed participants such as Jerry, Josina, Mary, Zama, Patisiwe and Montsheng also emphasised that they saw joining the project as a way of improving their livelihoods.

Lindi was born in 1950 in Taung. She attended school in the township until grade eleven. She married Johnny in 1976, and the couple had two sons. Lindi was not formally employed when she heard about Survive. She spent her days looking after her sheep and cattle: 'I was raising livestock to generate an income. Most of my livestock was stolen and I was left with ten sheep, three cows and some chickens and geese. My livestock was not providing enough income; that is why I got interested in the project'. She grew beetroots, cabbages, carrots, onions and tomatoes in a vegetable garden before becoming a beneficiary. The vegetables were all grown for home consumption. She is now the treasurer of the Survive project. Her others duties include irrigating, cleaning the house, cooking and cutting lucerne with a sickle. She told me that she was still active in the project because it was difficult to find a job, especially for a person of her age. Her husband continues to work in Taung. He reads water and electricity meters for the municipality and earns R3 000 a month. Bonolo, her son, is a waiter at the Taung Trust and sends her R200 every month, which she uses to purchase food.

Palesa, the secretary of Survive, was born in 1973. She completed school. She was a domestic worker before joining Survive. She has two children. Her daughter gets a child support grant of R200 a month, which she gives to her mother. Palesa's own mother also sometimes sends her money with which to purchase food. Palesa does not have a vegetable garden at home and has no livestock. She became interested in the land reform project because she had a 'love for agriculture'. She had also studied agriculture at school. Her duties in the project include irrigating, planting and baling lucerne with the tractor.

Sebini was among the group who initiated the project. She was born in 1974. A teacher by profession, she is among the better-off of the beneficiaries. She became interested in owning the land as she had had a love for agriculture from a young age. She is currently employed at a secondary school and earns about R5 000 a month. Her husband works on the mines. Before becoming a Survive beneficiary, Sebini was contractually employed at an Adult Basic Education and Training (ABET) centre, earning R2 000 a month. She maintains a vegetable garden, growing spinach for consumption and to sell to her neighbours. She also keeps chickens, which she sells at R30 each. Sebini is no longer an active member of the project because of conflict and misunderstandings but is still a member of the CPA.

Jerry is 46 years old. He left school when he reached grade six. He lives with his wife, Lerato, and their three daughters. He depends on piece jobs and earns R150 to R1 200 a month, depending on the type of job he finds. He was employed on a mine in Rustenburg until he was retrenched in 1995. He hoped that Survive would offer a means of escaping poverty, but no income was generated during the time that he participated in the project. He spends money on transport and food. The relatively high costs of travelling from Taung to Survive and back proved an insurmountable obstacle to Jerry's continued participation in the project. He would like to cultivate a vegetable garden but a lack of irrigation water limits his options.

He has 18 breeding chickens, though. This enables him to earn some money and also provides the family with chickens to eat. Like many others in Taung, Jerry had hoped that land reform would make a difference but the conflicts and misunderstandings that have bedevilled the Survive project have undermined these hopes.

Madipudi was born in 1967. She saw land reform as a key event in her life. As a domestic worker, she had never thought that she would be able to realise her dream to become a farmer. She saw Survive as the chance to make her dream come true. Unfortunately the project did not work out as she had expected. She has continued to keep livestock, though. She keeps chickens and geese for home consumption. She also owns three sheep. She plans to earn additional income by breeding her three sheep. She also has a vegetable garden and sells the surplus to her neighbours. She is proud that she is not entirely dependent on social grants.

The Dikgoho project

The Dikgoho project began when a group of retrenched farm workers decided to apply for an LRAD grant so that they could purchase a 21-hectare chicken farm whose owner, a Mr Florence, had gone bankrupt. A business plan was written and approved in 2001, and the sale went through in 2002.

The Dikgoho farm was valued at R3.5 million at the time of the transfer. The value of the beneficiaries' contribution, in the form of their labour, was set at R1.2 million. The balance of R2.3 million had to be paid by the beneficiaries over a period of 20 years. The Dikgoho project requested a loan of R448 070 from the Land Bank (NCDA 2001) in order for operations to start and to cover the working capital costs of the first year. At the time of my visit in 2007, the project was running up a substantial interest bill of more than R15 000 a month.

The farm was handed over to 60 beneficiaries, 35 women and 25 men. The beneficiaries argued that they had gained experience at managing the farm while working for Mr Florence and did not need training. When I began collecting data in 2007, I was told that the number of beneficiaries active in the project had dwindled to nine. Twenty-seven were no longer active, twelve had become permanently employed elsewhere, four were sick, four had died and four had been absent from the start of the project. I interviewed eight active and seven inactive members of the project.

Ms Mamabele, who hails from Warrenton, introduced herself as the chairperson of the project. She had started working on the farm in 1992 as a labourer, earning between R360 and R600 a month. I asked her to show me around. We first walked in the direction of the chicken houses. I jokingly asked if the chickens were asleep as I couldn't hear them. Ms Mamabele replied that there were no chickens. I asked why this was the case. She told me that the project no longer kept live chickens. 'We buy from commercial farmers in the region and sell to local retailers. We purchase 1 000 live chickens and slaughter twice per month and sell them at R19.70 per kilogram. We charge R3 to slaughter a chicken and we charge a lesser fee of R2.50 when the offal is removed and left with us.'

Most of the information about the history of Dikgoho came from Ms Mamabele. She spends most of her time in the office, running the administration.

The other beneficiaries work in the slaughterhouse. Gert, the white foreman who had worked on the farm for the previous owner, Mr Florence, had been part of the project in the beginning but had left. According to Ms Mamabele,

> Mr Florence left him with us so that he could manage the project for the new owners. As the new owners we felt that we had to get rid of him as we wanted to farm our way and also to manage it ourselves. We started the project in 2002 with 68 000 live chickens. In 2004 we started to experience high mortality rates amongst the chickens because of lack of ventilation in the chicken houses. We had no money to purchase chicken feed, and we were accumulating a debt with the Land Bank. We had only a one-year contract with the Correctional Services at a fixed price, which expired.

The loss of the contract to supply chickens to Correctional Services produced such a cash-flow problem that the very survival of the project was threatened. One of the solutions was to ask some of the beneficiaries to leave the project temporarily. Some of those who were no longer active in the project told me that they had been asked to leave but could return when the project began to make money. The beneficiaries who were still active on the farm saw things differently. Ms Mamabele told me that people had left because of the serious challenges that the project was facing. They had not been asked to go. She would not invite them back since 'they ran away from the problems'.

The nine remaining beneficiaries occupied themselves by cleaning the abattoir and slaughtering chickens for other people twice a month. They had a lot of time for socialising. They consumed the offal of the slaughtered chickens and also grew vegetables. They considered their vegetable gardens to be one of the main benefits of the project. They had no alternative source of employment. Unemployment had been the motive for joining the project in the first place: 'I had the interest in the project because I was not working and a person of my age is not easy to be employed'. Although the project did not generate sufficient income, it was better than nothing: 'If we slaughter for the public, we can earn R30 on that day'.

I asked the beneficiaries to compare their present situation on the farm with the situation when they had been workers. They admitted that it had been better when they did not have to face the problems of the farm directly themselves. The farm had also had a market for its produce. At least they had earned about R500 a month from Mr Florence. One of the beneficiaries, Malehlakana, conceded that they had made a mistake by deciding not to continue with the mentor. It was too late to rectify the situation, however.

Leadership and decision-making

In effect, the Survive and the Dikgoho projects are owned by their respective chair-persons. They often take decisions without consultation. The other beneficiaries do not have the courage to challenge the chairperson's decisions. The Survive chairperson is not engaged in day-to-day project activities such as irrigating, weeding and ploughing. The chairperson of the Dikgoho project sits in the office while others slaughter chickens, clean the abattoir and weed the vegetable gardens. This can partly be explained by different skills and educational backgrounds. Both leaders have managerial experience. Mr Shield has an ABET diploma and worked as a senior administration officer for the North West Development Cooperation. In the course of running their projects, leaders like Mr Shield and Ms Mamabele develop a style of leadership that effectively turns them into a local elite (Platteau 2004). The role of these 'big men' (and women) in land reform projects cannot be ignored.

One of the consequences of the top-down management style of Mr Shield and Ms Mamabele is that the constitution of the CPA becomes a meaningless document (see Bradstock 2003; De Wet and Mgujulwa 2010). Land reform has created a space for local leaders to emerge. This phenomenon does not always benefit the land reform process itself. Embedded in a 'traditional' or conventional set of social relations, a set of everyday relationships evolves that contrasts sharply with the policymakers' ideas of equity, social justice and human rights.

Conflict, mistrust and lack of transparency were not supposed to be part of land reform projects. The CPAs are based on the principle of cooperation. Instead, land reform projects have frequently been characterised by division and competition. The two projects discussed in this chapter clearly show that land reform has unintentionally created or contributed to the formation of new, previously non-existing social categories, the most powerful and easily observable of which are the active land reform beneficiaries and the non-active land reform beneficiaries. A distinction has also come to exist between the beneficiaries with active leadership roles and power positions and those who do not have much say in decisions about daily operations. Gender is another obvious social category which helps to explain everyday life at land reform projects. The two women in the Survive project, for example, engage in domestic activities such as cleaning the house, while the men work the fields. The only time that the collective nature of a land reform project becomes more than virtual reality is when the project needs financial assistance from the Land Bank, since this requires the signatures of all its members.

Concluding remarks

At present, the Survive and the Dikgoho projects are neither socially nor economically viable. This has resulted in the majority of the beneficiaries withdrawing from the projects. Twenty-seven beneficiaries have left the Survive project, citing a range of reasons: lack of incentive, motivation and trust among group members; poor communication; a failure of leadership; and the desire to pursue other professions/careers. An equal number of beneficiaries have left the Dikgoho project.

They attribute their decision to leave to nepotism; a lack of a sense of ownership; and leadership issues. Contrary to the expectations of the policymakers, the social capital – trust and collaboration, in particular – that is required to make institutional forms such as CPAs work has not yet materialised. This is hardly surprising when the 'rent-a-crowd' nature of the beneficiary groups is considered. The backgrounds and aspirations of the beneficiaries are simply too diverse to create a cohesive collective agricultural enterprise.

This study also suggests that the beneficiaries should not be treated as if they were all the same. Age, for example, is important when it comes to accessing state pensions, which serve as a springboard for a range of activities. Beneficiaries also differ in terms of skills, abilities and education levels.

This account of the livelihoods of the Survive and the Dikgoho beneficiaries accords with other livelihood studies in the NCP and elsewhere in South Africa. Much of this research examines a combination of resources and related activities. These resources are not purely material in nature, but include relations with next of kin, other family members, employers and the state. Like the majority of the people in the NCP, most of the active and non-active beneficiaries in the Survive and the Dikgoho projects derive their livelihood from social grants (pensions, disability grants and child support grants) as well as seasonal, casual and other salaried work (Bradstock 2003, 2005b, 2011).

While the distinction between active and non-active beneficiaries is an important explanatory factor when it comes to understanding the everyday dynamics of land reform projects, the distinction is not significant when it comes to explaining livelihoods and determining whether or not land reform has had an impact on them. The evidence suggests that participation or non-participation in a project hardly affects people's livelihoods. If anything, non-active beneficiaries generally tend to be better off than the still active beneficiaries. In either case, agriculture is not the major contributor to income or enhanced food and social security. Land reform has not broken the pattern whereby rural people supplement non-agricultural activities with some agricultural activities in order to procure a livelihood.

Interestingly, when it comes to understanding the everyday practices at land reform projects, the distinction between active beneficiaries and non-active beneficiaries is an important explanatory factor. Active or not, the evidence points to livelihoods that are virtually unchanged and continue to revolve around multiple resources. People joined the LRAD projects because they were looking for social and economic security. The LRAD projects offered them the prospect of improving their livelihoods. Unfortunately, land reform has not dramatically transformed rural peoples' livelihoods. These livelihoods continue to revolve largely around non-agricultural resources. The contribution of agriculture and land-based resources is still marginal. Active land reform beneficiaries tend to be among the marginalised people in the country whose livelihoods have not been boosted by post-apartheid transformations. Land reform has become a resource for people to fall back on when the labour market does not provide opportunities. It works the other way as well, though. When a project does not perform as planned or expected, beneficiaries turn to the labour market for work. Maintaining relations with land reform projects is just one element of a complex survival strategy in the Northern Cape province today.

References

Bradstock, A. 2003. *Key lessons learned from working with six land reform communities in the Northern Cape province of South Africa*, London: FARM-Africa.

Bradstock, A. 2005a. *Changing livelihoods and land reform: evidence from the Northern Cape province of South Africa*, London: FARM-Africa.

Bradstock, A. 2005b. *Key experiences of land reform in the Northern Cape province of South Africa*, London: FARM-Africa.

Bradstock, A. 2005c. *Supporting land reform in South Africa: participatory planning experience in the Northern Cape province*, London: FARM-Africa.

Bradstock, A. 2011. 'Land reform and its effect on livelihoods in the Northern Cape province of South Africa', in P. Hebinck, and C. Shackleton (eds) *Reforming land and resource use in South Africa: impact on livelihoods*, London: Routledge.

De Wet, C. and E. Mgujulwa. 2010. 'The ambiguities of using restitution as a vehicle for development: an Eastern Cape case study', in A. Bohlin, R. Hall, T. Kepe and C. Walker (eds) *Land, memory, reconstruction and justice: perspectives on land restitution in South Africa*, Athens: Ohio University Press.

DLA (Department of Land Affairs). 1997. *White Paper on South African land policy*, Pretoria: Department of Land Affairs.

James, D. 2007. *Gaining ground? Rights and poverty in South African land reform*, Johannesburg: Wits University Press.

Khwene, M.W., D. Ogane, S. Mpandeli, J. De Bruin, J. Domola and J. Mamabolo. 2004. *The development of a project framework for land reform at the Vaalharts Irrigation Scheme of the Northern Cape province, South Africa*, Agricultural Research Council, Field Study Series No. 4, Northern Cape.

Low, A. and A. Rebelo. 1998.*Vegetation of South Africa, Lesotho and Swaziland. Second edition*, Pretoria: Department of Environmental Affairs and Tourism.

NCDA (Northern Cape Department of Agriulture). 2001. *Dikgoho business plan*, Kimberley: Northern Cape Department of Agriculture.

NCPG (Northern Cape Provincial Government). 2007. 'Budget vote speech for 2007/08', Department of Agriculture and Land Reform, Kimberley.

Platteau, J.P. 2004. 'Monitoring elite capturing in community-driven development', *Development and Change*, 35(2): 223–246.

9 Locating policies in the daily practices of land reform beneficiaries: the Mighty and Wales land reform farms

Malebogo Phetlhu

This chapter views land reform in South Africa through an ethnographic lens. It addresses two general but fundamental questions: what is happening on land reform farms, and how do different actors develop strategies to make sense of land reform policies? The chapter provides an account of the everyday life experiences and ideas of those actors who are directly involved with land reform. An essential requirement of an ethnographic study of land reform is that it should not begin with preconceived ideas. A consideration of the views and experiences of those involved is the key ingredient of an open-minded approach to the study of social life on land reform farms. Anyone who has been engaged in ethnographic research of this sort soon realises where the challenges lie. The researcher cannot fully disconnect him/herself from the views expressed in the public, academic and media domains. Preconceived views have to be continually revised as more data is collected and new questions arise. Another difficulty is that land reform has different meanings for different beneficiaries. There is no single answer to the question about how land reform has reshaped people's lives. It soon becomes apparent that the nature of the interactions between key actors has important empirical and analytical consequences. These largely shape people's interpretation of land reform, which, in turn, colours their everyday life experiences.

This chapter focuses on the interactions between land reform beneficiaries and extension officials on two land reform farms in the Northern Cape province. The analysis of the Mighty and Wales land reform projects builds on the idea that land reform is often a conflictive and ambiguous process (Hebinck 2008; Moyo and Hall 2007). Its complexities can only be understood if beneficiaries are not seen as a homogeneous group. One of the tasks of this chapter, therefore, is to deconstruct the category 'beneficiary'. The other actors who are involved in land reform – extension officials, policymakers and the politicians who have pushed the land and agrarian reform agenda in South Africa – cannot be seen as belonging to homogeneous groups either.

The outcomes of the two projects that are discussed in this chapter, I argue, have largely been shaped by the various ways in which diverse groups of beneficiaries attribute their own meanings and understandings to the land reform programme, as well as by the nature of the interaction between the various groups of beneficiaries and the extension workers who are involved in the implementation of the Mighty and Wales projects. The objectives of the post-apartheid government with regard to land reform are laudable: the reconstruction of rural development by means of agrarian reform. The evidence presented in this chapter suggests, though, that the process of policymaking has failed to take into account the reality of the beneficiaries' everyday experiences.

Meeting the beneficiaries of the Wales and Mighty farms

In the sections that follow, I describe the two projects in terms of their infrastructure and economic activity and then discuss the beneficiaries' views and experiences of them. The analysis focuses on the interactions between the actors involved, and the everyday dynamics on the two farms.

Mighty farm project

The distance from Kuruman to Mighty farm is roughly 50 kilometres. It takes longer to undertake the journey than this distance suggests, however. The first 30 kilometres of the road from Kuruman is tarred. The road then turns to rocky gravel, before becoming sand and, finally, rock and shrubs. Only a four-wheel drive vehicle can make it all the way to the farm, and even then it is slow going. 'It requires somebody to be really desperate to decide to drive on this road or even to go to this farm,' I thought to myself the first time I drove along the road.

Mighty was acquired through the land redistribution programme in 1999. According to some of the beneficiaries, an extension officer recruited 110 beneficiaries to apply for the land. The present extension officer in the area told me that it had been necessary to mobilise the people of Drieloop (the village where Mighty farm is located) because they had not known about the land reform programme.

The beneficiaries had to contribute labour, assets or capital to the project if they wanted to participate in it. The farm was intended to be used for goat farming when it was handed over. Many of the beneficiaries left the project when they realised that they would not be allowed to bring their own animals to the farm. Apparently this rule contradicted a promise that had been made by the recruiting extension officer. Only 60 of the original beneficiaries remained as a result. The number of beneficiaries dwindled even further over the next few years. This led the local extension officer to start recruiting people who wanted to join the Mighty goat project in 2002. He did this in order to keep the project alive and to make up the numbers.

Some of the beneficiaries who remained on the farm also recruited new beneficiaries, mostly friends or family members. Some of the new members also invited people whom they knew to join. The new recruits did not always have assets or capital to contribute. It was agreed that they could work on the farm as a form of 'in-kind' contribution. Most of these people had been dependent on government pensions and child grants.

The fact that new beneficiaries were recruited to join the project has brought an interesting dimension to the Mighty project. Different actors from different backgrounds, with various skills and assets, have become involved in the common project of owning Mighty farm and making a living from it.

I discuss below the different beneficiaries according to their role in the project. Whether people contribute in kind in the form of labour, or in the form of goats makes a big difference. Along with family relationships, it is the major factor that shapes the relationships on the farm.

Ramatlho and his family

Ramatlho is the chairperson of the Mighty goat project. He is an outspoken man and is popular with the extension officials. His wife and daughter are also project beneficiaries. Ramatlho lives in a large, bright green house in Drieloop. A painted house is a rarity in a village in which most houses are built of mud or unplastered cement blocks. Ramatlho worked on the mines until he quit in 1995 because of ill health. He bought a *bakkie* (small pickup truck) with his pension fund payout and started a taxi business, transporting local people to and from town. He also transports animal feed and medicine to the farm, for which he gets paid from the project funds. None of the other beneficiaries possesses a car, although a few have donkey carts.

Ramatlho was among the beneficiaries that joined the farm in 2002. He says he joined because he was aware of the benefits that goat farming could bring. When I asked Ramatlho why he was still running his taxi business, he said, 'I have survived for years from transporting people and I make a living out of it. I cannot stop now.' Ramatlho is happy with circumstances on the farm but he complains that some members are not cooperative. Although he refused to name them, it was clear that he was referring to the people who were supposed to make their contribution to the project in the form of labour. He described the labour contributors as 'owing the project'.

Some of the other beneficiaries told me that Ramatlho's wife and daughter were rarely seen on the farm although they were beneficiaries. Ramatlho countered this by saying that his work on the project fulfilled his family's obligations.

Angelina, a former member

Angelina, a resident of Drieloop village, quit the Mighty goat project because she saw no reason to stay. She had been recruited in 2002 by one of the members. She contributed in kind, looking after the goats with another member who was in the same situation. They rotated the task. Angelina was very optimistic and motivated at first: 'The work was tiring because we had to walk long distances from the village to the farm, but I was determined to make it work'.

This changed when Ramatlho's wife and daughter joined the project. They brought more goats but did not help to look after them. Angelina saw Ramatlho's wife on the farm only twice. It was rumoured that Ramatlho's daughter lived in Johannesburg. Angelina and her friend, Bontle, left the project in 2004 because they felt that they were being overworked without sufficient compensation. She feels unfairly treated by the other beneficiaries. Bontle now works as a domestic worker in town. Angelina has not yet found a job. She survives on the government child grant that she gets for her two children.

Raditamati, an original member

Raditamati was one of the first people to join the Mighty land redistribution project in 1999. He is still a member even though he also has a job on a mine. He has always had a love for farming and spent most of his childhood herding his father's animals. When he grew older, he began keeping animals of his own.

Raditamati spends his leave and weekends on the farm. Mighty is a blessing for him, he says, because he knows that his cattle are taken care of while he is away at work. His wife passed away before he joined the project and his children are married. He has no one else to look after his animals. Mighty provides Raditamati with access to cheap labour and a safe environment for his animals. He clearly considers the cattle that he contributed to the project to be his property rather than a communal asset. The chances are that he will take his animals back to his village when he stops working on the mine.

Rooiland

Finding the former Mighty project beneficiaries was often difficult. Angelina told me that I would find a woman named Mpho in the village. When I knocked on her door, however, I learnt that Mpho had left four weeks previously on the truck that takes seasonal labourers to work on the commercial farms in Upington, about 300 kilometres away from Drieloop. I was ready to call it a day when I met an old man outside the agricultural office. I asked him if he knew any of the Mighty beneficiaries. He responded by directing me to the house of a man named Rooiland.

I walked up to an unfenced two-roomed house. It had a low door and two small windows which were stuffed with old rags. It was built from clay bricks and was plastered with red mud. A woman and a small boy were eating boiled maize from a big yellow enamel mug in front of the house. A small, three-legged black pot stood in the middle of an open dung fire next to them. I greeted the woman and the boy and asked if this was Rooiland's home. The woman asked if I wanted to see him. I said that I did. She brought me an old 20-litre paint drum on which to sit and a small mug of boiled corn to eat. She told me that Rooiland had gone to the shop to buy tobacco and would soon be back.

Rooiland returned after half an hour. He was a huge man. He wore old, heavy-duty builders' boots, and his arms were covered with tattoos. His face looked as if he had spent much of his life in the sun. I introduced myself and told him what I had come for. Rooiland sat flat on the ground and rolled a cigarette with newspaper. He smoked for a while before passing the cigarette to his wife. Then he began to speak.

Rooiland says he was recruited along with some other new members in 2002 by a woman named Anna, one of the original beneficiaries of Mighty farm. Anna had not told them much, he maintained, only that they had to make a contribution in the form of labour, assets or capital. Rooiland liked the proposal and decided to join. He asked his brother to lend him a goat, which he then gave to the project as his contribution. He was also asked to contribute a monthly amount of R50 but could not afford this amount. In any event, he did not wish to contribute cash because he knew that it would be used to buy food for Ramatlho's goats. He was not prepared to help make another man rich while he struggled. Rooiland quit the project in 2005, taking with him his brother's goat and the four goats it had given birth to on the farm. He gave his brother two of the young goats and kept the other goats himself. His flock has increased to five since then. I asked him whether he knew of any other beneficiaries who had left the project I could talk to. He told me that the few that he knew of had gone to work in Upington as seasonal workers. I gained the impression that Rooiland was an honest and happy man who was determined to make it on his own by rearing his own goats.

Dorkie, Ramatlho's wife

It took me two months to find Ramatlho's wife, Dorkie. I had heard many rumours about her and wanted to hear her side of the story. I finally came across Dorkie in her husband's taxi. A short woman with a very sharp voice, she works as a cleaner in one of the supermarkets in town and travels there every morning with her husband.

Dorkie told me that everything was going well on Mighty farm. She responded to my question about her relationship with the other members by saying that everyone worked well together and was hoping to achieve the same goal. I asked how she managed to combine her job with her duties on the farm. Dorkie told me that she was too tired to work on the farm after working all day as a cleaner. It was not a problem, though, since her husband took care of her share of the duties on the farm. She told me that she and her husband had decided to send their daughter to complete a computer course in Johannesburg. The daughter would therefore not contribute directly to the project for the time being. Dorkie said that it had not been necessary to inform the other members about this since they seldom visited the farm anyway. From the way that Dorkie spoke, it was clear that Ramatlho considers Mighty as his farm and takes decisions as he sees fit.

Muzi, the extension officer

As the extension officer responsible for Mighty farm, Muzi's task is to ensure that progress is made on the project. He maintains that he has not seen any improvement on the farm since he began working with the Mighty beneficiaries. The beneficiaries of Wales, with whom he worked previously, are more dedicated than those of Mighty, in his opinion. He accuses the Mighty beneficiaries of not being willing to work together. They seldom attend meetings and are lazy, he says. Muzi does have a good relationship with Ramatlho, however. He has Ramatlho's mobile number and contacts him whenever he needs information about the project.

The Wales project

Wales, formerly a commercial cattle farm of 1 344 hectares, was acquired through the LRAD programme. The project started in 2003 with a herd of 76 cattle: the beneficiaries contributed 18 cattle themselves, while 55 cows and 3 bulls were bought with LRAD funds.

The beneficiaries grew out of a group of people who had been encouraged to apply for a land reform farm by the local extension officer. The Department of Agriculture had mandated him to make people aware of the land reform programme. This group invited friends and relatives to join them. The beneficiaries initially consisted of 23 people, including ten people who were related to each other. The beneficiaries all come from Dinns, a village about 50 kilometres away from the farm. The farm itself is located just outside the town of Kuruman. The beneficiaries depend on hired transport to get to the farm since none of them has a vehicle.

Loesboy

Sixty-year-old Loesboy is one of only two men in the project. He worked as a seasonal worker on white-owned farms before joining the project. He would harvest maize, raisins or cotton for two months of the year, accompanied by his wife or one of his children. He now works full-time on Wales farm. Loesboy has seven children. One of them is married. The other six, and his four grandchildren, rely on him for food and accommodation. Loesboy spends most of the week looking after the project's cattle. He is paid by the other project members to do this. Loesboy also sells vegetables and fruit from his garden to the other beneficiaries.

Ma Tumelo

Ma Tumelo is another of the 23 members of the Wales project. She receives a state pension which she describes as 'Mandela's money'. She does not stay on the farm because she looks after her four grandchildren in the village. Their mother comes home only on weekends. It is difficult to get to the farm, she complains. There is not much transport available.

I first met her when she came to attend a meeting on the farm about the end-of-year cattle sale. She was sitting in front of Loesboy's house, washing spinach from the garden. She was preparing a meal for the rest of the members, who had gone out to fetch the cattle before the meeting. Her grandson was inside the house, making a fire for her to cook on. Ma Tumelo told me that he was going to stay on the farm and help Loesboy during the school holidays.

Ma Tumelo does not know much about what is happening on the project. She is not sure about the number of cattle on the farm, for example. She trusts Loesboy to look after the farm and the cattle. Like many other Wales beneficiaries, she goes to the farm only on important occasions, such as farmers' days and cattle-sale meetings. They can usually rely on the extension official for transport but sometimes have to hire a local van, which costs them R400.

Along with the other beneficiaries, Ma Tumelo receives a share of the profits from the sale of cattle. This is most important to her. She accuses four beneficiaries, who are supposed to make their contribution in the form of labour, of being lazy. They are not entitled to a share of the profits from the cattle, in her opinion, because they are not involved in the farm at all and have not contributed any assets or capital to the project.

Dinky, a former member

Dinky, an unmarried mother of four, lives with her ailing mother. Before joining the project, she worked as a cleaner in her village and as a seasonal worker on commercial farms. She also relied to some extent on her mother's old age pension. Dinky says she was very happy when she was invited by the chairperson, Marta, to join the project. She thought her seasonal working days were over as she would be able to derive an income from belonging to the project. She hoped to be able to spend her days looking after her mother.

It was agreed that Dinky would sometimes work on the farm because she did not have money or animals to contribute. She describes her first few months on the project as a happy time. Everyone was busy on the farm. Only a few old or employed people did not show up. The beneficiaries built a small house in which the cattle feed could be kept. Dinky considered her participation in this task to be her contribution to the project. At the end of the year, though, Dinky and the other beneficiaries who had contributed labour did not get a share of the proceeds. Nor were they consulted about this, as had been agreed. The chairperson ignored them when they asked about the decision to exclude them. Dinky and three other women in the same position decided to quit the project. They had no one to complain to about the way in which they had been treated because the chairperson and the extension officer were friends. Dinky has returned to working as a seasonal worker and as a cleaner.

Mr Nix, the 'stay at home' beneficiary

I had never seen Mr Nix on the farm. His niece, Marta, the chairperson of the project, gave me his address. I located his house in Dinns village on a hot Friday morning. A young man who was busy fixing the gate told me that Mr Nix was inside. I found him talking to another old man. He asked me to be quick since he was about to leave to visit his son in another town.

Mr Nix told me that he had worked on the mines before he was asked to become a beneficiary of Wales. He joined the project but left the farm when he became too old to work on it. He is a diabetic who has to live close to where he can get his medication. He lives off a government pension and the sale of sheep. He is not worried that the people at the farm might take decisions without informing him: 'My niece always keeps me updated on the progress of the farm. Marta is very good and is keeping things under control on the farm'. Marta keeps him informed about matters pertaining to the sale of cattle on the farm. After half an hour, Mr Nix's son arrived in a white van and I had to end the interview.

Conclusion

Both the land reform projects discussed in this chapter could be seen as providing evidence that land reform has failed. This would support the findings of those commentators who have emphasised that land is being wasted by giving it to people with no resources and few relevant skills (Du Toit 2004; Kariuki and Van der Walt 2000). The stories of many of the beneficiaries reinforce this conclusion. They have become disenchanted with land reform. Their experiences have been determined by the social inequalities that result from a person's ability or inability to contribute resources to a project. Labour contributions have a low value. Clearly, land reform has not diminished class differences among rural people. On the contrary, it has sharpened and strengthened them. This means that beneficiaries are often involved in struggles over resources, meaning, and institutional legitimacy and control (see Long 2004).

The two projects also invite a different set of conclusions, however. Land reform is not a linear and harmonious process. It is a complex, conflictive process that demands close observation and analysis. It is important, therefore, to move away from a linear and ideological interpretation of policies (as expressed in policy documents, which come with a set of prescriptions about how things should be done and what should be achieved) to a consideration of the everyday lives and practices of the beneficiaries. It is here that policies play themselves out in multiple and unpredictable ways (Koponen 2004; Long 2001). The case material suggests that the land reform process produces not only intended outcomes, such as the transfer of land and the deracialisation of land ownership, but also a series of 'unintended and unforeseen consequences' (Hebinck 2008: 40). Increasing inequalities and new, policy-induced social categories (contributors in kind versus those who contribute cash or animals) are perhaps the most significant. Mighty provides a good example of how the beneficiaries who enjoy substantial economic resources, such as Ramatlho, become dominant. They are able to shape projects in line with their own views and interests. The beneficiaries on the two projects clearly interpret land reform plans and projects in their own ways. Loesboy, for example, sells produce from his own garden on the farm to fellow members and co-owners. Dorkie and Mr Nix are beneficiaries only when it is convenient for them. Raditamati makes his livelihood off the farm and uses land reform as a way of fulfilling his 'hobby' of being a farmer. Rooiland has left the project to 'make it on his own'. The variety of different actors' responses to the opportunities presented by land reform makes it extremely difficult to draw generalised conclusion about the failure or success of the programme. Land reform is always unfinished business (Lipton 2009).

References

Du Toit, P. 2004. *The great South African land scandal,* Centurion: Legacy Publishers.

Hebinck, P. 2008. 'Land reform, scripts and social space: emergent properties in rural South Africa', in P. Hebinck, S. Slootweg and L. Smith (eds) *Tales of development: people, power and space,* Assen: Royal van Gorcum.

Kariuki, S. and L. van der Walt. 2000. 'Land reform in South Africa still waiting', *Southern Africa Report* 15(3): 19–20.

Koponen, J. 2004. 'Development interventions and development studies', in T. Kontinen (ed.) *Development intervention: actor and activity perspectives,* Helsinki: Helsingfors.

Lipton, M. 2009. *Land reform in developing countries: property rights and property wrongs,* London: Routledge.

Long, N. 2001. *Development sociology: actor perspectives,* London: Routledge.

Long, N. 2004. 'Actors, interfaces and development intervention: meanings, purposes and powers', in T. Kontinen (ed.) *Development intervention: actor and activity perspectives,* Helsinki: Helsingfors.

Moyo, S. and R. Hall. 2007. 'Conflict and land reform in southern Africa: how exceptional is South Africa?', in A. Adebajo, A. Adedeji and C. Landsberg (eds) *South Africa in Africa: the post-apartheid era,* Pietermaritzburg: University of KwaZulu-Natal University Press.

10 Where are the youth in land reform? The Vuki case

Petunia Khutswane

This chapter concerns the role of youth in rural development and land reform in South Africa. I argue in this chapter that reducing poverty and generating employment through land reform can be achieved only if such reforms capitalise on all the resources in society, including the involvement and commitment of all stakeholders: men and women, adults and the youth. The role of the youth in development is especially critical. The World Youth Report of 2005 (United Nations 2005) emphasises that development with a youth focus is important not only for the future of development but also to mitigate the intergenerational transmission of poverty. Growing up in a globalising world, the youth of today are able to use and employ new technologies. Theirs is a generation that is relatively well educated as regards information and communication technologies. However, there are many young people, particularly in the South, who lack the economic power to benefit from the opportunities that the contemporary world offers in this respect. Development, therefore, has to be seen as a process of negotiation between groups and generations over accessing, distributing and using resources for livelihood enhancement.

Surprisingly, generational issues and relationships between the older and younger generations are not considered in many land and agrarian studies. The youth is absent in most analyses of land reform processes. Where there is a focus on the socially differentiated impact of land and agrarian reform, the predominant focus is on income groups (Aliber 2011; Seekings and Nattrass 2006) or class (Bond 2000; Cousins 2011; Lahiff 2007). Gender has also received a great deal of attention (see, for instance, chapter 13, this volume; Walker 2005).

This chapter's contribution to the land reform debate is the problematisation of the relationship between the youth and land as a resource, and the factors that advance or inhibit the participation of the youth in the South African land reform programme. Little is known about why young people rarely engage in land reform projects. The majority of land reform beneficiaries in South Africa are older people whose livelihoods combine land ownership and old age pensions. This raises questions about the future of land reform.

Anyone who visits a land reform project is struck by the fact that the youth play little or no role. Is this because the land reform process itself has failed to create conditions in which the youth could participate and engage meaningfully in projects, or is it because the youth themselves do not see land reform as a vehicle for development? Do the youth actually want to farm? Does the frequently heard demand for land from young people, especially young men, arise from a view that small-scale farming would support a better lifestyle, or is it chiefly attributable to the failure of the wider economy to generate employment (Bernstein 1996; Walker 2005)? Whatever the answers to these questions, the perceptions of the youth in relation to land have important implications for the politics of land in the country. In this chapter I explore the matter of youth and the land by focusing on the intergenerational dynamics at a specific land reform project, Vuki farm, where I spent six months during 2008 and 2009.

Analytical focus

Youth is a dimension of generation and I treat it as a relational concept: age is socially constructed, institutionalised and controlled in historically and cultur-ally specific ways. One of the most significant issues in relation to the use of the category 'youth' concerns the degree of symmetry between biological and social processes (Wyn and White 1997). Youth is a transitional phase from childhood to adulthood. Young people go through a process of intense physiological, psycho-logical, social and economic change, in the course of which they begin to identify themselves as adults and are recognised as such by others. Youth refers, there-fore, to a stage in life. The transition to adulthood often includes leaving school, entering the labour market, participating in politics, establishing an independent homestead and having children.

The transition to adulthood is contingent on a social and cultural idea of what it means to become an adult. The category 'youth' is not merely biological; it is also social, based on criteria that a society deems to be important for being an adult. For this reason, it is necessary to find out how the transition to adulthood is conceptualised by members of a specific society during a particular period in time. Different societies allow the youth different degrees of room to manoeuvre and freedom to negotiate with members of the older generation, especially powerful people. Age, too, is subject to sociocultural, economic and political factors. Although a person's lifespan can be measured by the passing of time, cultural understandings about the growing-up and ageing processes are socially shaped (Leccardi and Ruspini 2006).

Plug et al. (2003) argue that the point of transition between receiving an education and entering the labour market is no longer as clear-cut as it used to be, resulting in a blurring of the distinction between youth and adulthood. Being a youth is no longer restricted solely to the period of secondary and tertiary education. Individuals frequently perform tasks that were formerly associated only with the phase of youth (education) or with the phase of adulthood (work). A young person, for example, may undergo education while also holding a job and being a parent. A person might return to full-time education after having been permanently employed for a number of years. Education and employment no longer seem to coincide unambiguously with a particular life-phase. Contemporary young men and women appear, therefore, to live somewhere between youth and adulthood.

Governments and demographers generally stipulate a specific range of years, such as 15–24, as the period of youth. This has a statistical and practical function. It is not the same as the legal age of adulthood, when a person is given full responsibility by the law for his/her decisions and actions; this is often referred to as the age of majority. The legal age is frequently set at 18 but differs from country to country. The standard UN definition of youth includes people between the ages of 15 and 24 (United Nations 2005). The South African government defines the youth as people between the ages of 14 and 35 (National Youth Commission 1997). I use these parameters in my discussion of the role of young males and females in the Vuki project, as I look at young people who work as seasonal workers as well as at those who form part of shareholders' households.

Vuki

Vuki is an interesting case for many reasons. It went through several changes of ownership before it ended up as a group-owned farm. The present beneficiaries were part of the process of transformation over the years. As a result, they have had a range of experiences on the farm, first as workers, then as equity shareholders and now as the owners of the farm. Unusually for a land reform project, the Vuki beneficiaries come from similar cultural backgrounds, even though some are black and others are coloured. Both adults and young people are present on the farm. In addition, conditions on the farm are conducive to production and the creation of employment opportunities.

Vuki farm, formerly known as Whitehall, is 310 hectares in extent. It is situated in the Grabouw area of the Western Cape and is currently managed as a Communal Property Association (CPA). Whitehall fruit farm was restructured as an equity share scheme in 1992, the first in the country to follow this route and thus the first to follow a land reform model that has been most common in the Western Cape. The scheme was initiated by the former owner of the farm. He wished to solve his financial problems and also share the profits of the farm more equitably with his workers. Initially, he wanted to make 30 per cent ownership of the farm available to workers, but the Development Bank of Southern Africa (DBSA) advised him to 'make a clean deal' by selling 50 per cent of the farm. The farm workers acquired a loan from the DBSA, the Independent Development Trust and commercial banks in order to purchase their 50 per cent stake in the holding. These loans were secured through bonds on the property.

Participation in the equity scheme was voluntary. Shares in the Workers' Trust were, however, allocated to permanent workers only. The number of shares for which a person was eligible was calculated on the basis of length of service and income. As part of their in-kind contribution to the scheme, most workers forfeited their annual bonuses. The Whitehall Workers' Trust and the Hall Family Trust each had 50 per cent of the shares in the Whitehall Landholding company, which owned the immovable property, and the Whitehall Farming Trust, which owned the movable property. The original holding was separated into two companies for tax reasons. The structure of the deal meant that the beneficiaries incurred a higher debt burden than would have been the case if they had applied for a land reform grant in the normal way.

The trustee board consisted of eight members in the 1990s; four of them represented the workers and four represented the Hall family. In addition, a dispute resolution mechanism was specified. Decisions on the day-to-day running of the farm were made by the management team, which was composed of a general manager, a production manager, an assistant production manager and a personnel manager.

This scheme passed through several phases. The initial phase involved trust-building, getting to know one another and reaching agreement on the principles of management. Time was allowed for external agents to facilitate processes that would help to improve interracial understanding. Despite a promising start, the scheme experienced serious problems due to a decline in fruit prices, a steep rise in interest rates and adverse production conditions during the latter half of the 1990s. As a result, the farm went through a liquidation process in 2001 and the Whitehall Farming venture was liquidated in 2002.

Vuki emerged from the proverbial ashes of the Whitehall Farming venture. The government-appointed liquidator retained the employees to run the operation. He then appointed an experienced business recovery specialist to assist the workers and to act as the general manager. The farm workers subsequently applied for and received a Land Redistribution for Agricultural Development (LRAD) grant from the Department of Land Affairs. Vuki was officially handed over to a total number of 42 beneficiaries by the former minister of agriculture in the Western Cape, Mr Dowry, on 5 August 2005.

The social dynamics at Vuki farm

Different categories of social actor on Vuki farm benefit from the social transformations that were initiated by the land reform policies that began in 1994. Vuki serves as an example of successful land reform because of its production history. Against all odds, the farm has managed to continue producing quality fruit for export and local markets. It is also recognised as a Fairtrade-certified farm. The premiums from its Fairtrade status are used for the social development of the Vuki community. The view of Vuki as a success story is widely held by both commentators and officials of the Department of Agriculture. It is based on Vuki's ability to continue high-level production, rare among South African land reform farms (CDE 2005, 2008), and the way in which some of the project's benefits are extended to non-land reform beneficiaries, such as seasonal workers. This is largely an outsider's interpretation, however.

For analytical purposes, I categorise the Vuki actors according to the role that they play in the production process on the farm and also according to generation. I distinguish, therefore, between shareholders and non-shareholders, experienced and inexperienced workers, adults and the youth, and people residing on and off the farm. I use a combination of interviews and observation in order to explore the internal dynamics of Vuki. I describe how the farm work is organised and what various beneficiaries actually do on the farm. The interviews reveal something of what Vuki means to different actors. I conclude the chapter by analysing Vuki through a generational lens in order to offer some comments about the future sustainability of the project.

Managers and workers

Only managers and directors engage in planning and decision-making at Vuki. They are assisted by a mentor chosen by the Department of Agriculture and sometimes consult other shareholders. The workers are divided into groups every day. The groups formulate a programme of action for the plans made by management. Each group is composed of shareholders (permanent workers), non-shareholders (seasonal workers) and a foreman. Everybody in the group helps to execute its programme of action. This arrangement has created room for social interaction between shareholders and non-shareholders. As a result, there is no noticeable distance between them in the workplace. They share topics of conversation, laugh together, and share food and drink. The foreman also enters into the group spirit, even though he also has to monitor the progress of the work.

Mr Xolane is a permanent worker and therefore a shareholder. He has 45 years of farming experience, mostly accumulated while working on various farms in the Western Cape. He joined Whitehall in 1976. His knowledge is widely respected. He told me something of the history of the farm:

> We all came as individuals and met here for the first time as workers on Whitehall farm. We shared accommodation. This setting allowed us to get to know and understand each other. We all struggled to maintain our livelihoods. We had to send remittances back to our rural homes. As a team we survived the harsh working conditions and the discriminatory wages. Your skin colour determined your daily wage. We all witnessed the downfall of Whitehall and this was a threat to our livelihoods as the future was uncertain. We elected skilled people from among ourselves who had the capacity to represent us.

He was elected to sit on various committees because of his experience. Currently he serves as the production and farm manager and is also involved in various agricultural associations, such as Agri-Western Cape and the Water Usage Council, on behalf of Vuki. 'Farming is a process that needs careful decisions and a good response to immediate challenges,' he says. He vividly recalls the 1990s fruit industry collapse that led to the downfall of Whitehall. Things have changed since then:

> Now we manage the farm collectively. As a team we are able to handle different operational challenges, especially those that cannot be predicted, like the increase in fuel, food and electricity prices. The daily operation of the farm is challenging, particularly during the harvest season when we need more workers for a short period.

Most of the seasonal workers are unskilled people who need proper training. It is best to hire many of them at a time, in his opinion, because the harvest season is short. He comments on the lack of participation of the youth in the work on the farm:

> I have personally noticed that the youth on the farm fear farming because they see that their parents work very hard. I wish that in future we can have a programme where learners who study agriculture as a subject can be given a chance to practise what they learn at school. We need to find an effective way to do this, though. It should not have a negative impact on production because every minute on a farm counts.

He is especially proud of the farm's Fairtrade initiative:

> Our priority is community development and that is why we are now Fairtrade-certified. The extra premium from Fairtrade is deposited into our individual accounts. We have formed a structure called a joint body which ensures that the money is used for the social development of the entire Vuki community.

At 36 years of age, Sophie is the youngest shareholder at Vuki. She started working on the farm in 1993, after completing high school. A friend had told her that the farm needed workers during the harvest season. She has been on several training courses, such as entomology and a supervision course at Elgin Community College. She was made a general manager in 2002 and was appointed as one of the directors of the farm in 2005. These positions have sharpened her interest in farming. She also raises funds for stationery, food and school uniforms for the children on the farm. In this way, she partly fulfils her dream of becoming a social worker.

Mr Xolane and Sophie are the kind of managers who drive things on the farm. They are planners and initiators who also maintain close contact with the government and other institutions. They ensure that all the decisions that are taken are implemented by organising the necessary materials and delegating duties where appropriate. Sophie talks about the challenges of leadership:

> It's difficult when you are young and working with older people. I have
> learned to always be respectful to elders because we do not see life the same
> way. My motivation is that they taught me everything that I know now. I
> came here with no experience about farming or agriculture.

In her opinion, all the workers at Vuki are equal. Living together has made them
behave as though they are relatives, although most of them are not actually
related. I observed, during my stay at the farm, that duties are executed in an
atmosphere of mutual trust and support.

Nomsa is originally from the North West province. I found her cleaning the
crèche. She was picking up toys while the children slept. She started working
seasonally on Vuki in the late 1990s. Her brother joined Vuki first and then
recruited her husband, who was hired as a mechanic to repair farm implements.
Her role is to take care of children at the crèche. She finds life at Vuki much better
than it was in North West because there are many developmental activities on the
farm, especially for the youth. She says: 'Even though we earn a low wage, the
farm has many things that improves our lives, especially the lives of our children.'
She is happy with the sewing lessons and other self-development lessons that
people on the farm can attend. She values the benefits that come with living on
the farm, such as housing, free electricity, access to water and a school uniform
voucher, which her family receives because her husband is a shareholder. 'All
my children's educational needs are taken care of. For example, my 21-year-old
son went to college on a farm bursary to study electrical engineering, while my
12-year-old child travels free on a bus to the nearby school.' She is also excited
that the farm encourages the youth to study even though they are not obliged
to come back and work on the farm. Instead, they are encouraged to explore the
outside world so that they do not become like their parents, working on a farm
with no alternative means of making a living.

Zama migrated to the Western Cape from the Eastern Cape, in search of better
opportunities after completing high school. He settled in the nearby location
of Rooitak. He looked for a job until he found one on Vuki. He is not entirely
committed to the farm:

> Poverty drove me to this farm; my dream was to get a job at a firm in Cape
> Town but unfortunately it was not as easy as I thought it would be. I do not
> have any interest in agricultural activities. It is hard work, and we work in
> harsh weather conditions. This is just a temporary means of maintaining a
> livelihood while searching for a better job.

He believes that it would be better if he had a permanent position. Seasonal
workers are in a difficult position. They perform the same duties as the permanent staff but do not enjoy the same benefits. They earn nothing on rainy days,
for example. Zama rents accommodation in Rooitak and has to send remittances
home every month.

Vuki through a generational lens

In order to gain a generational perspective on the Vuki land reform project, I interviewed several of the children of shareholders. These young people indirectly or directly benefit from land reform without being actively involved in the work on the farm. Instead, they commute by bus to a nearby school. They stay in after-care and do their homework after school. I also interviewed two groups of youth residing elsewhere. One group lives in Napier and is currently unemployed. The second group is undergoing a one-year learnership programme with the Western Cape Department of Agriculture in Bredasdorp.

Zaza is 16 years old. Her mother is a permanent worker and shareholder at Vuki. She told me that seeing her mother wearing overalls and sweating daily to make a living breaks her heart. She dislikes agricultural activities as a result. Her fear of spraying herbicides and insecticides led her to get involved in a school project called 'How to use chemicals safely'. This was an opportunity for her to find out why it was important to spray only at certain seasons or times and the effects that chemicals have on workers. She had to discover this information herself, at school, because her mother was always too tired to talk to her. Zaza goes to school every day, then attends after-care and does her homework. She watches television or joins a singing group in the evenings. Her dream is to become a psychologist. She says: 'The only thing I know is that our parents here are working hard so that we do not end up being farm workers like them.' She appreciates the fact that her parents' lives are a little better than those of others on other farms. Zaza knows nothing about land reform; it makes no difference to her whether her mother is a shareholder on the farm or just an ordinary farm worker.

Suzi is the 18-year-old granddaughter of the woman who works in the farm kitchen. She has lived on the farm since 2004. She is not interested in agriculture. To her it simply represents hard work. Her dream is to become a lawyer: 'Farm life taught me to think a lot about my future because I do not want to be like my parents who cannot read or write, and I also do not like the hard work that they do'. She appreciates the facilities and opportunities on the farm, though. Vuki hires teachers who coach mathematics on an individual basis. The youth also have access to computers and stationery and receive a free meal after school. She was embarrassed at first because her friends at school made jokes about people who lived on farms, but later she realised that she was much better off than they were.

Twenty-year-old Kago has lived with her parents on the farm since graduating from high school in the Eastern Cape. She says of life on the farm: 'Farm life is boring but I think teenagers on the farm are much better off because they do not get involved in drugs, alcohol abuse, roaming the streets and there is no problem of teenage pregnancies'. She is doing a nursing course at Providence College in Bellville, funded by a farm grant. This is a benefit which her father has earned as a result of his long service on the farm. She dislikes agriculture because she sees how her parents struggle to make a living and have no other choice.

Thozi is 17 years old and grew up on the farm. He is interested in farming and often asks his parents about their activities on the farm. Despite his interest, he is not allowed to engage in any farming activities because of his age. Recently he won a bronze medal in a competition in which 217 learners from various schools had to test soil samples and identify plants that could grow well in different types of soil. This has encouraged him to study agricultural management when he finishes school. Most of the older people on the farm do not think that a young person should study agriculture. He aims to change their perceptions by showing them that a farmer can lead a good-quality life. He especially appreciates the communal nature of life on the farm: 'Here we live like we are relatives; every elder, and not just your parents, has the right to discipline you when you misbehave'.

Thabo also considers agriculture to be a good option. He is the son of one of the managers and has achieved good grades at school. After a school tour to Stellenbosch University, he expressed an interest in agriculture as a career. His mother was not impressed: 'My mother thought that I would end up working like them, pruning trees in the sun, but I explained that the situation would not be the same'. The management team on the farm have helped him to follow his chosen career in agricultural economics. He says, 'Farm life shaped my future because now I know what I want from life; I can't even wait for January 2009. I have been admitted to the course and my accommodation has been arranged.'

Vuki as an arena of struggle

Vuki fits the description of an arena in which different groups of actors interact on a daily basis. The case material shows that the older and younger generations often have different expectations about the future. These perceptions are also influenced by whether a person is a shareholder or not. This greatly affects a person's sense of ownership of the project. It matters a great deal whether a person is a shareholder or a seasonal employee and whether she/he is young or old. Older shareholders are in a position to exercise authority and take on leadership roles such as those of director, manager or foreman. These people make the plans and decisions on the farm and make sure that they are put into practice. While the shareholders are not necessarily related by kinship ties, there are long-standing relationships between them, based on trust and reciprocity. They share a common identity and history as farm workers on Whitehall. The younger generation, by contrast, is largely made up of seasonal workers who come from the Eastern Cape. Unlike the shareholders, most of them live in a nearby location and commute to Vuki every day.

Vuki displays many of the features of what Lahiff (2008) has called 'capitalist collectivisation'. This describes a situation in which the state puts pressure on a group of land reform participants to use agricultural land in a collective manner but to achieve the market-oriented objectives that are associated with single-owner farms. The Vuki shareholders have adopted a management style that resembles that of a single owner running his own farm. Power is not distributed equally; the institutional patterns on Vuki express class (shareholder and non-shareholder), gender (male and female) and age (adult and youth) inequalities.

While decisions are taken in boardroom management style, the daily operations and activities of the farm are characterised by cooperation, collaboration and equality. Shareholders and non-shareholders execute similar duties. Group coherence is reinforced by the sharing of skills, knowledge and experience. Vuki invokes the spirit of *ubuntu* or humanness, the idea that 'a person is a person through other people'. The fact that people at Vuki know one another also creates an environment that is conducive to the collective management of resources. People tend to respect collective decisions even if they disagree with them. Principles of sharing and caring inform daily interactions on the farm. Most people use 'we' instead of 'I' when talking about the project. Solidarity is more common than competition or struggle between members.

The question remains as to how long the spirit of *ubuntu* will persist on the farm. The interviews with seasonal workers reveal the extent of the inequalities that exist between permanent and seasonal workers. These workers complain that their duties are the same as those of the beneficiaries but they do not receive equal benefits. Their jobs are temporary and insecure. Living off the farm results in their having to pay for transport, accommodation and basic services even though they earn the same wages as the permanent workers do. They are not eligible for the tangible benefits such as houses and school uniform vouchers that the permanent workers and their spouses enjoy. The fact that managers and foremen are drawn only from the ranks of shareholders entrenches unequal power relations. The non-shareholders are told what is to be done, how and by whom. They form a subordinate group on the farm. They comply with orders and rules in the hope that this will increase their chances of being permanently employed. They can do nothing that might threaten their employment on the farm.

Gender inequalities also persist on the farm. Women have a subordinate position on land reform projects in general because their participation is often mediated by their matrimonial status (Walker 2005). Vuki is no exception. Only 9 of the 37 shareholders are women. Many of the female seasonal workers also form part of male shareholders' households. The unequal gender relations that characterise households are automatically transferred to the work environment.

The situation at Vuki is evidence of land reform policies not resonating with the aspirations of the youth. Farm operations at Vuki are structured in such a way that the youth are prevented from actively participating in them. The farm rules do not allow the young people who live on the farm to work on it. Instead, they become passive recipients of development. Their needs are identified and addressed without actively consulting them. The perception exists among both shareholders and non-shareholders that farm work is only suitable for uneducated people. The stage of youth is equated with schooling, not with agriculture.

Farm work equals illiteracy in most people's minds. The young people who are employed as seasonal workers see this work as a stopgap while they look for other jobs. Almost all the youth on the farm, both residents and those who reside off the farm, regard agriculture as an occupation that requires hard labour and possesses low prestige. They see agricultural activities as dirty work. It belongs to the past; it is for the older generation, not for them. The youth, as a group, have no interest in agriculture and view it with either disdain or apathy.

The negative attitude of the youth towards agriculture raises a number of questions. Who will work on Vuki farm in the future? What will be the long-term consequences of the lack of participation by young people in agricultural production on farms? How can generational continuity be ensured? Although the youth dislike agriculture, it is clear that the Vuki project has had a positive socio-economic impact on their lives. This, as we have seen, is acknowledged by the young people who live on the farm. They are better off than their peers. They have access to resources such as computers and are not as susceptible to alcohol and drug abuse or teenage pregnancy.

Conclusion

Land reform in South Africa has proved to be far more complex than the policy-makers envisaged it would be. Vuki is held up as a rare success story because a group of beneficiaries initiated a land reform project themselves and transformed an almost bankrupt farm into a commercially viable enterprise. The farm has even obtained Fairtrade certification. It provides a relatively healthy, safe and non-exploitative working environment. There is an investment in community development.

Despite these undoubted successes, social transformation at Vuki has, at times, also proved to be contradictory. This is especially true when Vuki is considered from a generational perspective. Although Vuki is commercially viable and improves the lives of those involved on the farm, the youth on the farm have little interest in pursuing farming as a career. The youth are not encouraged to participate in the agricultural activities on the farm and it would seem that there are no plans to ensure the future continuity of the project. Little effort is made to transfer the knowledge and skills of the ageing group of shareholders to the next generation. The failure to make a succession plan will create significant problems in the future. If things continue as they are at present, the next generation will not build on what their parents, the current shareholders, have spent their lives developing. This trend has consequences not only for Vuki. The lack of youth involvement in land reform will jeopardise the transformation process that has been set in motion by the post-apartheid reform programme more generally.

References

Aliber, M. 2011. 'Anger, policy, data: perspectives on South Africa's "poverty question"', in P. Hebinck and C. Shackleton (eds) *Reforming land and resource use in South Africa: impact on livelihoods*, London: Routledge.

Bernstein, H. 1996. 'The agrarian question in South Africa: extreme and exceptional?' *Journal of Peasant Studies*, 23 (2/3): 1–52.

Bond, P. 2000. *Elite transition: from apartheid to neoliberalism in South Africa*, London: Pluto Press.

CDE (Centre for Development and Enterprise). 2005. *Land reform in South Africa: a 21st century perspective*, Research Report No. 14, Johannesburg: Centre for Development and Enterprise.

CDE. 2008. *Land reform in South Africa: getting back on track*, Research Report No. 16, Johannesburg: Centre for Development and Enterprise.

Cousins, B. 2011. 'What is a '"smallholder"? Class-analytic perspectives on small-scale farming and agrarian reform in South Africa', in P. Hebinck and C. Shackleton (eds) *Reforming land and resource use in South Africa: impact on livelihoods,* London: Routledge.

Lahiff, E. 2007. '"Willing buyer, willing seller": South Africa's failed experiment in market-led agrarian reform', *Third World Quarterly*, 28(8): 1577–1597.

Lahiff, E. 2008. 'Capitalist collectivisation? How inappropriate models of common property are hampering South Africa's land reform', unpublished paper.

Leccardi, C. and E. Ruspini. 2006. *A new youth? Young people, generations and family life*, Aldershot: Ashgate.

National Youth Commission. 1997. *National youth policy*. Accessed 23 April 2008, http://www.polity.org.za/polity/govdocs/policy/intro.html.

Plug, W., E. Reijl and M. Dubois-Reymond. 2003. 'Young people's perception on youth and adulthood: a longitudinal study from the Netherlands', *Journal of Youth Studies*, 6(2): 127–144.

Seekings, J. and N. Nattrass. 2006. *Class, race and inequality in South Africa*, Pietermaritzburg: University of KwaZulu-Natal Press.

United Nations. 2005. *World youth report 2005: young people today, and in 2015*, Geneva: United Nations, Department of Economic and Social Affairs.

Walker, C. 2005. 'Women, gender policy and land reform in South Africa', *Politikon, 32*: 297–315.

Wyn, J. and R. White. 1997. *Rethinking youth*, Australia: Allen and Unwin.

11 Land compensation in the upper Kat River valley

Robert Ross

Land compensation is by definition about history. The whole process is concerned with redressing the injustices caused by the racist nature of South African society and the racist measures of the South African state between 1913, a couple of years after the foundation of the Union, and 1994, the end of the apartheid era. Claims to land, and thus to compensation, have to be made on the basis of historical events, and indeed the standards of proof required to make a successful claim have been those of historical enquiry, not those of a court of law. In this way, as in others, the new South Africa attempts to redress the inequities of the old.

The problem with such laudable proposals is that history has sometimes developed in too complicated a way for the simple assumptions of the Land Claims Commission to be fulfilled. In this chapter I discuss one such case, that of the upper Kat River valley in the Eastern Cape. This has become one of the last areas of the country in which land claims have still to be settled. The cynic would suggest that part of the reason for this is that many, though by no means all, of the claimants are either whites or people of Khoisan descent. More generally, though, it has to be realised that the history of the valley, in particular the history of land ownership and allocation, has been extraordinarily complex.

The region in question lies in the upper catchment area of the Kat River valley in the Eastern Cape, to the north of Fort Beaufort. Essentially, the valley is a basin cut into the outliers of the Amathole mountains by a number of small streams which come together to form the Kat and the Blinkwater rivers. Just below the confluence of these two streams, the combined river runs through a narrow gorge, known as the Poort, before passing Fort Beaufort on its way to join the Great Fish River, and thence to the sea. In the upper Kat valley, the streams have eroded away a number of relatively broad areas of fertile bottomland, which is surrounded by rough grazing and, higher up, a corona of mist forest.

The area straddles the great ecological divide of southern Africa: the region where agriculture on the basis of summer rains was possible and the region where it could not be practised with the crops that were available in pre-colonial times. The valleys, which run north into the hills of the Amathole and the Tyhume

Valley to the east of the Kat, were historically areas of Xhosa settlement. In fact the area formed the heartland of the Ngqika chieftainship during the early nineteenth century. In contrast, the Koenap Valley to the west of the Kat never had a significant number of Xhosa inhabitants. In the nineteenth century it became a centre of sheep farming and one of the richest areas that were controlled by white settlers (Ross 1993: 59).

The Kat basin itself would seem to have enough rain at the right time of the year to grow summer rainfall crops. Seymour, for instance, a town in the centre of the upper valley, receives 534 millimetres a year. However, in practice sorghum and maize do not do well in the basin, according to local farmers. This obviously has had consequences for the development of the valley's population. This was especially true in pre-colonial times, when ethnicity and language were closely tied to economic activity (Ross 1980). Khoekhoe pastoralists in the eighteenth century used the valley as grazing on a seasonal basis. At the same time it was on the transhumant routes of the most westerly of the amaXhosa (Peires 1981). Undoubtedly, hunter-gatherers also still lived in the area, as they were not far to the north in the nineteenth century and there are still a number of rock-art sites in the valley. Although there were conflicts between the two groups, which resulted, for instance, in the destruction by the amaXhosa of the Khoekhoe Inqua kingdom well to the west of the Kat, there do not seem to have been any serious conflicts between amaXhosa and Khoekhoe in the Kat River valley itself. At least there are no reports of any such conflicts in the traditions that have survived. Things changed in the second and third decades of the nineteenth century, however. The pressure on the area from settlers of European descent was beginning to mount. The area of Cape colonial settlement had moved east to the area of Graaff-Reinet and Somerset East, and the Dutch settlers had overcome the last major outbreaks of Khoisan resistance in the region with the crushing of the Servants' Revolt of 1801 to 1803 (Newton-King and Malherbe 1983). At the same time, the British presence in the area was increasing, with military interventions in both 1813 and 1819, when the British triumphed over the amaXhosa at the Battle of Grahamstown, primarily as a result of the timely arrival of Khoekhoe auxiliaries (Maclennan 1986). The Kat River valley had already become a place of uncertainty before these events, however. The first mission to the amaXhosa was founded there, and Ntsikana, now hailed as the first Xhosa convert to Christianity, but a man with his own spiritual vision, died and was buried in present-day Tamboekies Kloof (Hodgson 1980). Maqoma, the head of the right-hand house of the amaNgqika, moved away from his father, whose main residence was in the Tyhume Valley, to establish himself in the Kat River valley itself, in the area still known as Maqoma's Hoek (Stapleton 1996). He was accompanied by a substantial number of Xhosa families who hoped to find sufficient sustenance and good rains in the new area. Whether or not they really would have been able to establish a sustainable agricultural settlement on the basis of pastoralism and rain-fed agriculture in the valley is a moot point; they were not given the opportunity to try.

The presence of such a large Xhosa population in the valley was seen as a threat by the European farmers who had occupied land in the valleys to the west of the Kat, notably the Koenap and the region around Fort Beaufort. The farmers included Sir Andries Stockenström, the man who was at that stage commissioner-general of the Eastern province and thus someone who was able to exert influence over the actions of the British colonial apparatus. He was determined to have Maqoma expelled from the Kat River valley. He was presented with an opportunity when Maqoma launched a series of raids on some of the abaThembu to the north, near the headwaters of the Black Kei River. As a result, Stockenström sent in the British army to drive Maqoma and his followers back across the hills into the Tyhume Valley. Maqoma himself never relinquished his determination to return to live in the valley, and indeed his descendants have regained what he lost and hold authority in parts of the valley today (Stapleton 1996).

In the place of the amaXhosa, the British decided to fill the valley with Khoekhoe settlers, who would thus, for the first time, be able to hold land on their own account. They were to form a 'breastwork' that would protect the British against future Xhosa attacks on the colony (Stockenström 1854: 5). In order to do this, they needed to live in a relatively close settlement pattern, quite different from the extensive sheep farms with which the European settlers covered the region. Restrictions were placed on the sorts of houses they could build and on the agricultural enterprises that could be pursued. In the Kat River Settlement, as it came to be called, there were around 400 small farms, of between 2 and 10 hectares each, held in blocks with communal irrigation systems. The Kat River people grew crops on the fertile valley bottomland, using a gravity-fed, and surprisingly sophisticated, network of water channels. Surrounding each block there was a broad area of commonage, on which the Khoekhoe were able run their stock. The higher slopes of the valley also contained forest. The Khoekhoe cut timber, especially in times of agricultural distress. They established a relatively prosperous small peasant community.

The threats to the Kat River Settlement were continuous and came from both sides. The white people in the Eastern Cape generally hated the settlement, both because it occupied land which they themselves coveted and because it clashed with their racist assumptions about how society should be organised. The amaXhosa, on the other hand, were still involved in an intermittent contest for land with the Europeans and, led as they often were by Maqoma, were particularly keen to regain the Kat River valley for themselves. It was not easy to be caught in the middle of the border conflict, without heartfelt support from either side.

In the quarter century after the foundation of the settlement in 1829, conflict between the Cape Colony and the amaXhosa, always latent, tipped into full-scale war on three occasions. In all three wars, the upper Kat River valley and its inhabitants were at the centre of the operations. In both 1835, during what subsequently came to be known as Hintza's war, and in the War of the Axe, just over a decade later, the valley was laid waste by Xhosa attacks; many of the houses were burnt and the fields were stripped of their crops. In both cases the Khoekhoe fought in great numbers on the side of the British, who were not always as convinced of Khoekhoe loyalty as they should have been. There were numerous rumours that the Khoe were going to defect to the amaXhosa. These were fostered by the Xhosa chiefs as a form of propaganda, but do not seem to have had any basis in fact. On the contrary, the Kat River men fought longer and harder than any other members of the colonial militias and in 1846, in particular, their actions at the battle of Burn's Hill, when they rescued the colonial ammunition wagons, saved the British from a devastating defeat. At the same time, the women and children of the valley were forced to congregate in what amounted to concentration camps, and levels of poverty, sickness and death were very high.

In Mlanjeni's war, which broke out in the last days of 1850, matters were different. The Khoekhoe had been heavily disillusioned both by their treatment as soldiers in the previous war, and by a particularly vicious assault on their rights in subsequent years by colonial officials who belonged to the British settler community that was implacably opposed to Khoekhoe advancement. In addition, Hermanus Matroos, also known as Ngqukumeshe, the son of a runaway slave and a Xhosa woman who had worked as an interpreter for the British, had established a substantial community, mainly of Xhosa and Thembu descent, to the west of the valley. He too had been badly treated despite his service in the War of the Axe and this time decided to join the amaXhosa in their assault on the colony. He managed to coerce a number of the Khoekhoe to join him, and others did so willingly (Ross 2004). In all, about a third of the Khoekhoe inhabitants of the valley revolted against the colony. Many fought in the mountains for several years, often with considerable success. The other two-thirds remained on the side of the English. Indeed, both they and a number of ex-rebels fought well and long for the colonial forces. Nevertheless, as a result of the actions of the rebellious minority, the status of the district was changed. The valley would no longer be an exclusively Khoekhoe settlement. In practice this meant that the colonial authorities would ensure that people of European descent were given land in the valley wherever possible.

In order to facilitate this policy, the British began by confiscating the land of all the *erfholders* (plot owners) in the valley who had rebelled. The only problem was that it was illegal under Roman-Dutch law, and thus under Cape law, for the government to dispossess people of their land, even those who had gone into rebellion. The British were forced, as a result, to compensate those rebels who had illegally lost their land. This was not a development which pleased the British colonial officials, especially as the first claimant to receive his land back was none other than Andries Botha, who had been convicted of high treason in a show trial in the aftermath of the rebellion – and who was then quickly and quietly released on the authority of the man who had led the prosecution against him, which perhaps gives some indication of what he had thought of the evidence he had presented to an all-white jury. Be that as it may, there was no option but to institute a commission to investigate the 134 cases of those who had been deprived of their land and requested its return. The grounds the commission invoked in those 114 cases in which it decided that the claim for restitution was unproven related largely to the conditions under which the land had originally been granted – namely, that the land was to be occupied and improved and a substantial house built on it. Whether this had really been the case was open to question, and the effects of the War of the Axe were not taken into account. In any event, it was a remarkable form of legalism that restored land to those who had been convicted of treason only to remove it again 'for the misdemeanour of a lack of glass windows' (Cape Parliamentary Papers 1859; Elbourne 2002: 372).

The consequences of opening up the upper Kat River valley to white settlement was predictable. Where land was available as a result of confiscation, it went exclusively to Europeans. The Khoekhoe were unable to expand their holdings, and, given the partible system of inheritance, each small parcel of land became increasingly subdivided until there were often dozens of owners on what had begun as a single plot (Cape Parliamentary Papers 1903). In 1905 an Act was passed which essentially made the continued subdivision of plots illegal and forced their owners to register and survey their land, generally at a prohibitive cost. On the other hand, white people began to buy up, exchange and generally engross the land, until they were very often able to obtain the enclosure of the commonage. This was obviously to the advantage of those who held a lot of land in a particular block. In some parts of the valley, notably Wellsdale, Gonzana and Ebenezer West, the land blocks were consolidated and quite large. Elsewhere, in Readsdale, for instance, the parcels of land could be very small. The signs of the redistribution of the commonage are clear on the cadastral maps today, as narrow strips run from the boundaries of the original *erven* (plots) to the edge of the former commonage. Furthermore, white control over the legal and judicial apparatus facilitated the dispossession of those Khoekhoe who had held on to their land. In the immediate aftermath of the rebellion, for instance, the magistrate Louis Meurant was able to ensure by dubious legal means that his cronies, and indeed his son, acquired areas of the valley. Most famously, in the first half of the twentieth century, a small-town lawyer named Fenner-Solomon effectively defrauded many Khoekhoe of the small parcels of land that they had retained. The provision of small loans at usurious interest rates often led to the forfeiture of possession and title, especially as the Khoe were generally required to lodge their title deeds with Fenner-Solomon's office (Peires 1987).

Slowly, then, in the course of the later nineteenth and early twentieth centuries, the upper Kat River valley was transformed into an area of white-owned farms. To some degree it was an extension of the citrus-growing region around Fort Beaufort, and Kat River oranges, from both parts of the river's valley, were, and remain, an important crop. In addition, some farms grew tobacco and a few, higher up the valley, produced fruit, notably peaches. The area's relatively rich bottom soil, with access to water for irrigation, is also suited to the growing of cabbages and potatoes. These crops were grown by the first Khoe settlers in the 1830s.

An area of white-owned farms in South Africa did not mean an area in which the inhabitants were predominantly white. As in all such regions, there was a large population of black farm labourers, many of whom had remained on the same piece of land for generations and were more rooted in the region than the white landowners were. In some places, they effectively farmed on their own account, as semi-legal tenants of the white owners. My impression is that this occurred, for instance, in Readsdale, an isolated sub-valley up against the mountains. In addition, there remained a substantial number of descendants of the Khoekhoe Kat River settlers, either living in the valley or retaining some rights to land within it. Their most notable concentration was in Tamboekies Vlei, above the church village of Hertzog, which had been granted as a single farm to the commandant of the original Khoekhoe forces, Christiaan Groepe, and was held in joint ownership by all his numerous descendants, although about half of this land had been made over to his second wife and remains a separate parcel of land. Elsewhere, too, there were still a number of pieces of land owned by coloureds, as the Khoe descendants came to be called. Many of their fellows were scattered in various places around the valley although they didn't own any land. These included Piet Draghoeder, whose lament for his lost community provides one of the greatest recorded instances of Afrikaans oral poetry (Peires 1988).

In 1982 matters changed drastically. The upper valley, then known as Seymour District, was transferred from the Republic of South Africa to the putatively independent Republic of Ciskei. The Xhosa rulers of the Ciskei could make a claim to the land on the basis of Maqoma's occupation. The Pretoria government considered the land transfer to be one of the cheapest ways to expand the bantustans. It would also help to acquire some credibility for the states they were attempting to create. More cynically, the Kat River valley was an area of individual tenure that could be given as private property to members of the Ciskei elite, in contrast to the communal tenure that prevailed elsewhere in the Ciskei. It is thus not surprising that the farm Lorraine, an orange farm which had the reputation of being the finest in the region, ended up in the possession of the Ciskeian president, Lennox Sebe, probably through the intermediation of the Ciskei Agricultural Corporation, Ulimcor.

There were several consequences that attended this transfer of territory. In principle, the dispossessed landowners were dispossessed and compensated. In terms of acreage the majority of these landowners were white but a substantial number of coloured people who had managed to hold onto some land were now also dispossessed. A number of them managed to retain their presence in the valley, however, although it is not evident what the legal basis for this was. Indeed, the main problem which accompanied the transfer of the valley to the Ciskei was the loosening of the tenure arrangements which had been built up over the previous century and a half. A number of the farms were handed over to the Ciskeian elite. While the boundaries and ownership of these farms were fairly clear, farming operations, for the most part, did not continue on anything like the level at which they had previously been pursued. In a number of places, the previous farm labourers effectively took control of the farm on which they had been working and were able to keep the farm in reasonable working order. Elsewhere, there was a steady incursion of amaXhosa. They took over the land which they regarded as having been theirs in the past and established their dwellings on abandoned and unclaimed land.

With the change in the political order of South Africa after 1994, the situation in the valley became even more confused. The area is not as poverty-stricken as much of the rest of the former Ciskei, though such matters are relative. As in many of the former bantustans, the main source of income is state grants, notably old age pensions. Nevertheless, there are places where some level of market gardening has developed, taking advantage of the same rich bottomland and water for irrigation that have formed the basis of Kat River agriculture since the 1830s. There have been areas, notably in the centre of the valley, around Hertzog and Fairbairn, where the small farmers of the Hertzog Agricultural Cooperative have been able to resuscitate the agricultural base. But it is a slow, difficult process. The cooperative has not been able to fulfil all the expectations of its early members or of the academics who wrote about it in glowing terms. As always, marketing problems have been the major obstacle to maintaining the profitability of small-scale commercial agriculture. The traders of Fort Beaufort, on whom the Kat River farmers depend to market their produce, have been able to exploit what amounts to a monopsonist or, at least, an oligopsonist situation. Citrus farmers are often able to plug into the long-existing Kat River Citrus Cooperative, which still has a fair number of white farmers – those whose land remained outside the Ciskei. These, it seems, have been generally able to do better than the small-scale vegetable farmers, in part because they are better capitalised.[1]

Nowhere in the valley was land title certain or transparent. Major claims were entered under the provisions of the land compensation legislation. In principle, several categories of people had claims to the land. First and foremost were the descendants of the Khoekhoe settlers who had lost their land either as a result of the 1982 dispossessions or earlier, when they had been victims of racially skewed market dynamics that were manipulated by corrupt white operators. It was unclear whether Fenner-Solomon's actions constitute a case for the descendants of those whom he effectively robbed to make a claim against the state, but there were many who believed this to be the case. The white farmers who had acquired their property under the legal dispensation that was effectively in force between 1853 and 1982 also had a case. Many of them had invested more in their operations than they received in compensation from the apartheid government. This group might indeed include individuals who had purchased a small block of ground with the intention of building on it in due course, but who later discovered that it had been taken over by the Ciskei without compensation because they were considered to be absentee owners. A third group of potential claimants consisted of people who had acquired land from the Ciskeian administration, either directly or by purchase from the original grantees. Some of these had farmed their land with a degree of success.[2] Fourth, there were the farm labourers, some of whom belonged to families that had been in the valley for generations. These families occupied the land on which they had long been working, usually without title. Finally, of course, there were those who had simply moved into the region and taken land for themselves. They had attempted to set up a livelihood for themselves, sometimes as clients of Ciskeian notables but more often on their own account.

Not surprisingly, these conflicting claims were accompanied by political competition. Sometimes this competition took symbolic form. Ntsikana's grave was refurbished and used to claim occupancy. In response, the descendants of Commandant Groepe made sure that his grave was well cared for and adorned with a copy of a painting that had been made of him in the 1840s. The conflict also sometimes turned violent. Crops were destroyed. Rumours circulated to the effect that the mayor of the town of Seymour, one of the semi-urban centres in the valley, had thrown his opponent off the Seymour dam or had himself suffered this indignity. The Kat River valley is undoubtedly a complex place, even though there are pockets of harmony, such as the Bellvale and Elands River valleys in which the old irrigation canals have been brought back into use. More symptomatic of the overall situation, however, is the abandonment of the canal in the Maasdorp valley, which had been in use since the 1830s.

It is obvious that land restitution cannot be implemented in the valley without many complications. Many questions arise. To whom, for example, should land be returned? In principle there can be up to five *de jure* or *de facto* claimants for every hectare of ground: those Khoekhoe descendants who feel they lost their land as a result of fraudulent, racially determined legal practices; those white people who bought the land over the period from 1856 to 1982; the amaXhosa who received land under the Ciskeian government after 1982; the farm workers who have been on the land for generations; and finally those who have moved in as squatters since 1994. It is difficult to see how these competing claims can be reconciled. Should any of the current occupiers be dispossessed, and if not, where are those with a legitimate claim to be placed? The cynic might say that the fact that many of the claimants are white has delayed the implementation of the restitution process. At the very least, the legitimacy of the various claims has not been tested in court, or agreed in any other way. This too creates complications. To compensate the former white owners of the farm Lorraine would seem to go against the spirit of the Act, as they were in categorical terms beneficiaries of apartheid. But so was Lennox Sebe, the president of the Ciskei, who took over the farm from them. Those with the strongest moral and political right to the land may well be those who have the weakest legal right. Some sort of debate about the potential conflicts between the various value systems would seem imperative, but in the fraught world of the Eastern Cape, where poverty drives a ruthless competition for resources, this seems unlikely. What is clear, however, is that the solution to the problems caused by the sheer complexity of land claims in the valley can come only if land restitution is accompanied by a major programme of land redistribution. Only in this way will some sort of justice and tenurial certainty be provided – the precondition, I would argue, for the fertile and well-watered valley to once again fulfil its potential. But whether there is any body, or combination of bodies, with the desire, the power and the political will to drive such a solution seems to me to be significantly unlikely, unless the provincial government of the Eastern Cape takes it upon itself to do so.

Notes

1   The literature on these developments is considerable. See, especially, Binns and Nel 1997, 1999; Hill and Nel 2000; Kyle 2005; Nel, Hill and Binns 1997.

2   This was not always the case. Some land was allowed to run to ruin, and, in a related and symptomatic matter, I have never drunk a worse cup of coffee than the one I ordered in the Seymour hotel in 1998.

References

Binns, T. and E. Nel. 1997. 'Learning from the people: participatory rural appraisal, geography and rural development in the "new" South Africa', *Applied Geography*, 17(1): 1–9.

Binns, T. and E. Nel. 1999. 'Beyond the development impasse: the role of local economic development and community self-reliance in rural South Africa', *Journal of Modern African Studies*, 37(3): 389–408.

Cape Parliamentary Papers. 1859. *Cape Parliamentary Paper G 18. General report of the commission appointed by his Excellency the Governor to inquire into claims for compensation for the loss of erven in the Kat River Settlement*, Cape Town: Saul Solomon.

Cape Parliamentary Papers. 1903. *Cape Parliamentary Paper G 27. Report of the select committee on the Boedel Erven, Stockenstrom District*, Cape Town: Saul Solomon.

Elbourne, E. 2002. *Bloodground: colonialism, missions, and the contest for Christianity in the Cape Colony and Britain, 1799–1853*, Montreal: McGill University Press.

Hill, T. and E. Nel. 2000. *An evaluation of community-driven economic development, land tenure and sustainable environmental development in the Kat River valley*, Pretoria: Human Sciences Research Council.

Hodgson, J. 1980. *Ntsikana's great hymn: a Xhosa expression of Christianity in the early 19th-century eastern Cape*, Cape Town: Centre for African Studies, University of Cape Town.

Kyle, P. 2005. 'Building capacity for community economic development: the case of the Kat River valley, South Africa', unpublished PhD thesis, University of Sussex.

Maclennan, B. 1986. *A proper degree of terror: John Graham and the Cape's eastern frontier*, Johannesburg: Ravan Press.

Nel, E., T. Hill and T. Binns. 1997. 'Development from below in the new South Africa: the case of Hertzog, Eastern Cape', *The Geographical Journal*, 163(1): 57–64.

Newton-King, S. and V.C. Malherbe. 1983. *The Khoikhoi rebellion in the eastern Cape (1799–1803)*, Cape Town: Centre for African Studies, University of Cape Town.

Peires, J. 1981. *The house of Phalo: a history of the Xhosa people in the days of their independence*, Johannesburg: Ravan Press.

Peires, J. 1987. 'The legend of Fenner-Solomon', in B. Bozzoli (ed.) *Class, community and conflict: South African perspectives*, Johannesburg: Ravan Press.

Peires, J. 1988. 'Piet Draghoender's lament', *Social Dynamics*, 14(2): 6–15.

Ross, R. 1980. 'Ethnic identity, demographic crises and Xhosa–Khoikhoi interaction', *History in Africa*, 7: 259–271.

Ross, R. 1993. 'Montagu's roads to capitalism: the distribution of landed property in the Cape Colony in 1845', in R. Ross *Beyond the pale: essays on the history of colonial South Africa*, Hanover and London, Wesleyan University Press.

Ross, R. 2004. 'Hermanus Matroos aka Ngxukumeshe: a life on the border', *Kronos: Journal of Cape History*, 30: 47–69.

Stapleton, T. 1996. *Maqoma: Xhosa resistance to colonial advance 1798–1873*, Johannesburg: Jonathan Ball.

Stockenström, A. 1854. *Light and shade as shown in the character of the Hottentots of the Kat River Settlement, and in the conduct of the colonial Government towards them*, Cape Town: Saul Solomon.

12 In the shadows of the cadastre: family law and custom in Rabula and Fingo Village

Rosalie Kingwill

This chapter is concerned with land tenure in the Eastern Cape, with a specific focus on the problems of conjugating customary and common-law notions of ownership. It examines the complex ways in which living customary approaches to land ownership articulate with the legal prescripts of ownership in South Africa, which are derived from common law. This chapter charts the lived and living interpretations of land ownership in a selected social field[1] – African freehold – drawing on evidence from two field sites, a rural locality and a suburban township. In both cases, normative practices involve a hybrid of custom and state law.

Customary practices cannot be reduced to official customary law (Bennett 2008: 138). The latter is, in any event, undergoing radical reinterpretation, in part due to the distortions imparted by Western attitudes and prejudices in the framing of customary law during the late colonial period. Customary law was subjected to the demands of a colonial state with an increasingly capitalist orientation towards productive resources. The effect was to ring-bind African customs into a body of law that was secondary to the dominant state law, which was implemented by a segregated administrative regime of native administrators and authorities. Common law evolved according to the norms and customs of colonial and apartheid society; it was insulated from the influences of African custom due to the strict separation of legal systems that was adopted in the late colonial period (Chanock 2001: 292), a tendency that still survives today. The democratisation of South African society calls for a more nuanced perspective of customary law, one which allows us to see beyond its legal status (Claassens and Mnisi Weeks 2009: 494; Mnisi Weeks and Claassens 2011: 826; Van Niekerk 2006: 12).

In the shadow of the cadastre

James Scott (1998: 49) describes the universal contest between state-imposed systems and the social systems they attempt to override. The gulf between 'land tenure facts on paper and facts on the ground' is widest during periods of social upheaval:

> We must keep in mind not only the capacity of state simplifications to transform the world but also the capacity of the society to modify, subvert, block, and even overturn the categories imposed on it … there will always be a shadow land-tenure system lurking beside and beneath the official account in the land-records office. We must never assume that local practice conforms to state theory.

Evidence emerging from my field research in South Africa does indeed reveal that there is a deep contradiction between the meaning of ownership as defined by law and the meaning of ownership as practised by a large proportion of South Africans of African descent. There would appear to be a 'shadow' land-tenure system 'lurking' beneath the official Deeds Office records.

Under the colonial and apartheid orders, white settler-citizens and even white foreigners 'owned' land, while the indigenous inhabitants of the country were accorded inferior occupational rights that were subject to highly discretionary administrative law. Today the Constitution affirms the commitment to equalising ownership rights. But where is ownership itself defined and interrogated? What does it mean to own land in South Africa? What is ownership?

The default legal position takes ownership to mean the common-law definition of ownership. Statutes confer a range of land rights, but ownership is a discrete category, which comprises an amalgam of rights. Ownership according to the common law is realised when specified legal criteria are met, most obviously registration in the Deeds Registry. 'The current registration system depends strongly on the well-understood concept of real rights' and its corollary that 'in principle, rights in land that do not meet the stringent requirements of recognition as real rights may not be registered' (Pope 2010: 3). At the very minimum, stringent requirements entail compliance with the national cadastre, which consists of the formal national land information system.

The South African cadastre (like most modern cadastres) is multidimensional. First, there is a spatial component: the geometric description of land parcels. Second, linked directly to the spatial dimension, is a textual component, which comprises the records or registers recording the real rights in the land parcels, such as ownership, bonds (mortgages) and servitudes. Both spatial and textual records must reflect up-to-date information, which means that every time a change occurs, such as sales transactions or inheritance, or spatial alterations such as subdivisions or servitudes, it must be duly registered. Three characteristics of this three-dimensional land information system are: (i) the core unit is the land 'parcel', which is a discrete unit, and which, according to statutes governing survey standards, must be surveyed within an extremely fine range of accuracy; (ii) registered owners of real rights have some degree of autonomy from other users of the property in deciding about the use and disposal of the property, though users have some legal protections; and (iii) registered owners of real rights have fiscal obligations: property registers are linked to other registers, such as records for purposes of income tax and servicing.

A grid of property information is superimposed on the terrestrial dimension of land. The multifaceted aspects of ownership are gathered into a thoroughly quantifiable private property regime that is legible to both central and local state organs as well as the wider public. The ownership grid is associated with a language of measurable indices, identified owners (named and registered) and inflexible boundary lines marked as coordinates on the survey map.

Community-based or family property regimes display characteristics that are not easily quantified. The social relationships within which access to property is embedded are visible, but state law regards them as private and beyond its reach. The margins of access have a fuzzy quality since property relations hinge on kinship or community networks that are fluid and shifting. The prevalence of labour migrancy, which results in multiple sites of residence, further encourages fluidity in claims to property. These regimes thus resist assimilation into an inflexible property grid.

Attempts are sometimes made to pin down these differences by categorising tenure in terms of a dualistic divide between individual and communal tenure. Conceptualising land tenure in terms of different *forms* of tenure, however, glosses over the deeper property relationships that exist between individuals in relation to the 'thing owned' (Hann 1998: 8; Lund 2001: 158; Moore 1998: 33).

Competing normative and legal orders in Rabula and Fingo Village

The two case study localities, Rabula and Fingo Village, represent what Tamanaha (2008: 375, 378), drawing on Moore (1978: 220), characterises as social arenas, typified by interaction and competition between state law and customary practices – in this case in respect of land tenure. Rabula is a rural locality near King William's Town in the district of Keiskammahoek, a core district of the former Ciskei bantustan. Fingo Village is a suburb of Grahamstown. These two localities are among a handful of black settlements in the Eastern Cape in which freehold title was introduced in the mid-nineteenth century.

The Rabula plots are smallholdings of between 4 and 37 hectares, while the plots in Fingo Village are roughly 1 000 square metres in size. These are large pieces of land by colonial and apartheid standards. Though the formal surveyed boundaries have changed very little in Rabula, there is evidence of a great deal of informal subdivision of land among individual siblings, both male and female. Properties have only rarely been formally subdivided through surveys and registration. Related families live in separate homesteads on the edges of the surveyed plots.

In Rabula, land arrangements are complicated by the presence of settlements without land title. The state purchased land from former white owners during the course of the territorial consolidation of the Ciskei homeland and redistributed plots and grazing rights to so-called squatters. New residential areas with access to agricultural plots and pastoral commonage were created under state tenancies called trust tenure, which resembled communal tenure with Permission to Occupy certificates, but with tighter administrative control and limited heritability. These differences diminished over time (De Wet 1987: 465; 1995: 129, 146–149, 176; Mills and Wilson 1952: 93–95,150–151). This form of tenure was regulated, not by the Deeds Registry, but by administrative imperative, with powers of land allocation delegated to native commissioners who were assisted by 'traditional' authorities. The family members of some of the titleholders also moved into these settlements. The varied tenure arrangements represent a complex mix of landholding, and illustrate the interpenetration of state law, customary practice and competing sources of authority.

Landowners in Rabula tend to identify themselves as 'people who bought [land]' – *nothenga*[2] – rather than as freeholders. Locally, the distinction between them and those without title is usually attributed to their independence from chiefs and headmen, rather than to their integration into the formal deeds system. A core set of shared norms and customs characterises diverse family practices regarding allocation and transmission of rights, as recounted by the landowners. These are clearly at odds with state law. The assumptions of state law presuppose the strict application of legal procedures regulated by the common law. The logic of the common law is strongly influenced by the laws of the market with regard to alienation and asset accumulation. These assumptions are not supported by evidence from the field sites, which show a disjuncture between normative and legal orderings of property.

Case 1: the contest over the meaning of ownership

Tatase (Stewart), Matolokazi (Virginia) and Ntsomi (Dickson) Ncanywa, and their families, live in Rabula on family land, acquired in 1868 by their great-grandfather, Ncanywa, whom they call *ukhokho* (ancestor, meaning the first ancestor traceable in memory). Ncanywa subsequently acquired other properties, though this is considered the original family land that was passed on to his eldest son. The other two sons received an adjoining property in the valley below, through which the main road to Keiskammahoek now runs. The family split into two branches. Each family traces its genealogical and social history from the acquisition of the additional plot. Two smaller plots acquired by the family play a minor role in this history.

The branch with which this story is concerned is named after Ncanywa's eldest son, John, known to the family as *utat'omkhulu* (grandfather). His grandson, Tatase, was in charge at the time of the interviews. As he was very ill, his sister (the eldest child of John), Matolokazi (Virginia), was planning to take over as manager. She lives on the property and has retained the Ncanywa family name, passing it on to her three children. The wife of a sibling born out of wedlock also lives with her children on the property.

The government wanted to establish an irrigation scheme in Rabula in 1959. An aqueduct was planned to pass through the Ncanywas' property. Officials needed to trace the owner in order to survey the strip and draw up a servitude. The property was still registered in the name of the original grantee, 'Canywa'. Registration had skipped two generations. Over 20 letters and memoranda were exchanged between various officials in the offices of the bantu affairs commissioner, the chief bantu affairs commissioner, the legal division of the Department of Bantu Affairs, the Native Appeal Court and the Deeds Registry, spanning a period of four years. The fastidiousness and attention to detail were extraordinary. Marriage and baptismal records were sought, family trees were drawn up and Professor Kerr, a customary law professor at Rhodes, was consulted (Republic of South Africa: SAB. NTS 51/337).

The white officials never reached agreement. The matter drew to a close only when they discovered that a titles commissioner had been appointed in terms of another legal imperative, with no direct connection to the water scheme. The titles commissioner was appointed to sort out lapsed titles in the whole of Rabula. Commissioners exercised their powers (and still do) in terms of special legislation that had been passed earlier in the century when government recognised that freehold and quitrent titleholders generally failed to transfer title into the name of the current owner, as strictly required by the Deeds Registry.[3] The commissioner awarded the property to Simon Ncanywa, son of John. This concluded the matter as far as the state was concerned and the file was closed.

Only Simon was consulted before the commissioner awarded the property to him in 1962. He made a sworn statement to the native commissioner of Keiskammahoek in 1959, witnessed by a female relative, in which he stated: 'As far as I am aware my father John was not regarded as the sole heir, it being understood that the children inherited jointly.' He listed the names of 40 family members, male and female, with possible rights in the property. In spite of his statement he was later identified as the true owner by virtue of official customary law rather than common law. John's eldest (and already deceased) son was skipped over because he had had only daughters.

The main legal issue with which these officials were grappling was whether to apply the common or customary law of succession.[4] There was some doubt because the original grantee was assumed to have married by 'native custom'. Officials fastidiously checked church records but could find no record of a Christian marriage. They did, however, find the marriage records of Ncanywa's eldest son, John, who had married according to Christian rites.

It was not clear whose property it was. As the title deed was still registered in the name of the first grantee, one line of highly technical legal argument concluded that the property still belonged to him in law. This required careful conveyance through each successor to the present owner. Moreover, if customary law applied, the property should devolve by custom through the male line, bypassing the eldest son's bevy of daughters and passing on collaterally to a younger brother's son. If, on the other hand, the land was the valid property of Ncanywa's unregistered heir, John, it would possibly devolve by common law because of John's marriage by Christian rites. If it devolved through this route, it first had to be established whether the estate was inherited before or after the law of succession changed in 1927, in terms of the Native Administration Act (No. 38 of 1927). A notorious result of this Act was the removal of the 'community of property' implications of Christian and civil marriages without prenuptial agreements. This would have meant that property would be owned jointly and passed on to all the children.

It also had to be established whether one of four mid-nineteenth-century colonial laws applied,[5] as there remained a remote possibility that one of these validated customary law. There were further intricate legal complications concerning a great-granddaughter who had borne children out of wedlock and a grandson who took a customary wife after the death of his first wife. These questions were never resolved (or resolvable) legally, but the administrative solution satisfied state requirements.

The family was unaware that there had ever been a 'succession crisis'. They have continued to devolve property according to family custom. All family members, male and female, have rights in the property within a patrilineal system of descent. Arable land is informally subdivided among the children, and women inherit fields as long as they are domiciled within the patrilocal residence. The sister of the current family head expects to take over the headship from her brother, a fairly unconventional step for women, by Rabula standards.

Two themes, among others, stand out in this story.

(i) The devolution of property follows norms drawn from a social code that takes patrilineal descent as its point of departure, as is common throughout Rabula. Respondents stressed that arrangements regarding family land were private and that 'families differed' in the way that they legitimated internal access and claims. In reality, practices reflect a consistent pattern of normative behaviour despite differences in detail, and despite situations where norms are being stretched, especially with regard to gender relations.

(ii) The suggestion of immutability that is associated with social identity traced by descent is tempered by historical contingency. There is interplay between membership of the family and family property. The interaction perpetuates, and is perpetuated by, an accepted version of the family lineage. Since the family's genealogy is invariably orally transmitted, 'as far as memory goes', the version accepted in the present is relatively adaptable to circumstance, but not absolutely so.

Many modern Rabula landowning families trace their genealogy from the period *after* the first properties were acquired – that is, from the second generation, when many families branched into two or three lineage offshoots, sometimes more finely categorised by anthropologists as lineage 'segments' or 'remnants' depending on the exact circumstances. This phenomenon arose when additional land was available for purchase by sons other than the firstborn (who generally inherited the family property), the capital for which was raised from the sale of livestock (Mills and Wilson 1952: 47). Subsequent generations had limited opportunities for acquiring additional land because land for African purchase and occupation was frozen within native reserves. The properties acquired then are, to a large extent, the properties owned now. The delimiting of African land within legally defined boundaries coincided with the contraction of the agrarian economy in African areas. This was manifested in third-generation offspring commuting or migrating to work in urban areas, in many cases to sustain rural-based livelihoods that were undermined by a lack of capital to intensify production and by the difficulty of acquiring more land.

Case 2: the tension between ownership and custodianship

Lilian Kate (family name Xhayimpi) is regarded as the custodian of the family property in Fingo Village. I interviewed her there in August 2006. In terms of the common law, her nephew, Archibald Xhayimpi, was meant to inherit the property from his mother, Nontusi, Lilian's sister, who died without a will. Nontusi was the oldest adult in the family, and the title was registered in her name. The family was relieved to learn that the title was still in her name, as Archibald had insinuated that the property had been transferred into his name. Prior to this, it was registered in the name of David, the sisters' uncle, and, after him, his wife, who passed it on to Nontusi. The family expected, in accordance with custom, that responsibility for the property would fall on Lilian after Nontusi's death. The family claims this was discussed with Nontusi and agreed to prior to her death. Lilian is, therefore, regarded as the present custodian of the property. She is seen as the 'responsible person' who manages the household affairs, including the bills.

Archibald, who did not live on the property and had his own house elsewhere, realised his power in terms of the law and went to lawyers who confirmed his status as Nontusi's heir. An eviction notice was served on the Xhayimpi family occupying the property: they were notified that they had to vacate the property within a month. The legal notice referred to them as 'tenants'. The family had felt vulnerable before the notice was served on them and had already consulted the Legal Resources Centre (LRC). They suspected that Archibald intended to sell the property, and indeed he later made these intentions clear. In terms of the Intestate Succession Act No. 81 of 1987, Archibald, as the child of the registered owner, had a clear right to inherit his mother's property. The LRC notified Archibald's lawyers that the family intended contesting the case. However, Archibald died a few months later, and the threat of eviction was removed.

Kinship, family property and property rights

The patrilineal mode of tracing descent is considered the norm in the Keiskammahoek District and is not restricted to any particular type of tenure (Mills and Wilson 1952; Wilson et al. 1952: 46–48). Family members, male and female, are affiliated as a group through the male line. There is strong evidence suggesting that the practice remains widespread among many people of African descent in South Africa, particularly along the eastern seaboard among people who speak the Nguni languages (Preston-Whyte 1974: 178). Homesteads are established on the basis of patrilocality, meaning that married women customarily go to live with the husband's family. Offspring are considered to be members of the paternal kinship group or patrilineage. The women themselves retain their original lineage and clan identity (Wilson et al. 1952: 48–49). The combination of patrilineal and patrilocal social arrangements inform the holding and passing on of property, a conclusion deduced from both oral and documentary evidence which shows that land is transmitted through the traceable kinship network of the landholding lineage, rather than through marriage.

Despite profound changes to property and gender relationships, the descent system endures and frames both family organisation and property. The kin group determines their relationships with one another on the basis of the male line, and traces their lineage to a common male ancestor, identified as the progenitor, *ukhokho*, of the family. Interestingly in the case of freeholders, customary descent is traced to the progenitor who procured the original title.

Notwithstanding shifts in internal power relations, the practical examples given by people attest to the strength of the continued relevance of patrilineage as a means of identifying close relatives and to the importance of the cluster of patrilineages that comprise a clan (see Wilson et al. 1952: 47, 49). Clans are important for framing broad customary rituals and marriage rules; the lineage determines rights of access to property. Ancestors are strongly associated with both the lineage and the property, forming the links in an all-male chain.

Freeholders view ownership in terms of customary claims based on historically constructed kinship relations developed over time: ownership is a process. Rights to newly acquired land are subject to relationships that adhere over time. Rights with regard to family property are associated with where and how one fits into the loose corporation of the extended family, which corresponds to a lineage, even though it may be quite shallow. No individual, not even if he or she is registered as the 'owner', controls the property to the extent of having the power to dispose of it, or to identify heirs to the exclusion of others, except in certain limited situations, such as those that concern children born out of wedlock who are not recognised as belonging to the patrilineage.

The language of family tenure is captured by the idea of belonging. 'People *belong* to the extended family; land *belongs* to the whole family; family members *belong* to the family land. Ownership functions to maintain family bonds, promote interaction and protect the family' (Kingwill 2008: 196). The Rabula and Fingo Village narratives interweave the sense of belonging as both inclusive and exclusive, moving between the poles of inclusion of lineage members and exclusion of non-lineage members. The line is drawn at the margins of open-ended inclusivity on the one extreme and commodification on the other.

Succession, kinship and property rights

Historically, the position and gender of the person assuming responsibility for the homestead was crucial to the undergirding of the customary concept of succession with regard to both the customary estate and accession to office. Land did not constitute property as a heritable object. It was not a scarce resource that required retention within the family; it did not pass from generation to generation as an asset in itself. Rather, it was associated with other productive resources, such as cattle, which were the main form of property that could be inherited.

Given this history, the application of succession rights to immovable property presents a number of problems and anomalies. The inheritance of land as a rule-bound legal concept was introduced by colonial governments. The traditional succession system, which was associated with status and responsibility and which followed the rules of male primogeniture, now became linked to the inheritance of material property. The native administration cemented these rules in administrative proclamations that had the force of law. This was tantamount to codification and also entrenched the patriarchal social structure.

The more circumscribed customary context of succession as position rather than heir is slowly transforming into a more nuanced approach to property management. The stress remains on functions of responsibility rather than proprietorship, consolidated in an identified individual's ability to manage property. In English the term used is 'responsible person', somewhat congruent with an executor of a deceased estate in the common law. In isiXhosa the expression most frequently used is *'umngcini ekhaya'* (the person who looks after the home), derived from the verb *'ugcina'*, meaning 'to take care of'. Heritable status is no longer a blueprint, but has blended into personal attributes of commitment and capacity, such as quality of home maintenance, permanent domicile, sobriety and stability. This means that sometimes a younger person might be preferred to an older one or a female to a male; the children of siblings might be considered more suitable than a person's own children. In short, a genealogical schema can be overridden, since eligibility is based on actual relationships. Rights are in practice congruent with the degree and quality of participation in family matters. These practices are not only deeply at odds with the common law, which predetermines heirs and vests them with proprietary power, but also varies from customary law with its emphasis on the authority of the eldest male.

Baninzi, a school principal from Fingo Village whom I interviewed in March 2010, could not at first identify a contemporary isiXhosa term to replace *indlalifa*, which he considered outdated. When pressed, however, he preferred *'imeli'* (representative) 'because … it's not like he is the heir to the property'. He described the tension between *indlalifa* and modern approaches:

> … families differ … in terms of our family, this is how we do things … Other families, they will say automatically the eldest son will inherit the property; other families will say automatically the youngest will inherit. So,

it differs from family to family. And in some cases they look at the contribution of the children – if they feel maybe the eldest doesn't assist in terms of building the family, maintaining the house and all that, they may choose another one, whom they know has made a huge contribution in terms of the property and in terms of sustaining and assisting the parents. In the past, it was the eldest, but somehow that's beginning to change. *Indlalifa* to me is a person who *automatically* inherits; there is nothing attached to that. If … the family says *indlalifa* is the eldest son, no matter what, that is the person who will inherit. But … if you add 'provided you do ABC', then to me, it cannot be *indlalifa*. *Indlalifa* was used in the olden days to say *indlalifa* is the eldest and that is that. Whether the others have worked or whatever, if they want something here, they have got to consult the *indlalifa* … [W]e don't have *indlalifa* here. If … the family says [the person] who inherits is the eldest, then that is *indlalifa*. But now if you attach other things, you cannot say that is *indlalifa*. You … use one of the words … like *ugcina ekhaya … ugcina bazali* [parents]. But if that person, for example, had not looked after the parents, had not looked after sustaining the home, that person would not inherit that property. Therefore you cannot call that person *indlalifa*. He inherits because of ABC.

There is a tension between *inkhulu* and *indlalifa*. The former is the firstborn while the latter is the customary heir. In the past, the two usually coincided. Today, though, the two terms are more clearly distinguishable, although there is still a degree of interconnectedness between them. The focus has shifted to contingency. Though many families nowadays do not employ the term *indlalifa* in its conventional sense, there are certain inheritance practices associated with the firstborn. Mostly the *inkhulu* label denotes an honorary position of respect: one would always consult, but not necessarily seek permission from, the *inkhulu*. Property distribution and decision-making are reached through discussion and agreement, not necessarily without conflict.

Gender, kinship and property rights

Balancing inclusivity and patriliny with female ownership and inheritance is becoming a vexed problem as the pressure for gender equality mounts and the moral authority of the Constitution finds its place in local norms. The central importance of a common ancestor is, ironically, reinforced in the context of title because the first member of the family to have been granted the title (always male) is regarded as the common ancestor. All subsequent descendants are traced through him. While the patrilineal model does not in itself exclude the rights of women to property, the conditions under which women are able to negotiate not just property rights but the entire spectrum of rights associated with their status in relation to the lineage are circumscribed, especially since residence is strongly patrilocal.

The distinction between a woman's place of origin and her place of marriage and partnership is captured by the Xhosa terms *ikhaya* (home), where you are born; *indlinam* (from *indlu,* house), where you move to if unmarried; and *emzinam* (from *umzi,* homestead), where you move to if married. The Mona sisters of Fingo Village stated in an interview in January 2008: 'At *emzinam* we conduct my husband's ceremonies and at home we conduct my family ceremonies.' 'Home' continues to be associated with the place and lineage of a woman's own kin. Relatives affiliated to the mother's kin are regarded as members of another lineage. The incidence of females staying at or returning to their natal home is becoming more widespread, though. Daughters no longer automatically get married. Men often have the means to move and establish a new home or retain long-term employment elsewhere. The family home is, in some cases, treated as a repository for the young and aged, and women are frequently left in charge. These modern relationships impact on patrilocality and the patrilineage.

In-laws are potential threats to property and lineage. The power of women as wives or daughters-in-law is always more circumscribed than that of a sister/ daughter in property matters. Strict taboos prevent infiltration of lineage property by in-laws. In Fingo Village, the case of a sister-in-law who tried to leave contested family property to her sister's children by means of a will elicited allegations of dishonesty, fraud and 'evil' intent.

Can titles be harmonised with customary law? How can women's rights be safeguarded? Recent Constitutional Court judgments underline the pluralistic sources of law, but within a framework of parity. While the judgments cannot give content to land rights, they do reinterpret customary law to take into account notions of 'living customary law' or the 'living law', acknowledging the dynamic quality of the law that people embrace in their everyday lives, under radically changed and changing circumstances.

In the absence of commonly accepted legal concepts of customary ownership and succession, statutory measures tend to adopt common-law approaches to safe-guard property rights for women and children. Gender discrimination in inheri-tance, for example, is being addressed by way of blanket measures that apply to all South Africans, moving away from the discriminatory, racially based measures that applied in the past under the guise of customary law, which favoured male primogeniture. In the absence of a will, statutory law now provides for mandatory equitable division of property between the spouse and children.[6] The fact that this approach is derived from common law, however, is a clear sign of the direction in which 'living customary law' may evolve in future.

Conclusion: '... a normal part of the present'

The case material shows that 'property' and 'ownership' are the result of socially constructed processes. The event of purchasing land is seen as initiating and witnessing an exchange, but does not embody the essence of 'ownership'. The common-law construct of ownership, on the other hand, creates a legally binding relationship represented by the contract in law. The moment of transfer creates a new relationship between the present owner and the object of possession. To change this relationship requires another snapshot event. The spatial dimension and the materiality of the object are emphasised by the system of registration. By contrast, systems that are informed by customary norms and values emphasise social relationships.

The common-law tradition has been instrumental in producing an ideal of ownership based on Western law to which many aspire. The freeholders of Fingo Village and Rabula, however, continue to adapt 'custom' to their 'private property' arrangements in ways that resist complete assimilation. The evidence provides a more nuanced perspective than one that characterises the general inability of the South African state to develop a unified common law as a process that 'deliberately failed' (Chanock 2001: 292).

The recently struck down Communal Land Rights Act (CLRA) No. 11 of 2004, while seeming to redefine a stream of ownership for black rural citizens known as 'communal tenure', in fact situated communal ownership within a problematic schema partially consistent with common-law individual rights. It made no attempt to recognise property in terms of familial or kinship relationships, nor did it allow for decentralised relationships of authority to tie in with the layered levels of local authority, building up from families and clans (Cousins 2008: 23). The CLRA reverted instead to the increasingly discredited binary formula of subdivision and transfer of property ('property-as-object') on the one hand, or forced tribal membership under centralised authority on the other.

The very notion of communal tenure is embedded within discourses suggesting synergy with 'indigenous systems'. The relationship between customary and common law, however, is left unclear, and the rights glossed as communal are relegated to the internal administration of local, 'traditional' structures, which historically acquired their authority, not from indigenous sources of law, but from colonial sovereignty. The confusion created by these legal binaries stems, in my view, from the inability of the new state to confront and redefine the very essence of what legal ownership involves despite clear evidence of different normative orders associated with ownership in South Africa. The divergences do not correspond to a simple opposition between individual and tribal identities. Chanock (2001: 357) reminds us of ZK Matthews's attempt to demystify customary law, to see it as a 'normal part of the present, something that should have a future'. Writing in 1934 from the perspective of a Western-educated African who favoured the integration of law systems, he declared, '[T]here is ... after all ... nothing mysterious about native law'.

Notes

1   I am using Moore's concept of the 'semi-autonomous social field' here (Moore 1978: 54; Tamanaha 2008: 392).

2   *Thenga* is the isiXhosa word for 'buy', the prefix *no-* being a formative noun denoting, in this context, person.

3   Under the Native Administration Act No. 38 of 1927, which evolved into the current
     Land Titles Adjustment Act No. 111 of 1991.
4   'Succession' is the common-law term for identifying heirs for purposes of devolving
     property; it is also the English term for succession to positions of office. Succession
     in African custom was formerly confined to replacement of heritable offices, though
     white legal officials used the term in customary law in both senses.
5   Promulgated in British Kaffraria, the forerunner of the native reserve that became the
     Ciskei, minus a large slice reserved for white settlement.
6   Recognition of Customary Marriages Act No.120 of 1998.

References

Bennett, T. 2008. 'Official vs "living" customary law: dilemmas of description and
    recognition', in A. Claassens and B. Cousins (eds) *Land, power and custom: controversies
    generated by South Africa's Communal Land Rights Act*, Cape Town: Legal Resources Centre
    and UCT Press.
Chanock, M. 2001. *The making of South African legal culture 1902–1936*, Cambridge:
    Cambridge University Press.
Claassens, A. and S. Mnisi Weeks. 2009. 'Rural women redefining land rights in the context
    of living customary law', *South African Journal of Human Rights*, 25(4): 491–516.
Cousins, B. 2008. 'Contextualising the controversies: dilemmas of communal tenure
    reform in post-apartheid South Africa', in A. Claassens and B. Cousins (eds) *Land, power
    and custom: controversies generated by South Africa's Communal Land Rights Act*, Cape
    Town: Legal Resources Centre and UCT Press.
De Wet, C. 1987. 'Land tenure and rural development: some issues relating to the Ciskei/
    Transkei region', *Development Southern Africa*, 4(3): 459–478.
De Wet, C. 1995. *Moving together, drifting apart: betterment planning and villagisation in a
    South African homeland*, Johannesburg: Wits University Press.
Hann, C.M. 1998. 'Introduction: the embeddedness of property', in C. Hann (ed.) *Property
    relations: renewing the anthropological tradition*, Cambridge: Cambridge University Press.
Kingwill, R. 2008. 'Custom building freehold title', in A. Claassens and B. Cousins (eds)
    Land, power and custom: controversies generated by the Communal Land Rights Act, Cape
    Town: Legal Resources Centre and UCT Press.
Lund, C. 2001. 'Questioning some assumptions about land tenure', in T. Benjaminsen
    and C. Lund (eds) *Politics, property and production in the West African Sahel: understanding
    natural resources management*, Uppsala: Nordiska Afrikainstitutet.
Mills, M. and N. Wilson. 1952. *Keiskammahoek rural survey vol. 4. Land tenure*,
    Pietermariztburg: Shuter and Shooter.
Mnisi Weeks, S. and A. Claassens. 2011. 'Tensions between vernacular values that prioritise
    basic needs and state versions of customary law that contradict them: "we love these
    fields that feed us, but not at the expense of a person"', *Stellenbosch Law Review*, 22(3):
    823–844.
Moore, S.F. 1978. *Law as process: an anthropological approach*, London: Routledge & Kegan Paul.
Moore, S.F. 1998. 'Changing African land tenure: reflections on the incapacities of the
    state', *European Journal of Development Research*, 10(2): 33–49.

Pope, A. 2010. 'Getting rights right in the interests of security of tenure', *Law, Democracy and Development*, 14(1): 1–23.

Preston-Whyte, E. 1974. 'Kinship and marriage', in W.D. Hammond-Tooke (ed.) *The Bantu-speaking people of southern Africa*, London: Routledge & Kegan Paul.

Republic of South Africa. SAB (Central Archives Depot, Pretoria). NTS, Archives of the Department of Native Affairs. SAB. NTS 51/337. Correspondence 1959–1962. Bantu Affairs Commissioner: Keiskammahoek: N8/20/3(5): 20/07/1959, 18/08/1959, Chief Bantu Affairs Commissioner: (47) N8/20/3/7 12/07/1959, 13/02/1960, 4/02/1960, 29/09/1960, 18/01/1961, 23/09/1961, 2/12/1961, 21/04/1962, Secretary for Bantu Administration and Development: NTS 51/337 Rabula Irrigation Scheme 8/06/1960, 22/08/1960, 29/08/1960, 17/07/1961, 28/10/1961, 5/03/1962, 6/06/1962, 11/06/1962.

Scott, J.C. 1998. *Seeing like a state: how certain schemes to improve the human condition have failed*, New Haven, CT: Yale University Press.

Tamanaha, B. 2008. 'Understanding legal pluralism: past to present, local to global', *Sydney Law Review*, 30(3): 375–411.

Van Niekerk, G. 2006. 'Legal pluralism', in J.C. Bekker, C. Rautenbach and N.M. Goolam (eds) *Introduction to legal pluralism in South Africa*, Durban: LexisNexis Butterworths.

Wilson, M., S. Kaplan, T. Maki and E. Walton. 1952. *Keiskammahoek rural survey vol. 3. Social structure*, Pietermaritzburg: Shuter and Shooter.

Court case

Tongoane and others v Minister for Agriculture and Land Affairs and others. 2010 CCT 100-100-09.

13 Land reform, tradition and securing land for women in Namaqualand

Karin Kleinbooi

This chapter focuses on the gendered nature of land tenure in the Namaqualand region of the Northern Cape. It discusses the ways in which women are beginning to assert their right to land, and shows how a few women manage to secure such rights, despite the fact that the land reform programme does not support their efforts. The chapter is derived from a study carried out between October 2003 and March 2005. In-depth interviews were conducted with some 65 women from the municipal areas of Steinkopf, Concordia, Leliefontein (including Kharkams, Rooifontein and Spoegrivier), Komaggas and the Richtersveld (Lekkersing, Kuboes, Eksteenfontein). The women were interviewed individually and in groups. A distinction was made between married, single and widowed women. Some of the women had access to land and some did not. The age of the women ranged from 18 to 65 years.

The setting

Namaqualand is situated in the north-western region of the Northern Cape province of South Africa. This vast, arid and semi-arid region borders the Atlantic seaboard and Namibia (Wisborg and Rohde 2004). Khoisan groups such as the Nama are native to the sparsely populated area. These groups were mainly pastoral-agriculturalists or hunter-gatherers. The gradual expansion of the colonial frontier and settler farming pushed the native inhabitants into small pockets of land, which were administered by mission stations by the early nineteenth century. At the end of the nineteenth century a total of 23 mission settlements in the Cape became known as the rural coloured reserves. They were proclaimed in terms of the Mission Stations and Communal Reserves Act (No. 29 of 1909).

Until 1994, land in the reserves (27 per cent of the total land area of Namaqualand) was formally owned by the state, but allocated to specific communities. The land in the reserves has always been held and managed communally, albeit with varying degrees of involvement by institutions of the church and state

(Archer 1993). Individual titles have been issued for some residential sites since 1995, but the great majority of the arable plots and communal grazing lands continue to be administered by local municipalities, which are now democratically elected.

There is a strong association between land and the family in Namaqualand. Marriage is virilocal since wives normally move to live with their husbands. Descent is traced through the male line only. Land rights are passed on along a patrilineal male line – fathers to sons, or to another male relative when sons are absent (Mann 2000). The right to occupy land in Namaqualand, which is linked to recognition of 'citizenship' (that is, community membership), is understood as the birthright of males born in Namaqualand. Independent tenure and use rights are reserved for men, although these remain somewhat insecure since the ownership of land is vested in the municipalities and does not involve individual ownership (Lebert 2004). A male inhabitant of Namaqualand can apply for the right to occupy land at the age of 18.

Missionary education introduced a membership system, based on the registration of citizens – 'burghers' – and the issuing of 'tickets of occupation' (Archer and Meer 1997; Boonzaier 1980). Women could not be considered as 'burghers' in their own right (Archer 1993). Ironically, the issuing of citizenship – 'burgherskap' – to men on behalf of their families was an attempt to safeguard against the further loss of land by the growing number of white settlers in the area, although not all commentators agree with this view (Boonzaier 1980; Wisborg 2007). The power of men as the heads of households was entrenched by the new system (Krohne and Steyn 1990). Given that the traditional system of land tenure was already gender-biased, women's land rights were seriously undermined.

Women's access to land as daughters or wives
Inheritance of land
The situation in relation to female inheritance of land appears to be ambiguous in Namaqualand at present, where it is customary for men to inherit land. However, some women are now beginning to inherit land in a context in which increased pressure on land means that inheritance is the principal means of gaining access to it.

There was considerable disagreement among the informants about which son should inherit, with some insisting that tradition dictates that it is the eldest son and others arguing that it must be the youngest. There are indications that the eldest was usually chosen in the past but that the younger son is often preferred nowadays. Another key factor is who shows the most interest in farming. In one instance, a father chose a middle son as his heir because he considered him the most dependable:

> My husband inherited a *saaiperseel* [arable plot] from his father. His father
> called his 12 children together and informed them of his decision to give

the land to my husband, and all 12 children had to sign the transfer agreement. This was to ensure that the children would not fight about who should get the land on his passing. When his father passed away my husband took the letter to the municipality and the land right was transferred into his name. My husband's brothers drink and smoke and their father felt he couldn't trust them to keep the land in the family. His choice fell on my husband, who was the second eldest, because he thought my husband would look after the land and would ensure that it was kept in the family.

In rare cases, land is subdivided as a pragmatic solution to rivalry between sons.

The dominant view is that daughters rarely inherit land if there is a son in the family. Women's exclusion has led to their taking a back seat when it comes to land. Women are 'not entitled' to land but we noted some shifts in patterns of inheritance in Namaqualand over the years. A married woman from Lekkersing, for example, who had inherited land from her mother, argued that the land would go to her daughter because she showed the greatest affinity for the land and the livestock, but the son would inherit the status of head of the family: 'That is how the tradition works'.

Daughters' positions in relation to parental land are very different from and more tenuous than those of mothers and of wives. There is a general reluctance to bequeath land to them since they may alienate the family from their land when they get married. Respondents argued that the practice of excluding daughters from inheriting land was justified as the land could easily end up in the husband's family after marriage:

> Most fathers focus on their sons when it comes to farming, with the understanding that they will become the breadwinners one day. They see women as a potential risk. They get married into another family and might take the land out of the family, and in any case if you are lucky you get married to a man that has land in his family. Our parents have the same attitude or belief when it comes to education … Our parents believe they cannot invest in a daughter who will live with someone else's son … The sons in the family later become the providers for the mother and the father.

The imperative to keep land in the family through inheritance and the preference for males in the succession system might involve the extended family as well. In some cases, fathers bequeath land to another male relative (or even return the land to the municipality) rather than leave it to their daughters: 'My brother works in Cape Town and he is next in line for the farm. My father often says that if my brother is not interested, then he will have to go and talk to one of his brothers' sons'. While this approach represents a deviation from cultural practice, it excludes women from accessing land through inheritance.

Marriage and access to land

Marriage provides a substantial form of leverage for women who wish to access land. Women who marry a man with land are often described as 'lucky' and those who do not as 'unlucky': 'I was lucky and married a man who received land from his father. Otherwise I would probably not have been involved [in farming] at all'.

Land rights often pass to the widow on the death of a husband, but this is not always straightforward. A woman from Steinkopf explained:

> I will take the land right over from my husband. In turn, when I die, my two sons will get the right to have the land transferred into both their names … My daughter will get married and leave the home or the land [would] get alienated from the family.

However, widows generally act as only interim holders of the land right, usually until their sons are old enough to take over. In effect they receive a 'temporary inheritance' from their husbands, an informal family arrangement on the death of fathers with young sons. Holding land in this way prevents women from freely disposing of land as they wish or making certain decisions regarding its use.

Women do seem to have considerable say in who should be vested with hereditary land rights in the event of their own passing. One woman from Steinkopf told me that she wanted to have the land formally transferred into her name on the death of her husband. This arrangement would allow her to continue farming, and afford her time to assess who should be the next in line to inherit the right.

When no formal mechanism, such as a will, is in place to ensure that a widow inherits the right of occupation of the family land, she might experience delays and other difficulties in having the land registered in her name. Getting land re-registered on becoming a widow is not a straightforward process. In many cases, accumulated outstanding tax debts make re-registration unaffordable for the widow, and the land often remains in the deceased husband's name as a result. This happened to a widow from Komaggas: 'My residential plot is still in my late husband's name because I do not have the money to pay the taxes in arrears'. The difficulty posed by what is often a tedious local government process was raised as another reason for widows keeping the family land registered in their deceased husband's name. One of the women in Leliefontein complained: 'During the referendum of 2003 I applied for the land to be registered in my name but it is still in the system and not in my name yet.'

There are indications that widows are beginning to inherit land rights directly from their husbands. The statements of two women from Steinkopf and Concordia corroborate this:

> It has become common to transfer land from husband to wife. In my case, if my husband dies the land will come to me and I will then pass it on to our son if I am not interested or am not able to farm.

> Land always had to be [in the name of] the husband. It was only later, in my father's time, that they were able to leave the land to their wives.

Opportunities for married women to obtain rights to land are clearly limited and uncertain, yet the situation is far more fluid than many analysts acknowledge. Some women have inherited land rights because of a lack of male descendants:

> In 1978 my father passed away and I got the farm from him. There were only five girls; we were raised like boys. We harvested, sowed, ploughed, milled and did everything with the livestock that had to be done. In the end I was the only one left on the farm, and I was also my father's favourite daughter. I knew I would get the farm.

Women are much more likely to benefit from inheritance of livestock or the family home than they are to inherit land. A woman from Concordia confirmed that women generally get a share of the family assets even though they do not get land as such: 'We do get something out even if it is just one sheep. When my mother passed away the livestock were divided between the four of us [two sons and two daughters] and the farm went to my eldest brother'.

I came across two cases of married women who inherited land from their mothers. Both indicated they would allow their daughters to take over the land from them one day. A woman from Leliefontein said: 'The land will go to my daughter because she loves the land, and the livestock and the house will go to my youngest son.'

Independent access to land

Prior to 1994, women rarely obtained independent land rights directly from the authorities. Even today, what are seen as 'traditional' forms of land tenure in Namaqualand are rarely challenged. Only a handful of women manage to circumvent the barriers and gain some degree of access to land rights, mainly by exploiting variations within the context of 'traditional' forms of land tenure.

Allocation by a municipality
A minority of women in the sample managed to acquire land in their own names, whether by default or by processes which work to keep land in the family. A woman from Steinkopf, for example, was able to apply to the council for unoccupied land that had previously belonged to her parents. Here, it appears, direct descent from the previous landholder was important:

> Earlier the farm was in my father's name. When my father passed away the land was transferred to my mother. My mother wasn't able to continue with the farming on her own and gave the land back to the council. In

1996 I moved back here and I heard there was an application for the same piece of land. I also applied for citizenship and the same piece of land was registered in my name.

In a similar fashion, a 78-year-old woman in Spoegrivier obtained a *saaiperseel* (arable plot) as a single woman as far back as 1955. Her family's interpretation of who was an eligible land-rights holder differed from the mainstream belief that land should not be held by women. The woman was the secondary rights holder in this case, partly because her husband was regarded as an 'incomer' from Komaggas, another part of Namaqualand. In line with the town's traditional norms, this meant that he was not eligible to hold land in Spoegrivier:

> When I was 25 years old I asked my father how he would feel if I applied to get occupational rights to land. My father gave his permission and I got access to land. This piece of land was handed to me for occupation in 1955. When this man [my husband] married me I already had this land. My husband is an incomer ['married in'] ... He won't get land here.

Informal access to land

Some women have resorted to the unauthorised occupation of land in cases in which the right to use the land has reverted back to the municipality due to a default in payment by the registered user. One woman in Kharkams identified a piece of land as unused and erected a stock post, without receiving the necessary permission from the municipality:

> My stock post is [located] as you come into town. There are two corrugated iron huts on that land. I just invaded that land. Nobody gave it to me. I have never registered the land. I just use it. I must probably go to the municipality to get it allocated to me.

This is not a frequent occurrence, however, and the invasion of unoccupied land does not guarantee that it will eventually be registered in the occupant's name. Security of tenure cannot be assured in this way and women remain vulnerable to the loss of the land. Transferral of the right becomes problematic in the event of death if it is not registered. Intergenerational inheritance cannot occur and no claim can be made to the land by family members.

A more common arrangement is that women access land by entering into informal land-sharing arrangements, usually with male relatives. Such arrangements reduce risks, such as stock theft, and enable women to share the cost and risks of farming with the people whom they partner. One woman from Concordia makes use of close familial ties in this way: 'I farm with my brother. Actually my brother farms and I have livestock on his farm'. Another woman from Komaggas entered into a sharing arrangement with her brother-in-law. Unfortunately she struggled to make ends meet after the man passed away: 'I worked with my one brother-in-law but he passed away. The costs for medicines, the herder and animal feed were shared between the two of us'.

The study indicates that women generally find it easier to gain access to residential land informally rather than by formally applying for commonage and *saaiperseel* rights. Although a woman's access to land may increase after marriage, this does not create a legally recognisable right, and women usually act only as interim rights holders and as guardians over land until their sons are old enough to become the primary rights holders.

Women's involvement in farming

Historically there has been a gendered division of labour in farming systems in Namaqualand. Women have been seen as the caregivers in the family and have thus prioritised activities that supported their reproductive role, like harvesting natural resources, such as medicines, food and firewood, close to the home. Although women in Namaqualand historically engaged in farming alongside their fathers and husbands (Vedder 1928), they had less status, power and control over resources (Archer and Meer 1997). While women had access to the land on the basis of their familial ties, it was their labour more than their control over resources that formed the basis of their involvement in farming.

In Namaqualand today women are mostly involved in growing vegetables and animal fodder on dryland plots. Some of them also run poultry projects. A few of my informants saw themselves as the primary farmer in the household, while some regarded themselves as equal partners in the farming enterprise. Most were clear, though, that their role in the household was a subordinate one: 'My husband is the head and is foremost'. My field study suggests that in reality women play much more than a support role in agriculture. A woman from Concordia, for example, described how she helped her father with practically everything on the farm when she was young. Many women in Concordia farm with their husbands. All the women emphasised the central role that women play in relation to land-based livelihoods. Men often have a reduced role in farming activities as a result of the shift to wage labour. In the words of one of the women: '[My husband] is a "guest" on his livestock post.' Yet women themselves are reluctant to recognise their increased role in agriculture. A woman from Spoegrivier articulated a sentiment shared by the majority of the respondents:

> As women, most of us are afraid to make or take decisions about anything. We grew up with the stigma that a woman should keep quiet and leave the husband's area alone. So in the end you become your husband's helper. You go with him and assist with the livestock. You trek with the animals, and you do everything else that needs to be done, but what is sad is when we trek the land just lies fallow and I would want to do something [with

it]. In the past women were seen as unwise, you know – it was a question of 'what do you know?' And in many cases we didn't know where to go to get the land tilled and tested. So I was always afraid to raise things with my husband because I expected him to think I was stupid or was asking stupid questions. And besides, the farm was his area; he made the decisions.

Women start working on their parents' dryland plots at an early age, often alongside their mothers, but also alongside their fathers, and perform tasks such as herding, milking, lambing, ploughing, planting and harvesting. Later, however, women's involvement in a range of farming activities remains relatively autonomous from their husbands or other male relatives, with a primary focus on vegetable and poultry production. Nowadays, women often become involved in livestock farming as well: 'My husband works during the week so I am responsible for everything until he comes back. I move the livestock or do what needs to be done. [On] weekends we do everything together'.

Is land reform in Namaqualand leveraging more secure land access for women?

The two most important land reform programmes that have been implemented in Namaqualand since 1994 are land redistribution, which involves the purchase of new farms through the municipal commonage programme, and tenure reform, through the Transformation of Certain Rural Areas Act (TRANCRAA) No. 94 of 1998. How have these affected women?

Municipal commonage

The municipal commonage programme allows municipalities to acquire land for use by the poor. More land has been acquired under this programme in Namaqualand than in any other part of the country (Benseler 2004). The aim is twofold: to relieve pressure on existing grazing lands and to provide land to larger herders wishing to expand into more commercial production (the so-called stepping stones approach) (Lebert 2004). Anderson and Pienaar (2004: 10) note that 'a material difference with "new" commonage is that the title conditions make it clear that the land was not set aside for the use of inhabitants in general, but that it must be earmarked for use by the "poor and less privileged"'. However, this places little emphasis on the proactive provision of land to previously marginalised groups such as women, enabling male herd owners to become the primary beneficiaries of land redistribution.

Predictably, since they were not targeted directly, women had little expectation of accessing land acquired through the municipal commonage programme. The women in the study knew little about the programme. Many thought that such land was available only to men, and some felt that the process was being dominated by better-off men. Dissatisfaction was expressed about the great distance to these farms, which makes them inaccessible for women in areas such as Concordia, Leliefontein and Komaggas. They also resented the grazing fees that were being charged by the municipalities. One woman from Leliefontein said: 'I am not interested in the new farms. It is too far out and if you do not have transport it is difficult. You also have to pay for your animals per head. I do not pay at the moment.'

When women did express an interest in the new farms, it was largely linked to their husbands' involvement. They did not intend to apply for grazing rights on the new lands in their own names. A woman from Komaggas summed up the situation: 'We [women] do know about the new farms but everything is done in our husbands' names. We are bound to tradition and our husbands are very dominating.'

Women's literacy and their economic status were important factors in determining their capacity to negotiate and maintain access to land. In Steinkopf, a group of poverty-stricken women applied to the municipality for access to a small piece of land on the new commons, to use as a vegetable garden. They complained about the length of time and the bureaucratic processes involved. They needed the land immediately. They were not always aware of what was happening and did not know where to go with their complaints. There is clearly a gap between women's land needs and government's ability to respond timeously to them. Even when women exert their agency, they encounter intractable institutional obstacles. It took two years before the women were granted access to the land and could start their community vegetable project:

> I could see that many women were suffering in poverty. They didn't have husbands as breadwinners and had children to support. I also knew we could live off the land. These women were all eager. I wrote a business plan. It took two years before we were informed by the municipality that it has been successfully granted to the women's group.

TRANCRAA and tenure reform in Namaqualand

The Transformation of Certain Rural Areas Act (Act No. 94 of 1998) represents the first major attempt by the state to address communal tenure in post-apartheid South Africa. It makes provision for the transfer of former mission land or coloured reserves (areas defined as rural by the Rural Areas Act No. 9 of 1987), currently held in trust by the minister in charge of land affairs, to either a municipality or a Communal Property Association (CPA). It is likely that this Act will impact greatly on the property rights of most people in the six coloured rural areas in Namaqualand – Komaggas, Leliefontein, Steinkopf, Pella, Concordia and Richtersveld – which are currently administered by the commonage committees of the local municipalities of Richtersveld, Khai-Ma, Kamiesberg and Nama-Khoi (May and Lahiff 2007).

TRANCRAA emphasises individual rights but allows for community decisions about land ownership. 'Replacing authoritarian, permit-based control, TRANCRAA honours the rights of residents by requiring that people must be consulted about land ownership, that their user rights will be respected and that future land governance will be democratic and non-discriminatory' (Wisborg and Rohde 2004: 3). The Act gives municipalities a central role in the implementation of tenure reform and in governance. Unfortunately, however, the Act is gender-blind. It stipulates general principles for municipalities to follow in implementing tenure reform (for example, all residents must be afforded an opportunity to participate in the decision-making processes regarding the governance of communal resources) and prohibits discrimination against any resident. But it is silent on the particular needs of women (Wisborg and Rohde 2005). At best the Act neutrally refers to 'he or she'. Given the history of women's invisibility and dependent status in land matters and the fact that their land needs remain largely unarticulated, this is hardly surprising, but it remains a major disappointment.

Widespread consultation and referenda with regard to the consequences of the Act have taken place in nearly all the rural areas in Namaqualand: in Leliefontein, Pella, Richtersveld, Concordia and Steinkopf, but not in Komaggas. Some leaders demonstrated a preference for municipal ownership on behalf of communities. This preference was based on (i) their fears of financial exclusion if the state's financial obligation ended, thereby increasing communities' liabilities, and (ii) the belief that municipalities could potentially safeguard access to land for vulnerable groups such as women and the poor (Wisborg and Rohde 2005). Many women had strong views about the way the consultative process unfolded and participated in it to varying degrees, but many admitted they had a limited understanding of what was actually at stake (Kleinbooi and Lahiff 2007). Their responses were mixed:

> Many women participated and I think they understood. When it comes to land everybody knows what they want.

> Many people attended the meetings and, yes, women did come to the information sessions.

> No, I didn't know about the voting. We are much divided and I am too stupid to participate. But I went to the meetings.

Many women deferred to their husbands or to other men in the community, as is generally the case in matters related to land. A woman from Concordia mentioned that women participated in partnership with their husbands rather than independently: '[Women] participated with their husbands. That's how it works here with such community processes and, as with farming, women stand behind their husbands'.

Opinions about community control of the land varied. A greater degree of 'ownership' was equated with handing control of the land to a community structure. A few women thought that having control over land by a structure closer to them would restore their dignity and strengthen the tradition of livestock farming. Others feared the possibility of elite capture:

> The land should be transferred to the community. It will make coloureds feel that we do have something. It will also give the value of farming back to our children. At this stage they are not interested because you do not own the land your livestock are grazing on. Where in the world do people farm like that?

A woman from Steinkopf preferred the continuation of the status quo because she feared alienation from the land as a result of detrimental actions by the municipality or the community: 'I prefer that the land remains in trust with the minister. We may lose the land if the communities control it. The municipality may take decisions without involving the communities'. A strong streak of cynicism about public institutions was evident in numerous comments.

None of the respondents related the process of land reform, land rights and governance directly to women as such. Minimal engagement in policy processes reflected the status of women in relation to land; they are either invisible or secondary to men. There was very little comprehension about what benefits the land reform processes could bring for women in terms of strengthening their access to and control over land.

Conclusions

Women have found it difficult to obtain and hold on to land in their own names. This situation has not changed significantly since the advent of democracy in the country. Strong social conventions dictate that land cannot be inherited by daughters, other than in exceptional circumstances. Young women are resigned to the fact that they will be passed over as fathers bequeath family land to younger sons or other male relatives. Widows generally inherit land rights from their late husbands, but there is a sense that they are merely looking after the land for their sons. In many cases, the land rights are not formally transferred into the name of the wife anyway. Prior to 1994, women were unlikely to be allocated land in their own name by the local council. This is changing, but very slowly.

Although women contribute significantly to both reproductive and productive activities, they generally occupy a position subordinate to their husbands or other male relatives. They are involved in a range of farming activities, from small-scale vegetable and poultry production to extensive grain and livestock farming. Some consider themselves to be equal partners with their husbands, despite not having land or livestock in their own name, but most emphasise that they play a supporting role and defer to the authority of their (often absent) husbands.

They are least involved in those aspects of farming that entail relationships with the wider world – buying inputs, selling livestock or produce, hiring labour and participating in local committees.

Some women, including unmarried women, widows and wives, engage in farming relatively independently of men. These women face a range of obstacles: lack of skills, lack of transport, poor access to finance, vulnerability to stock theft and the 'double burden' of domestic responsibilities in addition to farm production activities. Despite these obstacles, some women have acquired substantial herds of livestock by means of individual sales, land sharing and the pooling of group resources. They may also be involved in a range of commercial activities. Since these activities typically occur on land to which women do not have formal rights, they usually depend on a variety of sharing arrangements with men, both within and outside the immediate household.

Land reform processes in Namaqualand – mainly TRANCRAA and the municipal commonage programme – do not address the specific needs of women, which are not clearly articulated by anyone. These needs centre on land for poultry and vegetable production as well as for livestock production on a relatively small scale. The rights of women to family land also need to be strengthened. While TRANCRAA intends to strengthen the position of existing rights holders, it does not address entrenched social practices such as inheritance of land exclusively by males. The newly acquired municipal commonages might offer potential for improving women's access to land, if the land that is made available is close to where they live, inexpensive and suited to a variety of purposes, including cropping. The focus on semi-commercial or commercially oriented livestock should be accompanied by comprehensive support services for both new and existing women farmers. Such farmers need training, technical advice and access to credit. Women are not benefiting from land reform in Namaqualand at present, but if they had strong and independent access to land, they would be in a better position to contribute to the livelihoods of themselves and their families.

References

Anderson, M. and K. Pienaar. 2004. *Debating land reform and rural development: municipal commonage*, Policy Brief No. 6, Programme for Land and Agrarian Studies, University of the Western Cape.

Archer, F. 1993. 'Research about the future of Namaqualand: a preliminary report. A working document on the role of women in Namaqualand', discussion document, Cape Town, Surplus People Project.

Archer, F. and S. Meer. 1997. *'A woman's work is only recognised when it's done': women, land tenure and land reform in Namaqualand's coloured rural reserves*, Cape Town: Surplus People Project.

Benseler, A. 2004. 'The role of local government in common pool resource management: the case of municipal commonage in the Northern Cape', unpublished MA thesis, University of the Western Cape.

Boonzaier, E. 1980. 'Social differentiation in the Richtersveld, a Namaqualand rural area', unpublished MA thesis, University of Cape Town.

Kleinbooi, K. and E. Lahiff. 2007. 'Women's access to land in the communal areas of Namaqualand', *Journal of Arid Environments*, 70(1): 799–817.

Krohne, H. and L. Steyn. 1990. *Land use in Namaqualand: towards a community-based management strategy for agricultural use in the Namaqualand Reserves, Leliefontein, Steinkopf and the Richtersveld*, Cape Town: Surplus People Project.

Lebert, T. 2004. *Municipal commonage as a form of land redistribution: a case study of the new farms of Leliefontein, a communal reserve in Namaqualand, South Africa*, Research Report No. 18, Programme for Land and Agrarian Studies, University of the Western Cape.

Mann, M. 2000.*Women's access to land in the former bantustans: constitutional conflict, customary law, democratisation and the role of the state*, Occasional Paper No. 15, Programme for Land and Agrarian Studies, University of the Western Cape.

May, H. and E. Lahiff. 2007. 'Land reform in Namaqualand, 1994–2005: a review', *Journal of Arid Environments,* 70: 782–798.

Vedder, H. 1928. 'The Nama', in C. Hahn, H. Vedder and L. Fourie (eds) *The native tribes of South West Africa*, London: Cass & Co.

Wisborg, P. 2007. 'Land tenure reform in a Namaqualand rural area, South Africa: contesting Komaggas', in B. Derman, R. Odgaard and E. Sjaastad (eds) *Conflicts over land and water in Africa*, Oxford: James Currey.

Wisborg, P. and R. Rohde. 2004. *Contested land tenure reform in South Africa: the Namaqualand experience*, Occasional Paper Series No. 26, Programme for Land and Agrarian Studies, University of the Western Cape.

Wisborg, P. and R. Rohde. 2005. 'Contested tenure reform in South Africa: experiences from Namaqualand', *Development Southern Africa*, 22(5): 409–427.

Part 3

Competing knowledge regimes in communal area agriculture

14 What constitutes 'the agrarian' in rural Eastern Cape African settlements?

Paul Hebinck and Wim van Averbeke

In this chapter we examine what makes up the agrarian in present-day Guquka and Koloni, two rural African settlements located in the central part of the Eastern Cape, previously known as Ciskei. In our understanding, the agrarian presents itself in three important dimensions. Firstly, there is the economic dimension, where agrarian refers to agricultural activities and practices associated with farming and the provision of goods and services linked to it. Cultural landscape makes up the second dimension of the agrarian. Cultural landscape refers to specific patterns of land use – that is, the outcome of the interaction between people, their livelihoods and the physical landscape. In the literature this interaction is referred to as 'co-production' (Hebinck 2007; Van der Ploeg 2010, 2013) or 'co-evolution' (Norgaard 1994). Cultural landscape reflects how land resources are utilised and spatially organised. Lastly, there is the sociocultural dimension of agrarian, which refers to value systems, social networks, symbolism and cultural meanings of natural resource use. These three dimensions are interdependent and mutually shape one another. For this reason, they can be expected to change together.

The work presented in this chapter builds on the book edited by Hebinck and Lent that was published in 2007 and is largely based on two livelihood surveys conducted in 1996 and 2010 using the same instrument. These surveys enabled assessment of what constituted the agrarian in the two settlements during the post-apartheid period and the changes that had occurred in its composition during the 14-year period that separated the two surveys. Our findings confirm the weakening link between rural and agrarian in South Africa, described by many others. There is clear evidence of de-agrarianisation: long-term processes of occupational adjustment, income-earning reorientation, social identification and the spatial relocation of rural dwellers away from strictly agricultural modes of livelihood (Bryceson 2002). This reality contrasts sharply with the content of policy documents, which continues to equate the rural with the agrarian and assumes that rural areas are populated by farmers who work on the land and have livelihoods that revolve around cultivating crops and rearing livestock. The chapter starts with short summary descriptions of the livelihood resources at Guquka and

Koloni and the agrarian transformation that has occurred in these two villages. These descriptions are based on Hebinck and Lent (2007). They contextualise the empirical part of the chapter, in which the 'agrarian' in the two villages is analysed and the changes that have occurred during recent times are discussed. The findings show that the shift from production to simple reproduction and supplementing, which started many decades ago, is continuing.

Rural transformation in Guquka and Koloni: a brief history

Guquka

Guquka is located in the upper part of the Tyhume River valley in the shadow of the Hogsback Mountain in the former Victoria East Magisterial District. Receiving about 650 millimetres of rain annually, this area is suitable for dryland crop production. Oral evidence indicates that Guquka was first settled in around 1830. Cattle rearing dominated the farming system at that time with mountain pastures, forests and wetlands being used as feed resources. Maize and sorghum were cultivated on small parcels of land near the Tyhume River. Hunting and gathering were also important. Communal tenure[1] applied until 1899, when a land survey introduced new land-use categories and a new tenure system. The 1899 survey demarcated land for crops, referred to as garden lots or arable allotments, which were between three and four morgen (2.5 to 3.4 hectares) in size; and plots for residential purposes (building lots of about 2 500 square metres). The remaining land was designated as 'commonage'. Quitrent tenure, which is a form of individual tenure but with rights subject to the annual payment of a rental fee and use to the commonage being shared among the holders of quitrent deeds, was introduced. Throughout the nineteenth century the livelihoods of the people of Guquka remained agrarian.

During the twentieth century, livelihoods of people in Guquka became progressively diversified, mainly as a result of male migrancy. During the first half of the century, homestead production in Guquka was supported by remittances and by male migrants returning home from the mines specifically to plough their fields. Labour migration hinged on fairly well-defined cycles of working in urban areas and returning to rural homesteads. Time spent in the mines tended to coincide with the winter period, which enabled the men to remain actively engaged in cultivation at their homesteads during the summer months. Men invested part of their wages in cattle. From about 1930 onwards, however, the duration of mining contracts became longer and the visits to rural homesteads shorter. Returning home also increasingly coincided with the festive season around Christmas and New Year and visiting male migrants came to view their short stay at home as a holiday: a time to rest and participate in the social events that demanded their presence, rather than a time to toil behind a plough and span of oxen. Midsummer is also not the most appropriate time to plant crops, because it tends to coincide with a dry spell (Laker 2008). Aerial photographs confirm that fallowing of fields was fairly common as early as 1939. White farmers who occupied land across the river interacted with their black neighbours. A few of the men living in Guquka worked for white farmers and some of the women were employed as domestic workers in white homesteads. Men of Guquka purchased cattle from white farmers and borrowed threshers, sometimes in exchange for labour. White traders who operated in the area purchased grain from both black and white farmers. By 1970, all white farming families had left that part of the Tyhume valley, as a result of stricter implementation of the Native Trust and Land Act (No. 18 of 1936). This was also the time when Guquka farmers started to experience difficulties with marketing their produce.

Betterment planning[2] was implemented in Guquka after World War II. First, a few eroded fields were excised from the arable allotments and one homestead located on a steep hillside was relocated to the current site of the village. The second intervention occurred during the 1960s and involved subdivision of the commonage into grazing camps and the curtailment of livestock populations. Guquka residents resisted these state interventions. Fences that separated the grazing camps were stolen, re-erected and stolen again.[3] Next, the Department of Forestry fenced off part of the mountain pasture above the village and planted trees. This deprived the village cattle of a valuable feed resource. Again, the people from Guquka were up in arms and set fire to the young plantation, leading to a court case in which they were charged with committing arson. As a result of the loss of mountain pasture and the disastrous impact of the 1982/83 drought, the cattle herd of Guquka shrank considerably during the 1980s. During this period Guquka also experienced an influx of people who had been evicted from white-owned farms in the Border region.[4] These new settlers were provided with a residential site but lacked the right to arable land and to the use of the rangeland for the purpose of rearing livestock.

Koloni

Koloni forms part of the former Middledrift Magisterial District. Its climate and soils are poorly suited to rain-fed crop production. The natural vegetation makes it suitable for livestock farming. In contrast to Guquka, Koloni's history is associated with planned settlement by the British during the troubled period of the Frontier Wars during the 1850s and the accommodations that followed. While Koloni has had a similar history to Guquka with regard to labour migration and land cultivation, it did not have to accommodate a sudden influx of people from elsewhere in the region. Expansions of the village were largely planned and seemingly uncontested.

Koloni was established between 1853 and 1890, near the Perksdale Mission. The exact date is unknown and disputed. The presence of Perksdale Mission attracted dispersed Xhosa and small groups of Mfengu, who could then be found in every frontier town, on smallholdings, at mission stations and elsewhere. The area around Perksdale was surveyed in 1874 by order of the minister of native affairs. Categories of land use similar to those in Guquka were introduced. Settlement in Koloni was a gradual process in which families obtained land allocations when they had accumulated the necessary resources to do so.

In 1936, the principal of the nearby Fort Cox College of Agriculture suggested to the chief native commissioner that Koloni could be a suitable test case for betterment planning. In stark contrast with most other villages in the region, which opposed betterment, the people of Koloni showed interest and cooperated. As a result, the state favoured Koloni whenever it allocated resources. The arable land was terraced to conserve the soil; the perimeter of the arable allotments was fenced to protect crops from cattle; fodder plots were established; watering holes were expanded to ensure year-round water for livestock; separate bull camps were created to control reproduction; the cattle herd was improved by introducing the Shorthorn and Afrikaner breeds; and the rangeland was subdivided into camps to enable rotational grazing and resting. These interventions sought to ensure more constant cattle numbers and to balance stock herding with soil and water preservation measures. Betterment officials introduced 'good-quality' rams into the Koloni sheep flock to improve wool production, and farmers were trained in sheep-shearing and wool-classing, and assisted in marketing the village clip. There was also the imposed reduction in livestock numbers (Figure 14.1). A Ciskei betterment report (Bantu Affairs Commission 1962) states that '… stock numbers have been determined and the carrying capacity fixed, and stock culling has already been applied'. Since local people hated to let go of their cattle – people in Koloni were no exception – and goat ownership was still prohibited at that time, sheep were selected for disposal to achieve the imposed reduction in livestock numbers. This probably explains the substantial reduction in the number of sheep between 1938 and 1961 (Figure 14.1).

Figure 14.1 Livestock numbers in Koloni, 1938–2010

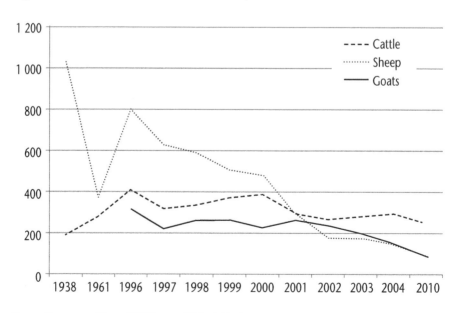

Source: Bennett and Lent (2007); unpublished 2010 survey

Koloni's inhabitants were first in line when tractor services became available. Aerial photographs of the village taken in 1963 suggest that the terraced arable land was cultivated using heavy equipment. Cultivation was diversified to prevent the traditional monoculture of maize or sorghum. Oral evidence indicates that until the end of the 1960s there was 'no need to seek work elsewhere', because crop and livestock production provided more income and satisfaction than could be obtained from migrant labour.

The decline in arable production occurred during the 1970s. Most homesteads lost access to draught animal power, especially that of oxen. The 'inability to plough' resulted from the decline in livestock numbers, set in motion by the compulsory culling of herds. During recent times, there has been a further decline in livestock numbers, notably sheep. More than 800 animals were held at the village in 1996, but this had dropped to 153 animals in 2004, and to just 79 in 2010. Theft was the main reason for this recent drop in livestock numbers (Bennett and Lent 2007).

How agrarian are contemporary rural African settlements in the central Eastern Cape?

To answer this question, information collected in Guquka and Koloni from 1996 to 2010 was analysed, using agriculture and land use, cultural landscape, and socio-cultural expressions of the agrarian as themes. The initial idea of dealing with each theme separately before attempting integration was abandoned in favour of an integrated approach, which acknowledges the interrelatedness of these themes. Accordingly, livelihoods and land-use activities were used as organising themes and issues regarding landscape and sociocultural aspects are raised under these themes where appropriate.

Rural livelihoods
Table 14.1 summarises the various sources of income for Guquka and Koloni homesteads in 1996 and in 2010. Sources of income and their relative contribution to total homestead income are an indicator of the way in which livelihoods are structured. The table shows that in both 1996 and 2010, homestead income in the two villages was largely (75 per cent to 90 per cent) derived in cash and from sources external to the village. Important sources of such income were social grants, remittances and wages, but this phenomenon is not new. More than 60 years ago (Houghton 1955) rural incomes in the region already depended largely on externally derived monetary income (79.3 per cent) (Houghton 1955), but at that time remittances were considerably more important (49.4 per cent) than in recent years (8.7 per cent to 13.4 per cent). Salaries and wages rose in importance during the homeland era (1970–1990). In 1990, this source contributed on average 38.6 per cent to the income of rural homesteads in the Ciskei region and had overtaken remittances (32.1 per cent) as the most important source (Fabricius and McWilliams 1991). Salaries and wages have retained their relative importance as a source of income in both villages, but only

a minority of homesteads had salaries and wages as an income source (Table 14.1). This is particularly evident in Koloni, where the relative contribution of salaries and wages to total income rose from 39.1 per cent in 1996 to 48.6 per cent in 2010, but the number of homesteads who derived income from this source dropped from 20 in 1996 to 14 in 2010. Field data indicated a rise in qualification-based professionalisation among those in paid employment, resulting in higher remuneration levels.

Table 14.1 Relative contribution of various sources of income to total income and number of homesteads deriving income from these sources, Guquka and Koloni, 1996 and 2010

Income sources	Guquka				Koloni			
	1996 N=76		2010 N=58		1996 N=54		2010 N=51	
	(%)	n	(%)	n	(%)	n	(%)	n
Remittances	13.4	23	13.1	22	8.7	40	12.1	20
Pensions and grants	41.8	32	41.9	46	26.5	40	29.5	36
Salaries and wages	35.4	13	36.0	24	39.1	20	48.6	14
Agriculture	6.7	43	6.1	42	12.1	40	8.2	42
Other village-based economic activities	2.7	17	3.0	5	13.5	20	1.7	5
Total	100.0		100.0		100.0		100.0	

Source: Unpublished 1996 and 2010 surveys

In 1990, social grants, mostly in the form of old age pensions, contributed on average 20.5 per cent to the income of rural homesteads in the region (Fabricius and McWilliams 1991). Table 14.1 shows that the importance of this source has since increased. In Guquka it was the main source of income in both 1996 and 2010, and the fact that a large proportion of homesteads derived income from this source in both villages is also significant.

The data in Table 14.1 further demonstrate that as a source of homestead income, agriculture was not important in either of the two villages. In Guquka, the contributions made by agriculture in 1996 and 2010 were similar, ranging between 6 per cent and 7 per cent, whilst in Koloni there was a drop from 12.1 per cent in 1996 to 8.2 per cent in 2010, which tracked the decline in livestock (sheep) numbers over the same period. The relative contribution of agriculture to total homestead income in the Ciskei region has declined compared to 60 years ago, when agriculture contributed about 20 per cent. Nonetheless, a large proportion of homesteads continue to derive some income from agriculture: as Table 14.1 shows, between 1996 and 2010 their absolute numbers remained more or less constant in both villages, against a background of declining numbers of homesteads as a result of outmigration. This indicates that agricultural activities continue to play a role in the livelihoods of rural homesteads in the region.

Agrarian activities

Table 14.2 presents the participation rates of homesteads in the two villages in five agrarian activities, using reported material benefits as the indicator of this participation. The table shows that between 60 and 70 per cent of homesteads were growing crops for own consumption in both settlements, and between 30 and 50 per cent reared animals for this purpose.

Table 14.2 Participation rates (%) of homesteads in various agrarian activities through material benefits derived from these activities, Guquka and Koloni, 1996 and 2010

	Guquka		Koloni	
	1996	2010	1996	2010
	N=76	N=58	N=54	N=51
	(%)	(%)	(%)	(%)
Growing crops for own consumption	72	64	61	61
Growing crops for sale	17	12	19	12
Rearing animals for own consumption	29	50	33	41
Rearing animals for cash	13	15	50	31
Gathering*	75	75	78	80

Source: Unpublished 1996 and 2010 surveys

Note: * The data on gathering were obtained from the unpublished, 1996 survey and an unpublished 2005 survey.

Farming for the purpose of selling produce was less common, except for animal production in Koloni, in which 50 per cent of homesteads participated in 1996, dropping to 30 per cent in 2010. Participation in the production of crops for sale was low in both villages, ranging between roughly 10 and 20 per cent, and when the 1996 and 2010 data are compared, there is evidence of a declining trend.

Cultivation of crops

Crops can be grown in arable fields and home gardens, but Figure 14.2 shows that few fields were still being cropped and that the number of cropped fields had declined substantially between 1996 and 2010 in both villages. 'Fallow' and 'fallowing' are not part of the local discourse, nor is underutilisation. Instead, people refer to their fallowed allotments as fields that have not been 'ploughed', suggesting that the land is in a state of waiting to serve its intended purpose. Theoretically, growing crops is intimately connected to land ownership and land–people arrangements to access land. However, landlessness is not the prime factor for the very low cropping intensity on the arable allotments, because landlessness affects only 7 per cent of homesteads in Koloni and 39 per cent in Guquka. 'Absenteeism', which refers to an entire homestead that has left the village without transferring its arable and residential land to someone else, has been on the rise since 2000 and could have contributed to the declining cropping intensity on the arable allotments, although local accounts indicate that in Koloni absenteeism had already occurred soon after the place was settled.

Figure 14.2 Proportion (%) of total number of arable allotments cropped, Guquka and Koloni, 1996–2010

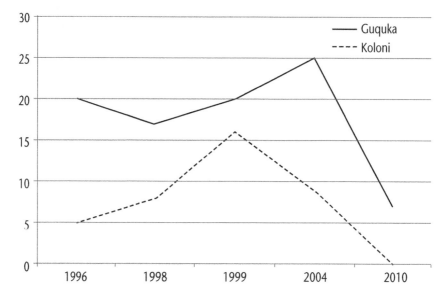

Source: Unpublished 1996 and 2010 surveys

Lack of access to resources other than land is probably the main reason for the lack of cultivation on arable land. In isiXhosa, cultivation of crops is referred to as 'ploughing'. Being 'able to plough' indicates access not only to land but also to labour and the means to plough. The monetary and social resources to hire a tractor or organise the animal draught power, labour and implements needed to cultivate the land are not readily available to all. 'No money to plough' is the usual answer to the question of why cultivation on the arable allotments has all but disappeared. No money to hire tractors or oxen to plough, or to buy seed, insecticides, fertiliser or manure and fencing, is what is really meant by this state-ment. The ageing population of landholders is another factor. When one gets older, 'one loses the power to work', a farmer in Koloni once remarked during a conversation about the decline of crop production in the village. When an alter-native source of labour (family or hired) is not available or affordable, 'ploughing' is no longer feasible.

The widespread fallowing of arable allotments has made home gardens the locus of crop production, but levels of production are limited by the small size of the gardens. On residential plots, the area that is cultivated typically ranges between 50 and 500 square metres. Accordingly, crop production contributes only a very small fraction to the food consumed by homesteads. The lion's share is purchased in town and replenishment of food stores is closely tied to the 'paydays' of salaries, wages or social grants. On these paydays, it is common in both settlements to see local taxis offloading passengers carrying bags of maize, cooking oil, sugar, canned food and other groceries that have been purchased in town. As the taxi arrives in the village, children come running out of the houses, pushing wheelbarrows to help transport the food to the homestead. Similarly, when crops are sold, usually to neighbours, the income earned is of little significance and typically is used to buy other food items or to take care of school fees. The use of fresh produce as gifts to neighbours, friends and homesteads in need, however, remains common practice.

The production of crops in home gardens is traditional practice among rural homesteads in the central Eastern Cape and has not replaced cropping on arable allotments (Houghton 1955). For this reason, cultivation in parts of the residential site should be viewed as a remnant of the historical cultural landscape and not as a recent addition. What is new, though, are the extensions onto commonage land, which some homesteads in Guquka have made to their residential sites. These extensions do not exceed 1 000 square metres, are fenced in and are invariably used to produce crops, primarily maize.

Rearing of animals

As in the past, ruminant livestock (cattle, sheep and goats) graze and browse on the commonage, whilst monogastric livestock species (poultry and pigs) are reared on the residential sites. However, in both villages livestock numbers and the proportion of homesteads that keep livestock have declined since 1996, goats in Guquka being the only exception (Table 14.3). Of particular significance is the dramatic reduction in the number of sheep in both Guquka and Koloni, the complete disappearance of equines in Koloni and the near-total collapse of pig production in Guquka.

The reduction in the number of ruminants in both villages is not due to limitations in forage and grazing. Stocking rates in the past were much higher (see Figure 14.1). Moreover, the fallowing of the arable allotments has expanded the grazing and forage resources available to livestock.

Interviews with participants indicate that the high risk of losing livestock through theft, on occasion involving violence, was the primary reason for the declining number of ruminants in the villages. Another factor that could have contributed to the particularly sharp decline in sheep numbers was the relative stability of the nominal price of wool during the period 1996 to 2010. This meant that inflation gradually eroded the real value of wool, making its production increasingly less lucrative. The disappearance of equines, mostly horses, in Koloni could be an indicator that monitoring livestock on the rangeland, which was often done on horseback, has become less intense in that village.

The virtual collapse of pig production in Guquka (from 82 in 1996 to just 8 in 2010) could be associated with the virtual abandonment of crop production on the arable allotments. In the central Eastern Cape, pigs are mostly reared in order to make money from selling meat. To support their growth, pigs are usually fed primarily maize grain.

Table 14.3 Livestock numbers and ownership (%), Guquka and Koloni, 1996 and 2010

	Guquka				Koloni			
	1996 N=76		2010 N=58		1996 N=54		2010 N=51	
	n	%	n	%	n	%	n	%
Cattle	154	30.3	131	22.4	286	55.6	248	51.0
Sheep	212	15.8	24	5.2	381	33.3	95	11.8
Goats	51	14.5	115	15.5	172	40.7	92	19.6
Horses/donkeys	6	3.9	2	3.4	14	11.1	0	0.0
Chickens	349	60.5	263	36.2	265	48.1	204	35.3
Pigs	82	43.4	8	5.3	11	22.2	4	7.8

Source: Unpublished 1996 and 2010 surveys

Cattle occupy a special place in the lives of people in the Eastern Cape. Besides their economic value (draught power, milk, investment), cattle also have a strong and shared cultural meaning. Rituals associated with male circumcision, marriage and death call for the slaughtering of a beast, which has to be purchased if it cannot be acquired from the own herd. Meeting the expectations associated with these rituals can place a considerable financial burden on homesteads, and this burden has been exacerbated by the rise in HIV/AIDS-related deaths. Local demand for cattle provides the main marketing opportunity for those who have cattle. Interestingly, young men, especially those who have been exposed to urban lifestyles, claim that they are no longer interested in accumulating cattle the way their fathers did. They prefer to put energy and resources into educational opportunities to enhance their chances of entry into the urban labour market.

Gathering of plants

The rangeland, the (fallowed) arable allotments and the home gardens are a source of wood fuel, herbs, wild vegetables, medicinal plants, clay dung and thatch (Lent 2007). Most homesteads take part in the gathering of these livelihood resources. Wood fuel is collected primarily from the commonage and is done by women. People of Guquka have to travel quite a distance to get to parts that are wooded, but in Koloni there is an abundance of thorn bush, and woody species have even colonised the arable allotments. The thick main stems of woody species are used as fuel for cooking and heating. Most homesteads have a sizeable stockpile (*igogo*) of this fuel on the residential site. The thinner branches of trees and shrubs are used to construct livestock enclosures (kraals) and to support wire fences around home gardens, with a view to making them impenetrable to poultry, pigs and goats. Livestock enclosures are located within the boundaries of the residential allotment or immediately adjacent to it when space is available.

Various plants or plant parts are collected for use in personal hygiene practices and for the treatment of human and livestock ailments. In 2005 in Guquka, a total of 65 different plant species were utilised for these purposes. People also collect weedy species for use as a vegetable (*imifino*). Among these, sow-thistle (*Sonchus* spp.), pigweed (*Amaranthus cruentus*), goosefoot (*Chenopodium* spp.), nightshade (*Solanum nigrum*) and stinging nettle (*Urtica urens*) were the most commonly used to prepare local dishes. Thatch grass, almost exclusively harvested from the fallow arable allotments, is used for roofing or as insulation under corrugated iron roof-sheets. A few homesteads buy thatch from local harvesters.

What makes up the agrarian in present-day rural African settlements in the central part of the Eastern Cape?

People in Guquka and Koloni largely rely on sources other than agriculture to make a living. In 2010, about 80 per cent of average homestead income in the two settlements consisted of salaries, wages and social grants. The contribution of salaries and wages, which was more or less the same as that of social grants, was important to a minority of homesteads only, most of them in civil service employment. Social-grant income, on the other hand, was widespread and the most important source for the majority of homesteads. The contribution of income from crop and animal production, in cash and kind, in 2010 was about 6 per cent in Guquka and 8 per cent in Koloni. On the whole, these findings indicate that contemporary rural homesteads in the two settlements no longer had agrarian livelihoods.

The extent of de-agrarianisation of livelihood activities was most aptly illustrated by the near-total abandonment of crop production on the arable allotments. Producing crops on a scale of one to three hectares requires homesteads to mobilise land, labour and capital, locally referred to as the 'ability to plough', and the evidence presented shows that all but a few no longer had the ability to plough, or that they were no longer interested in mobilising the necessary resources to plough, because of old age, alternative occupations or, in the case of the youth, an urban-oriented outlook on life. Due to migration, often drifting between rural and urban without securing a foothold in either environment, labour was only a temporal or a virtual resource, because many of those who could provide labour were in a mental state of 'waiting to leave', and this could happen anytime. Investing time and effort in the labour process of growing crops, which would last at least six months, would imply acceptance that moving to the city would not be for tomorrow. This idea was unacceptable, especially among the youth. Homesteads lacking one or more essential resources to 'plough', be it land, labour or capital, are not new in the region. In the past, reciprocity and collaboration among homesteads enabled them to deal with such resource constraints (Houghton 1955; McAllister 2001), but this ability appears not to exist any longer. At present, most of the crop production that still occurs takes place on small parcels of land located within or adjacent to residential sites. Cultivation is done using spades and hand hoes, and considering the small scale of production, this activity is best described as home gardening.

The rearing of ruminants on the commonage persists but animal numbers have dropped to historical lows. This applies particularly to sheep, which until about 1970 provided monetary income from wool sales. The risk of losing livestock due to theft appeared to be the principal reason for the decline in livestock numbers. The rearing of micro-livestock (poultry and pigs) has also diminished, probably due to the abandonment of field cropping, which provided homesteads with access to animal feed.

Gathering from 'nature' is still a widespread practice and has both economic (utilitarian) and cultural value (Cocks and Wiersum 2003). Gathering still helps to secure the reproduction of the homestead and cushion the homestead against extreme poverty (Shackleton and Shackleton 2011). However, most of the products obtained by gathering are consumed directly in the homestead and little, if any of it, is ever sold and barter trade is virtually absent. Migration and urbanisation and the urban orientation of food acquisition, with people in the villages getting increasingly used to purchasing their food in town, could reduce the importance of gathering as a livelihood activity, because gathering is embedded in the indigenous knowledge system, which relies on generational transfer for its reproduction (Faber et al. 2012).

Given the low intensity of contemporary agrarian activities and the limited contribution of these activities to homestead incomes, it is appropriate to refer to the majority of rural African homesteaders in the two villages, and probably also in other parts of the central Eastern Cape, as rural dwellers and not as peasants or smallholder farmers. Wage earners and homesteads with multiple social grants are among the relatively rich, whilst those without any of these sources of income struggle to make ends meet. The value of salaries, wages and social grants has been adjusted annually to account for inflation, stabilising the purchasing power of the majority of rural homesteads, which is important as most food needs are satisfied through cash exchanges. This picture of contemporary rural people in Guquka and Koloni is not unique to the two villages. As is evident from the case study of De Wet (2011) in Chata (Keiskammahoek), it probably applies to most other parts of the central Eastern Cape as well.

The decline in agrarian activities has impacted visibly on the cultural landscape. Abandonment of crop production on the arable allotments has resulted in the establishment of a grass-dominated cover on these plots, and in Koloni bush encroachment has also occurred. Land use has changed from actively working the land to harvesting nature, be it by livestock grazing or browsing or by people gathering products for various uses. New also, albeit limited in extent, is the excising of small parcels of land within the residential area for the purpose of producing crops on a small but convenient scale. Overall these changes in land use have blurred the once sharp lines that divided the landscape into the three distinct land-use categories (commonage, arable and residential) which had been imposed by the authorities at various stages in the histories of the two villages. In a way, the cultural landscape appears to be reverting back to pre-colonial patterns. Environmentally, these changes, especially the abandonment of 'ploughing', are beneficial because the establishment of natural vegetation on the arable allotments protects them against soil erosion.

Cultural repertoires in the form of rituals and ceremonies remain important in both villages. Many former residents who work and live in the city return home during the festive seasons of Easter and especially Christmas. It is during these special times that most rituals and ceremonies take place. However, the persistent ties of people with the rural place have more to do with cultural traditions than with agrarian repertoires.

The rural reality described in this chapter indicates that new and creative thinking and policy processes are needed to revive the agrarian in African rural settlements of the central Eastern Cape. Land is underutilised and opportunities to generate agrarian livelihoods are available. Land, particularly arable land, is locked up and ways to free this land need to be found. Old landowners, who constitute the majority, might be convinced to lease their land or engage in sharecropping relations. Likewise, migrants who hold land might be convinced that land improvements, such as irrigation, hold opportunities for increasing the economic value of the land. Recent fieldwork (Van der Horst 2013) has shown that landowners were open to the idea of availing their arable allotments to others provided valuable and viable options were on offer.

Notes

1   'The essence of communal tenure is that members of a settlement share certain rights in the land attached to their settlement [...and] have exclusive rights to this land for as long as they are domiciled in the settlement. Rights may be inherited but cannot be sold' (Mills and Wilson 1952: 8).

2   The key concern of betterment planning was to protect and rehabilitate natural resources. Government introduced policies aimed at limiting livestock numbers to address perceived denudation of the rangeland, and engaged in the construction of contour banks in an attempt to prevent soil erosion. Implementation started in the late 1930s, but was subject to much resistance, thus proceeding rather slowly. At a later stage, betterment objectives were broadened to include education and health (Beinart 2003; De Wet 1989).

3   The few times Guquka can be traced in the Cape colonial archives is when fences were reported stolen and a budget was drafted to ask for funds to re-erect them.

4   The Border region covers the area to the west and the east of the Kei River. During the colonial period, the area was heavily contested between the colonial state and Xhosa settlers.

References

Bantu Affairs Commission. 1962. Reclamation and settlement of Koloni Location, File no. 60 N2/11/3/12. Middledrift District, King William's Town.

Beinart, W. 2003. *The rise of conservation in South Africa: settlers, livestock, and the environment 1770–1950*, New York: Oxford University Press.

Bennett, J. and P. Lent. 2007. 'Livestock production and forage resources', in P. Hebinck and P. Lent (eds) *Livelihoods and landscapes: the people of Guquka and Koloni and their resources*, Leiden/Boston: Brill Academic Publishers.

Bryceson, D. 2002. 'The scramble in Africa: reorienting rural livelihoods', *World Development*, 30(5): 725–739.

Cocks, M.L. and K. Wiersum. 2003. 'The significance of plant diversity to rural households in Eastern Cape province of South Africa', *Forests, Trees and Livelihoods*, 13(1): 39–58.

De Wet, C. 1989. 'Betterment planning in a rural village in Keiskammmahoek District, Ciskei', *Journal of Southern African Studies*, 15(2): 326–345.

De Wet, C. 2011. 'Where are they now? Welfare, development and marginalisation in a former bantustan settlement in the Eastern Cape, post-1994', in P. Hebinck and C. Shackleton (eds) *Reforming land and resource use in South Africa: impact on livelihoods*, London: Routledge.

Faber, M., A. Oelofse, P. van Jaarsveld, F. Wenhold and W. Jansen van Rensburg. 2012. 'Availability and household consumption of African leafy vegetables at selected sites in KwaZulu-Natal and Limpopo provinces', in A. Oelofse and W. van Averbeke (eds) *Nutritional value and water use of African leafy vegetables for improved livelihoods*, Gezina: Water Research Commission.

Fabricius, M. and J. McWilliams. 1991. *Population development survey of five magisterial districts in the Republic of Ciskei*, Research Report 42, Institute for Planning Research, University of Port Elizabeth.

Hebinck, P. 2007. 'Investigating rural livelihoods and landscapes in Guquka and Koloni: an introduction', in P. Hebinck and P. Lent (eds) *Livelihoods and landscapes: the people of Guquka and Koloni and their resources*, Leiden/Boston: Brill Academic Publishers.

Hebinck, P. and P. Lent (eds). 2007. *Livelihoods and landscapes: the people of Guquka and Koloni and their resources*, Leiden/Boston: Brill Academic Publishers.

Houghton, D.H. 1955. *Life in the Ciskei: a summary of the findings of the Keiskammahoek rural survey 1947–51*, Johannesburg: South African Institute of Race Relations.

Laker, M.C. 2008. 'Challenges to small fertility management in the "third major soil region of the world", with special reference to South Africa', in S. Haneklaus, C. Hera, R-M. Rietz and E. Schnug (eds) *Fertilizers and fertilization for sustainability in agriculture: the First World meets the Third World – challenges for the future*, Iasi, Romania: Terra Nostra.

Lent, P. 2007. 'Gathering from the land', in P. Hebinck and P. Lent (eds) *Livelihoods and landscapes: the people of Guquka and Koloni and their resources*, Leiden/Boston: Brill Academic Publishers.

McAllister, P. 2001. *Building the homestead: agriculture, labour and beer in South Africa's Transkei*, Aldershot: Ashgate.

Mills, M. and W. Wilson. 1952. *Land tenure, Keiskammahoek rural survey vol. 4.* Pietermaritzburg: Shuter and Shooter.

Norgaard, R. 1994. *Development betrayed: the end of progress and a coevolutionary revisioning of the future*, London: Routledge.

Shackleton, C. and S. Shackleton. 2011. 'Exploring the role of wild natural resources in poverty alleviation with an emphasis on South Africa', in P. Hebinck and C. Shackleton (eds) *Reforming land and resource use in South Africa: impact on livelihoods*, London: Routledge.

Van der Horst, B. 2013. 'Land, people, livelihoods: irrigation', unpublished MSc thesis, Wageningen University, the Netherlands.

Van der Ploeg, J.D. 2010. 'The peasantries of the twenty-first century: the commoditisation debate revisited', *Journal of Peasant Studies*, 37(1): 1–30.

Van der Ploeg, J.D. 2013. *Peasants and the art of farming: a Chayanovian manifesto*, Black Point, Nova Scotia: Fernwood Publishers.

15 The Massive Food Production Programme: a case study of agricultural policy continuities and changes

Klara Jacobson

The main purpose of this chapter is to explain why recent agricultural development interventions have been largely unsuccessful in improving the lives of the rural poor (Aliber and Hall 2012; Hajdu et al. 2012; Jacobson 2009). The chapter presents a critical discourse analysis (Chouliaraki and Fairclough 1999; Fairclough 1995, 2001) of the Massive Food Production Programme (MFPP), implemented by the Eastern Cape Department of Agriculture[1] from 2003 onwards. Case material from three villages where the MFPP has been operative will provide some empirical contexts to debate the extent to which the MFPP has managed to break with the heavily criticised apartheid development interventions in the region and to critically examine the assumptions underlying the formation of the MFPP. The MFPP's major aim is to reduce rural poverty by raising crop yields. The programme has experienced many practical problems, such as the delayed payment of funds which resulted in late planting, which in turn led to failure in raising yields and reducing poverty. These practical failures have been acknowledged both by programme management (Jacobson 2009), in an external audit, and in other publications on the programme (Damgaard Hansen 2006; Hajdu et al. 2012; Masifunde Education and Development Project Trust 2010). I argue, however, that in order to understand why the programme has failed to achieve its aims we need to focus, not on its practical implementation problems, but on the underlying assumptions about how smallholder agriculture should be transformed (Hajdu et al. 2012; Jacobson 2009).

The MFPP, its aims and guiding assumptions

The analysis in this chapter draws on 11 policy documents on the MFPP, acquired either directly from the senior manager for resource planning at the Eastern Cape Department of Agriculture, who was the administrative head of the MFPP at the time of its initiation (6 documents), or from other researchers investigating the MFPP (5 documents). The department's 'Strategic Plan 2003–2006' (ECDA 2003) guided agricultural development in the province at the time when the MFPP was implemented in the villages studied for this chapter. The strategic plan is included in the analysis to reveal the extent to which the ideas about agricultural development and smallholder farming presented in the MFPP are specific to the programme or representative of the policy view at provincial level.

The aim of the MFPP is to alleviate poverty and improve food security by raising agricultural yields, increasing market orientation and reducing degradation in targeted areas (ECDA n.d., 2005). The goals are spelled out in the 'Massive Food Programme: Notes and Observations 2004' (ECDA 2004a: 1, 2), a document issued by the Eastern Cape Department of Agriculture: the MFPP should fundamentally transform smallholder agriculture through employing two strategies – namely, introducing 'modern technologies' and making smallholders see farming as a business. The 'modern technologies' included high-yielding hybrid or genetically modified (GM) maize seeds, chemical fertiliser, and the control of weeds and pests either by chemicals and/or by the introduction of herbicide-resistant or insect-resistant GM crops (Hobson 2004; Jacobson and Myhr 2013). The MFPP 2004 documents promoted the 'modern technologies' and 'scientifically based technical solutions' because these are understood to be superior to and fundamentally better than the so-called traditional production methods that are currently used by the targeted smallholders, as these methods only 'lead to massive soil erosion and land degradation, rendering many thousands of hectares of lands useless' (ECDA 2004a: 3).

A core reason for the low agricultural production in the target areas was, according to the MFPP, that smallholders had become dependent on government support and therefore did not take responsibility for their own farming. This dependency had allegedly been created by pre-democratic agricultural interventions:

> Too often, enthusiastic, sympathetic and well-intentioned Government grants have had a negative effect on the very entrepreneurs who should be enhanced; these grants tend to create a dependency syndrome, which is counterproductive to truly stimulating sustainable economic growth in rural communities. (ECDA 2002: 3)

The MFPP envisioned itself to be radically different from these schemes:

> the Schemes [the MFPP] must be communicated in a manner which emphasises their essential difference from the past Tractor Schemes ... These new Schemes are to produce entrepreneurs and self-sustaining food production for local and export requirements. (ECDA 2002: 6)

To eradicate dependency, the MFPP introduced grant conditionality to ensure that smallholders would take responsibility for their situation (ECDA 2004b). Grants were supplied only on condition that beneficiaries followed programme guidelines. Smallholders would have to contribute increasing financial amounts towards input costs as the programme proceeded (as described in more detail in chapter 16, this volume). The idea was that as yields increased due to the use of 'modern' inputs and the business-oriented approach to agriculture, smallholders would have the financial means to pay for the inputs themselves after five years (Jacobson 2009).

It should be highlighted that while previous governments were explicitly given responsibility for the allegedly widespread dependency syndrome, structural limitations to farming in the targeted areas, such as lack of market access, land or credit, are not once explicitly described in the documents as being the result of past or present government policies. Thus the picture that emerges from the documents is that smallholder agriculture is underproducing because smallholders are employing backward agricultural methods and do not take responsibility for increasing agricultural production since they have been trained to rely on grants.

The Eastern Cape Department of Agriculture 'Strategic Plan 2003–2006', like the MFPP policy documents, emphasises the importance of 'changing of the mindset of the average farmer, our primary client, from the culture of entitlement to that of a proactive trendsetter and business leader' (ECDA 2003: 13). There is a sense that officials and experts know better than locals how to manage local resources and thus the strategy aims to plan rural agriculture from above. The local situation is pictured as one of 'conditions of sustained internal decay and low motivation' (ECDA 2003: 6). In contrast to this picture, situating smallholder farming in a historical context reveals that the long-term systematic discrimination against smallholders has greatly reduced the possibility for farming in the former homelands. A historical perspective also reveals strong continuities in the way that smallholder farming and agricultural development are portrayed in policy.

The history of agricultural production in the former Transkei

The Natives Land Act, passed in 1913, marked the beginning of the implementation of a series of increasingly comprehensive discriminatory policies. These policies deliberately undermined African farmers in order to reduce their competitiveness, and access to land was restricted in order to force Africans out of agriculture so that they would become a source of cheap labour for the mining industry. Colonial farmers were simultaneously encouraged by state subsidies, the availability of credit facilities and improved infrastructure (Bundy 1988). The process of undermining African agriculture culminated in the implementation of the homeland system by the apartheid government in the 1950s. The homelands confined the majority of the population to only 13 per cent of the land in the country (Kepe 2009). The chronic shortage of land, in combination with local labour shortages due to the enforced migration for wage work, clearly limited the possibility to live off agriculture in the homelands. Farming in the homelands was dependent on money and labour from the migrant mineworkers and seldom met even subsistence needs (Bundy 1988; McAllister 1992).

The guiding assumptions of the MFPP in a historical perspective

Low agricultural production and land degradation in the homelands resulting from the discriminatory government policies became a problem to those in power when it threatened to undermine the capacity of the homelands to provide cheap labour (Hendricks 1990). Beginning with the Betterment Proclamation in 1939, various government programmes aimed to address the problem of low agricultural production and degradation of agricultural land in the homelands. As in the contemporary MFPP, the local situation was attributed to the inhabitants' unsustainable farming methods, and the solution was seen to lie in top-down planning, reorganising local communities and teaching homeland residents economically viable and environmentally sustainable farming practices (Fay 2003a; Hendricks 1990). In contrast to their envisioned improvement of agriculture and rural livelihoods, these schemes have been criticised for further undermining local possibilities to derive a living from farming (Aliber and Mokoena 2003; Beinart 1984; Beinart 2002; Bernstein 1997; De Wet 1990; McAllister 1992). For example, many people had expanded their gardens as labour shortages made it hard to sustain agricultural production in the field (Andrew and Fox 2004). The consolidation of villages made this impossible (McAllister 1992) at the same time as the relocations during betterment often resulted in increased distance between the homestead and the fields (De Wet 1990). The relocation of houses and fields also meant considerable economic costs and hard manual work for rebuilding houses and breaking new land for farming (McAllister 1992). It is important to mention that local people did not passively accept all the changes imposed by these programmes, and indeed this meant that they seldom were implemented as fully as originally planned. Both more quiet struggles, such as breach of contracts and various forms of non-collaboration, as well as numbers of accounts of violent rural resistance, including the Pondoland uprisings (Bundy 1988; Hendricks 1990), bear testimony to this. Regarding the strong focus on reducing degradation, it is also important to acknowledge that the degree of the problem of land degradation in the homelands has been debated and that the degradation problem was also acknowledged as a problem in 'white' farmer areas. Furthermore it has been claimed that state interventions to reduce erosion in the homelands simply worsened the problem (Beinart 1984).

The maize production schemes, described by De Wet (1990), also intended to increase agricultural production through top-down-planned-and-implemented schemes in the homelands. As in the MFPP, large-scale commercial farming was the blueprint and agricultural production was to be raised through mechanisation, the introduction of hybrid seeds and agrochemical inputs. This top-down planning and implementation undermined local agricultural practices, and the large-scale commercially oriented design reduced the flexibility of local land use. The costly inputs used meant that while economic gains were made in good years, years when there were unfavourable rain patterns or severe pest outbreaks resulted in economic loss. Those who did not have sufficient funds to create a buffer for variations between years thus often became indebted to the schemes. The fact that programmes encouraged people to exchange their local maize varieties for high-yielding but fertiliser-dependent and costly hybrid varieties (De Wet 1990) is likely to have exacerbated the effects of environmental fluctuations, as hybrid varieties developed for large-scale farming often are less tolerant to environmental fluctuations than locally used varieties (Mercer et al. 2012). Monoculture plantings and the ban on picking green maize further undermined subsistence needs (De Wet 1990). The combined effects of the betterment programmes were that the possibility of subsistence agriculture often was reduced (De Wet 1990; Hajdu 2006). The MFPP, while claiming to be something radically different from these past schemes, still employs almost exactly the same top-down approach and introduces the same tools and practices without considering their compatibility with local social and ecological contexts. As the next section reveals, the effect of this is a failed programme which, if it had been fully accepted by smallholders, would, like its predecessors, have reduced the flexibility of local land use and the possibility of agriculture to provide for subsistence.

Contemporary rural livelihoods: case material from three villages participating in the MFPP

The data drawn on here were collected during five months of fieldwork between 2006 and 2009 in three villages participating in the MFPP. The material includes 265 household surveys, participant observation and in-depth interviews with selected households. A fuller description of the materials and methods can be found in Jacobson (2009).

The three villages in this case study belong to the same traditional authority and are located in the former Transkei homeland region of the present-day Eastern Cape province. The case study locality is deeply rural: the nearest town is a 40-minute drive away, using local minibus-taxi transport on a dirt road of variable quality. After the betterment reorganisations in 1977, every household has a small garden, and most households have a field in the designated field area. The distance between households and fields varies from a couple of hundred metres to several kilometres. There is no piped water or electricity, so people have to carry water from streams and collect firewood, which is important even in households that can afford paraffin and gas. Chores like this take up a considerable amount of time, especially in poorer households who cannot use cattle or pay for labour to perform these tasks.

While agriculture was important for subsistence in virtually all households, the forced adaptation to labour migration in agriculture, the betterment reorganisations of land and the lack of infrastructure and extension services had led to a subordinate role for agricultural production in providing a livelihood for many households. Monetary incomes, mainly from welfare payments but also from remittances, local business and employment, were commonly regarded as more important and as a prerequisite for being able to engage in farming. As described by Fay (chapter 18, this volume), welfare payments were of key importance in the context of a shrinking availability of wage employment.

Smallholders repeatedly emphasised the importance of having an income for being able to farm the field. An analysis of the effects of poverty[2] on agricultural production confirmed this. Poor households were significantly less likely to plant their field: in 2008, 81 per cent of the wealthiest households cultivated their fields but only 56 per cent of the poorest ones did so. There were a range of reasons for this. Poor households had significantly fewer cattle than wealthier households. As a result they commonly relied on others for ploughing and thus planted late, when cattle were available. Many poor households also failed to plant because they did not possess their own cattle for ploughing, and were unable to pay others to plough for them. While average household size did not differ significantly between wealth groups, poorer households also experienced labour shortages to a greater extent than the wealthier. They were harder hit by disease and as a result of their monetary poverty they had to spread their labour more thinly to access sufficient resources, which negatively affected their capacity to engage in farming. While the wealthier households could use their own cattle and pay for extra labour, for example, which meant that they could engage in more farming, they were, however, still highly constrained by the effects of long-term marginalisation. Surplus production was made difficult by lack of storage space. Bad roads placed limitations on transportation to the market and long-term lack of sufficient and suitable extension support had resulted in limited local knowledge on how to best select and use seed and other agricultural inputs to maximise production.

The MFPP on the ground

Villagers were enrolled in the programme in 2003 on condition that fields were allocated in the larger units organised during betterment, to facilitate mechanisation, and had not been fallowed immediately before the programme, to avoid problems with weed removal. This excluded the poorest disproportionally, as they more frequently had failed to plant their fields.

With the intention of stimulating entrepreneurial development and avoiding dependency, training was very limited. Participants were in essence expected to negotiate deals with the private sector for traction, seeds and agrochemical inputs, with minimal government support. This completely disregarded the participants' very low levels of experience in running farming as a business and their low degree of knowledge about different seeds and agrochemicals.

The practical agronomic instructions also went counter to local practices. Practices and inputs of large-scale commercialised farming were uncritically introduced to smallholders. The hybrid and GM maize seeds provided do not grow well when recycled, and are protected by patents and plant-breeders' rights which place bans on sharing and recycling seed. These are, however, important local strategies to ensure seed supply in the face of limited financial means. Monoculture maize plantations were promoted to assist mechanisation and herbicide application. This also contradicted local practices of spreading risks and ensuring subsistence through plant diversity.

Local people did not, however, simply accept programme conditions. Contrary to the intentions of the programme, the chief distributed seeds and inputs to those households that had initially been excluded because their fields were uncultivated or unfavourably located. Many participants recycled the seeds distributed by the MFPP, and continued to plant local seed varieties and other plants along with the new hybrid or GM seeds. Policy-level interviews reveal that these ways of trying to modify the programme to suit local conditions were interpreted by programme management as incompetence and lack of respect for the programme and led to tensions between the programme management and targeted communities. This, in my view, highlights the dominance of the view that smallholders are incompetent and that agricultural development means 'doing like the already successful farmers (those who have been supported through decades of discriminatory policies) do'.

In the words of one policymaker involved in the MFPP, interviewed in East London in 2008 and commenting on the failure of the programme to transform smallholder communities:

> I can just say this: I'm coming to the conclusion that the lack of development, lack of progress or lack of modernisation … It's more a perception problem, it's a world-view problem, it's a confidence problem, it's a mindset problem … We have struggled to get people to adopt new agricultural techniques, and yet in the last eight years there are more women wearing jeans in rural areas than there have ever been before … Where was the workshop? Where was the big government promotion scheme?

Continuities in agricultural policy in the Eastern Cape and their current effects

Despite its attempt to break with the history of failed agricultural interventions, the MFPP demonstrates several continuities with these interventions. I argue that this is a core reason that it failed in its practical implementation. In essence, the view of smallholders and their farming practices as being the major obstacle to agricultural development is apparent from colonial times to the present, as evidenced by the MFPP. The local case study shows that farming is constrained by a shortage of labour and money in poor households and thus a certain level of wealth must precede further engagement in agriculture in poverty-stricken households. This is supported by other research in South Africa (Carter and May 1999) and elsewhere (Ellis 2000; Ellis and Freeman 2004; Holmén 2005). However, the MFPP interprets the failure to plant the field as laziness and grant dependency. In the words of one policymaker: 'They could produce two tonnes of maize entirely by hand. Why don't they do it? Because they don't need to because they've got child-care grants, the pensions and it is easier to buy it [maize].'

Connected with this is the likewise historically rooted belief that if small-holders start behaving like large-scale farmers and use the tools that they use, they will prosper. This ignores the fact that the large-scale commercially oriented farming sector in South Africa has long been served with the best-quality land, good infrastructure, access to credit and extension services, and immensely cheap labour which was made possible by the simultaneous marginalisation of small-holders. The absurd practical result of ignoring history is that the MFPP promoted business orientation but hardly provided any support to farmers in how to achieve this. Apart from historical continuities (Hebinck et al. 2011), others have emphasised the contemporary neo-liberal view of development as central to this disregard of local contexts and structural inequalities (Hajdu et al. 2012). The choice of inputs, in particular the choice of maize seeds, also follows the idea of large-scale commercial farmers being the blueprint and is thus deeply insensitive to local practices and conditions. The high-yielding hybrid and GM maize varie-ties introduced by the MFPP are developed to suit large-scale, high-input farming. They are expensive, heavily fertiliser-dependent, not suitable for recycling and are intolerant of environmental dynamics (Gouse 2012; Jacobson and Myhr 2013). In contrast, there are other varieties on the market which are suitable for recycling, significantly cheaper and better adapted to the dynamic environmental condi-tions (Gouse 2012; Jacobson and Myhr 2013; McCann et al. 2006) that commonly typify smallholder environments (Altieri et al. 2011). Because of the dominance of the view that agricultural development means doing as the large-scale farmers do, the programme and its predecessors have completely ignored this. Luckily, this case study shows that smallholders have not followed the programme slavishly and therefore its negative effects are less than they would have been otherwise.

A brief look ahead

A look ahead shows that something is happening in the discourse of agricultural development in the province. While the 2006–2009 strategic plan still empha-sises the need for 'changing the mindset' of smallholders (ECDA 2006: 18), the most recent strategic plan 2010/11–2014/15 acknowledges the structural histor-ical inequalities as a core reason for widespread rural poverty and low agricul-tural productivity (ECDA 2010). Not once in the document is the situation in the rural areas blamed on the mindset of smallholders. This manifests a definite break with previous policies. Acknowledging the effects of structural inequalities on the potential for commercialisation, the document emphasises the impor-tance of infrastructure support and increased availability of agricultural extension services as core target areas. This is radically different from past policies and must be welcomed as a major improvement in its cognisance of local realities. However, the plan retains the one-sided focus that smallholders should become commercial farmers at the same time as it does not make clear to what extent this means adopting the inputs and practices that large-scale farmers use. As is shown in this chapter, this is in essence what commercialising has meant in past policies. This case study shows that to truly benefit smallholders, agricultural policy must not only be targeted at mitigating historical inequalities, but it must also acknowledge social and ecological realities and adapt technology and practices to suit local conditions. If future development interventions do so, they are much more likely to reduce poverty and raise levels of agricultural production than if the perspective of large-scale farming as a blueprint is retained.

Notes

1   Since 6 May 2009, the former Department of Agriculture in the Eastern Cape province has been renamed the Department of Agriculture and Rural Development. The former name is used in this chapter when referring to documents and practices occurring before 6 May 2009, and the latter name is used when referring to actions and documents produced by the new department.

2   Poverty levels were defined in a participatory wealth-ranking exercise in which villagers developed categories of wealth, defined the characteristics of each category and ranked each household according to these categories. Not only monetary assets or cattle were important for defining wealth, but also factors such as the health of family members and social networks. In all three villages, people settled on four levels: rich, middle, poor and very poor. In total, 40 per cent of the households were classed as 'very poor'. The remaining households were evenly distributed among the 'poor', 'middle' and 'rich' categories, with 20 per cent of the households in each group. It is important to note that these were relative measures of wealth; most of the households classed as 'rich' in the villages would be considered poor by many other poverty measures.

References

Aliber, M. and R. Hall. 2012. 'Support for smallholder farmers in South Africa: challenges of scale and strategy', *Development Southern Africa*, 29(4): 548–562.

Aliber, M. and R. Mokoena. 2003. 'The land question in contemporary South Africa', in J. Daniel, A. Habib and R. Southall (eds) *State of the nation: South Africa 2003–2004*, Cape Town: HSRC Press.

Altieri, M.A., F. Funes-Monzote and P. Petersen. 2011. 'Agroecologically efficient agricultural systems for smallholder farmers: contributions to food sovereignty', *Agronomy for Sustainable Development*, 32(1): 1–13.

Andrew, M. and R. Fox. 2004. '"Undercultivation" and intensification in the Transkei: a case study of historical changes in the use of arable land in Nompa, Shixini', *Development Southern Africa*, 21(4): 687–706.

Beinart, W. 1984. 'Soil erosion, conservationism and ideas about development: a southern African exploration, 1900–1960', *Journal of Southern African Studies*, 11(1): 52–83.

Beinart, W. 2002. 'South African environmental history in the African context', in
S. Dovers, R. Edgecombe and B. Guest (eds) *South Africa's environmental history: cases and comparisons*, Cape Town: David Philip.

Bernstein, H. 1997. 'Social change in the South African countryside? Land and production, poverty and power', in Programme for Land and Agrarian Studies (ed.) *Land reform and agrarian change in southern Africa: an occasional series*, Cape Town: University of the Western Cape.

Bundy, C. 1988. *The rise and fall of the South African peasantry*, London: James Currey.

Carter, M., and J. May. 1999. 'Poverty, livelihood and class in rural South Africa', *World Development*, 27(1): 1–20.

Chouliaraki, L. and N. Fairclough. 1999. *Discourse in late modernity: rethinking critical discourse analysis*, Edinburgh: Edinburgh University Press.

Damgaard Hansen, K. 2006. *The Massive Food Production Scheme, Eastern Cape: design extension approach and scope for adoption of minimum tillage*, Copenhagen: Royal Veterinary and Agricultural University of Denmark (KVL), Department of Plant and Soil Science.

De Wet, C. 1990. 'The socio-ecological impact of development schemes in the "homelands" of South Africa', *South African Journal of Science*, 86: 440–447.

ECDA (Eastern Cape Department of Agriculture). n.d. 'Massive food production conditional grant scheme and rural mechanisation scheme, *Masilime Sihluthe*', Bisho: Eastern Cape Department of Agriculture. Accessed 22 May 2009, http://www.agr.ecprov. gov.za/index.php?module=sd_programmes&id=3.

ECDA. 2002. 'Memorandum: Massive Food Production Scheme through a conditional grant scheme for crop production and a rural mechanisation scheme 2002', Bisho: Eastern Cape Department of Agriculture.

ECDA. 2003. *Strategic plan 2003–2006*, Bisho: Eastern Cape Department of Agriculture.

ECDA. 2004a. 'Massive Food Programme: notes and observations 2004', Bisho: Eastern Cape Department of Agriculture.

ECDA. 2004b. 'Massive Food Production Scheme 2004', Bisho: Eastern Cape Department of Agriculture.

ECDA. 2005. 'Massive Food Programme: Siyakula & massive food components', Bisho: Eastern Cape Department of Agriculture.

ECDA. 2006. *Strategic plan 2006–2009*, Bisho: Eastern Cape Department of Agriculture.

ECDA. 2010. *Strategic plan 2010/11–2014/15*, Bisho: Eastern Cape Department of Agriculture and Rural Development.

Ellis, F. 2000. *Rural livelihoods and diversity in developing countries*, Oxford: Oxford University Press.

Ellis, F. and H. Freeman. 2004. 'Rural livelihoods and poverty reduction strategies in four African countries', *The Journal of Development Studies*, 40 (4): 1–30.

Fairclough, N. 1995. *Critical discourse analysis: the critical study of language*, London: Longman.

Fairclough, N. (ed.) 2001. *Language and power,* Harlow: Pearson Education.

Fay, D. 2003. '"The trust is over! We want to plough!": land, livelihoods and reverse resettlement in South Africa's Transkei', unpublished PhD thesis, Boston University.

Gouse, M. 2012. 'GM maize as subsistence crop: the South African smallholder experience', *AgBioForum*, 15(2): 163–174.

Hadju, F. 2006. 'Local worlds: rural livelihood strategies in Eastern Cape, South Africa', unpublished PhD thesis, Linköping University.

Hajdu, F., K. Jacobson, L. Salomonsson and E. Friman. 2012. '"But tractors can't fly…": a transdisciplinary analysis of neoliberal agricultural development interventions in South Africa', *International Journal of Transdisciplinary Studies*, 6(1): 24–64.

Hebinck, P., D. Fay and K. Kondlo. 2011. 'Land and agrarian reform in South Africa's Eastern Cape province: caught by continuities', *Journal of Agrarian Change*, 11(2): 220–240.

Hendricks, F. 1990. 'The pillars of apartheid: land tenure, rural planning and the chieftancy', unpublished PhD thesis, Uppsala University.

Hobson, F. 2004. 'Massive Food Production Programme: critical matters of implementation as at September 2004', Bisho: Eastern Cape Department of Agriculture.

Holmén, H. 2005. 'Spurts in production – Africa's limping green revolution', in G. Djurfeldt, H. Holmen, M. Jirstrom and R. Larsson (eds) *The African food crisis: lessons from the Asian green revolution*, Wallingford: CABI Publishing.

Jacobson, K. 2009. 'The mismatch between smallholder realities and agricultural development interventions: from "Betterment" to the Massive Food Production Programme', in S. Guyot and J. Dellier (eds) *Rethinking the Wild Coast, South Africa: eco-frontiers vs livelihoods in Pondoland*, Limoges: VDM Verlag.

Jacobson, K. and A. Myhr. 2013. 'GM crops and smallholders: biosafety and local practice', *Journal of Environment & Development*, 22(1): 104–124.

Kepe, T. 2009. 'Unjustified optimism: why the World Bank's 2008 "agriculture for development" report misses the point for South Africa', *Journal of Peasant Studies*, 36(3): 637–643.

Masifunde Education and Development Project Trust. 2010. 'Threats to the food security and food sovereignty in the Eastern Cape: impacts of the Massive Food Production Programme (MFPP), GMOs and cash crops in four villages in the Amathole District Municipality', Grahamstown: Masifunde Education and Development Project Trust.

McAllister, P. 1992. 'Rural production, land use and development planning in Transkei: a critique of the Transkei agricultural development study', *Journal of Contemporary African Studies*, 11(2): 200–222.

McCann, J., T. Dalton and M. Mekuria. 2006. 'Breeding for Africa's new smallholder maize paradigm', *International Journal of Agricultural Sustainability*, 4 (2): 99–107.

Mercer, K., H. Perales and J. Wainwright. 2012. 'Climate change and the transgenic adaptation strategy: smallholder livelihoods, climate justice, and maize landraces in Mexico', *Global Environmental Change*, 22(2): 495–504.

16 The Massive Food Production Programme: does it work?

Zamile Madyibi

A critical analysis of the different aspects of policymaking – design, implementation, monitoring and evaluation – requires a deconstruction of the idea of planned development. Its theoretical conceptions, its notions of time and space and its normative assumptions all have to be critically examined. This chapter aims to adopt this sort of critical approach towards development, taking as its object of study the Massive Food Production Programme (MFPP) in the Eastern Cape. Rather than approaching this programme as a linear practice, it views it as an embedded practice, shaped by negotiations and networks that cut across formal institutional boundaries. These negotiations and networks operate on multiple levels, and involve multiple values and realities. The outcomes of a programme such as the MFPP, I argue, are shaped by the ways in which human needs and desires are formulated as well as by the unfolding of organisational capabilities, the development of power relations, the growth of skills and knowledge, and the clash of different ways of ordering the world (Long 2001). It is essential, therefore, to look at how actors (individually or in a network) process social experiences and devise ways of coping with life under circumstances that are partly created by interventions such as the MFPP.

I begin the discussion of the programme by describing its design and implementation. I go on to examine the theoretical assumptions that underpin the intervention. I then explore the multiple realities of the rural Eastern Cape province in order to show the different ways in which rural beneficiaries have accommodated the MFPP in their agricultural activities. I focus on three cases which have been selected because they are representative of some of the different labour patterns and land tenure systems that prevail in the Eastern Cape. The cases are the Majali MFPP project in Buffalo City Municipality, representative of communal lands in the former Ciskei homeland; the Ngxakaxha MFPP project in Mbhashe Municipality, typifying communal lands in the former Transkei homeland; and the Ndakana farm project in Amahlati Municipality, which represents private land ownership in an area that was formerly known as a 'black spot', a small area in which black people were allowed to own land in the apartheid era.

The conceptualisation of the MFPP

Policymakers in the Eastern Cape conceived the Massive Food Production Programme (MFPP) as a potential solution to the problem of rural poverty and unemployment. The intervention was based on the recommendations of the research team of the Provincial Growth and Development Plan (PGDP) in 2003 that agrarian transformation should become one of the pillars of provincial growth and development (ECPG-UNDP 2003). Accordingly, during a state of the province address in 2004, the Eastern Cape premier, Nosimo Balindlela, announced:

> An integrated food security programme called Massive Food Production is being intensified ... to address poverty in all its dimensions, including hunger, service poverty, income poverty and vulnerability. The programme is intended to empower people in their respective localities to be active players in local economic development, thereby transforming the agrarian economy. (Balindlela 2004: 2)

The designers of the MFPP identified maize as the staple food of the Eastern Cape. Based on previous food consumption trends in the province, they calculated that 600 000 tons per annum of maize would be required to ensure the food security of the area. Maize production, they argued, would trigger other kinds of agricultural activity. Five hundred thousand hectares of land in the former homelands of the province were singled out as having high agricultural potential. A technical director for the then Provincial Department of Agriculture (PDA) told a gathering of the research team on PGDP strategies that he was 'of the view that if agriculture is developed to its full potential, we can produce tons of maize, we can be the bread basket of certain parts of South Africa' (ECPG 2004: 9). Similar sentiments were expressed by a member of the executive council for agriculture:

> In a province that is mainly rural in nature and is primarily dependent on agricultural development for its competitiveness, it is important that agriculture be developed to its fullest potential and that government support projects, programmes and schemes that support emerging farmers, while sustaining commercial agriculture. (ECDA 2003: 6).

The MFPP has become the flagship programme of the province's efforts to improve the socio-economic situation in the province. The objectives of the MFPP are twofold: to increase food production, particularly that of maize and other staple foods, and to encourage the development of rural entrepreneurs who will create employment for the poor. The programme consists of two different schemes, both of which are financed by conditional grants. A mechanisation scheme has been established to enable local contractors to acquire equipment such as tractors, harrowers and ploughs. The mechanisation scheme resembles the

tractor hire schemes set up by the apartheid government in the days of its betterment programme and similar schemes run by the homeland governments. The
second part of the programme involves a production scheme that is meant to help
aspiring farmers acquire the necessary inputs for farming: hybrid seeds, inorganic
fertilisers, herbicides and insecticides.

Both schemes are accompanied by prescriptions and conditions. In the case of
the mechanisation scheme, local emerging contractors obtain a soft loan in the
form of a conditional grant if they meet specific minimum requirements relating
to the size of their business and its future outlook. This enables them to buy tractors and appropriate equipment on a contractual basis from certain farmers. They
are expected to repay the loan over a period of six years. The production scheme
requires prospective farmers to lodge an application in which they indicate an
interest in participating in the MFPP as a producer. Upon meeting minimum
requirements, they are awarded a conditional grant to enable them to purchase
essential inputs and to cover mechanisation costs (such as ploughing, disking and
planting, and herbicide/insecticide application). The grant covers 100 per cent of
the costs associated with producing three tons of maize per hectare on contiguous
blocks of lands in the first year. The grant recipients have to fund 25 per cent of
these costs themselves in the second year, 50 per cent in the third year, 75 per cent
in the fourth year and everything thereafter (ECDA 2002).

The production scheme includes another essential prescription. This relates to
the prevailing communal land tenure system. The PDA decided that all aspiring
farmers who were operating in terms of the communal tenure system and who
intended to participate in the MFPP should organise themselves so that the project
members would work contiguous blocks of 50 hectares of land. The 50-hectare
size of the blocks was initially regarded as an agronomic criterion for determining
the viability of an MFPP project. It has now come to be used chiefly as an administrative figure and as a means of determining the level of a conditional grant repayment. Private landowners are allowed to participate as individuals irrespective of
the size of their fields.

The schemes were intended to be implemented simultaneously on a scale
which would create jobs and enhance food security in the rural areas. Eight
hundred tractors were to prepare 64 000 hectares of arable land, with an estimated
yield of 160 000 tons of maize. This would provide food for over 1.2 million
people per annum. The value of the projected crop would be R352 million. The
programme would serve as the baseline for more rapid development and rural
transformation in the province (ECDA 2002).

Assumptions of the MFPP

It is important, as several commentators have noted, to identify and examine
the assumptions underpinning the MFPP (see chapter 1, this volume). At least
four assumptions become evident when reading the MFPP policy documents and
talking to the policymakers who framed them.

Economies of scale

Policymakers perceive the small size of fields to be a limiting factor when it comes to achieving agricultural development. The fact that the communal tenure system allocates African farmers in the Eastern Cape an average of 1.5 hectares of land each is seen as problematic. The MFPP has aimed to circumvent this size constraint by insisting on contiguous blocks of 50 hectares. These should be collectively managed as this reduces the transaction costs associated with managing small fields. The assumption is that lumping fields together will increase the size of agricultural operations and result in increased and more profitable production. The simultaneous implementation of the mechanisation and production schemes will also reduce the cost of production and increase the economies of scale in the region (ECDA 2002).

Public–private partnerships

The programme assumes that public–private partnerships provide access to production inputs, mechanisation and technical assistance which will help to speed up the commercialisation of agriculture in the province. The private sector has been assigned a key role in the MFPP. 'Mentors' are employed to guide the beneficiaries and impart skills to them. The provincial coordinator of the MFPP has indicated that

> [t]he vast majority of agricultural extension officers responsible for Siyakhula/Massive Food Production projects have little experience in the practice and production management of commercial agriculture at the level required to ensure a high probability of commercial viability of the projects. (ECDA 2009: 9).

Rural livelihoods

The MFPP assumes that rural people in the Eastern Cape are primarily farmers who depend on agriculture to provide food security for their (extended) families but who lack the means (such as land, inputs and knowledge) to farm on their own account.

The MFPP as an instrument of policy implementation

When the new member of the executive council for agriculture joined the PDA in 2004, he established a 'six-peg' policy framework hinging on five principles: stakeholder mobilisation, institutional arrangements, participatory planning and implementation, and sustainable development. This process has culminated in the launching of a 'green revolution' approach, as this is understood as the perfect strategy to partner with stakeholders in the planning and implementation of agriculture-oriented policies for sustainable development. All of this assumes that the state is the chief initiator of development.

The realities of the MFPP

The Majali MFP project

Majali is one of the locations that was proclaimed by the Native Trust and Land Act No. 18 of 1936 as part of the government's 'betterment planning programme' (see chapter 2, this volume). It is located four kilometres north-east of Bisho, and falls within the Buffalo City Municipality. Most of the land in the area is held under the communal tenure system, which means the land falls under the direct authority of traditional leaders, although the state is the ultimate custodian. Rural dwellers hold a 'Permission To Occupy' (PTO) certificate which entitles them to about 1.5 hectares of land in a designated arable land area.

According to Mr Xola, the extension officer (EO) responsible for facilitating agricultural development in Majali, a brief awareness campaign about the MFPP was conducted by the PDA in the area encouraging community members to decide to participate. One of the participants told me that she saw the programme as a means to bridge the gap between subsistence and commercial agriculture: 'When the programme was introduced, I saw an opportunity to realise my dream of farming commercially. Farming is the main source of livelihood for my family'. She still considers agriculture as a major source of income and food. In this she is in the minority. The number of people whose main source of household food comes from growing it themselves in South Africa has decreased significantly, from 33 per cent in 2000 to 6 per cent in 2006 (Stats SA 2008).

With the assistance of the EO, the Majali community filed an application for more than a hundred hectares of land with the PDA. Due to the financial constraints of the MFPP, the department granted only 50 hectares to Majali. They looked for ways to use the remaining 50 hectares of land. This they found in adapting the benefits that accrued from the programme to the land that was available. In a meeting they divided the arable fields into three blocks of 50 hectares each. Thirty-four beneficiaries were assigned to the first block. Interestingly, only ten members (30 per cent) of this block have a PTO certificate. Twenty-four members (70 per cent) do not hold PTO rights to land in that block. They instead lease land from community members who are not interested in working the land themselves. One of them complained about the land tenure system in rural South Africa:

> The democratically elected government promised to redress the imbalances of land tenure through a new land reform programme, but even today … I do not own a piece of land or entitlement to support my family. I have leased land from a community member who is not interested in agriculture. I appeal to the South African government to do something about people aspiring to be farmers.

The project's first production season was in 2004/2005. The land is worked collectively in terms of rules devised by the participants themselves, within the MFPP guidelines. No one works his/her own piece of land, as was previously the case.

An elected executive committee coordinates the project. All the operations are carried out according to a strict production plan. This plan includes a mechanisation protocol that is devised and controlled by an external contractor. The executive committee and the EO for the service area are responsible for procuring inputs and mechanisation services. A mentor has been appointed by the PDA. He is supposed to offer advice about every aspect of production. The participants hardly ever see the mentor, however – a fact that is corroborated by the EO. All the members are expected to be on site on scheduled days to perform tasks such as the thinning of maize seedlings, top-dressing with inorganic fertilisers and applying insecticides.

Many participants resent the rigid model that has been imposed by the MFPP. They feel that the MFPP disregards traditional methods of cultivation, undermines local practices and knowledge, and disturbs prevailing labour patterns. Many of the technologies that they are compelled to use are not user-friendly or compatible with local conditions. They argue that whole process has been implemented from above:

> The PDA once visited our community in order to evaluate and identify resources. We told them our aspirations and ambitions but never received any feedback until we were told about the MFPP as the agricultural intervention that was intended to be implemented in the rural areas of the Eastern Cape.

They feel they have been forced to accept preconceived ideas about agricultural production while their own forms of production and decision-making have been suppressed.

Each member of the project is given 10 bags of maize (50 kilograms) after each harvest for his or her own use. The rest of the crop is sold as the project's consignment. The project established a niche market for its green maize (sweetcorn) harvest in the 2006/2007 production season. This has bolstered its income levels significantly.

Table 16.1 Production trends (maize) of the Majali project

Season	Area planted (ha)	No. of participants	Yield (kg)	Revenue (R)
2005/6	50	34	117 600	164 662.00
2006/7	50	34	102 450	174 189.40
2007/8	50	34	180 548	361 097.40

Source: Own data

While the MFPP has its shortcomings, it has undoubtedly increased production in areas such as Majali, as Table 16.1 shows. The production trends in the Majali project are consistent with those of the MFPP at provincial level (see Table 16.4). Good production levels are attributable largely to the commitment shown by

project members. Mr Quthubeni is one of the Majali members who has contributed greatly to the success of the project. He was one of 24 people who had to
lease land before he could join the project. He is also an executive member of
the project. He was born in Majali in 1955 and is married with five children. Mr
Quthubeni started working with Spoornet in 1975 but was retrenched in 1993.
After that he established a herd of eight cattle and leased about 1.5 hectares of
land for food production. This supplements his Spoornet pension. His wife has no
source of income but grows food in a backyard garden. Mr Quthubeni is happy
with the MFPP:

> Ever since MFPP was introduced to the Majali community, my life has
> changed. As a member of the project, I know what I am going to do for the
> day when I wake up in the morning. Moreover, I can put food on the table
> on a daily basis because of the proceeds from the project.

The Ngxakaxha MFP project

The Ngxakaxha project is situated in the Mbhashe Local Municipality, near the
national road (N2) between East London and Mthatha. This is a pilot area for
the 'green revolution' in the Eastern Cape. The project was founded by members
of the Masincedane Farmers' Association. Consisting of 94 members, all from
Ngxakaxha location, the association welcomed the MFPP with great enthusiasm
when it was launched in 2004. An application was made with the assistance of a
local EO, and the Ngxakaxha MFP project came into being. People expressed their
dissatisfaction about their lack of participation in the design and planning phases
of the project unequivocally. Although an arable block of about 300 hectares
of land belonging to the whole community of Ngxakaxha was available, only
a contiguous block of 50 hectares of land was accepted to become a part of the
MFPP. The MFPP mediated and identified 22 potential project members. Although
the 22 members operate under the 'umbrella' of a 50-hectare land project that is
coordinated by an executive committee, each member works his/her own piece
of land separately within the project. The project has received perimeter fencing
and a mechanisation package for maize production. This includes two tractors
provided by the PDA. All the participants receive free mechanisation services;
however, they have to pay an annual maintenance fee. The project did not do
well and has dwindled in terms of size and membership. By 2008/2009, only 16
of the original 22 members remained (see Table 16.2). They cultivated only 25 of
the original 50 hectares of land. One of the members explained why he had left
the programme:

> The intervention is too modernised and rigid; it ignores valuable and cost-
> effective traditional methods. Almost all the operations are mechanised. I
> decided to leave the project and follow my own way of farming as I could
> not afford the high costs of production any longer.

Table 16.2 Production trends (maize) of the Ngxakaxha project

Season	Area planted (ha)	No. of participants	Yield (kg)	Revenue (R)
2005/6	50	22	–	–
2006/7	50	22	104 200	156 300
2007/8	50	22	115 800	194 544
2008/9	25	16	n.a.	n.a.

Source: Own data

Note: n.a. – data were not available.

The production levels of the Ngxakaxha project have been below the provincial average (see Table 16.4). This may well be related to the rigid approach of the MFPP, which clearly prevented proper consultation with the relevant stakeholders. In the case of the Ngxakaxha project, the MFPP failed to take into account the viable livelihood strategies that were already in place. Although a stakeholder analysis was conducted during the design stage of the MFPP, it did not go far enough. A representative of the farmers' association observed:

> Social dialogue is important for the future of this intervention as many participants never display and exercise ownership of the programme. Key stakeholders were left out of the processes.

Many of the members of the Ngxakaxha project have leased land from community members so that they can continue cultivating crops individually, in their own way, free of the obligation to conform to the MFPP guidelines. They claim that their traditional methods are still valuable for their livelihoods. They regard the intracropping and intercropping of maize, beans and pumpkins as the best system because it produces different kinds of food from the same piece of land. They rely on draught animals for ploughing and use modified five-litre oil tins for top-dressing maize plants with inorganic fertilisers. In addition, the Ngxakaxha project leader also expressed his concerns about the financial implications of the PDA's initiative:

> Some of us have decided to lease unused land outside the project so that we can incorporate some traditional methods to reduce the costs. We cannot afford the mechanisation costs when the grant period lapses.

The Ndakana farm project

Ndakana farm is situated 10 kilometres south of the Stutterheim sub-district in the Amahlathi Local Municipality. It is privately owned by Mr Shota. The farm was previously categorised as a 'black spot'. Mr Shota owned a building contracting business and produced only food for his family on his land. After he became eligible for the MFPP, he reduced the time spent on his business and devoted more of his energies to farming. Although he holds 179 hectares of land, Mr Shota managed to get only 50 hectares of it accepted for the MFPP due to grant policy stipulations. On the 50 hectares he produces mainly maize. The remainder of his land is for livestock farming. He has 82 cattle, 68 sheep and 34 goats. Mr Shota also produces other crops – sweetcorn, dry beans and potatoes – on his 50 hectares, chiefly to demonstrate to the PDA that they should diversify the MFPP. Mr Shota is especially passionate about livestock farming and has lobbied the PDA strongly to include it in the MFPP:

> Whenever I meet the MFPP district coordinator, I raise the issue of diversification of the MFPP to include other commodities. It is working for me already. Production inputs for the previous production season arrived very late from the contracted supplier and I resorted to planting maize for silage. I managed to repay the grant deposit for the 2007/2008 production season from the proceeds of livestock production.

Mr Shota relies on a locally hired workforce. He complains that 'African people do not recognise another African as their employer. They still have the old mentality and do not acknowledge me as the owner of the farm.' He recounted an incident when the employees went on holiday, on the understanding that they would work for three days between Christmas and New Year's Day. They returned to work only after New Year. Moreover, Mr Shota has mixed feelings about the mentoring programme that has been introduced by the PDA to bridge the skills gap between commercial and previously disadvantaged farmers. Although he acknowledges that their advice is useful, he also laments the lack of real commitment on the part of the mentors:

> I last heard from the mentor in October, when we discussed plans for the 2008/2009 production season. I rely more on advice from a commercial farmer – a friend of mine – from the East London area for further improvements in my farm. The mentor service means nothing to me.

While Mr Shota has achieved considerable success on his farm, Ndakana's maize production levels, as reflected in Table 16.3, are far below provincial average yields (see Table 16.4). This can partly be explained by the fact that a portion of his maize is harvested as green maize (sweetcorn) for the niche market that he has identified in the area. The revenue base of the farm has clearly been strengthened by crop diversification. This is especially important since maize production has not been at optimal levels.

Table 16.3 Production trends of the Ndakana farm project

Season	Type of crop	Area planted (ha)	Yield (kg)	Revenue (R)
2005/6	Maize	45	75 000	90 000
	Beans	1	1 750	14 000
	Potatoes	4	15 450	46 350
2006/7	Maize	45	25 000	30 000
	Beans	1	–	–
	Potatoes	4	20 000	40 000
2007/8	Maize	45	42 500	85 000
	Beans	2	1 000	8 000
	Potatoes	4	–	–

Source: Own data

The MFPP at provincial level

A simplified cost-benefit analysis of the MFPP in terms of food security from its inception in 2003/2004 until 2007/2008 is presented in Table 16.4 below.

Table 16.4 Simplified cost-benefit assessment of the MFPP for a five-year period

	2003/4	2004/5	2005/6	2006/7	2007/8
Budget (production & administration) (R)	41 000 000	50 000 000	69 000 000	70 000 000	40 000 000
Area planted (ha)	9 000	12 000	15 000	15 000	13 133
Number of projects	192	247	413	424	350
Average yield (tons/hectare)	1	1	3.2	3.6	3.89
Quantity of maize (tons)	9 000	12 000	48 000	54 000	51 087
Commercial trade value of maize (less transport costs) (R/ton)	1 300	600	900	1 300	1 900
Total value of maize per annum (R)	11 700 000	7 200 000	43 200 000	70 200 000	97 065
Profits received by contractors and input suppliers expressed in maize product (tons)	1 362	1 661	2 292	2 325	1 247
Jobs sustained in economic chain	256	313	431	438	250

Source: Adapted from ECDA 2007

Clearly the implementation of an intervention of the magnitude of the MFPP was new to all the major stakeholders: government officials, contractors, input suppliers and especially the project members. This is one of the reasons why an average output of only one ton per hectare was achieved for the first two seasons instead of the targeted three tons per hectare. In economic terms, the success of the intervention looked uncertain. The breakeven point was attained, however, during the fourth season of the programme (2006/2007), when average yields of 3.6 tons per hectare were obtained. This level of production realised a profit since the average production cost per hectare was R6 316.40. The people who benefited most, however, were not the producers but the input suppliers, mechanisation contractors and mentors. They received the standard payments that had been agreed between them and the MFPP for their services, regardless of production levels. In addition, the mentors received a special bonus when a project that they had mentored exceeded the targeted yields.

An interactive internal auditing of the MFPP that was conducted in 2004/2005 by the monitoring and evaluation unit of the PDA reflected gross omissions in the process of developing and introducing the programme. Based on an ad hoc evaluation, a mentorship programme was then introduced with the purpose of imparting skills to the participants in order to increase production levels. This resulted in over 30 000 tons more maize being produced by the end of 2005/2006 than in either of the previous two seasons (see Table 16.4). Various interactions between the different actors triggered an adaptive process that took greater cognisance of the multiple realities of development. The course correction factor that was implemented after the evaluation report yielded a positive spin-off and contributed to a dramatic turnaround, as is shown in Table 16.4.

The available data confirm that prior to the ad hoc evaluation (internal audit) in 2004/2005, only 4 per cent of the projects achieved a yield of four tons per hectare or greater. After the introduction of the amendment projects, this increased to 18 per cent and later to 30 per cent of the projects by the end of the 2006/2007 season (ECDA 2007).

Conclusions

The three cases discussed in this chapter clearly show that the MFPP is not a homogeneous phenomenon. Each of the three projects implemented and engaged with the MFPP in different ways. Each project having taken on a life of its own, their progress cannot be reduced to a predictable chain of events. This means that the MFPP as a whole should be perceived as a transformational process, influenced by the internal organisational and political dynamics of its different projects, rather than as a linear, technocratic programme with knowable outcomes.

The cases also suggest that MFPP policymakers have failed to properly acknowledge and understand the potential contribution of the smallholder agricultural sector to the mainstream economy. The view that large, capital-intensive farms are more economically efficient than small farms is driven by beliefs about economies of scale in farming. It also replicates one of the illusions of agricultural modernity: a farm looks efficient because it possesses tractors and machinery. The major challenge facing agriculture in the Eastern Cape, in my opinion, is the removal of the structural constraints that inhibit the growth of a vibrant commercial smallholder sector. Despite the relative success of the MFPP, forcing small-scale farmers to combine their lands and form blocks of 50-hectare projects is clearly not the long-term answer to creating sustainable rural livelihoods in the region. One of the issues, frequently mentioned by rural dwellers themselves, is greater access to markets. Farmers also said they needed processing facilities such as maize hammer mills in their areas. A growing body of evidence suggests that developing markets for resource-poor smallholders would have large-scale spillover effects on their productive capacity as well as on income and local employment. Policy interventions need, therefore, to ensure that smaller producers are integrated into agro-food markets.

The MFPP is undeniably a good example of a community-based development approach in many ways. It gives community representatives a mandate to distribute resources provided by the state under the supervision of government institutions. More often than not, though, the advantages of delegating distribution tasks to local representatives are undermined by the phenomena of 'elite capture' and 'social exclusion'. Platteau (2004) and Platteau and Gaspart (2003) argue that rural elites in African communities are often able to direct benefits to themselves because of poor information and communication systems. The MFPP is a case in point. It was advertised in the local newspapers and communities had to apply and qualify to participate in it. Very few of them managed to apply in time. Only those groups with good networks managed to get the information and apply in time. These were usually linked to rural elites. The result was that many areas with good resource potential, as required by the programme's contractual conditions, were not considered, while areas with less potential for maize production were included in the programme (ECDA 2007).

Real agrarian reform cannot be limited to the sort of intervention practice that is promoted by the designers of the MFPP. Planned interventions are often part of the development problem. They import packages that delegitimise local bodies of knowledge, organisational forms and resources and thus become a major obstacle to locally driven development. The MFPPs sought to establish new patterns of local economic development by the externalisation of farm labour through mechanisation and the modernisation of key agricultural resources. However, the MFPP technology package and knowledge was not crafted to resonate with the life-worlds of the people targeted by the intervention, the 'intervened'. Most of the technology employed at MFPP sites was not compatible with existing production systems. Given the level of 'underdevelopment' of the agricultural sector in the countryside of the Eastern Cape, the massive modernisation of agriculture can be sustained only through subsidy schemes. All the evidence, including that from the cases discussed in this chapter, suggests that such subsidies only retard the creativity of smallholder farmers.

The way that the MFPP has been designed and implemented clearly shows signs of continuity in the policymaking arena in the province. It rests on a model in which development is parachuted into communities without regard for the particularities of specific lived-in worlds. The failure of numerous, large-scale, top-down schemes around the world has led to a renewed interest in self-reliant and 'bottom-up' rural development strategies in recent years. There has been a critical rethinking of centrally driven approaches and a revaluation of the dynamics of indigenous decision-making and innovation (Nel et al. 1997). There is a growing realisation that a rigid adherence to the ideas connected with economies of scale and the pursuit of state-driven green-revolution-style strategies will not contribute significantly to the creation of sustainable livelihoods for poor rural households. The MFPP only strengthens the trend that was set in motion in the 1930s (Beinart 1992) whereby only an elite few who manage to combine wage income with agricultural activities can begin to cultivate more land and obtain higher yields. The rest of the rural population falls by the wayside. What is needed, therefore, is an endogenous development approach that builds on local realities and practices and is bolstered by the use of appropriate technology. Only then will agriculture become an effective vehicle for sustainable development in the Eastern Cape. The MFPP does not represent such an approach. Indeed, the MFPP resembles what Scott (1998) calls 'seeing like a state'.

References

Balindlela, N. 2004. 'Eastern Cape state of the province address'. Accessed 4 June 2009, http://www.polity.org.za/article/balindlela.

Beinart, W. 1992. 'Transkeian smallholders and agrarian reform', *Journal of Contemporary African Studies*, 11(2): 178–199.

ECDA (Eastern Cape Department of Agricuture). 2002. 'Memorandum: Massive Food Production Scheme through a conditional grant scheme for crop production and a rural mechanisation scheme 2002', Bisho: Eastern Cape Department of Agriculture.

ECDA. 2003. *Strategic plan 2003–2006*, Bisho: Eastern Cape Department of Agriculture.

ECDA. 2007. 'Record of potentially the most significant course correction of the Massive Food Programme (MFP) towards achieving sustainable socio-economic success', unpublished internal report, Eastern Cape Department of Agriculture.

ECDA. 2009.'Report on the performance of Siyakhula/Massive programme in terms of crop yields with regard to the objectives over the programme and results from course corrections in the programme (course correction factor 2007)', unpublished internal report, Eastern Cape Department of Agriculture.

ECPG (Eastern Cape Provincial Government). 2004. *Eastern Cape provincial growth and development plan 2004–2014*, Bisho: Eastern Cape Provincial Government.

ECPG-UNDP (Eastern Cape Provincial Government with United Nations Development Programme). 2003. 'Strategic framework for growth and development 2004 – 2014', Bisho: Eastern Cape Provincial Government.

Long, N. 2001. *Development sociology: actor perspectives*, London: Routledge.

Nel, E., T. Hill and T. Binns. 1997. 'Development from below in the new South Africa: the case of Hertzog, Eastern Cape', *The Geographical Journal*, 163(1): 57–64.

Platteau, J.P. 2004. 'Monitoring elite capturing in community-driven development', *Development and Change*, 35(2): 223–246.

Platteau, J.P. and F. Gaspart. 2003. 'The risk of resource misappropriation in community driven development', *World Development*, 31(10): 1687–1703.

Scott, J. 1998. *Seeing like a state: how certain schemes to improve the human condition have failed*, New Haven, CT: Yale University Press.

Stats SA (Statistics South Africa). 2008. *South African Statistics 2008*, Pretoria: Statistics South Africa.

17 'Still feeding ourselves': everyday practices of the Siyazondla Homestead Food Production Programme

Henning de Klerk

The Siyazondla Homestead Food Production Programme (Siyazondla HFPP) was launched in Mbhashe Local Municipality in 2004/2005. *Siyazondla* can be translated as 'we nourish ourselves', 'we feed ourselves' or 'we look after ourselves'. The level and pace of social mobilisation that occurred among the potential participants was consistent with the high profile that politicians were affording the Siyazondla HFPP, but soon outstripped the limited institutional capacities and budgetary resources of the Department of Agriculture in the municipality. During the first three years, women from villages in each of Mbhashe's 24 wards (subsequently expanded to 26 wards and later to 31 wards) organised themselves into 15-member clubs or groups. This was the condition set by the then Department of Agriculture (DOA, currently Department of Agriculture and Rural Development) extension officers for participation in the Siyazondla HFPP. By the end of the first three years, 265 such village-level clubs (with a total of almost 4 000 members) had been established, each with a constitution detailing its objectives, its membership, and the roles and responsibilities of its members and executive. At the time of writing, only about one in every five of the Siyazondla clubs in Mbhashe had received the assistance from the DOA to which they were entitled (Blaai-Mdolo 2009).

This chapter documents a case study in which I describe and discuss the experiences of the members of 10 Siyazondla clubs that fall under a single administrative area (formerly headman's location) in the Eastern Cape's Mbhashe Municipality. My perspective is somewhat unusual. My account of what happened is not intended to be read as an evaluation of the programme design, the efficacy of its implementation or its performance in terms of its own goals and indicators. Instead, I approach Siyazondla HFPP from the perspective of women and women's groups who view themselves as prospective participants in the programme and as potential recipients of its benefits. Their stories form the main focus of this case study. Despite having complied, at no small cost in terms of time and money, with the administrative and bureaucratic procedures required for them to become participants in the programme, they have not been able to gain access to the benefits it provides.

I argue that the response of homestead food producers to their experience of exclusion needs to be taken into account in debates about governance and development interventions at local municipal level. Unfulfilled expectations and experiences of exclusion have a major impact on social relationships among homestead food producers at village level and on relationships between homestead food producers and local DOA officials. While the municipality's lack of action seems to be an instance of 'non-intervention', I will argue that its inertia actually constitutes an intervention.

The role of household food gardens in the livelihood portfolios of women in Mbhashe

Most Mbhashe residents' lives are connected to a homestead (*umzi*) in a rural locality. The rural homestead is the primary location of the household's domestic, agricultural and ritual activities. Daily activities in the rural homestead include collecting water from communal taps in the neighbourhood, collecting firewood from grazing fields in the vicinity of the homestead, attending to domestic animals, performing various seasonal tasks in the food garden, and maintaining and expanding infrastructure. The homestead is also periodically transformed into a ritual space. A variety of rituals, including funerals, beer drinking and ceremonies in which an animal is slaughtered, may be performed in it. Many of these rituals are associated with the rites of passage of the living or deceased members of the household. The homestead becomes a public space during rituals because these events are usually open to the residents of the neighbourhood and to visitors from further afield. The homestead generally consists of a house or houses, a cooking shed, a firewood stack, an outside courtyard, an animal byre and a fenced food garden. The garden has sections allocated for fruit trees, annual vegetables and staple crops such as maize, beans and a variety of pumpkins and squashes. Homesteads occur in loosely clustered neighbourhoods that are located on hillocks and are connected by footpaths and by gravel roads that usually are in a poor condition.

In each neighbourhood there are a few shops selling a small variety of consumer items including prepaid electricity and cellphone coupons. A few shebeens sell alcoholic beverages. Residents prefer to buy only small amounts from local businesses as the prices are high when compared with those in wholesale stores in towns. Once a month, a centrally located open space is transformed into a hub of economic activity. This is the time when grant recipients are paid out. The vehicles and officials of the South African Social Security Agency, armed security guards, travelling traders and debt collectors (such as burial societies) converge near the grant queues. Although some residents do their primary monthly shopping at these grant payouts, most prefer to travel into town at least once a month, not only for shopping but also to access health, financial and administrative services.

A number of places in Gatyana (Willowvale), Dutywa or Gcuwa (Butterworth) become part of the life-world of the Mbhashe residents during their monthly, bimonthly or emergency trips to these towns. These include the wholesale shops where basic food items are sold in bulk; feeding lots where small and large stock are sold for slaughter; streetside hammer mills where harvested or purchased maize can be milled; various local municipal offices where government services are accessed; restaurants; bars; hair salons; furniture, electronics and appliances stores; outlets that offer communications, banking or credit services; offices of lawyers or funeral societies; doctors' surgeries; pharmacies; and hospitals and various meeting and waiting places. Importantly, the banks and the wholesale shops in the towns are places where the income that is obtained from government social welfare grants, remittances and other sources can be accessed and converted into cash. Taxi ranks and bus stations are important spaces connecting the villagers to South Africa's distant metropolitan, mining or labour-intensive agricultural areas. Johannesburg and Cape Town, the two principal migration destinations for residents of these 10 villages, are respectively about 900 kilometres and 1 300 kilometres away.

The places in which prospective participants in the Siyazondla HFPP engage in many of their livelihood activities are an integral part of the broader livelihood context in which homestead food gardening occurs. In the former Transkei there has been a close association between long-distance labour migration and household food production systems for more than a century. Together they comprise a strategy to reduce vulnerability and retain a degree of autonomy in the face of continuous and varied attempts by authorities to control rural life (Beinart 1982; Beinart and Bundy 1987; Mayer 1980; McAllister 2001). Both the type and the extent of household food production systems have altered significantly during this time, however. For at least the last half-century, household food production has adapted to dwindling household resources through an increase in production in homestead food gardens with an associated decline in production in ploughing fields located some distance from the homestead (Andrew 1992; Andrew and Fox 2004).

Migrants have experienced significantly reduced access to secure employment in urban areas since the mid-1980s (Bank and Minkley 2005; Beinart 1991; McAllister and Deliwe 1994; Southall 1991). This has meant that those household members who remain in rural areas have experienced less and less reliable access to remittances from migrant household members. As a result, they have become increasingly dependent on state social welfare grants as well as on a range of informal economic activities and natural resources in the local economy and environment (Palmer et al. 2002). Migration levels among women are still significantly lower than among men, and women still have significantly poorer access to employment opportunities in migration destinations (Hunter 2007; Sharp and Spiegel 1990; Tsikata 2009). Nevertheless, over the last decade and a half, women have experienced increased access to cash income in the local economy through a variety of state social welfare grants (see chapter 2, this volume). Improved access to cash income enables women to play a greater role in household decisions about the allocation of resources. These include decisions that relate to investments in homestead food production, such as infrastructure like fencing, or production inputs (Case and Deaton 1998; Posel 2001a, 2001b; Posel et al. 2006).

The degree of participation in homestead food gardening among residents of Mbhashe's rural localities varies greatly. Some individuals do not engage in cultivation at all (apart from collecting wild green edibles [*imifino*] and harvesting the pumpkins and squashes that come up opportunistically in gardens, along hedges and in between homesteads), while others cultivate a range of vegetables throughout the year. People might hand-irrigate a part of the garden during the dry months but will probably allocate most of the garden to the cultivation of the main dryland seasonal crops: maize, beans and a range of cucurbits (pumpkins and squashes). Cultivation practices range from the superficial clearing of tiny plots by hand-held hoe, to ploughing by ox-, horse- or mule-drawn plough or deep ploughing and disking by tractor.

Homestead food gardening is generally well integrated with keeping chickens, pigs, goats and cattle. Composted animal manure is applied to the garden. In turn, the animals are often fed on produce from the garden or allowed to forage on weeds and insects in it. Homestead food gardening also generally goes hand in hand with the use of natural resources in the vicinity of the homestead: fencing poles are manufactured from trees harvested in nearby forests; ox-drawn sleds are made from the beams, sticks and weaving materials found in local forests; a variety of baskets, mats and strainers are manufactured from local reed- and grass-based fibres and used in the harvesting, transport and processing of produce; grain-milling stones are sourced in nearby rivers. The integration of animal husbandry and natural-resource-use activities produces significant cost-saving benefits for homestead food production.

Maize, beans and cucurbits are sown in one, two or three different sowings in different sections of the garden at different stages of the season, depending on the arrival of summer rains and the perceived risk of drought. Because of the involvement of draught animals, ploughing is regarded by some cultivators as a male activity, although household demographics often mean that men, women and children are all involved in soil preparation. The remaining vegetable crops are cultivated in a separate part of the garden, usually located next to the buildings that comprise the homestead. This part of the garden is sometimes separately fenced. A range of vegetable crops are cultivated, with care being accorded to the specific needs of each type of vegetable. Sowing, planting, transplanting, weeding and harvesting occur throughout the agricultural season. When a patch is harvested and cleared, a different crop is soon sown or planted in its place. Although practices of intercropping, rotational cropping and mulching do take place, the extent to which these are undertaken varies from one household to another. Pesticides are applied to particular crops, such as cabbage and maize, which can be greatly affected by insect pests.

Most labour in homestead gardens comes from members of the household: hired labour is rare. A tractor and driver might be hired to plough the homestead food garden and casual labourers are sometimes hired to hoe weeds. Cooperative labour arrangements in the study area are not as extensive as they are in other localities in Mbhashe (cf. Heron 1990; McAllister 2001). For the most part they are limited to the sharing of teams of oxen for ploughing purposes, as well as to the harvesting, preparation and transport of fencing poles from the forest. Women generally provide the bulk of agricultural labour while having only marginal control over farming resources and income. The gendered nature of homestead agricultural production is deepened in societies that have been dependent on migrant labour for several generations (Charman 2008). The capacity of women to bear the major responsibility for agricultural work is often severely limited by their unpaid labour in the domestic sphere, in particular their disproportionate role in providing care for the sick and the elderly, which is accentuated by the high prevalence of HIV and AIDS (Bak 2008; Mashiri et al. 2009; Ogunmefun and Schatz 2009; Razavi 2009; Tsikata 2009). HIV and AIDS also redirects household income towards caring for the sick, accessing health services and paying for funerals. Household assets often need to be sold in order to meet these expenses. The pandemic also shapes farming patterns by its impact on knowledge and skills transmission and the effect that the death of household members might have on a household's access to land (Oglethorpe and Gelman 2008; Slater and Wiggins 2005; White and Morton 2005).

Home gardens are fenced to exclude livestock and wild animals. Fencing is as important as hand-irrigation facilities and water-harvesting systems. Together they allow households to cultivate a range of vegetables for much of the year. Some households manage to harvest vegetables throughout the year.

Very few homesteads produce enough food in their gardens to be sold either locally or in town. The exception is a handful of experienced and well-resourced gardeners who produce a small surplus of certain crops, most notably maize, potatoes, sweet potatoes, cabbage, onions and spinach. Homestead food gardens generally enable a household to cut back on expenditure on fresh vegetables (and the associated cost of travelling to town and transporting the purchases back) during all but the driest months of the year (July to September), while improving a household's access to the vitamin- and mineral-rich fresh produce that is necessary to supplement the carbohydrate-rich staple foods that can be bought relatively cheaply in bulk from wholesalers in towns. They also can serve as a source of cash, supplementing grants and wages.

The implementation of the Siyazondla HFPP and the response of its intended beneficiaries

The Siyazondla HFPP, together with the Massive Food Production Programme (chapters 15 and 16, this volume), the Comprehensive Nutrition Programme and the Integrated Agriculture Infrastructure Programme, forms part of the Eastern Cape's Provincial Growth and Development Plan (ECPG 2004). Similar to the MFPP, the strategic objective is to promote agrarian transformation and in particular to strengthen household food security through household gardens. It has the potential to assist even the most small-scale of producers to improve food production (Pillay and Zimmerman 2004).

Siyazondla HFPP came into being as a co-production between academia and the provincial government, initiating a policy process in the form of public participation and consultation and in the form of a detailed experts' report based on case studies (Ainslie 2003; Andrew 2003; Fay 2003; FHISER 2003; Westaway and Minkley 2003). Interventions should build on current trends in livelihood strategies and activities if they are to be sustainable. The intensification of food production in individually held homestead food gardens in different areas of the Eastern Cape emerged as a viable and less risky cultivation strategy than field cultivation in a context of significant resource constraints. A strategic element of Siyazondla HFPP was to build grass-roots-level social structures composed of women, which is clearly in line with recent trends towards the democratisation and liberalisation of agricultural extension services through participatory, bottom-up approaches emphasising self-help and ownership (Charman 2008).

An initial budget allocation of R250 000, supplemented by a R150 000 contribution from the Office of the Premier, allowed the 60 members of four different Siyazondla clubs in the Gatyana sub-district to purchase production inputs (seeds, seedlings and fertiliser), various gardening tools (wheelbarrows, rakes, spades, watering cans, and so on) and, most valuable of all, a 2 500-litre rainwater storage tank.

The women in the study area learnt of these pilot projects through their informal social networks. They often meet friends and relatives from different administrative areas during trips to Gatyana and Dutywa, at funerals and church gatherings, and during rituals and celebrations. When they heard about Siyazondla, a few cultivators contacted the DOA in Gatyana to find out about the programme and how they could participate in it. The extension officers told the women that they had to organise themselves into groups or clubs of 15 members each (women only); draw up a constitution detailing their aims and objectives, membership, decision-making procedures and financial management; and open a bank account. They were also told that new clubs would be selected to participate in the programme on the basis of the commitment they showed to cultivating their gardens. Extension officers encouraged the women to order and buy seedlings in the name of their clubs through the DOA, which sourced seedlings from a commercial supplier in East London and sold them to homestead food gardeners from their offices in Dutywa, Gatyana and Xhora. The department kept records of seedling orders so that they could measure a club's commitment to cultivation by looking at the amount of seedlings it purchased.

An already existing farmer association facilitated the distribution of information regarding the requirements of the Siyazondla HFPP. The process of club formation revolved around a small group of women in each village. These were often senior women of pensioner age who were experienced and active homestead cultivators. Groups of women organised themselves into clubs of 15 members each during 2005 and 2006. One club was formed in each of seven of the ten villages in the administrative area. In an eighth village, significantly more populous than the others, three clubs were formed.

Each club complied with the DOA's requirements and registered the name of the club and the bank account details at the DOA offices in Gatyana. In addition, the 10 clubs formed an overall executive committee. Each club collected start-up funds through contributions from the membership. Decisions over the allocation of the club's funds were taken during club meetings. Expenses included items such as seedlings, groceries for club meetings and the transport costs of club representatives who travelled to Gatyana to meet with extension officers or to purchase seedlings.

A renewed enthusiasm for gardening characterised the clubs' energetic involvement in homestead food production during the initial period. For two agricultural seasons, several gardeners produced a harvest of vegetables that exceeded their own consumption needs. In some cases they produced more than was marketable in the local economy, with the result that a lot of produce – cabbages in particular – rotted before it could be eaten or sold. Part of the reason for the surplus harvest was the understanding among club members that one of the key criteria that extension officers would use when selecting future groups to participate in and benefit from the Siyazondla HFPP would be the level of production of its members in their homestead gardens. The 'carrot' of receiving free production inputs, gardening tools and rainwater harvesting equipment provided enough motivation for the newly formed groups to continue to buy seedlings from the DOA, despite the fact that they were not included among the additional clubs that received support in subsequent budget years.

The budget for Siyazondla HFPP in Mbhashe rose from R610 000 in 2005/2006 to R1 000 000 in 2006/2007. In Gatyana, this money was used to expand the pilot project to all eight wards. Eight more clubs were selected to receive assistance in the second and third years of the programme's implementation. Although an effort was made to select one club from each of Gatyana's eight wards, no attention was given to the fact that each ward consisted of two or more administrative areas. The additional clubs were all taken from the same administrative areas as those that had already been selected. In effect, some administrative areas, such as the one in the study area, were systematically excluded from becoming beneficiaries of the programme. Members of clubs in the study area were keenly aware of this fact. Their concern and frustration became more and more noticeable, both in meetings among themselves and in visits to the DOA.

Figure 17.1 The budget for Siyazondla HFPP in Mbhashe, 2004–2011 (R)

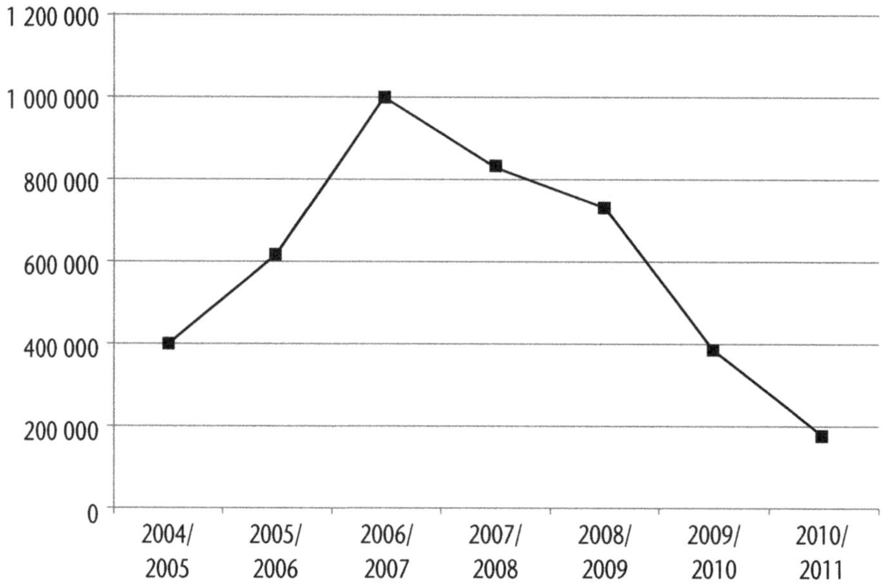

Source: ECPG 2004

The increase in the budget was not sustained and declined in every year after the 2006/2007 season (see Figure 17.1). The Siyazondla coordinators in the Gatyana and Dutywa offices of the DOA were not involved in the budget process. They could not explain the dramatic reduction, which clearly flew in the face of the project's prominence as one of the DOA's flagship programmes, proudly proclaimed in the provincial minister's policy speeches year after year. Since neither of the coordinators felt that they had the authority to reveal the department's annual service-delivery reports to the researcher, the reasons behind the dramatic cuts in budgetary allocation remain unclear and speculative.

The budget cuts had serious consequences for the 'self-organised' clubs that were on the DOA's waiting list. While eight additional clubs were again selected in both 2007/2008 and 2008/2009, they were provided with production inputs only and told that they would have to share toolkits with existing clubs. No rainwater tanks were distributed. The Siyazondla budget was reduced so dramatically during 2009/2010 and 2010/2011 that no additional clubs received any support from the DOA at all. At present, the budget is being used to provide production inputs to existing clubs only.

The Siyazondla club members have become increasingly disillusioned and demoralised. Despite the extensions officers' promises, they were not among the clubs selected to participate in the programme in the fourth, fifth and sixth year. Neither the reason for not receiving support through the programme nor the procedure for the selection of additional clubs was properly communicated to the clubs. On several occasions, representatives of the 10 clubs travelled to the offices in Gatyana at their clubs' expense in order to inquire about their status as 'self-organised' clubs on the DOA's waiting list. They were not provided with transparent information and instead were told to keep on purchasing seedlings and to be patient. Finally, the overall executive committee of the 10 clubs wrote a letter of complaint to the manager of the Gatyana office of the DOA. The manager and the Siyazondla coordinator in the Gatyana office then called a meeting where Siyazondla members were promised that the extension officer assigned to their area would be replaced. The office manager, the Siyazondla coordinator and the Siyazondla club members all regarded the incumbent extension officer as the most important obstacle in the way of the clubs' receiving assistance from the programme. The office manager retired soon after the meeting, however, and no one in the office knew of any plans to replace the extension officer of the area in question. At the time of writing, the sixth year of the Siyazondla HFPP's active operation in Mbhashe, all the Siyazondla clubs in the study area are still on the 'waiting list' of 'self-organised' clubs. The experience of the 10 Siyazondla clubs is by no means unique. For every Siyazondla club in the Mbhashe Local Municipality that has received assistance from the department, there are four that have not.

There are good reasons for the mismatch between the enthusiasm with which prospective participants responded to extension officers' calls to organise themselves, and the ability of extension officers to follow up and provide assistance to these self-organised clubs. Apart from the constraints induced by limited budget allocations, the Gatyana DOA office, like most of its offices in Mbhashe Local Municipality, suffered from severe limitations in terms of human resources and institutional capacity (ECDA 2009). The extension services section of the office, which is responsible for the normal farmer support services of the department and the implementation of the Siyazondla HFPP, has only one departmental vehicle for its 13 extension officers to use. This problem is compounded by poor road conditions, a population that is dispersed over a vast geographic area and the broken topography of Gatyana sub-district. There has been little attempt to develop the capacity of the DOA staff to implement the programme. Neither the extension officers nor the Siyazondla coordinator has received any form of training that is specific to the purposes of the Siyazondla HFPP. Although the Siyazondla HFPP is an intervention that is aimed specifically at women homestead food producers, only 3 of the 13 extension officers in Gatyana are women. None of the extension officers has received any training regarding gendered practices of homestead food production. Not surprisingly then, the relationships between extension officers and participants in the Siyazondla HFPP are highly asymmetrical. Gender relations and education intersect in such a way that participants do not feel comfortable to ask all their questions and raise their problems in an open manner in meetings.

My primary concern in this chapter is to go beyond the DOA's weaknesses, and focus on the responses to Siyazondla HFPP among its prospective participants.

The efforts of prospective participants to organise themselves into units in accordance with the programme's requirements are especially remarkable in a context in which there are high costs involved in accessing town-based information and administrative and financial services. The consensus-based decision-making that led to the formation of neighbourhood-level clubs was a time-consuming process.

Club formation represents a formalisation of certain aspects of long-standing informal social networks at neighbourhood level. These networks have diverse historical origins. They emerge, in part, from the practices of mutual assistance and labour cooperation that are associated with the hosting of rituals and with certain agricultural tasks. The networks of women's church groups, informal savings clubs and burial societies are another precedent for the cooperative club networks. Relationships among club members are not ahistorical and neutral. Rather, they are based on histories of alliances and divisions, trust and mistrust, and cooperation and competition. While disagreements among members are to be expected, the clubs have the potential to function as vehicles for consensus-based decision-making. Disputes can be mediated in a constructive manner since the clubs are neighbourhood-based social organisations with a high degree of face-to-face interaction. Unfortunately, however, the common experience of exclusion from the Siyazondla programme is the main source of solidarity among club members at present. Club members tend to compare themselves with clubs in other administrative areas and to become envious of those clubs which are receiving benefits through the Siyazondla programme. This has resulted in attitudes of disillusionment and distrust towards extension officers and other officials from the DOA.

Potentials, benefits and unintended social impacts of development interventions

The levels of participation and the initial enthusiasm among prospective participants of the Siyazondla HFPP in Mbhashe are surprising in the broader developmental context of relatively low participation in projects (and willingness to assume ownership of them). The tangible potential benefits that the Siyazondla HFPP holds for participants clearly played an important role in motivating women in the area to form or join Siyazondla clubs. The garden tools and rainwater tanks possess both a monetary and a practical value. While the benefits of being part of the Siyazondla HFPP cannot be ignored, it still needs to be acknowledged that significant expenditures of time and money are involved in forming clubs.

As I pointed out earlier, women in the area have always participated at the neighbourhood level in various practices of mutual assistance, resource sharing and cooperative labour arrangements. The Siyazondla clubs in the study area were able to capitalise on the close ties, high levels of cooperation and trust, and informal insurance structures that characterise these long-standing social and economic networks.

Over the last three years, Siyazondla club members have increasingly expressed their awareness of the negative cost of their participation in the programme during meetings. Their experience of exclusion has affirmed and strengthened the mutually held prejudices that already existed between extension officers and homestead food gardeners before the launch of Siyazondla. Homestead food gardeners did not accept the department's excuse that its single vehicle was the main reason why extension officers did not visit their area on a regular basis. Siyazondla club members were also sceptical of the reasons provided for their not being included in the Siyazondla programme. Judging from the passionate speeches during club and inter-club meetings, the levels of respect and trust among homestead food gardeners towards extension officers deteriorated significantly as a result of their non-inclusion in Siyazondla HFPP.

This case also illustrates the important and difficult brokerage role extension officers play as the primary point of mediation between homestead food gardeners (and farmers in general) and those involved in policymaking and budgetary processes at the DOA. Since extension officers have an interest in demonstrating high levels of farmer participation in the Siyazondla project to their superiors, they may be unwilling to tell a 'self-organised' Siyazondla club that there is little or no possibility of being included in the programme in the near future. Instead, they might appeal to farmers to continue cultivating, go on buying seedlings from the department and exercise patience. This is especially critical in a context in which there is such a mismatch between the programme's limited budgetary allowance and the high levels of interest shown by prospective participants.

More positively, by virtue of being women only, the Siyazondla clubs demonstrate a number of characteristics that make them important social units for homestead food gardeners. They have the capacity to interact with both the DOA and other stakeholders in agricultural production and also to become involved in the marketing of agricultural produce. During the several club and inter-club meetings I attended between 2008 and 2010, the clubs spontaneously assumed a number of functions and responsibilities, including the pooling of resources to finance the transport costs of representatives who were commissioned to visit the DOA in Gatyana, to purchase vegetable seedlings at wholesale prices and to cater for meals during club meetings. Attending club members contributed cash and fresh produce from their gardens, while cooking was the responsibility of a single club, with clubs taking turns to cook.

During meetings, homestead food gardeners shared the knowledge that they had acquired through experience and experimentation and from observing other food gardeners. This strengthened their own knowledge regarding cultivation techniques, the treatment and prevention of pests, the cultivation of new crops, and the timing for the sowing and planting of different crops. The meetings also provided a platform for gardeners to discuss marketing issues. They discussed ways of synchronising the planting or sowing of specific crops, most importantly cabbages and potatoes, in order to be able to harvest at the same time and send the combined produce in a truck to the fresh fruit and vegetable wholesalers in Dutywa and Gatyana. Although the meetings always contained a variety of perspectives, and some women played a prominent role while others hardly spoke at all, the women-only Siyazondla club meetings nevertheless invited much more open discussion and wider participation than was the case in other development-related meetings in the same locality, in which both men and women were present.

The newly created clubs are social structures that have the potential to play an important role in (i) providing a platform where locally relevant, experience-based agricultural knowledge can be shared, (ii) protecting and expanding the shared interests of household food producers in overcoming production and marketing constraints, (iii) devolving some of the responsibilities of local government to neighbourhood-level farmers' organisations, and (iv) transforming gender roles in agricultural and developmental decision-making in rural areas. There is considerable irony in the fact that the potential of the Siyazondla clubs to take on these functions is strongest among the clubs that have not been incorporated into the Siyazondla programme and which have not enjoyed the formal benefits the intervention offers. The 'self-organised' (read 'excluded') Siyazondla clubs have been 'nurturing themselves' (*ukuzondla*), largely as a result of their not receiving support from the DOA. Through their very non-inclusion, the processes of mobilisation, empowerment and solidarity-building which characterised their formation have been strengthened. This has enabled them to take on the role of representing collective interests and negotiating as a bloc with the DOA extension officers. Recognising the importance and potential of the Siyazondla clubs, whether 'self-organised' or government-supported, and investing in their ongoing skills and capacity development would serve well any future interventions in homestead food production in Mbhashe.

This case study illustrates that the initial implementation stages of a development intervention such as Siyazondla HFPP is a politically sensitive process from the moment that the intervention enters local discourse. The process of participant selection is especially delicate. There is great potential for the development of unrealistic expectations among potential beneficiaries if the initial stages of an intervention are not managed carefully. Particular attention must be paid to clear, accurate and transparent communication between implementers and participants. If the participants' expectations are repeatedly crushed, the relationship between the implementers and the participants can deteriorate to such an extent that not only the long-term sustainability of the intervention will be threatened but also the likelihood of success of any future intervention.

References

Ainslie, A. 2003. 'Case study report no. 4: Ngqushwa Municipality, Peddie, Eastern Cape', *Eastern Cape agricultural and rural livelihoods study*, prepared for the Provincial Growth and Development Plan, Fort Hare Institute of Social and Economic Research, Alice.

Andrew, M. 1992. 'A geographical study of agricultural change since the 1930s in Shixini Location, Gatyana District, Transkei', unpublished MA thesis, Rhodes University, Grahamstown.

Andrew, M. 2003. 'Case study report no. 1: Willowvale', *Eastern Cape agricultural and rural livelihoods study*, prepared for the Provincial Growth and Development Plan, Fort Hare Institute of Social and Economic Research, Alice.

Andrew, M. and R.C. Fox. 2004. '"Undercultivation" and intensification in the Transkei: a case study of historical changes in the use of arable land in Nompa, Shixini', *Development Southern Africa*, 21(4): 687–706.

Bak, M. 2008. 'Townships in transition: women's caring keeps the township together', *Journal of Southern African Studies*, 34(2): 255–268.

Bank, L. and G. Minkley. 2005. 'Going nowhere slowly? Land, livelihoods and rural development in the Eastern Cape', *Social Dynamics*, 31(1): 1–37.

Beinart, W. 1982. *The political economy of Pondoland, 1860–1930*, Cambridge: University of Cambridge Press.

Beinart, W. 1991. 'Transkeian smallholders and agrarian reform', *Proceedings of the conference on political transition and economic development in the Transkei*, Institute of Social and Economic Research, Rhodes University, Grahamstown.

Beinart, W. and C. Bundy. 1987. *Hidden struggles in rural South Africa: politics and popular movements in the Transkei and Eastern Cape, 1890–1930*, London: James Currey.

Blaai-Mdolo, B. 2009. 'The green revolution and poverty alleviation: challenges faced by women in small-scale agriculture. An investigation into the Siyazondla Homestead Food Production Programme, Mbhashe Local Municipality, Eastern Cape', unpublished MSocSci thesis, University of Fort Hare, Alice.

Case, A. and A. Deaton. 1998. 'Large cash transfers to the elderly in South Africa', *The Economic Journal*, 108(480): 1330–1361.

Charman, A.J.E. 2008. *Empowering women through livelihoods-orientated agricultural service provision: a consideration of evidence from Southern Africa*, Research Paper No. 2008/01, United Nations University World Institute for Development Economics Research (UNU-WIDER).

ECDA (Eastern Cape Department of Agriculture). 2009. *Department of Agriculture annual performance plan 2008/2009*, Bisho: Department of Agriculture.

ECPG (Eastern Cape Provincial Government). 2004. *Eastern Cape provincial growth and development plan 2004–2014*, Bisho: Eastern Cape Provincial Government.

Fay, D. 2003. 'Case study report no. 2: Hobeni, Xhora District', *Eastern Cape agricultural and rural livelihoods study*, prepared for the Provincial Growth and Development Plan, Fort Hare Institute of Social and Economic Research, Alice.

FHISER (Fort Hare Institute of Social and Economic Research). 2003. *Eastern Cape agricultural and rural livelihoods study*, prepared for the Provincial Growth and Development Plan, Fort Hare Institute of Social and Economic Research, Alice.

Heron, G. S. 1990. 'Household production and the organisation of cooperative labour in Shixini, Transkei', unpublished MA thesis, Rhodes University, Grahamstown.

Hunter, M. 2007. 'The changing political economy of sex in South Africa: the significance of unemployment and inequalities to the scale of the AIDS pandemic', *Social Science & Medicine*, 64(3): 689–700.

Mashiri, M., J. Chakwizira and C. Nhemachena. 2009. 'Gender dimensions of agricultural and rural employment: differentiated pathways out of poverty – experiences from South

Africa', paper presented at the FAO-IFAD-ILO workshop on gaps, trends and current research in gender dimensions of agricultural and rural employment: differentiated pathways out of poverty, Rome, 31 March – 2 April.

Mayer, P. 1980. *Black villagers in an industrial society: anthropological perspectives on labour migration in South Africa*, Cape Town: Oxford University Press.

McAllister, P. 2001. *Building the homestead: agriculture, labour and beer in South Africa's Transkei*, Aldershot: Ashgate.

McAllister, P. and D. Deliwe. 1994. *Youth in rural Transkei: the demise of 'traditional' youth associations and the development of new forms of association and activity: 1975–1993*, Development Studies Working Papers Vol. 61, Institute of Social and Economic Research, Rhodes University Grahamstown.

Oglethorpe, J. and N. Gelman. 2008. 'AIDS, women, land, and natural resources in Africa: current challenges', *Gender and Development*, 16(1): 85–100.

Ogunmefun, C. and E. Schatz. 2009. '"Caregivers" sacrifices: the opportunity costs of adult morbidity and mortality for female pensioners in rural South Africa', *Development Southern Africa*, 26(1): 95–109.

Palmer, R., H. Timmermans and D. Fay. 2002. *From conflict to negotiation: nature-based development on South Africa's Wild Coast*, Pretoria: Human Sciences Research Council.

Pillay, P. and M. Zimmerman. 2004. *The provincial growth and development plan of the Eastern Cape: assessment of capacity to implement PGDP programmes*, Pretoria: Sizanang Centre for Research and Development.

Posel, D. 2001a. 'How do households work? Migration, the household and remittance behaviour in South Africa', *Social Dynamics*, 27(1): 165–189.

Posel, D. 2001b. 'Who are the heads of household, what do they do, and is the concept of headship useful? An analysis of headship in South Africa', *Development Southern Africa*, 18(5): 651–670.

Posel, D., J. Fairburn and F. Lund. 2006. 'Labour migration and households: a reconsideration of the effects of the social pension on labour supply in South Africa', *Economic Modelling*, 23(5): 836–853.

Razavi, S. 2009. 'Engendering the political economy of agrarian change', *Journal of Peasant Studies*, 36(1): 197–226.

Sharp, J. and A. Spiegel. 1990. 'Women and wages: gender and the control of income in farm and bantustan households', *Journal of Southern African Studies*, 16(3): 527–549.

Slater, R. and S. Wiggins. 2005. 'Responding to HIV/AIDS in agriculture and related activities', *ODI Natural Resource Perspectives* No. 98, London: Department for International Development.

Southall, R. 1991. 'The labour market, labour relations and trade unions in Transkei', paper presented at the conference on political transition and economic development in the Transkei, Institute of Social and Economic Research, Rhodes University, Grahamstown.

Tsikata, D. 2009. 'Gender, land and labour relations and livelihoods in sub-Saharan Africa in the era of economic liberalisation: towards a research agenda', *Feminist Africa*, 12(1): 11–30.

Westaway, A. and G. Minkley. 2003. 'Case study report no. 5: Chatha', *Eastern Cape agricultural and rural livelihoods study*, prepared for the Provincial Growth and Development Plan, Fort Hare Institute of Social and Economic Research, Alice.

White, J. and J. Morton. 2005. 'Mitigating impacts of HIV/AIDS on rural livelihoods: NGO experiences in sub-Saharan Africa', *Development in Practice*, 15(2):186–199.

18 Cultivators in action, Siyazondla inaction? Trends and potentials in homestead cultivation

Derick Fay

This chapter examines transformations and continuities in smallholder agriculture in southern Hobeni, in the Xhora District of the Mbhashe Local Municipality in the Eastern Cape, based on fieldwork in 1998 and 1999, 2005, 2009 and 2010, including household surveys in Hobeni (1998 and 2009) and neighbouring Cwebe (1998 and 2003).[1] The research findings reveal both recent change – a sharp decline in the cultivation of remote fields since 1998 – and long-term continuities – the expansion and intensification of cultivation in homestead gardens, manifested in increases in the diversity of gardens, in the cultivation of fruit trees and in the intensity of input application. Concurrently, the contribution of formal employment to livelihoods has declined considerably, while the contribution of welfare has expanded.

The research allows a partial assessment of two forms of state support to local livelihoods, the Child Support Grant (CSG) and the provincial Department of Agriculture's Siyazondla Homestead Food Production Programme (henceforth Siyazondla). Since 1998, the CSG has expanded to reach nearly two-thirds of the households in Hobeni, while Siyazondla began to assist households in southern Hobeni in 2007 with production inputs and training.

The chapter engages broader debates about the potential of direct cash transfers (Hanlon et al. 2010) and subsidised inputs for smallholders (Denning et al. 2009; Sanchez et al. 2009) to serve as strategies for rural development and poverty alleviation. Hanlon et al. synthesise the results of research on direct cash transfer programmes worldwide since the late 1990s, including South Africa's CSGs (2010: 38–43). They note the repeated conclusion that such programmes are affordable and efficient. Recipients use the money well and in ways that promote long-term economic growth and human development (2010: 2). Cash transfers encourage other forms of livelihood enhancement by facilitating increased labour migration and investment and experimentation in agriculture (2010: 53–58, 75, 31–32). Nutrition is improved through purchases of more nutritious and diverse foods. They also identify two areas of continuing debate: 'should smaller grants be given to many people or larger grants to a few?' and 'should recipients be asked to satisfy conditions?' (2010: 3). At present in South Africa, old age pensions and CSGs reach far, to 85 per cent of the population aged 63 and older and 55 per cent of all children in 2009 (2010: 38–39). Both grants are means-tested but are otherwise unconditional. This chapter will suggest that in rural Mbhashe, direct cash transfers have facilitated both an increase in school enrolment and the diversification and intensification of cultivation, and should continue.

Debates over agricultural subsidies have been more contentious. Attacked by World Bank structural adjustment policies in the 1980s and 1990s, subsidies have found favour again with the realisation that neo-liberal policies have widely led to declines in productivity and household food security (Denning et al. 2009: 2–3). The Malawian example illustrates benefits of subsidies. In defiance of donors, Malawi has been using targeted subsidies since 2005 to produce record maize harvests and end food imports (Denning et al. 2009: 4–6). These policies have now gained support from the UN Development Programme and the Gates Foundation–supported Alliance for Green Revolution in Africa (Sanchez et al. 2009: 38), which have promoted hybrid seeds and nitrogen-rich fertiliser as well as modified cultivation techniques (Denning et al. 2009: 6–7). Doubts have focused on the promotion of genetically modified crops (often with increased input requirements), environmental and economic equity consequences, and the concern that promotion of new inputs is 'a corporate strategy for colonizing Africa's food and agriculture systems' (in Helm 2008). As this paper shows, subsidies can effectively foster agricultural intensification, even without the controversial package of 'African green revolution' inputs, by promoting the dissemination of new crops and more intensive use of local resources. The success of both cash transfers and agricultural subsidies – in the form of basic pieces of agricultural equipment, seedlings, fertiliser and insecticide – has contributed to the expansion and intensification of garden cultivation in Hobeni.

Livelihoods in Hobeni in the late 1990s

Xhora District was long considered by officials as one of the most 'backward' in the Transkei. A short period of commercial cultivation of maize and tobacco ended by the 1930s (Fay and Palmer 2002). Primary education has been available locally only since the 1960s. For most of the twentieth century, Hobeni was a labour reserve, with the majority of migrants composed of men working in the mining industry. By 1996, remittances from mineworkers provided roughly 36 per cent of total income in Xhora District, more than any other district in the Eastern Cape (Malherbe 2000: 10–11). The district made national headlines in 2000 when a Statistics South Africa survey declared it the poorest in the country (cited in Shackleton et al. 2007: 137).

In the late 1990s, commercial agriculture was all but absent. Rain-fed agriculture for local consumption remained widespread, however, facilitated by annual rainfall averaging over 1 100 millimetres (Timmermans 2004: 19). Hobeni residents, like many of their neighbours in Gatyana District (Andrew 1992; De Klerk 2007; De Wet and McAllister 1983; chapter 17, this volume), expanded the cultivation of homestead gardens in the mid-twentieth century. These gardens were closer to homesteads, fenced and generally smaller than fields. Unlike the people of Gatyana and much of the rural Eastern Cape, though, residents of Hobeni and nearby areas did not abandon their more distant fields. These trends put them at odds with administrative limits on garden size and removals under 'betterment' policies. Betterment was implemented only in the mid-1980s, and many people began returning to their pre-betterment sites by the early 1990s, in Hobeni itself and across the Xhora District (see Fay 2003a, 2012).

Cultivation in the late 1990s took place in gardens near homesteads and in more distant fields. Typically, the agricultural cycle began with the first significant rains in September, when young men and older boys started ploughing the fields and gardens of members of their ploughing company. Some people would arrange to plough early and plant a crop of beans prior to sowing maize. Most would fertilise their gardens and fields with kraal manure, but only a handful used purchased fertiliser. While women, and some men, weeded their own gardens and fields as the maize plants grew, access to outside labour for hoeing and weeding, in the form of work parties and direct hiring, was vital for maize to flourish.

Local geographical and sociocultural factors explain the persistence of field cultivation in Hobeni and neighbouring Cwebe after it declined elsewhere (cf. Timmermans 2004: 137–138). Fields in Hobeni and Cwebe are relatively productive, especially on the large flood plains of the Mbhashe and Ntlonyane rivers, which do well in dry years when household gardens yield poorly. It is likely, too, that population pressure played a role in discouraging the abandonment of fields since Xhora has long had one of the highest population densities in the Transkei (Muller and Mpela 1987). Low wages and poor job prospects meant that people continued also to depend on local cultivation. The gendered division of labour also facilitated continued cultivation: until the late 1990s, only men of working age generally migrated, leaving behind a relatively large, mainly female, labour force in the district. Work parties and ploughing companies meant that labour and traction remained highly mobile, helping poorer homesteads to continue cultivating.

Transformations since 1999

Retrenchments and welfare

Since the late 1990s, livelihoods in coastal Xhora have changed in several directions at once: formal employment has declined, welfare income has increased, migration has diversified and field cultivation has declined while garden cultivation has increased and intensified. Employment has been adversely affected by shifts in the mining economy. By 2002, the practices of downsizing and subcontracting on the mines (Buhlungu and Bezuidenhout 2008) had reduced mining employment to about 55 per cent of its 1990 level nationwide (Seekings et al.

2004: 15). The impact in Xhora was especially severe: in Cwebe, the number of households receiving remittances dropped from over 40 per cent in 1998 to 13 per cent in 2003 (Pade et al. 2009: 42). The Rustenburg-based platinum industry, the most common destination for migrants from Hobeni and Cwebe, led the way in the turn to much-lower-paid subcontracted jobs, accounting in 2005 'for by far the most subcontracted workers ... a staggering 36 per cent of employment in the sector' (Buhlungu and Bezuidenhout 2008: 276). In addition, part-time employment of household members increased from 7 per cent of households in 1998 to 24 per cent in 2009.

Table 18.1 Income sources in Hobeni, 1998 and 2009 (%)

Year	Full-time employment and welfare	Full-time employment	Welfare only	Neither
1998	21	26	24	28
2009	9	19	56	16

Source: Own data

The loss of jobs has been partly offset by the increase in access to state grants. The distribution of income sources in 1998 and 2009 illustrates their growing importance (see Table 18.1). The CSG, not available in 1998, accounts for much of the increase. Its reach has gradually expanded to include 'children under 14 years of age in 2005' (Ferguson 2007: 77). By 2009, 62.5 per cent of households in Hobeni were receiving CSGs, while the proportion receiving old age or disability pensions had increased from 45 to 55 per cent. These payments make up a greater and greater proportion of income in the area and increased women's bargaining power and autonomy because the CSGs are typically paid directly to women (see Posel 2001; Posel et al. 2006).

The pattern of migration has also changed; interviews and survey data reveal that migrants are seeking jobs in more diverse locales and economic sectors and increasingly working in part-time or temporary and contract positions. In a context where the mining sector is in a restructuring process, the old pattern of male, mining-focused migration is being replaced by a more diverse pursuit of employment by more household members. This has led to an increase in female migration. The proportion of absent household members increased from 20 to 28 per cent between 1998 and 2009. Women made up most of this increase. The ratio of male to female absentees decreased, from nearly two men for every absent woman in 1998, to about six men to five women in 2009.

Field abandonment
Land use and agriculture have also changed markedly. There has been a pronounced decline in the cultivation of distant fields (see Table 18.2), while the proportion of households cultivating home gardens has remained steady.

Table 18.2 Field and garden cultivation in Hobeni, 1998 and 2009 (%)

Year	Cultivating in gardens	Cultivating in fields
1998	80	65
2009	82	22

Source: Own data

It is difficult to determine the precise reasons why people have abandoned field cultivation. Studies in Gatyana have identified declines in per capita cattle numbers, male outmigration, deteriorating soil fertility and damage by bush pigs as contributing factors (Andrew 1992: 88; Timmermans 2004: 41–42). Additional reasons that can be advanced for the decline of field cultivation in southern Hobeni include changes in settlement patterns, which make unfenced fields more vulnerable to livestock damage, and increases in school enrolment, which reduce the labour available for herding or guarding fields. Another possible disincentive to cultivation is increased access to cash from CSGs.

Local residents themselves generally attribute the decline in field cultivation to a lack of fencing. As Table 18.3 indicates, complaints about lack of labour and traction remained infrequent between 1998 and 2009, while there was an eightfold increase in the proportion of people who complained about a lack of fencing.

Table 18.3 Reasons reported for disused land in Hobeni, 1998 and 2009 (%)

Reason	Proportion of respondents reporting (multiple answers allowed)	
	1998	2009
Lack of labour/weakness	6.25	11.25
Lack of traction	6.25	7.5
Lack of fencing	5	40
Lack of money	3.75	–
We don't want to	2.5	–
Distance from fields	–	3.75

Source: Own data

Informants probably mentioned fencing as a complaint because the 2003 Dwesa-Cwebe Development Plan, which included plans to fence fields in Hobeni, had still not been implemented by the Amathole Municipality (the fields remained unfenced as at March 2012).

The salience of fencing also reflects shifts in settlement patterns. Beginning in the early 1990s, many of the people who had been moved under betterment schemes in the 1980s moved back to pre-betterment sites, which they were using as fields. In addition, new homesteads have been established on former fields throughout southern Hobeni since 1999. These areas have seen the greatest decline in field cultivation, while the smallest decline is in fields situated on the Mbhashe floodplain, far from settled areas.

Finally, there is some evidence linking the decline in field cultivation to the CSG. Correlation matrices, in general, reveal no statistically significant relationships between the presence or absence of field cultivation and demographic or economic variables. The one exception is an inverse correlation between the number of CSGs a household receives and the presence of field cultivation. The mean number of CSGs is 0.94 for households which cultivate their fields, while the mean for households which do not cultivate their fields is 2.29. This raises the question of whether this correlation reflects changes in labour or changes in expenditure. Are households with CSGs putting children in school, rather than having them look after ripening mealie fields, or are they spending the grants to buy the maize and other food that they cultivated in the past? Interviews suggest the former: informants were emphatic that school enrolment had increased since the advent of the CSGs, spurred by upgrades to schools and roads that have made school attendance more attractive and feasible.

Whatever the cause, the trend is unmistakeable and in line with patterns observed much earlier in other parts of the Eastern Cape (for example, De Wet and McAllister 1983; Hebinck 2007): Hobeni residents are giving up cultivation in distant fields but continuing to cultivate homestead gardens. At the same time, there have been significant changes in the way that people use their gardens.

Garden crop diversification and the expansion of fruit tree cultivation

The decline of field cultivation has been accompanied by an increase in garden crop diversity and input application. In August 2009, I chatted with Joe Savu, a local government councillor. He claimed that 'nobody will buy cabbages in town this year'. His comment drew attention to a clear expansion of garden cultivation and the growing of crops for sale that had taken place in recent years. These trends are evident across the sample as a whole but they are particularly concentrated among members of the Siyazondla clubs.

De Klerk, in chapter 17 of this volume, recounts the history and organisation of Siyazondla in the Eastern Cape and in Mbhashe Municipality in particular. Beginning in 2004/2005, the programme called for cultivators to form 'clubs' of 15 members each. Members were eligible to receive agricultural training, production inputs, gardening tools and, in some cases, a 2 500-litre rainwater tank. Siyazondla, as it has been implemented in Hobeni, builds incrementally on existing homestead strategies and landholdings, following recommendations that researchers had made for years (for example, Fay 2003b; McAllister 1992, 2001). Beginning in 2007, Hobeni residents organised 15 clubs. Two of these actually received inputs from Siyazondla. The 80 households surveyed in Hobeni in 2009 included 17 members of Siyazondla clubs, including 9 members of the two clubs that had received inputs. Siyazondla members have been at the forefront of garden intensification in the area.

The 1998 household survey gives a baseline for recent crop diversification. In 1998, most homesteads in Hobeni grew only two or three crops. Agriculture took place only in the rainy summer, centred on maize, beans and pumpkins for home consumption. All the homesteads that practised cultivation grew maize. There was an almost even split between beans (11) and pumpkins (8) as the second crop among the 19 homesteads that grew two crops. Nearly all the 26 households that produced three crops grew both beans (24 of the 26) and pumpkins (23 of the 26). Home-grown maize was usually pounded, not ground, and eaten with beans as samp (*umngqusho*). Fields were given over almost exclusively to maize, with beans and/or pumpkins intercropped.

From 1998 to 2009, the crop mix in fields (among those who still cultivated fields) remained low and consistent. In gardens, however, the variety of crops cultivated increased substantially. The mean number of crops cultivated for the sample as a whole increased from 2.3 (1998) to 3.6 (2009). The 2009 mean was 4.9 for Siyazondla club members overall and 6 for members of the clubs that had received inputs from Siyazondla.[2]

Several trends are evident: first, garden cultivation is partially substituting for field cultivation (see Table 18.4). Maize cultivation in gardens has increased; all but one of the households cultivating in gardens in 2009 grew maize. The cultivation of both beans and pumpkins in gardens, on the other hand, has decreased, alongside the decline in cultivation of these crops in fields. The decline in bean cultivation may reflect a shift to a less 'traditional' staple diet, with maize being eaten as stiff pap (cooked maize meal) rather than as samp (*umngqusho*).

Second, the proportion of households cultivating root vegetables (potatoes, sweet potatoes and beetroot) has roughly doubled. Of the 32 households cultivating root vegetables, 27 grew only one, while 5 cultivated both potatoes and sweet potatoes.

Third, the proportion of households growing leafy green vegetables (cabbage and spinach) has more than tripled, with Siyazondla members disproportionately represented. In the majority of cases (20 out of 34), growers of leafy green vegetables cultivated both cabbage and spinach.

Fourth, there has been a small increase in the sale of crops, from 8.75 per cent of households in 1998 to 12.5 per cent in 2009. The raw data reveal that in fact there has been a complete turnover: none of the seven households that were selling crops in 1998 were still doing so in 2009, while others had begun to sell their produce locally and at welfare payout points.

Finally, 20 per cent of households have begun growing crops in the winter, mostly cabbage and spinach. This has been facilitated by the installation of communal water taps in four of the six neighbourhoods of southern Hobeni, though 5 of the 16 households cultivating in the winter live in areas without water taps. Winter cultivation is probably linked to the installation of water storage tanks. The survey did not ask directly about water tanks. It did reveal, however, that the proportion of households living in a house with a corrugated iron roof (allowing for gutters and water tanks) increased from roughly 1 in 11 to nearly 50 per cent (Fay 2011).

Table 18.4 Crops and cultivation in Hobeni, 1998 and 2009 (%)

Crop	1998			2009				
	In gardens	In fields	Sold	In gardens	In fields	Sold	Grown in winter	Among Siyazondla members
Maize	70	65	–	81.25	22	1.25		100
Beans	59	23	3.75	52.5	7.5	3.75	1.25	65
Pumpkins	53	31	–	25	6	–	1.25	29
Sweet potatoes	15	–	–	29	1	–	3.75	23.5
Potatoes	7.5	1	3.75	11	–	–		6
Cabbage	7.5	–	1.25	34	–	7.5	15	76.5
Spinach	8.75	–	2.5	32.5	–	6.25	11.25	70.5
Tobacco	3.75	–	1.25	3.75	–	2.5	1.25	
Carrots	1.25	–	–	2.5	–	–	1.25	12
Tomatoes	1.25	–	1.25	5	–	–	1.25	12
Beetroot	–	–	–	3.75	–	–	2.5	18
Peri-peri	–	–	–	10	–	–	1.25	12
Onion	–	–	–	7.5	–	–	2.5	18

Source: Own data

Cultivation of fruit trees has expanded dramatically. In 1998, only 15 per cent of households had fruit trees, with only 12 trees among them. By 2009, 60 per cent of households had fruit trees, with a total of 106 trees. Table 18.5 illustrates the variety of cultivated tree species as well as the prominence of Siyazondla members among tree cultivators in relation to the entire 2009 sample. The increase in guava cultivation is attributable in part to the transplantation of non-native guavas from Cwebe Nature Reserve in the early 2000s under the Work for Water programme.

Table 18.5 Tree crops in Hobeni, 1998 and 2009 (%)

Tree	1998	2009	Siyazondla members
Guava	6.25	32	47
Peach	5	21	29
Banana	2.5	31	53
Lemon	1.25	1.25	0
Orange	0	3.75	6
Apple	0	1.25	6

Source: Own data

Cultivators attribute the rise in bananas to the Siyazondla clubs, explaining that the clubs shared banana plants among themselves and their neighbours, even though the plants were not provided by the Department of Agriculture.

Changes in agricultural inputs

In addition to diversifying garden cultivation, people have changed the way they cultivate, relying less on collective agricultural labour and more on other, local, organic inputs and externally purchased inputs. As Table 18.6 reveals, there has been an overall decline in the use of work parties for agricultural tasks.[3] The exception is the use of work parties for harvesting, which has increased, especially among households that still cultivate their fields.

Table 18.6 Agricultural work parties in Hobeni, 1998 and 2009

Type of work party	Proportion of households holding (%)			Mean number (among households holding)	
	1998	2009	Siyazondla members	1998	2009
Hoeing	55	36	23.5	2.3	2.3
Weeding	10	16	6	1.75	2.5
Planting	6	9	6	1.8	1.1
Harvesting	1	14	12	3	1.7

Source: Own data

The decline in the use of the work party appears related to the decline of field cultivation. Seventy-two per cent of the households that still cultivate fields continued to make use of agricultural work parties, while only 24 per cent of those who had abandoned field cultivation still did. There is also a pronounced generational aspect to the decline of field cultivation. Analysis revealed that most long-established households,[4] which tend to have older household heads, were still holding agricultural work parties in 2009, while only about 20 per cent of newer households were doing so.

The survey did not ask about the hiring of agricultural labour, but interviews suggest that hiring labour is increasingly replacing work parties, particularly among churchgoers who do not want alcohol at their homestead. In a separate survey of 38 households in Hobeni in March 1999, slightly over half the households (53 per cent) had hired people to hoe for them in the past season, providing a total of 184 work opportunities (Fay and Palmer 2002: 171–172).

The proportion of households cultivating with oxen remained consistent: 88 per cent in 1998 and 85 per cent in 2009.[5] Genealogically organised ploughing companies are the most common means of pooling oxen to form ploughing teams. While tractor hire has been available sporadically at the Hobeni Store, it has never been popular, as local cultivators generally prefer the longer-term security of belonging to a ploughing company.

The use of locally obtained organic inputs (kraal manure and compost) and purchased inputs (fertiliser and insecticide) has increased in gardens. Siyazondla members are at the forefront of these trends. Interestingly, the use of purchased inputs (fertiliser and insecticide) has also increased sharply among those who cultivate fields. Those who continue to cultivate fields are doing so in a more input-intensive way.

Kraal manure is the most widely used input besides land, labour and traction. Use of kraal manure has increased in gardens, from 57 per cent to 66 per cent of households, and the mean number of applications among users has increased from 1.15 applications to 1.3. Among those who still cultivate their fields, use of manure increased from 63 to 78 per cent of households. The total number of reported applications for fields and gardens combined was nearly the same in 2009 (85) as it was in 1998 (88). This suggests that manure that was previously allocated to fields is now being applied to gardens instead.

Compost use reveals a contradictory trend: while overall use decreased from 26 per cent of households to 16 per cent, the mean number of applications among users increased from 1 application to 1.54. Siyazondla members were nearly twice as likely as non-members to use compost in 2009. The use of compost in field cultivation remained constant, practised by about one in five households.

The increases in natural inputs have been matched by increases in the use of purchased inputs. The proportion of households using fertiliser in gardens increased from 12.5 per cent in 1998 to 22.5 per cent in 2009, and 29.5 per cent among Siyazondla members, and the average number of applications has increased from 1 to 1.33. Fertiliser use has also increased in fields. In 1998, only 15 per cent of those who cultivated fields (N = 52) used it; 55 per cent of those cultivating fields (N = 18) applied fertiliser in 2009.

Pesticide use in gardens increased from 5 per cent to 27.5 per cent. A similar increase occurred in fields, from a single household in 1998 to six, or one-third of the total, in 2009. Pesticide use is a concern, given the potential for overuse or misuse, although interviewees who received pesticide and sprayers from Siyazondla were able to explain the procedures for proper dilution and application.

The overall picture that emerges with regard to agricultural inputs is consistent with the patterns discussed earlier in the chapter. Hobeni residents have been intensifying their cultivation of homestead gardens. Siyazondla members have been particularly prominent in this process; they have increased not only their use of chemical inputs from Siyazondla, but also their use of locally available organic inputs.

Household case studies

This section presents more detailed accounts of three households in order to show the kinds of trajectories of livelihood change in the decade before 2009. The first case concerns a household in which the effects of unemployment have been partly offset by access to Siyazondla and CSGs.

The household of Elias and MaDingata Magqazolo was established at a site in MaVundleni in 1997. Elias's father had been removed under betterment in the mid-1980s. Elias, in his early 30s, moved back to his father's pre-betterment site in 1997. He was employed full-time on the mines, while his wife, a Zionist church member, remained at home with their three young children. They culti-vated maize, beans and pumpkins in their garden and in a field. At the time of the survey in 1998, they still had small stocks of all three of these crops. They applied manure and compost to their garden and compost to the field. They had held five work parties for various agricultural tasks during the year.

Their overall livelihoods and their approach to cultivation had shifted consid-erably by 2009. Elias was living at home, after being retrenched following an injury at work, and was in the process of trying to secure a disability pension. His only income came from occasional work for fishermen staying at the Haven Hotel. The couple now had five resident children of their own and were also taking care of two of MaDingata's sister's young children. All told, they had six CSGs, providing a monthly income of R1 200. All their school-age children were attending school. A daughter had married and moved to her husband's family about five kilometres away. They had received bride-wealth but this was cancelled out, they explained, by the cost of buying the supplies that the bride had to take to her husband's home.

MaDingata signed up as part of the first Siyazondla group in Hobeni in 2007. The couple had stopped cultivating their fields, attributing the decision to a shortage of cattle for traction and a lack of fencing. Both Elias and MaDingata worked in their homestead garden, however, cultivating maize, beans and five other vegetable crops as well as a dozen banana plants and two guava trees. They had increased the applications of kraal manure to three annually, along with one of compost, but no longer held work parties. They were able to water cabbages and spinach manually in the winter because they lived near a water tap, while Elias was building a cement stand to mount the rainwater tank they had received from Siyazondla. Elias and MaDingata's homestead nicely illustrates a number of the trends described earlier in this chapter: the shift in income patterns that has followed retrenchments, the expansion of the welfare system and the transformation of garden agriculture.

The case of Jomjom and NoAnswer differs from that of Elias and his family in many important respects. It is more typical of the older, previously mining-dependent homesteads, revealing substantial continuities between 1998 and 2009. Jomjom was in his mid-50s and working on the mines in 1998. He had recently moved his family to his father's pre-betterment site. They were growing maize and beans in their field and maize and sweet potatoes in their garden. They used manure in both field and garden. They had held four work parties for hoeing and weeding and had about 400 kilograms of maize and 50 kilograms of beans in storage.

In 2009, Jomjom had died, and NoAnswer had several children. They had added a rondavel, but not a 'modern' house suitable for rainwater collection. Their cultivation practices were largely unchanged: they still grew two crops (maize and beans) and held four agricultural work parties during the season, and remained in the same ploughing company, which continued to plough their land after Jomjom's death. At the time of the survey, they had about 450 kilograms of maize and 100 kilograms of beans on hand from the prior season. Not part of Siyazondla, generally tied into more conservative networks of neighbours and kin, Jomjom's homestead had continued to follow the old agricultural ways.

The third case, that of Zikhelele and NoFenitshala's homestead, illustrates intensification without Siyazondla support. This homestead escaped the retrenchments that had affected so many others and has expanded the agricultural component of its livelihood. In 1998, Zikhelele, about 40 years old, worked on the mines while NoFenitshala lived at home with the couple's four children. They grew the usual three crops (maize, beans and pumpkins) in their garden, with no additional inputs or work parties. The stocks from the last harvest had run out by the time of the survey.

By 2009, their oldest son had joined his father in full-time work on the mines. Three of the couple's six children and one resident grandchild were receiving CSGs. The family that had occupied their field during betterment had moved away, allowing Zikhelele and NoFenitshala to grow maize in the field. They had also added cabbage, spinach, potatoes and a peach tree to their garden, built an 'American Flat', a multi-roomed house with a corrugated iron roof, which would allow them to collect rainwater in the future, and had begun using manure, compost, fertiliser and insecticide in both their garden and their field. They said that the fertility of both the field and the garden had increased greatly. They relied on household and hired labour to cultivate and made no use of work parties. They also had sufficient oxen to put together a ploughing team on their own, maximizing their flexibility. While they did not have stored crops at the time of the survey, their overall trajectory has clearly been one of using cash income in order to diversify and intensify cultivation. Their example illustrates that enthusiasm for agriculture and a willingness to intensify and experiment among some younger households is found even among those outside of Siyazondla.

Conclusion

The overall picture that emerges from the 1998 and 2009 surveys is one of an increasing intensification and diversification of garden cultivation alongside a decline in field cultivation, partly shaped by changes in labour availability and welfare incomes. Given these findings, how can one evaluate existing state support for local livelihoods?

First, the recent downward trend in Siyazondla funding is troubling. It contradicts the international 'return to subsidies as a potential intervention for promoting food security and agricultural growth' (Denning et al. 2009: 3). The Siyazondla programme possesses great promise: with it, the Eastern Cape agriculture department is finally focusing on home gardens, in line with longstanding but largely ignored recommendations (such as McAllister 1992), and supporting the long-term trend towards garden intensification. Moreover, the programme successfully fostered intensification even without the 'African green revolution' package of hybrid seed and so on, promoted in the work of Sanchez, Denning and their colleagues.

Siyazondla in Hobeni has built effective networks for disseminating agricultural resources and information (notably with the cultivation of bananas, which is said to have spread through Siyazondla clubs, even though the agriculture department has not promoted bananas). It has also demonstrated the potential of homestead cultivation to enhance livelihoods, nutrition and food security. Siyazondla members stand out from the sample as a whole: they produce a greater diversity of crops and use more inputs, including locally obtained inputs (manure and compost). The programme has successfully fostered the use of existing resources to increase agricultural productivity without additional financial costs to the government or to the smallholders themselves.

It would be a tragedy if this support were allowed to languish. The programme's budget increased steadily until 2007. Since then, however, the budget has been cut, shrinking in 2010/2011 to less than a fifth of its 2006/2007 level, precluding distribution of inputs and tools to more recently formed clubs (see chapter 17, this volume). While 30 homesteads in Hobeni had received material support from Siyazondla in 2009, another 195 had joined Siyazondla clubs and would benefit if the programme's support resumed. There is also unrealised potential to expand the programme to reach homesteads such as Zikhelele and NoFenitshala's, described above, which are actively engaged in cultivation but which are not in a Siyazondla club. Twenty-one per cent of the homesteads which did *not* belong to Siyazondla clubs grew six or more crops in their garden in 2009, up from a single household (out of 80) in the 1998 survey. Faced with retrenchments and the prospect of chronic unemployment, many rural residents are eager to pursue garden cultivation as a way to enhance their livelihoods. The state should be supporting these initiatives, not allowing the networks built under the Siyazondla programme to decline.

A second conclusion that can be drawn from evaluating the surveys is that the effects of the CSG on cultivation appear positive. The CSG reaches women who are involved in garden cultivation on a day-to-day basis. Access to CSGs is positively correlated with garden crop diversity, which, in turn, benefits children's nutrition. While the availability of cash may have led some families to substitute purchased food for maize and beans formerly grown in fields, the decline in field cultivation has possibly been outweighed by the long-term benefit of higher school enrolment that follows from greater access to cash.

Neither the Siyazondla programme nor the Child Support Grant is likely to produce revolutionary changes in local livelihoods. Like any intervention, they may disappoint, create jealousy and have unequal consequences in an already differentiated rural population (see chapter 17, this volume). But both, by building on existing activities and aspirations while providing new capabilities and livelihood options, deserve continued support as part of a broad-based poverty-reduction strategy.

Notes

1   The Cwebe surveys were conducted by researchers from Rhodes University; all four surveys have been reanalysed here with the statistical software R, version 2.11.1.
2   The differences between these subsamples and the overall samples are statistically significant at $p < 0.05$.
3   There has also been a comparable decline in work parties for building (Fay 2011).
4   Details of the procedure used to classify households' position in the developmental cycle are found in Fay and Palmer 2002.
5   This figure does not represent the entire sample since a problem in the 2009 survey instrument led several of the interviewers to skip the question about ploughing.

References

Andrew, M. 1992. 'A geographical study of agricultural change since the 1930s in Shixini Location, Gatyana District, Transkei', unpublished MA thesis, Rhodes University, Grahamstown.

Buhlungu, S. and A. Bezuidenhout. 2008. 'Union solidarity under stress: the case of the National Union of Mineworkers in South Africa', *Labor Studies Journal*, 33(3): 262–287.

De Klerk, H. 2007. 'The mutual embodiment of landscape and livelihoods: an environmental history of Nqabara', unpublished MA thesis, Rhodes University, Grahamstown.

Denning, G., P. Kabambe, P. Sanchez, A. Malik, R. Flor, R. Harawa, P. Nkhoma, C. Zamba, C. Banda, C. Magombo, M. Keating, J. Wangila and J. Sachs. 2009. 'Input subsidies to improve smallholder maize productivity in Malawi: toward an African Green Revolution', *PLoS Biol*, 7(1):e1000023.

De Wet, C. and P. McAllister. 1983. *Rural communities in transition: a study of the socio-economic and agricultural implications of agricultural betterment and development*, Grahamstown: Rhodes University ISER.

Fay, D. 2003a. '"The trust is over! We want to plough!": land, livelihoods and resettlement in South Africa's Transkei', unpublished PhD thesis, Boston University.

Fay, D. 2003b. 'Case study no. 2: Hobeni, Xhora District', prepared for the Provincial Growth and Development Plan, Fort Hare Institute of Social and Economic Research, Alice.

Fay, D. 2011. 'Migrants, forests and houses: the historical political ecology of architectural change in Hobeni and Cwebe, South Africa', *Human Organization*, 70(3): 310–321.

Fay, D. 2012. '"The trust is over! We want to plough!": social differentiation and the reversal of resettlement in South Africa', *Human Ecology*, 40(1): 59–68.

Fay, D. and R. Palmer. 2002. 'Poverty and differentiation at Dwesa-Cwebe', in R. Palmer, H. Timmermans and D. Fay (eds) *From conflict to negotiation: nature-based development on South Africa's Wild Coast*, Pretoria: Human Sciences Research Council.

Ferguson, J. 2007. 'Formalities of poverty: thinking about social assistance in neoliberal South Africa', *African Studies Review*, 50(2): 71–86.

Hanlon, J., A. Barrientos and D. Hulme. 2010. *Just give money to the poor: the development revolution from the global south*, Sterling, VA: Kumarian.

Hebinck, P. 2007. 'Investigating rural livelihoods in Guquka and Koloni: an introduction', in P. Hebinck and P. Lent (eds) *Livelihoods and landscapes: the people of Guquka and Koloni and their resources*, Leiden/Boston: Brill Academic Publishers.

Helm, K. 2008. 'Gates Foundation's agriculture aid a hard sell', *Seattle Times* online, 20 January. Accessed 16 November 2010, http://community.seattletimes.nwsource.com/archive/?date=20080120&slug=gatesagriculture200.

Malherbe, Stephan. 2000. 'A perspective on the South African mining industry in the 21st century', unpublished report prepared for the Chamber of Mines of South Africa.

McAllister, P. 1992. 'Rural production, land use and development planning in Transkei: a critique of the Transkei agricultural development study', *Journal of Contemporary African Studies*, 11(2): 200–222.

McAllister, P. 2001. *Building the homestead: agriculture, labour and beer in South Africa's Transkei*, Aldershot: Ashgate.

Muller, N. and V. Mpela. 1987. *The population of Transkei – by magisterial district*. Umtata: University of Transkei Bureau for African Research and Documentation.

Pade, C., R. Palmer, M. Kavhai and S. Gumbo. 2009. 'Siyakhula living lab: baseline study report', unpublished ms, Rhodes University Department of Information Systems, Grahamstown.

Posel, D. 2001. 'Who are the heads of household, what do they do, and is the concept of headship useful? An analysis of headship in South Africa', *Development Southern Africa*, 18: 651–670.

Posel, D., J. Fairburn and F. Lund. 2006. 'Labour migration and households: a reconsideration of the effects of the social pension on labour supply in South Africa', *Economic Modelling*, 23(5): 836–853.

Sanchez, P., G. Denning and G. Nziguheba. 2009. 'The African Green Revolution moves forward', *Food Security*, 1(1): 37–44.

Seekings, J., M. Leibbrandt and N. Nattrass. 2004. *Income inequality after apartheid*, SALDRU/CSSR Working Paper No. 75, Cape Town: Centre for Social Science Research, University of Cape Town.

Shackleton, C., H. Timmermans, N. Nongwe, N. Hamer and R. Palmer. 2007. 'Direct-use values of non-timber forest products from two areas on the Transkei Wild Coast', *Agrekon* (46): 135–156.

Timmermans, H.G. 2004. 'Rural livelihoods at Dwesa/Cwebe: poverty, development and natural resource use on the Wild Coast, South Africa', unpublished MA thesis, Rhodes University.

19 Smallholder irrigation schemes as an agrarian development option for the Cape region

Wim van Averbeke and Jonathan Denison

Agricultural development is identified in the 'National Development Plan – Vision 2030' to drive the economic development of the rural areas in South Africa (NPC 2011). Irrigation is the 'driving force' in the proposed agricultural development strategy. It is argued that 0.5 million hectares of new irrigation land can be added to the current 1.5 million hectares of irrigated land, by using existing water resources more efficiently and by developing new water schemes. The aim of this chapter is to provide pointers that should be considered when planning new smallholder irrigation schemes in South Africa. This is done by analysing important factors known to affect scheme and farm performance on four schemes located in the Cape region, where smallholder irrigation scheme performance has been particularly poor relative to other parts of South Africa (Bembridge 1997, 2000; Commission for the Socio-Economic Development of the Bantu Areas within the Union of South Africa 1955; Fanadzo et al. 2010; Legoupil 1985; Van Averbeke et al. 1998). A framework of smallholder scheme development trajectories, based on local and international experiences, guided the analysis. The results of the analysis were used to identify what type of scheme development would be most likely to succeed under the various circumstances that occur in the Cape region and elsewhere in South Africa, and to highlight the key factors for consideration when a particular scheme development is opted for.

Smallholder irrigation schemes in South Africa

Irrigation is the artificial application of water to land for the purpose of enhancing plant production. Irrigation water can be abstracted from the source and conveyed to the field by farmers individually or in a group as an irrigation scheme. Accordingly, an irrigation scheme can be defined as an agricultural project involving multiple holdings that depend on a shared distribution system for access to irrigation water and, in some cases, on a shared water storage or diversion facility (Van Averbeke et al. 2011). The term 'irrigation scheme' is also used more broadly to refer to a multitude of entities that correspond to this definition, when these entities share the same bulk conveyance system (Reinders 2010). South African social policies of racial segregation and separation of the past also impacted on irrigation scheme development. Plots on schemes developed for white farmers ranged between 8 and 20 hectares and were on average about 10 times larger than the 1.5-hectare plots allocated to black farmers during the same period (Van Averbeke et al. 2011). This explains why the term 'smallholder irrigation scheme' is commonly used to refer to irrigation schemes on which the land is held by black people (Machete et al. 2004). Accordingly, Van Averbeke et al. (2011) defined 'smallholder irrigation scheme' in the South African context as an irrigation scheme that was constructed specifically for occupation and use by black farmers. In terms of a real cover these smallholder irrigation schemes are of secondary importance. In 2010, they covered 47 667 hectares (Van Averbeke et al. 2011), whereas in 2008, South Africa had 1 675 822 hectares of registered irrigation land of which 1 399 221 hectares were irrigated annually (Van der Stoep 2011).

Irrigation and rural economic development

Where water deficit is a limiting factor, which is the case in most of South Africa (Annandale et al. 2011), irrigation enables or improves crop production. Generally, irrigation increases crop income by raising crop yield, lifting the quality of produce, and allowing for multiple cropping cycles during a single year where the temperature regime is favourable. Multiple cropping cycles not only increase the labour requirement per unit area, but also spread it more evenly through the year than is the case with dryland farming. They also level the cash flow of farm enterprises. By removing the risk of yield reductions due to water deficit, irrigation provides farmers with the opportunity to intensify their cropping systems, which requires investments in fertilisers, superior crop varieties, labour and transactions. This process of intensification is the essence of the 'green revolution'. Enhancement of the backward and forward linkages to agriculture brought about by intensification forms part of the multiplier effect agriculture has on local and national economies. Making this happen is what the vision and strategy of the National Development Plan (NPC 2011) for rural economic development is all about.

Irrigation has contributed significantly to economic development and poverty reduction in rural areas of Asia (Turral et al. 2010). Studies on the effect of irrigation on poverty reduction have shown that the rise in farm income brought about by irrigation is sufficiently substantial to lift poor households out of poverty (Castillo et al. 2007; Gebregziabher et al. 2009; Huang et al. 2005; Huang et al.

2006). Although the economic performance of irrigation schemes around the world has been judged as good generally, it is widely accepted that irrigation developments over the last five decades have seldom performed to their design potential (Shah et al. 2002; Smith 2004; Turral et al. 2010). Generally, smallholder irrigation schemes have been less successful in Africa than elsewhere in the world (Inocencio et al. 2007) and South Africa is no exception (Bembridge 2000; Crosby et al. 2000; Van Averbeke et al. 2011).

Factors affecting irrigation schemes and smallholder irrigator typology

Backeberg (2002) identified eight factors that influence irrigation schemes across the domains of farm, scheme and external world. Somewhat modified, these factors are:

- natural resources;
- technology and infrastructure;
- policy, institutional arrangements and social resources;
- location in relation to markets;
- human resources (knowledge and skills of smallholders);
- financial services;
- farming system feasibility; and
- agricultural support services.

This multitude of different interacting factors highlights the complexity of successful irrigation scheme development. Categorisation by means of a typology is a useful way of dealing with complexity. In Table 19.1, the typology of South African smallholder irrigation schemes developed by Denison and Manona (2007) and adapted by Van Averbeke et al. (2011) is presented. The idea behind this typology is that smallholder irrigators can be differentiated in terms of risk-taking and why and how they farm and irrigate, and that the factors that characterise smallholder irrigation schemes have a determining influence on the type of farmers and the type of farming that will occur on an irrigation scheme.

In what follows, four case studies of smallholder irrigation schemes in the Cape region, with different characteristics, are described in the light of the eight factors that influence irrigation schemes and the irrigation scheme typology shown in Table 19.1. In the final part of the chapter, the case studies are analysed with a view to identifying lessons for future irrigation scheme development as envisaged in the National Development Plan.

Table 19.1 Typology of South African smallholder irrigation schemes

Scheme type	Typical plot size	Typical irrigation system	Purpose of farming and farming system
Food plot	< 0.5 ha	Canal irrigation or movable sprinklers	Mainly for own consumption with some local marketing. Low external input approaches to production.
Peasant	1 ha to 2 ha	Preferably canal irrigation	Diverse purposes in line with diversified livelihoods of plot holders and diverse approaches to production reflecting risk appetite. Local (urban) markets dominate, but with assistance, distant city markets could be accessed.
Commercial farmer	> 2 ha	Relatively simple overhead or micro-irrigation	Full-time commercial farming that includes engagement with distant markets. Highly productive farming systems are necessary and access to finance could be a requirement.
Equity-labourer	Consolidated landholding	Complex overhead or micro-irrigation	Commercial farming with strategic partner who manages the enterprise, whilst plot holders are farm workers, who also receive a share in the profits for providing the land.

Source: Van Averbeke et al. 2011

Case studies

Eksteenkuil irrigation scheme (Northern Cape)

When the Northern Cape government instituted the Orange River Farmer Settlement Programme as an economic initiative in response to available water rights, its aim was to irrigate 4 000 hectares along the banks of the lower part of the Orange River, including the settlements of new farmers from previously disadvantaged groups. Eksteenkuil irrigation scheme, located about 50 kilometres south-west of Upington, has about 620 hectares under irrigation, used by 119 farmers primarily for the production of raisins. Lucerne and cotton are also grown. Farmers reside on their plots, which are about five hectares in size. Farming is generally a full-time activity and the primary contributor to livelihoods (Khundlande and Van Schalkwyk 2010). These farmers conform to the 'commercial farmer' typology.

After its inception farmers held their plots in terms of a kind of trust tenure. Promulgation of the Transformation of Certain Rural Areas Act (No. 94 of 1998) paved the way for the upgrading of tenure at Eksteenkuil from occupational rights to freehold. However, according to Khundlande and Van Schalkwyk (2010), only about one-third of plot holders have been issued title deeds to their plots.

Irrigation water is pumped from the Orange River and gravitated to individual plots by a conveyance and distribution system of lined canals. All farmers practise surface irrigation and the cost of water is subsidised by the state. Eksteenkuil is a member of a Water Users Association (WUA), which includes several commercial farmers and the urban area of Keimoes. The WUA manages the scheme's water abstraction from the river.

Although Eksteenkuil farmers work individually, 106 farmers are members of the Eksteenkuil Farmers' Cooperative through which they market a large proportion of their raisins. The cooperative has a standing arrangement with Traidcraft, an established fair-trade organisation based in the United Kingdom, which ensures that farmers receive reasonable prices for their raisins. Jordaan and Grové (2010) found, though, that Eksteenkuil farmers do not hesitate to sell their raisins on the spot market when lucrative opportunities arise. Traidcraft also makes a financial contribution towards the cooperative. This income, combined with membership fees, is used by the cooperative to purchase implements which can then be rented by its members. Since only one in four farmers at Eksteenkuil owns his or her own implements, the availability of jointly owned implements is of great benefit (Khundlande and Van Schalkwyk 2010).

At the time of writing, farming at Eksteenkuil was going well (Khundlande and Van Schalkwyk 2010). The area under raisin grapes has expanded, and incomes are reasonable. The average cash income of irrigator homesteads, with an average of 4.8 members, was R43 056[1] in 2004, well above the poverty line. Of this, 63 per cent was generated on the farm. Most homesteads hire additional labour from Keimoes during peak times, thus contributing to local employment. One constraint on the further expansion of raisin production is the high cost of establishing vines, estimated to range between R80 000 and R200 000 per hectare in 2008 (Khundlande and Van Schalkwyk 2010). This is a substantial investment considering that the estimated gross annual income from raisin production is only about R13 000 per hectare, whilst the annual operating costs are about R7 700 per hectare. Moreover, it takes between two and four years before income from newly planted vines is forthcoming.

Prince Albert commonage schemes (Western Cape)

Prince Albert is a small village located in the Great Karoo at the foot of the Swartberg mountains. The commonage was developed in terms of policy set out in the Department of Land Affairs (DLA) White Paper (DLA 1997) and is funded by the Land Reform Programme. The land is owned by the municipality. The commonage policy aims to provide access to land for the purpose of food security to emerging farmers who want to expand their enterprises without incurring land-purchase costs.

Irrigation is essential for crop farming on the commonage since the area is semi-arid. Two earth dams, fed by surface water run-off from seasonal rivers, supply irrigation water to pumped sprinklers. Water supply is variable, though, and in drought years the dams run dry. There are a number of supplementary boreholes which are used for irrigation in times of drought, but these are limited by their poor water quality and high saline levels. Aquifer levels are seasonably variable but generally replenish annually (personal communication, Dr R Murray, September 2011).

Small livestock and irrigation enterprises have leases on the commonage. Importantly, each enterprise has a separate lease agreement with the municipality and is distinct in terms of decision-making and financial control. Two smallholder irrigation initiatives on the commonage (vegetable producers and an onion seed collective) have been established as 'incubators' with the intention of providing a low-risk environment for farmers to develop production and marketing skills before attempting to farm on a bigger scale.

The vegetable producers farm individually but share pumping costs and irrigation system maintenance. Only about 15 per cent of the 10 hectares available to the vegetable farmers is used, mainly because of the insecure water supply and the fact that farmers hold jobs and can only farm part-time.

The farming approach conforms to the typology of the 'peasant farmer': part-time, low-risk and geared to home food production with some cash sales. Production is subsidised by the Department of Agriculture. It has assisted with the capital costs of borehole refitting and has facilitated trials of potatoes, sweet potatoes, maize, beetroot, carrots, tomatoes, pumpkins, and melons. It provides substantial support, including an extension officer.

The onion seed collective has 35 members, mainly women. Farming and marketing is led, supported and subsidised by the DLA with the close involvement of the group. The DLA has brokered a seed-production contract with Japan. Although the enterprise is succeeding, there are a number of issues concerning the way in which the group will eventually take ownership of it. It remains to be seen whether it will be financially sustainable when government support is withdrawn. From the perspective of the land-rights holders an 'equity-labourer' relationship prevails even though the partner is the government. The enterprise serves to provide secure jobs for participants but its potential as incubator still has to be demonstrated over time (Aliber et al. 2011; Umhlaba 2010).

Horseshoe irrigation scheme (Ciskei region of the Eastern Cape)

Horseshoe irrigation scheme is interesting because it demonstrates how new farmers can be settled on irrigation projects. The scheme had a short life, though. It came into existence in 1991 and was closed down at the end of 1997, when Ulimcor ceased operations. The farming typology on which the scheme was developed was that of the 'commercial farmer', a near full-time individual farmer.

Horseshoe, about nine kilometres from King William's Town, was established on land in the Braunschweig area, purchased by the South African Development Trust for the purpose of consolidating the Ciskei homeland territory. In 1986, user rights to most of the released land around Braunsweigh were transferred to Ulimcor for commercial exploitation. A parcel of about 50 hectares along the banks of the Buffalo River was used by parastatal staff to produce vegetables under irrigation. In 1991, following changes in the agricultural policy of the Ciskei, Ulimcor was instructed to stop farming and instead focus on farmer development. Ulimcor decided to subdivide the irrigation farm into 18 plots under sprinkler irrigation of two hectares each for allocation to local people. The scheme design was implemented using existing pumps, pipes and sprinkler lines, providing each plot with independent access to water. Plots were laid out on well-drained soils, 14 moderately deep (> 800 millimetres) and 4 shallow (about 500 millimetres deep). Farm workers who had been retrenched by Ulimcor had first option to take up a plot; vacant plots were made available to other applicants. Forty applications were received from retrenched workers, but 36 withdrew after learning that they were expected to farm independently. The other 14 plots were allocated to applicants from surrounding settlements. Few of the 18 plot holders had been exposed to commercial agriculture previously and none to irrigated farming.

The plot holders farmed independently and had to pay for their operational costs. The on-site support services offered by Ulimcor were impressive, though. These included training and technical support, administrative and bookkeeping support, access to water and tractor services, produce transportation service and inputs through an ordering system. These services were provided by a total of 20 people, 10 of whom served as security officers, 3 as tractor drivers, 3 as clerical workers, 1 as truck driver, 1 as technician responsible for agrochemicals, 1 as extension officer and 1 as project coordinator. In addition there was a private workshop responsible for tractor and pump maintenance, owned by the three mechanics who worked there. A portion of the support services costs was recovered from farmers. In 1996, plot holders paid a monthly water levy of R50 for pumping (electricity costs) and pump maintenance, which covered only half of the actual operational and maintenance costs of supplying water to the plots. Plot holders paid R6.50 a litre for diesel for the tractors. Full cost recovery for this service, including maintenance and repairs, would have required a charge of R8.50 per litre of diesel. The rest of the support services were paid for by Ulimcor, amounting to R400 000 in 1996.[2] In that year, the gross cash receipts of the 18 farmers totalled about R100 000.

Plot holders were given a credit line by the Ciskeian Agricultural Bank to purchase inputs and get their enterprises running. The bank did not control the credit lines well, though, and allowed plot holders to get deeply into debt. Plot holders each owed the bank R13 000 on average, amounting to about two years of cash receipts from plot production. After the bank had suspended the credit facility the scheme assisted plot holders financially by allowing them to access tractor services on credit. Other services, though, including the monthly water levy, had to be paid on time in cash. This new financial arrangement acted as a self-elimination factor: nine of the original plot holders quit farming and left the scheme. Their plots were promptly taken over by new applicants. The new arrangement worked well and in 1997 plot holders owed the scheme only R20 000, an arrears of about two to three months. In addition some of the original plot holders who had remained were managing to repay their bank loans. Farming standards were improving but cropping intensity dropped because farmers planted only what they could afford on a cash basis.

Part of the success of smallholder vegetable production at Horseshoe from a production perspective was the favourable location of the scheme in relation to markets. Farmers could sell all that they produced as long as the quality was acceptable. About 60 per cent was sold to bakkie-traders and another substantial portion to a vegetable shop in King William's Town. A small portion was retailed to local consumers, and specialised produce, such as celery, was sold in East London.

The scheme stopped operating when Ulimcor closed. At the time of the closure, continued operations were dependent on retaining eight support staff. About 75 per cent of the cost of the three tractor drivers and the truck driver was already being recovered from farmers. The Department of Agriculture turned down a request for a budget of R25 000 a month, including a specialist extension officer, and Horseshoe was shut down at the end of 1997.

Ncora irrigation scheme (Transkei region of the Eastern Cape)

Ncora irrigation scheme is located near the town of Cofimvaba in the former Transkei homeland. The scheme is 2 830 hectares, making it one of only six smallholder irrigation schemes in South Africa larger than 1 000 hectares. The scheme receives water from the Ncora Dam on the Tsomo River and irrigation is by gravity pressure. Various types of overhead irrigation systems are used, including semi-solid set sprinkler systems, centre pivots, portable laterals and movable sprinklers connected to hosepipes. Although Ncora is still considered an operational scheme, only a small portion of the total command area is presently being used.

Ncora epitomises the smallholder irrigation scheme model of Loxton Venn and Associates, whose model has been applied in the design of several other schemes in the Eastern Cape, such as Keiskammahoek, Shiloh, Tyefu and Zanyokwe. Loxton Venn and Associates (1983) elaborated the principles that underpinned their model in their 'Master preliminary plan for Zanyokwe irrigation scheme'. They argued that the cost of constructing smallholder irrigation schemes was too high to be restricted to the social objective of providing poor rural people with irrigation land to grow food. To justify the expense of constructing schemes, they considered it necessary for projects to have an economic objective. They broke this down into three sub-objectives for poor rural areas: high production, high employment and high gross margins. They pointed out that under normal circumstances the social and the economic objectives were mutually exclusive, but argued that their model of scheme development made it possible to pursue both by separating these functions in the design of the scheme. They argued that the economic objective could be achieved by allocating a large portion of the irrigation land to a central unit which would be farmed as an estate using labour and sophisticated management. The holders of the land on which the scheme was to be established were required to give up part of their dryland allotments to make land available for the central unit. In return they received access to a smaller-sized irrigation plot that would enable them to produce crops for their own consumption and for sale, thus taking care of the social objective.

The implementation of the model at Ncora involved offering original landholders the choice between a 0.9-hectare tribal plot, which they would farm for themselves, or a 0.3-hectare food plot and a share in the group farm. The profits from the group would be used to support the scheme's social objectives. It was explained to landholders that their 0.9-hectare allocation would be subdivided into three parts or panels if they selected the food plot option. One panel would be for their use, while the remaining two would be transferred to the group farm. The profit made by the group farm on one of the two panels would pay for the inputs on the food plot, while the profit made on the other panel would be paid out annually as a dividend. A total of 419 landholders opted for the 0.9-hectare tribal plot and 805 chose the food plot option. In addition 69 landless homesteads were allocated a 0.2-hectare special food plot each. Three chiefs were given a 21-hectare farm and 23 homesteads were allocated 5-hectare commercial farms. The functional subdivision of Ncora is shown in Table 19.2. From the subdivision, it is clear that Ncora combined all four irrigation farmer typologies presented in Table 19.1.

The completed development included the establishment of economic and social infrastructure. Potable water, power systems, roads, workshops, storage facilities, housing for senior staff, recreation facilities and a landing strip for small airplanes formed part of the project. The headquarters consisted of a staff village, central stores, management, research and finance, marketing and engineering offices, and a training centre. The farmers resided in four villages at the edge of the scheme, each with a field centre made up of two large sheds and housing for field staff.

Table 19.2 Functional subdivision of Ncora irrigation scheme

Description of unit	Number of units	Total area (ha)
Ncora farm (central unit)	1	1 542
Group farm	1	488
Chief's farm	3	63
Commercial farm	23	104
Tribal plot	419	377
Food plot	805	242
Special food plot	69	14
TOTAL (planned area)		**2 830**

Source: Commision of Enquiry Appointed by the Eastern Cape Province (1996)

Production involved dairy and a selection of crops. In 1984, one year after the scheme had been decommissioned, the dairy herd consisted of 2 008 cattle and milk production amounted to 5 million litres (6.7 litres/day/animal across the herd). The most important crops were potatoes, silage maize, wheat, peas and dry beans. The scheme also boasted the largest cabbage enterprise in Africa (260 hectares) and produced asparagus and Cape gooseberry for canning on site.

The Ncora Project was never able to finance itself, let alone pay back its capital investments. It was dependent on the state to cover shortfalls between operating income and expenditure. This deficit amounted to about 12 per cent of total operating expenditure in 1984, when the project was running reasonably well. The deficit soared rapidly when problems arose as early as 1986. These problems stemmed from certain assumptions underpinning the model. Realisation of the economic objective depended on cheap and docile labour. When labour refused to remain cheap and docile, the economic wheels came off. The weakening of the project's economic base led to the undermining of its social component. Landholders at Ncora were in the 'privileged' position of having their plots cultivated, fertilised and planted by the central unit. Farmers had only to irrigate, weed and harvest certain crops themselves. Wheat, for example, was harvested by the central unit on their behalf. Services were supplied free of charge to food plot holders as part of the land exchange arrangement. The services were available on credit to holders of tribal plots, to be paid for by selling the crop through the central marketing service of the scheme. Rising financial deficits and labour at critical times in the cropping calendar resulted in a decline in the quality of service provision to farmers. The lack of profits from the group farm also made it difficult to adjust the value of the annual dividend in line with inflation. Increasingly, food plot holders felt cheated and started to call for the return of the land they had transferred to the group farm. Unrest among tribal plot holders developed, because the value of the crop they delivered to the central marketing service was rarely sufficient to pay for the services and inputs they had received from the central unit, and many found themselves in debt.

A political decision was taken to make the Ncora workers permanent employees with full benefits. This pushed Ncora's balance sheet further into the red. In 1994 the Eastern Cape government took over all parastatal projects from the Ciskei and Transkei homelands, including the Ncora irrigation scheme. The annual budget was a major financial burden to the provincial Department of Agriculture. During its final year of operation as a parastatal project, for example, the total income of Ncora was R2.8 million whilst total expenditure was R21.3 million, 78 per cent of which consisted of remuneration for 669 staff members (Commission of Enquiry Appointed by the Eastern Cape Province to Look for Sustainable Solutions to the Problems of Large Eastern Cape Irrigation Schemes, 1996). At the end of 1996 the Eastern Cape Department of Agriculture discontinued financing the parastatal projects it had inherited. All project staff were retrenched, and the scheme was transferred to its landholders. It soon became clear that the landholders had not been prepared to take over its management. Various revitalisation initiatives involving local and foreign agencies were implemented with little or no success. Being a gravity-fed scheme, irrigation at Ncora has continued but production has been restricted to small portions only, because ageing and vandalism have affected the irrigation system. Ncora was meant to be the ultimate example of sustainable smallholder irrigation development, with all the possible support systems that could be thought of available on site. In the end, Ncora proved to be little more than an expensive mistake. Yet the stream of public funding aimed at revitalising the project keeps flowing. The latest 'donation' of R280 million was made in July 2012 (Vhelapi 2012).

Lessons from the case studies

Referring to the eight factors that influence irrigation schemes, several lessons can be learnt from the four case studies that have been described.

Natural resources

In the past, the presence of a source of water, a dam site and irrigable soil was often sufficient justification to establish an irrigation scheme. It is now realised that this perspective was inadequate. Economic, human, institutional and social factors have been identified as critical for the sustainability of smallholder irrigation schemes in South Africa (Van Averbeke et al. 2011). This does not mean that natural resource factors, particularly the suitability of soils for irrigation, should be ignored when planning is done. As in the past, the quality of the natural resources must receive adequate attention.

Technology and infrastructure

Scheme design is concerned with decisions on irrigation technology and infrastructure, among others. The key elements of the technical system are indivisible, which brings about a degree of technical determinism over the development trajectory of the scheme. Any scheme can be consolidated and operated centrally, but the option for farmer management is reduced as the technical complexity of the system increases. Some schemes, well illustrated by Ncora, have little alternative but to continue operating as a centrally controlled farming operation by virtue of their size and complex technical design. Smallholders can neither operate the scheme themselves, nor can they generate sufficient profit to pay a management entity to operate it on their behalf. The only practical solution is a commercial partnership based on consolidation of the smallholdings into a larger land unit.

The canal system at Eksteenkuil, where most farmers fitted the 'commercial farmer' typology, allowed for individual enterprises to thrive, even though the system involved a shared pump station, which brought with it costs and risks. Farming was the main occupation and source of income of plot holders at Eksteenkuil and generated sufficient money to finance the pumping costs. The canal and furrow distribution system is simple and has low operational costs.

Canal schemes are durable, because many continue to function even though they are old and dilapidated. Canal schemes are better suited to local control than schemes with complex technology, and when gravity-fed, they are not affected by energy price externalities (Van Averbeke 2012). The link between technology choices, where system design either limits or accommodates individual rather than group farming, and the nature of the resulting irrigation enterprises needs to be fully appreciated to take smallholder irrigation forward in the Cape.

Policy, institutional arrangements and social resources

Of all the institutions that affect farming on irrigation schemes, land tenure is probably the least certain, particularly in terms of policy. One of the reasons why expansion by successful smallholder farmers is limited on irrigation schemes is the absence of land-trading institutions which facilitate exit from and new entry onto irrigated plots (Manona et al. 2010). The landholding at Ncora typifies the limitations of traditional tenure on smallholder irrigation schemes. Land-use rights are effectively held in perpetuity regardless of interest, capability or willingness to use the irrigation scheme land and its infrastructure. There is little opportunity for rentals or land exchange in any secure or formally administered way. Non-performing farmers have no reason to exit as there are no costs involved in holding onto the land asset and no gain to be had from handing it back to the tribal authority.

Prince Albert commonage presents a workable tenure option through leasing, because it intentionally facilitates land exchange. The lease system provides access to land and irrigation infrastructure for emerging farmers to develop their competencies and networks. Leases are secure, and the coordinated presence of a range of established agencies to support the farmers in an incubator context aims to enhance the chances of success. There is no attempt to force everyone into the same farming arrangement; people can farm individually or enter into cooperative arrangements. If the farmers do not succeed in the early and more risky stages of enterprise development, they can exit in a formal way and others can take their place. The role of the municipality in administering leases and facilitating the exit of those who were not using the land successfully was crucial in the Prince Albert case. A similar arrangement applied at Horseshoe. Another option is the use of new legal instruments to upgrade long-term occupancy to title deeds, such as at Eksteenkuil. This enables market-based exchange through lease or sale, and also allows land to be used as collateral for production loans, overcoming a critical financial constraint to farming.

The landholding arrangements at Prince Albert and Horseshoe (formal lease) and at Eksteenkuil (tenure upgrade) are models of how opportunities can be provided to access irrigation resources, allowing land to change hands when farming fails or personal choices lead to an exit. However, these approaches require bold political engagement because they remove the power of the traditional authorities over the land. Given the high level of state investment in infrastructure, and the low utilisation of irrigation land and other resources, a bold approach seems justified.

Policy and institutions governing water is also of critical importance for smallholder irrigation. Given the reality of competing demands and a water-stressed state, the future of (smallholder) irrigation in South Africa will increasingly be dictated by water economics. On the one hand, making water available for smallholder farmers is a priority in policy and strategy in relation to water allocation reform (DWA 2010). However, the returns from this water are relatively low and market forces are going to result in a shift of water allocations from 'low-value' to 'high-value' users within the regulated water market (Nieuwoudt and Backeberg 2011). Currently such transfers take place only in a limited way. According to a Department of Water Affairs (DWA) report on its 'Integrated Water Resource Planning for South Africa' (DWA 2010), it '… might be sensible to make unused water (from smallholder irrigation schemes) available either for rural or urban domestic use or to meet other economic user demands (e.g. industrial, mining, forestry)'. This represents a critical shift in water resource management policy and will place increasing pressure on smallholder irrigators. Water for this sector is usually subsidised by the state and, due to the generally low production characteristic of newly established farmers, has low economic returns per unit of water. While the subsidisation of water, electricity, capital and production costs can be justified on the basis of historical marginalisation, the state's ability to exploit its economic value is likely to become the overriding consideration. What, we need to ask, can stop water being reallocated from smallholder irrigators (lower-value users in financial terms) to large-scale commercial agriculture and other high-value users? The answer to this question involves an analysis of the economic value of rural stability more broadly, as well as of national food security.

Location in relation to markets

Location in relation to markets is important for all types of schemes, but especially for 'peasant'-type schemes. Farmers on peasant-type schemes tend to purchase small quantities of inputs and their production is also relatively small and diverse. Proximity to a sizeable urban centre that has one or more farm-requisite or gardening stores provides farmers with the opportunity to fund the purchase of the inputs in small quantities from their normal cash flow. Being close to a town also facilitates marketing of peasant produce, usually by bakkie-traders and micro-traders who bring produce from the scheme to the town daily, using public transportation (Van Averbeke 2012). Evidence of this produce marketing process was presented for Horseshoe but has also been documented on schemes in KwaZulu-Natal (Cousins 2013) and Limpopo (Van Averbeke 2012). 'Commercial farmer' schemes, such as Eksteenkuil, and 'equity-labourer' schemes, such as the central unit at Ncora, are not as dependent on proximity to urban centres, because the size of their production makes bulk transportation possible. In the case of 'food plot' schemes, the local rural market is often large enough to absorb surplus production (Van Averbeke et al. 1998), especially in the context of declining dryland production in the rural areas (see chapter 14, this volume).

Human resources (knowledge and skills of smallholders)

Farming successfully involves the application of a wide range of skills that cover the production process of land preparation, planting date and spacing, nutrient application, cultivar selection, irrigation, plant protection, harvesting and post-harvest treatment. Added to that are finance, resource management and marketing. Traditionally, farming skills were transferred from generation to generation with young people learning from their parents whilst helping on the farm, an informal learning process, to which innovation contributed through experimentation and farmer-to-farmer exchanges. When a new farming system is required (irrigation, new crop choices, different fertiliser materials, use of agrochemicals), as in the case of irrigated and market-oriented production, the existing knowledge and skills base of farmers has to expand and considerable learning is needed. This learning requires external support but can be achieved, even when participants have little prior knowledge of farming of any kind, as was shown clearly in the Horseshoe case.

Financial services

Access to financial services is critical for 'commercial farmer' and 'equity-labourer' schemes. The scale at which production occurs brings about substantial production expenses, and these, in turn, present a serious risk to farmers. Farmers rarely have the financial reserves to pay all production expenses directly, and for this reason, access to credit or production loans is important, as well as access to insurance to cover the risk associated with credit or loans. Access to financial services is less important on 'food plot' and 'peasant farmer' schemes, because farmers usually pay for their production expenses using cash receipts from produce sales or income derived from other sources.

Farming system feasibility

From a financial perspective the feasibility of a farming system is determined by the difference between the cost of production and the income obtained. Farming systems of 'food plot' and 'peasant' schemes are more malleable to approaches that limit costs to improve margins (Van Averbeke 2008). This can be achieved by replacing capital with labour and by on-farm reproduction of resources. Examples of this are the use of canal irrigation, animal draught power, and the production and use of animal manure and compost instead of chemical fertilisers. Factors of scale are likely to limit such opportunities on 'commercial' and 'equity labourer' schemes.

Agricultural support services

The level of support established on the 36-hectare Horseshoe project, where 10 people provided training and support for 18 farmers, covering all aspects of irrigated farming, provides a perspective on just how much support is needed. Public outlay in support services can be seen as an investment in cycles of learning with a resulting upward ratchet effect in the capabilities of farmers, even when there are occasional failures. The agricultural learning curve is by nature slow and needs to be supported accordingly. Chancellor et al. (2003) argued that long time-lines of 8 to 10 years are needed to develop the relevant farming experience and essential skills for a sustainable agribusiness. Short-term support might be helpful in some instances, but success is likely to demand commitment from government or other development agencies over a period that is long enough to establish skills and stable institutional systems.

Are smallholder irrigation schemes an agrarian development option for the Cape region?

Irrigation clearly can increase food security and become a driver of local economic growth, but there are lessons from experiences in South Africa and abroad that need to be taken into account when electing to establish smallholder irrigation schemes. Technical planning and system design must be guided by farmers' objectives and capabilities. A commitment to provide support for about a decade is necessary to achieve the production and profitability outcomes that justify the high investment in schemes. Partnerships with commercial entities can fill critical gaps in production knowledge, finance, inputs and marketing, but must be approached cautiously and must be geared towards achieving developmental objectives, not just production objectives. Partnerships which centralise control of all aspects of the farming business do not encourage the promotion of individual farming skills and can marginalise landholders, locking them in the position of observers rather than active participants (Schreiner et al. 2010; Tapela 2012; Van Averbeke et al. 2011). While this arrangement might solve immediate financial resource problems, it rarely empowers smallholders with farming skills to create self-sustaining livelihoods.

Technology should always be appropriate to the farming typology that is being supported. Expensive technologies require commercialisation of the enterprise to cover capital repayment and operational costs, and are not appropriate to part-time farming or home food production. A more suitable solution for these farmers is gravity-fed canal irrigation which has low operational costs. This method has been scientifically proven to be 'waterwise' when used with the short-furrow method. Misperceptions about flood irrigation in academic, professional and government circles need to be countered so that this technique can be exploited in suitable contexts.

The imperatives of water allocation reform have to be weighed against the pressure to obtain maximum economic gain from a unit of water. To counter this inevitable shift away from the smallholder sector, there will have to be a dramatic shift in the production, management and marketing capability of farmers on smallholder schemes. Crafting locally appropriate and diverse irrigation responses, technically, institutionally and in terms of the on-farm production and marketing approaches, is critical. If diversity is not accommodated, and land administration and tenure security in particular are not addressed boldly, smallholder schemes are increasingly likely to be dominated by commercial partnerships, with a move away from individual farmer development. For smallholder irrigation to play any role in agrarian reform in future, revitalisation and new developments have to be done in ways that respond to site-specific opportunities and which match the *different* objectives and capabilities of participant farmers.

Notes

1   The June 2011 rand value of the stated amounts can be estimated by multiplying the stated amounts with a factor of 1.513, derived using the CPI data published by Statistics South Africa.

2   The June 2011 rand value of the stated amounts can be estimated by multiplying with a factor of 2.409 derived from the CPI data published by Statistics South Africa.

References

Aliber, M., M. Baiphethi, R. de Satge, J. Denison, T. Hart, P. Jacobs and W. van Averbeke. 2011. *Strategies to support South African smallholders as a contribution to government's second economy strategy, Volume 2: Case Studies*, Cape Town: Institute for Poverty Land and Agrarian Studies, University of the Western Cape.

Annandale, J., R. Stirzacker, A. Singels, M. van der Laan and M.C. Laker. 2011. 'Irrigation scheduling research: South African experiences and future prospects', *Water SA*, 37(5): 751–763.

Backeberg, G. 2002. *Requirements for sustainable irrigation development*, Pretoria: Water Research Commission.

Bembridge, T. 1997. Small-scale farmer irrigation in South Africa: implications for extension, *South African Journal of Agricultural Extension*, 26(1): 71–81.

Bembridge T. 2000. *Guidelines for rehabilitation of small-scale farmer irrigation schemes in South Africa*, WRC Report No. 891/1/00, Gezina: Water Research Commission.

Castillo, G., E. Namara, H. Ravnborg, M. Hanjra, L. Smith and M. Hussein. 2007. 'Reversing the flow: agricultural water management pathways for poverty reduction', in D. Molden (ed.) *Water for food, water for life: a comprehensive assessment of water management in agriculture*, London: Earthscan and Colombo: International Water Management Institute.

Chancellor, F., D. Shepherd and M. Upton. 2003. *Creating sustainable smallholder irrigated farm businesses (SIBU)*, DFID KAR Research Project R 7810, Report OD 149, HR Wallingford/UK Department for International Development.

Commission for the Socio-Economic Development of the Bantu Areas within the Union of South Africa. 1955. *Summary of the report*, Pretoria: Government Printer.

Commission of Enquiry Appointed by the Eastern Cape Province to Look for Sustainable Solutions to the Problems of Large Eastern Cape Irrigation Schemes. 1996. *Ncora irrigation scheme: summary report*, Alice: Faculty of Agriculture and ARDRI, University of Fort Hare.

Cousins, B. 2013. 'Smallholder irrigation schemes, agrarian reform and "accumulation from above and from below" in South Africa', *Journal of Agrarian Change*, 13(1): 116–139.

Crosby, C., M. de Lange, C. Stimie and I. van der Stoep. 2000. *A review of planning and design procedures applicable to small-scale farmer irrigation projects*, WRC Report No. 578/2/00, Pretoria: Water Research Commission.

Denison, J. and S. Manona. 2007. *Principles approaches and guidelines for the participatory revitalisation of smallholder irrigation schemes: Volume 2 – concepts and cases*, WRC Report No. TT 309/07, Gezina: Water Research Commission.

DLA (Department of Land Affairs). 1997. *White Paper on South African land policy*. Pretoria: Department of Land Affairs.

DWA (Department of Water Affairs). 2010. *Integrated water resource planning for South Africa: a situation analysis*, DWA Report No. P RSA 000/00/12910, Pretoria: Department of Water Affairs.

Fanadzo, M., C. Chiduza and P. Mnkeni. 2010. 'Overview of smallholder irrigation schemes in South Africa: relationship between farmer crop management practices and performance', *African Journal of Agricultural Research*, 5(25): 3514–3523.

Gebregziabher, G., R. Namara and S. Holden. 2009. 'Poverty reduction with irrigation investment: an empirical case study from Tigray, Ethiopia', *Agricultural Water Management*, 96(12): 1837–1843.

Huang, Q., D. Dawe, S. Rozelle, J. Huang and J. Wang. 2005. 'Irrigation, poverty and inequality in rural China', *The Australian Journal of Agricultural and Resource Economics*, 49(1): 159–175.

Huang, Q., S. Rozelle, B. Lohmar, J. Huang and J. Wang. 2006. 'Irrigation, agricultural performance and poverty reduction in China', *Food Policy*, 31(1): 30–52.

Inocencio, A., M. Kikuchi, M. Tonosaki, A. Maruyama, D. Merrey, H. Sally and I. De Jong. 2007. *Costs and performance of irrigation projects: a comparison of sub-Saharan Africa and other developing regions*, WMI Report 109, Colombo: International Water Management Institute.

Jordaan, H. and B. Grové. 2010. 'Analysis of the governance structure used by Eksteenkuil raisin producers: is there a need for more vertical integration?', paper presented at the Third African Association of Agricultural Economists (AAAE) Conference, Cape Town, 19–23 September. Accessed 3 August 2011, http://ageconsearch.umn.edu/bitstream/96645/2/193.%20Governance%20in%20raisin%20production%20in%20South%20Africa.pdf.

Khundlande, G. and H. Van Schalkwyk. 2010. 'Water resource management for profitable small-scale farming along the banks of the Orange River', WRC Project K5/1354 Draft final report, Bloemfontein: Department of Agricultural Economics, University of the Free State.

Legoupil, J. 1985. 'Some comments and recommendations about irrigation schemes in South Africa, Report of Mission 11 February – 3 March 1985', Gezina: Water Research Commission.

Loxton Venn and Associates. 1983. 'A master preliminary plan for Zanyokwe Irrigation Scheme', Bramley: Loxton Venn and Associates.

Machete, C., N. Mollel, K. Ayisi, M. Mashatola, F. Anim and F. Vanassche. 2004. *Smallholder irrigation and agricultural development in the Olifants River basin of Limpopo province: management transfer, productivity, profitability and food security issues*, WRC Report No. 1050/1/04, Pretoria: Water Research Commission.

Manona, S., J. Denison, W. van Averbeke and T. Masiya. 2010. 'Proposed land tenure and land administration interventions to increase productivity on smallholder irrigation schemes in South Africa', paper presented at the conference on 'Overcoming inequality and structural poverty in South Africa: towards inclusive growth and development', PLAAS SPII and Isandla Institute, Johannesburg, 20 September.

Nieuwoudt, W. and G. Backeberg. 2011. 'A review of the modelling of water values in different use sectors in South Africa', *Water SA*, 37(5): 703–710.

NPC (National Planning Commission). 2011. *National development plan 2030. Our future – make it work*, Pretoria: National Planning Commission, The Presidency.

Reinders, F.B. 2010. *Standards and guidelines for improved efficiency of irrigation water use from dam wall release to root zone application: guidelines*, WRC Report No. TT 466/10, Gezina: Water Research Commission.

Schreiner, B., B. Tapela and B. van Koppen. 2010. 'Water for agrarian reform and rural poverty eradication: where is the leak?', paper presented at the conference on 'Overcoming inequality and structural poverty in South Africa: towards inclusive growth and development', Johannesburg, 20 September.

Shah, T., B. van Koppen, D. Merrey, M. De Lange and M. Samad. 2002. *Institutional alternatives in African smallholder irrigation: lessons from international experience with irrigation management transfer*, Research Report 60, Colombo: International Water Management Institute.

Smith, L.E.D. 2004. 'Assessment of the contribution of irrigation to poverty reduction and sustainable livelihoods', *Water Resources Development*, 20(2): 243–257.

Tapela, B. 2012. 'The livelihood impacts of commercialization in emerging small-scale irrigation schemes in the Olifants catchment area of South Africa', unpublished PhD thesis, University of the Western Cape.

Turral, H., M. Svendsen and J.M. Faures. 2010. 'Investing in irrigation: reviewing the past and looking to the future,' *Agricultural Water Management*, 97(4): 551–560.

Umhlaba. 2010. *A review of experiences of establishing emerging farmers in South Africa: case lessons and implications for farmer support within land reform programmes*, Capacity Development in Food and Agriculture Policies 3, Rome: Food and Agriculture Organization of the United Nations.

Van Averbeke, W. 2008. *Best management practices for sustainable subsistence farming on selected irrigation schemes and surrounding areas through participatory adaptive research in Limpopo province*, WRC Report No. TT 344/08, Gezina: Water Research Commission.

Van Averbeke, W. 2012. 'Performance of smallholder irrigation schemes in the Vhembe District of South Africa', in M. Kumar (ed.) *Problems, perspectives and challenges of agricultural water management*, Rijeka: InTech.

Van Averbeke, W., J. Denison and P. Mnkeni. 2011. 'Smallholder irrigation schemes in South Africa: a review of knowledge generated by the Water Research Commission', *Water SA*, 37(4): 797–808.

Van Averbeke, W., C. M'Marete, C. Igodan and A. Belete. 1998. *An investigation into plot production at irrigation schemes in central Eastern Cape*, WRC Report No. 719/1/98, Gezina: Water Research Commission.

Van der Stoep, I. 2011. 'Irrigation water measurement – from voluntary management to pending regulations', paper presented at the Water Research Commission 40-Year Celebration Conference, Johannesburg, 31 August – 1 September.

Vhelapi, S. 2012. 'Project revived', *New Nation*, 25 July. Accessed 18 February 2013, http://www.thenewage.co.za/printstroy.aspx?news_id=57202&mid=53.

20 Cattle and rural development in the Eastern Cape: the Nguni project revisited

Ntombekhaya Faku and Paul Hebinck

This chapter examines the dynamics of the Nguni projects in the Eastern Cape. These projects are designed and implemented by a number of organisations, including the provincial Department of Agriculture and the University of Fort Hare. They are the result of policy initiatives to resurrect some of the developmental processes that were set in motion during the colonial and apartheid eras. Nguni projects target the so-called communal areas of the Eastern Cape and other provinces in the country. They cover the same areas that were set aside in the past, first as reserves and later as homelands.

A critical examination of the wider Nguni project reflects some of the particularities of post-apartheid policy dynamics. This chapter addresses the perspective that rural development should revolve around the Nguni as a pivotal element of plans to transform communal livestock farming. The 'Ngunisation' of the cattle stock in the communal areas also symbolises the redress of injustices of the past, which resulted in the Nguni gene pool's becoming owned and controlled by white commercial farmers. Returning the Nguni to their original custodians represents the reclamation of indigenous knowledge and wealth.

The chapter describes the historical shifts and changes that have attended cattle breeds, genetic make-up and ownership in the region. These provide the rationale for the design and implementation of the Nguni projects. We then examine the ideas and assumptions that underpin the Nguni projects. This is followed by an account of how people in the villages respond to the Nguni project initiatives. We conclude by examining the 'why' and 'how' of the Nguni projects.

Livestock and historical changes

Livestock has played an important role in the history and development of the people and landscapes of South Africa. Cattle production currently contributes between 25 and 30 per cent of the country's total annual agricultural output in the form of meat, milk and live animals. Cattle are also a major resource in culturally inspired rituals (such as funerals and weddings) and serve as a source of security in times of difficulty. The Eastern Cape province alone has over 3.2 million head of cattle (NDA 2008). Some 1.9 million of these, according to the Eastern Cape Veterinary Report (ECDA 2008), are owned and kept by African people who reside in the former homelands of the Eastern Cape: the Transkei and the Ciskei. Most of these cattle graze commonly managed rangelands with goats and sheep (Ainslie 2005a; Bennett and Lent 2007). This sort of cattle production is usually categorised by policymakers and researchers as 'subsistence' (Düvel and Afful 1996; Kirsten and Van Zyl 1998). Commercial farming largely takes place in areas where the land and pastures are privately held and managed, mostly by white farmers.

Unlike the commercial ranching areas of the drier Eastern Cape rangelands, where livestock numbers have declined, livestock numbers in the communal areas have remained stable over the past 50 to 100 years (Dean and Macdonald 1994). This contradicts the views that were held in the past – notably during the times of betterment planning (De Wet 1987, 1989; Hendricks 1989) – when it was common among policymakers and experts to view the communal range-lands as becoming progressively more overstocked (Bembridge 1979). This perception led the government to consistently follow a policy of destocking (Tapson 1993). Destocking has been an important focus of the government's agricultural agenda since the 1950s, both to reduce pressure on the available rangeland and to improve cattle production in the communal areas. While the census data is not readily available, there is growing consensus among researchers nowadays that livestock numbers and herd compositions fluctuate and change. De Wet and Van Averbeke (1995), Steyn (1981), Ntsebeza (2002), Vetter (2003), Bennett and Lent (2007) and Hebinck and Van Averbeke (chapter 14, this volume) all note that per capita livestock ownership has dropped and that fewer people nowadays own cattle. This average number per owner varies from area to area. People in the Transkei region tend to have more cattle than people in the former Ciskei do.

Development interventions, orchestrated by the provincial departments of agriculture in the Cape with the support of agricultural research, have also been guided by the imperative to cross-breed exotic breeds of cattle with the locally available breeds (Muchenje et al. 2008). Bembridge (1979: 167) notes:

> Since the early 1950s, the Agricultural Department has increasingly encour-
> aged the use of improved sires through subsidies to individuals and groups
> of farmers. However, improved breeding and selection even under good
> management is unlikely to lead to increased economic production unless
> the effects of environmental factors are sufficiently appreciated.

Exotic breeds are perceived to be superior to local, indigenous ones. A range of publications and opinions voice the view that the introduction of exotic breeds has resulted in the gradual disappearance of the indigenous Nguni and Nkone from the 'communal' areas of the Eastern Cape (Bester et al. 2003; Strydom 2008).

Large Nguni herds are primarily found today on commercial beef-cattle farms whose owners consider the Nguni to be an economical producer of quality and ecologically sound meat (personal communication, Mr Schenk, 24 March 2009; see also Ainslie 2002, 2005b). The former homeland areas are home to what are commonly referred to as 'African' cattle, depicted in most animal science literature as a nondescript, impure and mixed breed of cattle. While their exact origin cannot be ascertained, certain bloodlines are still recognisable (Faku 2009; Scholtz et al. 2008).

The Nguni is currently being revalued as an environmentally friendly, sturdy and easy-to-handle breed. This tendency is particularly evident in the numerous Nguni projects that are being implemented by various governmental bodies (for example, the provincial departments of agriculture, district municipalities and the Agricultural Research Council's Animal Improvement Institute) with support from Fort Hare's Agripark and the Kellogg Foundation. These 'Nguni projects' aim to reintroduce the Nguni to the former homelands of the Ciskei and Transkei and to other parts of the country as well. Since Nguni cattle, the argument goes, thrive in the harsh and variable natural environment of the former homelands, they offer good opportunities for the production of ecological meat in these areas. National and international niche markets exist for this meat: Nguni meat is considered to be lean and of good quality. The Nguni could become the backbone of commercial cattle production by African farmers. Policymakers and experts in the Eastern Cape often decry the lack of cattle breeds that are adapted to the needs of communal cattle farmers. The reintroduction of the Nguni would fill this gap.

The rationale behind the reintroduction of the Nguni

The set of ideas and assumptions that inform agrarian policy in South Africa is closely related to specific bodies of animal science, agricultural economics and management sciences. The principles of animal breeding that feed the Nguni projects are derived from animal science. Typical of many of the agrarian sciences is their decontextualisation: insights which form the basis for expert recommendations are disconnected from everyday practice and the sociocultural environment. Bembridge (1979: 164) asked the question, 'What do we really know about the peasant farmers?' several decades ago. He concluded: 'Unfortunately, we know very little.' The situation has changed since then. Agrarian science, with its cohort of expert advisors and consultants, has moved from the field to experimental farms, research stations, and university farms and laboratories (Hebinck et al. 2011). The cultural repertoires, beliefs and preferences of scientists and experts, deriving as they do from animal science, are not necessarily shared by cattle keepers themselves. Similar to Bester et al. (2003), we find that both past and contemporary efforts to address the constraints of cattle production in South Africa have ignored farmers' perceptions and their sociocultural and economic repertoires.

The data in this chapter are derived from a field study conducted in the Amathole District Municipality of the Eastern Cape (Faku 2009). Three villages were selected in the municipalities of Nkonkobe (Melani and Guquka) and Ngqushwa (Bell). We have focused on the Amathole District Municipality because many of its villages are enrolled in the Nguni Cattle Project. The three communities have been selected because they represent different lengths of time in, and degrees of exposure to, the Nguni projects. The Guquka community is on a waiting list to receive Nguni cattle; Bell became part of an Nguni initiative in 2006, initiated by the Fort Hare Agripark and the Kellogg Foundation; while Melani was enrolled in an Nguni project in 1998 as a result of its relationship with the nearby University of Fort Hare.

Why are Nguni cattle being reintroduced in communal areas in the Eastern Cape? The answer to this question is complex. It lies partly in the history of the Nguni breed in South Africa, its domestication and its adaptability to harsh environments. It is ideally suited to the conditions in the former homelands. Its renowned qualities also make it a worthwhile commodity for exchange. The long-term goal is to develop a niche market for Nguni beef and skins, and to enable 'communal' farmers to enter the global beef market through organic production and product processing (Raats et al. 2004).

The experts also argue that the conservation of the Nguni breed has become important because it constitutes a valuable genetic resource for future generations. At present, only white commercial farmers are aware of the advantages of Nguni cattle and maintain stock in the Eastern Cape (Ainslie 2002, 2005a, 2005b). The advantages of Nguni cattle are not as obvious to black communal farmers.

The history of the Nguni in southern Africa is not only one of the conservation of a pure African breed. It is also one of genetic erosion. This resulted from breeding and cross-breeding programmes implemented by the colonial and apartheid states and by white 'commercial' farmers. This history is also a history of the gradual shift of ownership and control of the Nguni gene pool from black to almost exclusively white ownership. The state-led introduction of exotic breeds before and during the betterment era has led to a situation in which the Nguni are largely absent from the Ciskei and, to a lesser extent, the Transkei. Returning the Nguni breed of cattle to its original owners is a post-apartheid gesture aimed at 'bringing back pride, dignity and heritage to the Xhosa people' (personal communication, J. Raats, 22 March 2009). This rationale for the Nguni projects turns out to be too simple, as our study reveals. For a start, it ignores the effects and aftermath of the 'great cattle killing' movement between 1856–1857, described by Peires (1989). It also fails to take into account the long-term effects of the complex settlement processes during the border wars (1820–1890) in which Xhosa people moved across the Kei River to settle in what was then virgin territory (Hebinck and Smith 2007). It is not clear, for example, whether people took their cattle with them, and what breeds these would have been if they did, or whether they purchased cattle from Afrikaner and English settlers.

The question arises as to what kind of Nguni cattle are now being reintroduced to the Ciskei and Transkei. The history of the breeding of the Nguni in the region means that the current Nguni breed is not the same as that of 50 or 100 years ago. In-situ and ex-situ breeding has changed the genetics of the breed. There is also the question of the relationship between 'communal' farmers and the Nguni. They have been exposed to new breeds over the last 60 years as part of programmes to upgrade the quality of the indigenous stock and have learned to appreciate the traits of the 'African' cattle that have resulted from this history of cross-breeding.

The Nguni and breeding

The history of the Nguni breed has been widely associated with human migration. Epstein (1971) traces the origin of Nguni cattle to the Nile Valley. He refers to records of domesticated cattle in Africa that show that people and their cattle began to move southwards from the Nile Valley by 400 BCE. The driving force of this migration was environmental change and pressure, combined with wars which displaced both people and cattle. The trading of cattle also occurred (Hanotte et al. 1998). Bester et al. (2003) and Scherf (2000) detail the arrival of Nguni and Sanga breeds in what is now South Africa between 300 and 700 CE. Bachmann (1983, cited in Strydom 2008) argues that these breeds soon dominated the cattle populations of southern Africa. The migration southwards simultaneously spurred processes of natural selection as a response to environmental challenges, such as the tsetse fly and East Coast fever. What resulted was an animal type that was anatomically and physiologically adapted to harsh conditions (Strydom 2008: 87). The Sanga and the Nguni evolved as low-maintenance cattle that were ideally suited to the natural environment of southern Africa and to the communal nature of cattle rearing and keeping in the region (Bester et al. 2003).

The gradual transformation of the cattle economy, from one that catered for local needs – food, *lobola*, hides and skins – to one that is linked to regional, national and global markets, has had a major impact on cattle breeds and their genetic make-up. The emphasis has shifted from quantity to quality. The arrival of commercial feedlots in South Africa in the 1970s also left its mark. It became increasingly common practice to feed cattle for the market in a feedlot. This contributed to a decline in the popularity of indigenous cattle (Bachmann 1983, cited in Strydom 2008: 87) since grass-feeding and late-maturing *Bos taurus* breeds came to be regarded as inferior and were decimated by government decree (Bester et al. 2003). The perception that local breeds were inferior led to a gradual dilution of the genetic pool through replacement and cross-breeding with exotic breeds (Strydom 2008: 87, 88). The Nguni were particularly badly affected.

This is not the whole story, however. Strydom (2008) notes that a number of interventions to preserve the indigenous breeds have taken place since the 1940s. A committee to conduct a survey on the nature and number of indigenous cattle breeds and their conservation was appointed by the state in 1949 (Scholtz 2006). The committee recommended that immediate steps be taken to arrest the deterioration of indigenous cattle in the 'native reserves'. Due to the infusion of exotic bloodlines and the use of inferior sires, indigenous cattle breeds had gradually been eroded. The committee also recommended that a purebred herd of not less than 500 Nguni should be established in order to investigate the potential of the breed. This led to the establishment of the Bartlow Combine Breeding Station in KwaZulu-Natal in 1954 to accommodate the herd. This herd played a significant role in the development of the Nguni breed and formed the foundation of the initial 'seed stock' industry (Kars 1993). The formation of the Drakensberger Breed Society in 1947 and the Bonsmara Breed Society in 1964 was also an organised attempt to arrest the degradation of the gene pool of indigenous cattle (Strydom 2008). The process was later driven by the scientific arguments of Professor Bonsma. Bonsma found support in a committee that was appointed by the state in 1985 to report on the desirability of a germ-plasm bank to maintain the hardiness of the various Sanga breeds. Strydom (2008) points out that this led to the revival of the Nguni's popularity, specifically among commercial breeders whose numbers were increasing exponentially at the time.

Betterment and homeland agricultural policies

Ironically, the attempts to rescue the Nguni and other local breeds produced a situation in which the Nguni stock and gene pool was owned and controlled by commercial cattle farmers while the provincial and national departments of agriculture promoted cross-breeding and the introduction of exotic breeds in the homelands. The upgrading of local stock by crossing them with new breeds in the Ciskei and Transkei was a central component of the betterment planning exercise.

The scene was set nationally and locally during the 1930s for a series of inter-ventions in African (read 'pastoral') farming (Beinart 2003). Hendricks (1989) describes the reports of soil erosion and desertification that reinforced the view among experts and policymakers in the 1930s that Africans had an 'irrational' desire to accumulate large numbers of livestock (see also Cousins 1996, 2007; De Wet 1989). The 'religious' outlook of African cattle owners contradicted 'scien-tific' farming methods and was considered to be the root cause of overstocking and erosion (Trollop 1985). Improving the land : livestock ratio was considered necessary to arrest the degradation of land. Overstocking was the official (that is, government- and expert-supported) explanation for the degradation of the land in the 'reserves' (Bennett 1996). It was tackled by a combination of culling and intro-ducing new breeds. The government introduced a proclamation (Proclamation No. 180 of 1937) aimed at upgrading the pedigree of livestock. A more compre-hensive 'enactment' (Livestock Control and Improvement Proclamation No. 31 of 1939) was passed two years later when it became evident that there had been no improvement, mainly because the quality of pasturage remained poor (Bennett 1996). Large numbers of animals were culled and Nguni bulls and other 'nonde-script' males were castrated. Beinart (2003) reports that in 1937 alone, 16 000 Afrikaner bulls were castrated in the Transkei and replaced by 1 000 pedigree bulls. The Department of Agriculture launched a breeding scheme in the Ciskei in 1949 that provided stock owners with subsidies to purchase sires of specific breeds (Steyn 1981). Brown-Swiss sires were particularly favoured by the department since the breed was associated with high milk production and sturdiness. Dipping programmes were introduced to prevent tick- and skin-borne diseases. These efforts were accompanied by well-established extension programmes emphasising the message that improved breeds would provide more draught power, milk and meat. Rural families were also encouraged to reduce their holdings in order to save the rangelands from overgrazing and degradation (Beinart 2003). At the same time the introduction of Afrikaner bulls in the Transkei and Ciskei was criticised. Although Afrikaner cattle were sufficiently hardy to survive in the communal areas and were good beef and draught animals, their progeny were poor milkers.

During the betterment period emphasis was placed on implementing rotational grazing management systems. According to a writer cited by Bembridge (1979: 167), 38 per cent of the land had been 'brought under grazing control' by 1970. This is confirmed by research in Guquka and Koloni (Hebinck and Lent 2007). The policy began to change only later (Ainslie 2005a: 79). Ainslie (2002, 2005a) questions the 'official' view that the communal areas were overstocked. He argues that the communal areas in South Africa had been sustaining high stock numbers for decades. There was no sudden increase in the cattle population and thus no new problem that needed urgent solution.

The Department of Agriculture of the Ciskei homeland government continued to implement the stock improvement policies that had been pursued by their predecessors. It encouraged the introduction of pedigree bulls and the elimination of 'scrub' males.

Recent research in the communal areas of the Eastern Cape, particularly in the former Ciskei, demonstrates that the policies of stock improvement had a lasting impact (Ainslie 2005a, 2005b; Bennett and Lent 2007; Faku 2009). Mixed 'African' or 'nondescript' cattle predominate. A range of exotic and local breeds have gone into the mix: Angus, Hereford, Sussex, Brangus, Bonsmara, Drakensberger, Brahman, Jersey, Holstein-Friesland, Ayshire, Guernsey, Brown-Swiss, as well as local breeds such as the Afrikaner and Nguni (Faku 2009). Most of these breeds – the Afrikaner and Brown-Swiss in particular – were introduced as a result of state efforts; others arrived in the villages through local purchases and exchanges. Earlier commentators tended to underestimate the effect of the state's interventions in the region. In his evaluation of agricultural development in the 'Black States', Bembridge (1979: 165) argued that the overall impact of agricultural policy was minimal. Communal cattle farming largely nullified the effect of the interventions:

> In fact, the very developments which have done so much to improve livestock production in South Africa have contributed towards grazing deterioration in the Black States. If people continue to treat grazing land as they are doing today it is only a matter of time before our best pastoral land will become unproductive. The lack of conservation consciousness and ecological knowledge is a fundamental stumbling block to development of the livestock industry.

Bembridge attributed this state of affairs to the ineptitude of black governments: 'Since individual black state governments assumed responsibility for agriculture, the extent of grazing management has declined to almost zero' (Bembridge 1979: 165).

It is generally accepted today that betterment was heavily contested by rural actors. Ainslie (2002, 2005a) notes that communal farmers resented the dipping programme because they reasoned that the dipping of cattle allowed the authorities to count the numbers of their cattle, information they were not happy to divulge. Mager (1995, 1999) has documented the widespread opposition to government dipping in the communal areas of Peddie and neighbouring districts. Villagers in villages like Guquka still consider the culling of cattle as the reason for the permanent decline of animal husbandry in the area (Hebinck and Smith 2007: 100 ff.). Betterment policies contributed to a general feeling of bitterness and disenchantment with the authorities in a context of rising rural landlessness, drought, poverty and deprivation. The present genetic composition of 'African cattle' in the villages suggests, though, that the breeding and cross-breeding components of the betterment policies were much more acceptable than other aspects of them.

The Nguni projects

After years of cross-breeding and introducing exotics, the realisation set in, by the late 1970s, that the smaller-framed and more fertile breeds like the Nguni

> were in fact far better adapted to conditions in the reserve areas (for instance periodic grazing and water deficits and nightly kraaling regimes) than the introduced exotic breeds. When the Ciskei National Ranch was established in the early 1980s, two adapted breeds, the Nguni/Nkone and the Bonsmara, were vigorously promoted. Naturally, cattle-owners in the reserves were suspicious of these U-turns in official thinking, and Hundleby noted that there was 'consistently a problem with the perceptions of farmers in the communal areas against the Nguni in the late 1970s and early 1980s'. (Ainslie 2005a: 79–80)

The suspicion that attended the introduction of the Nguni in the 1970s and 1980s still plays a significant role some 30 years later. The relationship between the state and Nguni project officials, on the one hand, and communal cattle owners, on the other, is not as cordial as the Nguni project accounts would suggest.

The first programme that was specifically aimed at reintroducing the Nguni in the Eastern Cape began in 1998, when Nguni were introduced in Melani as part of a Fort Hare University–managed research programme. Since then more organisations and institutions have designed and implemented Nguni projects: Fort Hare Agripark, Kellogg Foundation, the Provincial Department of Agriculture

(PDA) and, to a lesser extent, the Agricultural Research Council and the Animal Improvement Institute.

It is difficult to obtain an accurate overview of the Nguni projects since the monitoring of the different programmes has been limited. It is clear, though, that the different projects follow different strategies and work in different areas. The PDA distributes bulls while the Fort Hare Agripark and the Kellogg Foundation distribute both bulls and heifers. The University of Fort Hare Nguni project gives two bulls and 10 in-calf heifers to selected villages so that the villagers can build up a nucleus herd (Nguni Cattle Project 2005). The plan is to replace the existing 'nondescript' bulls with registered Nguni bulls. Each village is expected to return two bulls and 10 heifers to the project after five or six years. These are then given to another village (Raats et al. 2004). By the end of 2010, some 75 villages were expected to have received Nguni.

Despite minor differences, the organisations that drive the 'Ngunisation' of the former homelands are united by the fact that their activities lack a sound understanding of current communal cattle farming. The projects are all based on the preconception that the rural economy should be modernised and commoditised. They also share the view that the Nguni should be preserved as a pure breed. Only then, the assumption goes, will their unique organic character be maintained and their place in national and global niche markets be assured. The prevention of cross-breeding is a commonly shared project philosophy, in stark contrast to widely held views and practices in the villages. Nguni project experts (most of them animal scientists) view 'nondescript', genetically mixed animals as a danger:

> It is alarming that many of the bulls used [by communal farmers] were classified as non-descript (35%) or Brahman types (18.2%). This clearly demonstrates a threat to the indigenous cattle breeds for which communal people have been the traditional custodians for many centuries. (Scholtz et al. 2008: 4)

Controlled mating is prescribed. The Nguni are reintroduced in the villages on condition that they are kept separate from the 'nondescript' 'African' cattle. In practical terms this means that villages have to have fenced camps before they are eligible to receive Nguni bulls and heifers. Another condition is that a rangeland management committee is required to monitor rotational occupancy of the camps at specified stocking rates.

The prerequisites of the programme have generated some discontent in villages. They also effectively limit the programme's reach to the former betterment areas since they seek to replicate the very systems that were established in most of the villages in the former Ciskei and large parts of the former Transkei that were subjected to betterment planning. The many villages, like Guquka, that resisted betterment in the past (Smith and Hebinck 2007) do not qualify. Not only does Guquka have no fenced camps for rotational grazing, but it also has to share its rangelands with four neighbouring villages (Van Averbeke and Bennett 2007).

Knowledge encounters and emerging issues

The communal farmers who participated in the project in Bell and Melani initially appreciated the programme and recognised the qualities of the Nguni. Some of them said that they could not reject their reintroduction since a gift of cattle, according to Xhosa cultural tradition, cannot be refused. They kept the Nguni in separate camps, away from their 'African' cattle. They themselves were responsible for the cost of keeping the animals fenced in. Having now worked with Nguni herds for 6 and 11 years respectively, they have noted some of the Nguni's drawbacks. A large majority (55 per cent in Bell and 80 per cent in Melani) complain that the Nguni do not produce enough milk to satisfy human requirements. Their 'African' cattle produce more. Brown (1959) notes that the Nguni cattle's udders and teats are small and not suited to hand-milking. The farmers complain about this, citing it as a reason why Nguni cows only produce sufficient for their calves. The Nguni are also not suitable for ritual purposes. Communal farmers prefer animals of a particular size, colour and horn shape for their rituals (see also Ainslie 2002). The Nguni also fail to make a sound when slaughtered, another ritual prerequisite.

In contrast to these perceptions about Nguni cattle, communal farmers have developed an appreciation for their mixed 'African' cattle breeds over the years. They particularly appreciate the capacity of 'African' cattle to yield milk along with meat, cash, social status and, to a lesser extent, bride-wealth. Cattle serve as a source of security in times of economic hardship. Cattle are consumed only if they die of old age or disease or if they have been ritually slaughtered. Some respondents told us that 'to own cattle is a Xhosa bank'. Others referred to their cattle as 'capital on the hoof'. Communal farmers have come to value their 'nondescript' herds, formed over years of breeding based on local exchanges, bride-wealth payments, gifts and purchases. They do not see cattle as just an economic investment: their appreciation of cattle goes far beyond that. This is well documented in the literature (Ainslie 2002, 2005a, 2005b; 1987; Comaroff and Comaroff 1987, 1990; Cousins 1996, 2007b; Steyn 1981). These practices and views directly affect stocking rates and the low off-take rates in the form of cattle sales and starving and dying animals during periods of nutritional stress. Ainslie (2005a, 2005b) argues that cattle production on communal lands effectively meets local expectations and does not require reform. In addition, it became clear to us that cattle improvement is understood by communal farmers to mean cross-breeding that results in high(er) milk yields and an increase in the size of the herds. They perceive crossing their 'African' nondescript cattle with an Nguni or Brahman bull as a form of upgrading. Some also consider an increase in herd size as cattle improvement. Cattle improvement for them also implies producing animals that are drought-tolerant, tick-resistant and able to calve every year.

Many researchers and experts, in contrast, have voiced their frustration with the attitudes of communal farmers about cattle, describing them as economically wasteful and destructive of natural resources (see, notably, Bembridge 1979;

Düvel and Afful 1996). Experts, though, base their cattle improvement and also the recent Nguni programmes on an anachronistic notion of 'traditional' cattle breeds rather than on an empirically grounded identification of current preferences. They are chiefly concerned with their potential to generate cash and transform the rural economy. They emphasise the functional efficiency of particular breeds: hardiness, ability to produce a calf every year and resistance to ticks.

Conclusion

This chapter has examined the tensions and dynamics generated by the attempts to 'Ngunise' livestock production in the Eastern Cape. The vision of the Nguni as the vehicle for modernisation (through, for example, marketing, upgrading the breed, and so on) does not resonate well with ideas and perspectives in the villages. Experiences with the Nguni project challenge the knowledge fundaments of current post-apartheid agricultural policies. This chapter has provided a picture of what happens when these contrasting bodies of knowledge and the narratives that support them meet in project settings like those produced by the Nguni programmes in the former Ciskei. The rural villages in which the Nguni projects are implemented become arenas, defined in this context as 'social encounters or series of situations in which contests over issues, resources, values and representations take place' (Long 2000: 190). The Nguni projects are the arenas in which the 'romanticised' narrative that glorifies the adaptable and indigenous nature of the breed encounters the village-based narratives that have been constructed over time in the course of villagers' interaction with the mixed breeds that were introduced in earlier eras. The Nguni projects failed to acknowledge that communal farmers bring their experiences with them to the negotiating table. These experiences have been accumulated and built up over long periods of time. They have also been influenced by past state efforts to upgrade their herds. In stark contrast, projects such as the Nguni projects work within a fixed time frame of about eight years and draw their knowledge from a mixture of scientific and idealistic, even romantic, views.

Paraphrasing Düvel and Afful (1996), we would argue that it is largely cultural routines that constrain sustainable cattle farming in the Eastern Cape. We thus fundamentally disagree with the view that communal farmers lack knowledge. Bembridge, the respected *éminence grise* and supporter of rural extension in South Africa's homelands, exemplifies this sort of attitude: 'The lack of conservation consciousness and ecological knowledge is a fundamental stumbling block to development of the livestock industry, since the essential base of knowledge is lacking. Tomorrow's farmer must be a conservationist or the consequences for future generations are grave indeed' (Bembridge 1979: 165).

What stands out in our analysis is that the Ngunisation of the rural economy requires considerable rethinking. The initiative needs to find ways to build on local views about cattle production and livelihoods. Taking up this challenge requires a less technicist approach to cattle and an appreciation that policy can provide a space in which various actors interact and negotiate. This entails a different set of relationships between the state and the communities with which it works.

References

Ainslie, A. 2002. *Cattle ownership and production in the communal areas of the Eastern Cape, South Africa*, PLAAS Research Report No.10, Programme for Land and Agrarian Studies, University of the Western Cape.

Ainslie, A. 2005a. 'Keeping cattle? The politics of value in the communal areas of the Eastern Cape province, South Africa', unpublished PhD thesis, University of London.

Ainslie, A. 2005b. 'Farming cattle, cultivating relationships: cattle ownership and cultural politics in Peddie District, Eastern Cape', *Social Dynamics: A Journal of African Studies*, 31(1): 129–156.

Bachmann, M. 1983. 'Early origins of cattle', *Farmer's Weekly*, 23: 18.

Beinart, W. 2003. *The rise of conservation in South Africa: settlers, livestock, and the environment 1770–1950*, New York: Oxford University Press.

Bembridge, T. 1979. 'Problems of livestock production in the black states of Southern Africa and future strategy', *Southern African Journal of Animal Science*, 9: 163–176.

Bennett, J. and P. Lent. 2007. 'Livestock production and forage resources', in P. Hebinck and P. Lent (eds) *Livelihoods and landscape: the people of Guquka and Koloni and their resources*, Leiden/Boston: Brill Academic Publishers.

Bennett, T.W. 1996. 'African land – a history of dispossession', in R. Zimmerman and D. Visser (eds) *Southern cross: civil law and common law in South Africa*, New York: Oxford University Press.

Bester, J, I. Matjuda, J. Rust and H. Fourie. 2003. *The Nguni: case study. FAO community-based management of animal genetic resources*, Rome: UNDP, GTZ, CTA, FAO.

Brown, D.L. 1959. 'The Nguni breed of cattle: a descriptive review', *Empire Journal of Experimental Agriculture*, 27(108): 277–290.

Comaroff, J. and J.L. Comaroff. 1987. 'The madman and the migrant: work and labor in the historical consciousness of a South African people', *American Ethnologist*, 14: 191–209.

Comaroff, J.L. and J. Comaroff. 1990. 'Goodly beasts, beastly goods: cattle and commodities in a South African context', *American Ethnologist*, 17: 195–216.

Cousins, B. 1996. 'Livestock production and common property struggles in South Africa's agrarian reform', *The Journal of Peasant Studies*, 23(2/3): 166–208.

Cousins, B. 2007. 'More than socially embedded: the distinctive character of "communal tenure" regimes in South Africa and its implications for land policy', *Journal of Agrarian Change*, 7(3): 281–315.

Dean, W.R.J. and I.A.W. Macdonald. 1994. 'Historical changes in stocking rates of domestic livestock as a measure of semi-arid and arid rangeland degradation in the Cape province, South Africa', *Journal of Arid Environments*, 26: 281–298.

De Wet, C. 1987. 'Betterment planning in South Africa: some thoughts on its history, feasibility and wider policy implications', *Journal of Contemporary African Studies*, 6(1/2): 85–122.

De Wet, C. 1989. 'Betterment planning in a rural village in Keiskammmahoek District, Ciskei', *Journal of Southern African Studies*, 15(2): 326–345.

De Wet, C. and W. van Averbeke (eds). 1995. *Regional overview of land reform related issues in the Eastern Cape province*, Alice/East London/Grahamstown: Agricuture Rural Development Research Institute (ARDRI)/Border Rural Committee (BRC)/Institute for Social and Economic Research (ISER).

Düvel, G.H. and D.B. Afful. 1996. 'Sociocultural constraints on sustainable cattle production in some communal areas of South Africa', *Development Southern Africa*, 13(3): 429–440.

ECDA (Eastern Cape Department of Agriculture). 2008. 'Eastern Cape veterinary report', in Department of Agriculture, Eastern Cape province, *Annual report 2008*.

Epstein, H. 1971. *The origin of domestic animals in Africa, Vol. 1. Africana*, New York: Publishing Corporation.

Faku, N. 2009. 'Reintroduction of Nguni cattle breed in the rural communities of the Eastern Cape, South Africa', unpublished MSc thesis, Wageningen University.

Hanotte, O., M. Okomo, D. Bradley, Y. Verjee, A. Ochieng, A. Teale and J.E.O. Rege. 1998. 'Geographical distribution and frequency of taurine *Bos taurus* and *zebu B. indicus* Y chromosome haplotypes amongst sub-Saharan African cattle breeds', in J.N.B. Shrestha (ed.) *Proceedings of the fourth Global Conference on the Conservation of Domestic Animal Genetic Resources, Nepal, 17–21 August*.

Hebinck, P. and P.C. Lent (eds). 2007. *Livelihoods and landscape: the people of Guquka and Koloni and their resources*, Leiden/Boston: Brill Academic Publishers.

Hebinck, P. and L. Smith. 2007. 'History of settlement: processes and patterns', in P. Hebinck and P. Lent (eds) *Livelihoods and landscape: the people of Guquka and Koloni and their resources*, Leiden/Boston: Brill Academic Publishers.

Hebinck, P., D. Fay and K. Kondlo. 2011. 'Land and agrarian reform in South Africa's Eastern Cape province: caught by continuities', *Journal of Agrarian Change*, 11(2): 220–240.

Hendricks, F. 1989. 'Loose planning and rapid settlement: the politics of conservation and control in Transkei, South Africa,1950–1970', *Journal of Southern African Studies*, 15(2): 306–325.

Kars, A. 1993. 'A genetic analysis of the Bartlow Combine Nguni cattle stud', unpublished PhD thesis, University of the Orange Free State.

Kirsten, J. and J. Van Zyl. 1998. 'Defining small-scale farmers in the South African context', *Agrekon*, 37(4): 551–562.

Long, N. 2000. 'Exploring local/global transformations', in A. Arce and N. Long (eds) *Anthropology, development and modernities: exploring discourses, counter-tendencies, and violence*, London: Routledge.

Mager, A. 1995. 'Patriarchs, politics and ethnicity in the making of the Ciskei, 1945–1959', *African Studies*, 54(1): 48–72.

Mager, A. 1999. *Gender and the making of a South African bantustan: a social history of the Ciskei, 1945–1959*, Portsmouth/Oxford/Cape Town: Heinemann/James Currey/David Philip.

Muchenje, V., K. Dzama, M. Chimonyo, J. Raats and P. Strydom. 2008. 'Meat quality of Nguni, Bonsmara and Aberdeen Angus steers raised on natural pasture in the Eastern Cape, South Africa', *Meat Science*, 79(1): 20–28.

NDA (National Department of Agriculture). 2008. 'National livestock statistics, 2008', in 'Directorate: agricultural statistics of the national Department of Agriculture, Republic of South Africa'. Accessed 20 October 2008, http:www.nda.agric.za/docs/Abstract_08.pdf.

Nguni Cattle Project. 2005. 'Progress report, January 2004–2005', Alice: Faculty of Science and Agriculture, University of Fort Hare.

Ntsebeza, L. 2002. 'Cattle production in Xhalanga District', in A. Ainslie (ed.) *Cattle ownership and production in the communal areas of the Eastern Cape, South Africa*, PLAAS Research Report No. 10, Programme for Land and Agrarian Studies, University of the Western Cape.

Peires, J.B. 1989. *The dead will arise: Nongqawuse and the great Xhosa cattle-killing movement of 1856–7*, Johannesburg: Ravan Press.

Raats, J.G, A. Magadlela, G. Fraser and A. Hugo. 2004. 'Re-introducing Nguni nucleus herds in 100 communal villages of the Eastern Cape province,' a proposed co-operative project between the University of Fort Hare, Agriculture and Rural Development Research Institute (ARDRI), the Eastern Cape Department of Agriculture and the Kellogg Foundation.

Scherf, B. 2000. *World watch list for domestic animal diversity. Third edition*, Rome: FAO.

Scholtz, M.M. 2006. 'The contribution of research performance recording and breed societies to the conservation of genetic resources', *Nguni Journal*: 55–71. Accessed 17 April 2013, http://www.ngunicattle.info/Documents/Journals/2006/THE%20 CONTRIBUTION%20OF%20RESEARCH.pdf.

Scholtz, M., J. Bester, M. Mamabolo and K. Ramsay. 2008. 'Results of the national cattle survey undertaken in South Africa, with emphasis on beef', *Journal of Applied Animal Husbandry and Rural Development*, 1(1): 1–9.

Smith, L. and P. Hebinck. 2007. 'Livelihood and mobility', in P. Hebinck and P. Lent (eds) *Livelihoods and landscapes: the people of Guquka and Koloni and their resources*, Leiden/ Boston: Brill Academic Publishers.

Steyn, G.J. 1981. *Amatola Basin rural development project, section III: present land use: animal production in the Amatola Basin*, Report No.6/81, Agricultural and Rural Development Research Institute, Alice: University of Fort Hare.

Strydom, P.E. 2008. 'Do indigenous southern African cattle breeds have the right genetics for commercial production of quality meat?', *Meat Science*, 80: 86–93.

Tapson, D. 1993. 'Biological sustainability in pastoral systems: the KwaZulu case', in R. J. Behnke, I. Scoones and C. Kerven (eds) *Range ecology at disequilibrium*, London: Overseas Development Institute.

Trollope, W.S.W. 1985. 'Third World challenges for pasture scientists in Southern Africa', *Journal Grassland Society of Southern Africa*, 2(1): 14–17.

Van Averbeke, W. and J. Bennett. 2007. 'Local governance and institutions', in P. Hebinck and P. Lent (eds) *Livelihoods and landscapes: the people of Guquka and Koloni and their resources*, Leiden/Boston: Brill Academic Publishers.

Vetter, S. 2003. *Rangelands at equilibrium and non-equilibrium: recent developments in the debate around rangeland ecology and management*, PLAAS, University of the Western Cape in association with the Rhodes University Botany Department and Leslie Hill Institute for Plant Conservation.

About the authors

Ben Cousins, DPhil. Professor, DST/NRF Research Chair in Poverty, Land and Agrarian Studies (PLAAS), University of the Western Cape, Cape Town, South Africa

Henning de Klerk, MSc. PhD student, Department of Anthropology, Rhodes University, Grahamstown, South Africa

Jonathan Denison, MSc. Director, Umhlaba Consulting Group, East London, South Africa

Ntombekhaya Faku, MSc. Animal scientist, Department of Agriculture and Rural Development, East London, South Africa, and member of the South African Council for Natural Scientific Professions

Derick Fay, PhD. Assistant Professor in the Department of Anthropology, University of California, Riverside, USA

Paul Hebinck, PhD. Associate Professor, Sociology of Rural Development, Wageningen University, the Netherlands, and Adjunct Professor, University of Fort Hare, Alice, South Africa

Klara Jacobson, PhD. Department of Urban and Rural Development, Swedish University of Agricultural Sciences

Petunia Khutswane, MSc. Department of Agriculture, Rural Development and Land Administration, Mpumalanga province, South Africa

Rosalie Kingwill, MSc. PhD student, PLAAS, University of the Western Cape, Cape Town, South Africa

Karin Kleinbooi, MPhil. Researcher, PLAAS, University of the Western Cape, Cape Town, South Africa

Zamile Madyibi, MSc. Senior manager, Eastern Cape Department of Rural Development and Agrarian Reform, East London, South Africa

Francois Marais, MSc. Senior lecturer, Cape Institute for Agricultural Training, Elsenburg, South Africa

Modise Moseki, MSc. Junior lecturer, Department of Development Studies, University of South Africa, Pretoria

Malebogo Phetlhu, MSc. Department of Agriculture and Rural Development, George, South Africa

Robert Ross, PhD. Professor, Institute for History, Language and Cultures of Africa, Leiden University, the Netherlands

Dik Roth, PhD. Assistant Professor, Sociology of Rural Development, Wageningen University, the Netherlands

Limpho Taoana, MSc. Agricultural Advisor (Dairy), Free State provincial Department of Agriculture and Rural Development, South Africa

Harriët Tienstra, MSc. Sociology of Rural Development, Wageningen University, the Netherlands

Wim van Averbeke, DSc. Professor, Centre for Organic and Smallholder Agriculture, Department of Crop Science, Tshwane University of Technology, Pretoria, South Africa

Yves van Leynseele, MSc. PhD student, Department of Sociology of Rural Development, Wageningen University, the Netherlands; part-time lecturer, Department of Human Geography, Planning and International Development Studies, University of Amsterdam

Index

Printed and bound by CPI Group (UK) Ltd, Croydon, CR0 4YY

16/04/2025

14658447-0002